Home Waters

Heritage Books by Cdr. David D. Bruhn, USN (Retired)

Battle Stars for the "Cactus Navy":
America's Fishing Vessels and Yachts in World War II

Eyes of the Fleet:
The U.S. Navy's Seaplane Tenders and Patrol Aircraft in World War II

Ingram's Fourth Fleet:
U.S. and Royal Navy Operations Against German Runners,
Raiders, and Submarines in the South Atlantic in World War II

MacArthur and Halsey's "Pacific Island Hoppers":
The Forgotten Fleet of World War II

Home Waters:
Royal Navy, Royal Canadian Navy, and U.S. Navy
Mine Forces Battling U-Boats in World War I
Cdr. David D. Bruhn, USN (Retired) and Lt. Cdr. Rob Hoole, RN (Retired)

We Are Sinking, Send Help!:
The U.S. Navy's Tugs and Salvage Ships in the African,
European, and Mediterranean Theaters in World War II

Wooden Ships and Iron Men:
The U.S. Navy's Ocean Minesweepers, 1953–1994

Wooden Ships and Iron Men:
The U.S. Navy's Coastal and Motor Minesweepers, 1941–1953

Wooden Ships and Iron Men:
The U.S. Navy's Coastal and Inshore Minesweepers,
and the Minecraft that Served in Vietnam, 1953–1976

To my old friend, shipmate and kindred spirit Geoff Goodwin with my best wishes.

Rob Hoole

27 April 2018

Home Waters

Royal Navy, Royal Canadian Navy, and U.S. Navy Mine Forces Battling U-Boats in World War I

Cdr. David D. Bruhn, USN (Retired)
and
Lt. Cdr. Rob Hoole, RN (Retired)

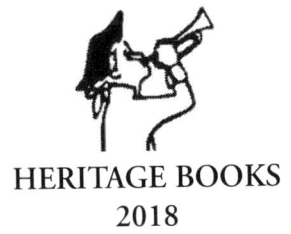

HERITAGE BOOKS
2018

HERITAGE BOOKS

AN IMPRINT OF HERITAGE BOOKS, INC.

Books, CDs, and more—Worldwide

For our listing of thousands of titles see our website
at
www.HeritageBooks.com

Published 2018 by
HERITAGE BOOKS, INC.
Publishing Division
5810 Ruatan Street
Berwyn Heights, Md. 20740

International Standard Book Number
Paperbound: 978-0-7884-5798-2

To the officers and men of the British, Canadian, and United States navies, who served aboard mine warfare ships in World War I, and to Ship Fitter 1st Class Rolf Bruhn, USN.

After serving aboard the armored cruisers *South Dakota* and *Colorado* between 1912 and 1916, Bruhn rejoined the Navy on 27 April 1918, and was assigned to the freighter *Westmount*, part of the Naval Overseas Transportation Service.

Westmount left Seattle on 23 May 1918, bound for Europe via the Panama Canal. Arriving at Bordeaux, France, on 29 July, she discharged her cargo, and sailed for America.

Westmount arrived at New York City on 9 October, and Bruhn was transferred from the ship to Willard Parker Hospital on 22 October. He died on 29 October 1918 of bronchopneumonia, one of the many non-combat casualties of the war, and one of over 5,000 U.S. sailors who died of influenza and pneumonia during the worst epidemic in American history.

Contents

Photos and Illustrations

Maps and Diagrams

Foreword

Many military and naval historians believe that World War One was the most significant event of the Twentieth Century. It was the first "total war" because for the first time, the destruction of the enemy's economy, and by extension, the civilian population's will to resist, became war goals. It was also the first war in which each nation's war effort included all the nation's resources. It is considered to be the first "modern war" because it featured the wide-spread use of automobile transport vehicles, and new weapons; tanks, aircraft, and submarines. But there was one other new addition to warfare, mine warfare on a massive scale. Taprell Dorling, in *Swept Channels Being An Account of the Work of the Minesweepers in the Great War*, published in 1935, set the number of mines laid by all the belligerents at 235,983.

Both sides entered the war unprepared for the minelaying and minesweeping operations that would be required. They literally started from scratch. Both sides converted outdated warships to minelayers and minesweepers, and both sides used former commercial vessels for the same purposes. Both sides also pressed fleets of fishing trawlers and drifters into service.

Along with the need for ships was the attendant need for crews to man them. The result was that both sides went to war with mine forces that were inexperienced and hastily trained. Their training was often "on-the-job-training." Many of those ships were lost to the very weapons they either employed, or were attempting to remove. The whole business of mine warfare is extraordinarily dangerous as illustrated in Chapters 1 and 9, which details the losses of the USS *Richard Bulkeley* and the HMS *Princess Irene*.

Commanders David Bruhn and Rob Hoole have done a masterful job of explaining and illustrating mine warfare equipment and its use. Minelaying had to grow from having the capability of laying a few mines to being able to lay whole fields in a very short time. Speed was important to working at night because of the need to get in and out quickly before the Germans discovered what was happening on their doorstep. Minesweeping was done under the same conditions, especially when the Germans and the British started mining the same areas, such as off the Horn Reefs.

None of the special mine warfare gear was on hand so, together with techniques for its use, it had to be developed and improved as the war went on. At the start of the war, British mines were deficient in many ways. The two they started the war with, the Service mine and the Elia mine, became something of a joke to the Germans, whose propaganda depicted British mines as being no concern to U-boat captains. In one propaganda account, an unnamed U-boat captain flaunted a recovered mine displayed on his boat's foredeck. The truth was that initially, the Germans assumed that British mines were as good as German mines. But they soon discovered that, with care, the U-boats were able to pass under and over British minefields. And if they blundered into a minefield, they might even be able to pass through it safely. But German captains did not develop a cavalier attitude toward British mines, which, despite their deficiencies, did sink U-boats.

But what British mines lacked in reliability was largely compensated for by laying them in huge barrages, in a "ladder" pattern, each rung of the ladder being a layer of mines. By 1917, the British were manufacturing the H2 mine that was a knock-off of the very effective German E-mine. The H2 mine was used to build the Folkstone-Gris Nez Deep Mine Barrage in November-December 1917, effectively closing the Dover Strait to the U-boats.

As one would expect, the initial British minesweeping attempts were rather primitive, and involved a great deal of danger. Imagine being on a ten-knot fishing trawler while dragging a steel cable, hoping to foul and snap a mine cable, allowing the mine to rise to the surface, wholly untethered. You now have a free-floating mine on the surface that you need to destroy before it drifts off and becomes a wandering, ship-sinking explosive charge. You shoot at it with a rifle, no easy feat when firing from a rolling, pitching deck and aiming at a bobbing floating target. The book's clear explanations and sharp illustrations allow you to understand the process as it developed through the war and culminated in 1919 with the clearing of the Northern Mine Barrage. This was probably the most hazardous undertaking accomplished, since the mines being swept were the American Mark VI, so sensitive that almost anything would cause it to explode.

Bruhn and Hoole have laid out these things in a well-organized narrative that puts the Royal Navy's mine warfare in the greater context of the war at sea, 1914-18. The result is a book that is entertaining, interesting, and informative.

Dwight R. Messimer

Foreword

There is a famous quote from George Santayana: "Those who cannot learn from history are doomed to repeat it." Military historians have traditionally focused on the land battles of World War I. Commanders David Bruhn and Rob Hoole have written a commendably well-researched and presented history of mining and mine clearing by the British (with help from Americans and Canadians) and German navies in the German attempt to isolate Britain and defeat her by strangling her commerce from the sea. As I read the many detailed chapters I had an uneasy feeling: Is this prescient as well as historical? More about this later.

I have a deep admiration for the sailors who crew minesweepers. In 2002, shortly after taking command of the U.S. Navy's Mine Warfare Command, I had the pleasure of riding USS *Avenger* (MCM-1), a minesweeper conducting training operations in the Gulf of Mexico. The ship was constructed of wood (with fiberglass sheathing covering the hull to reduce maintenance) to minimize the metallic signature of the ship, and the interior outfitting of the ship was primarily wood, including such simple furniture as the chairs at the wardroom table. For someone who doesn't understand the full mine clearing process, minesweepers actually navigate through minefields hoping that their own acoustic and magnetic signatures don't set off the mines they're trying to clear and that the mines are detonated by the magnetic influence or acoustic sweep gear towed behind the minesweeper. There's a lot of confidence in the ability of modern minesweepers to safely sweep mines, but in the World War I anecdotes in this book, technology frequently failed the operators.

As noted in Dwight Messimer's foreword and elsewhere in this book, over 200,000 mines were laid during World War I. At the start of the war the British Admiralty had little appreciation for the use of sea mines, either offensively or defensively. As German mines took their toll on British and allied shipping the Admiralty developed a belated respect for mines, mine laying and mine clearing. Have our current naval leaders learned the lessons of history and paid adequate attention to mine warfare?

Fast forward one hundred years from the end of World War I. It's now 2018 and the western world is concerned about threats from North Korea, Iran, China and a resurgent Russia. At the start of the Korean War, Rear Admiral Allan Smith, in charge of the advance force at Wonsan, cabled the Navy's Washington headquarters that "we have lost control of the seas to a nation without a Navy, using pre-World War I weapons, laid by vessels that were utilized at the time of the birth of Christ."[1] His words and the experience at Wonsan would invigorate the Navy's mine warfare community for several years.

As explained in this book, minesweeping is technically difficult. I remember being briefed in 2002 on the mine warfare community's vision of using advanced technology to "get men out of the minefield." Sixteen years later we're still not there and we're still using minesweeping and minehunting ships with a lot of the same technology used in World War II, which isn't much different from the technology used in World War I!

As I read the fascinating story of repeated British and German mining and mine clearing efforts in the North Sea, I could only think about the modern Persian Gulf. Several tankers and a U.S. Navy frigate struck mines during the "tanker war" (Iraq-Iran War) in the 1980s. When allied forces liberated the port of Umm Qasr in southern Iraq, during Operation Iraqi Freedom, several covertly converted minelayers were found with mine rails full of mines. Iran has repeatedly threatened to mine the Strait of Hormuz. Do the allies have the capability and capacity to expeditiously clear modern minefields?

Commanders Bruhn and Hoole discuss the challenges both Britain and Germany had fielding effective mines during World War I. Offensive and defensive mining has been relatively ignored in modern Western military thought, almost from a chivalric perspective that "gentlemen don't lay mines." In fact, the U.S. Navy hasn't developed a new mine since the 1980s. Are we ignoring a critical component of naval warfare?

---

[1] Edward Marolda, Mine Warfare. Naval History and Heritage Command, https://www.history.navy.mil/research/library/online-reading-room/title-list-alphabetically/m/mine-warfare.html

I thank the authors for their thorough research and for highlighting an under-appreciated aspect of naval warfare. I hope this book also serves as a call to action. The mine strike damage to USS *Samuel B. Roberts* during the "tanker war" in 1988, and USS *Tripoli* and USS *Princeton* in 1991 during Operation Desert Storm all highlight the vulnerability of modern warships to inexpensive asymmetric weapons.

Paul J. Ryan
Rear Admiral, USN, retired.

Foreword

I joined the Royal Navy to be a Diver, to be a Minewarfare and Clearance Diving Officer, to be exact. I grew up with my younger life revolving around a swim team and watching Jacque Cousteau (that amazing military leader, scientist, film maker and inventor of the aqua lung) on television as he dived in the far flung oceans of the world. I was drawn to the sea.

Achieving my ambition, I found myself in the Persian Gulf in 1988-1989 plying my specialist minewarfare and clearance diving trade on the frontline in the aftermath of the "tanker war," serving in the same task group as Rob Hoole. Together we were part of the effort that laid the foundation for the Royal Navy's *Hunt*-class mine countermeasure vessels' (MCMVs) success at clearing Saddam Hussein's minefields off the Iraqi Coast in 1991. Whilst the Royal Navy's specialists were prepared to face and deal with the threat from sea mines during Desert Storm, others in that Service were less so. The same can also be said of the U.S. Navy which had been drawing down their ability to counter the threat of sea mines for the previous decade. Senior decision makers, driven by reducing financial resources, had prioritised elsewhere.

I witnessed no clearer demonstration of this than on 18 February 1991. My ship HMS *Atherstone* was easing slowly into the area that intelligence suggested had been mined. I had just come up from a seabed search dive to classify a sonar contact, and was standing dripping water on the bridge wing next to my captain, as I debriefed him on the dive. I asked him whether all the frigates and destroyers on the horizon knew something we did not—about the extent of the potential minefields in the area—as they were steaming back and forth, ploughing a furrow on the chart table with classic Williamson turns at the end of their tracks. Gazing over to the distant ships, we had our answer: the stern of USS *Princeton* lifted out of the water as she detonated a Manta sea mine. A $10,000 mine had neutralised a billion-dollar warship.

My captain calmly announced on Main Broadcast that the mine threat warning was now red! There is an old saying in the Minewarfare community, "Where the Fleet Goes, We've Been," except we had not been over in that destroyer and frigate holding area before they got there. Every one of those frigates and destroyers crash stopped and called for the MCMVs to lead them south and into deeper, safer waters. Approaching a British Type 42 destroyer with every man on the upperdeck and above the waterline, the worried captain hailed from the bridge and expressed his surprise as the task group had been in the same area all day. He had forgotten that sea mines can be equipped with a ship count mechanism before detonation. Everyone that day relearnt the age-old lesson that any ship can be a minesweeper, once.

Twenty-six years later, I am still involved in minewarfare and diving. As Deputy Commander Naval Striking and Support Forces NATO, I am responsible for delivering Exercise Baltic Operations (BALTOPS), which earlier this year amongst a Task Force of 40 ships of various sizes and capabilities, included a Task Group of 25 MCMVs from 12 different countries exercising their skills on GPS-positioned sea mines air dropped from USAF B1s and B52s in precise locations across the Baltic Sea. We train hard in the challenging conditions of the Baltic Sea in order to fight easy.

It is a complex area of the world. Much has been made of Russia's increasingly capable long-range air and surface missile systems that have been incorporated into the Anti-Access Area-Denial (A2AD) measures in the Baltic Region. The goal of this concept is to prevent an opponent from entering into a theatre (Anti-Access) and deprive him of freedom of action in this theatre (Area-Denial). Whilst the term A2AD might be new, the concept is not. This is exactly what a minefield is designed to do; stop the enemy from entering an area and if he does deprive him of his room to manoeuvre.

The threat from mines is as prevalent and real today as it was in the many conflicts discussed in this book. We forget the lessons from our past and from those who served before us at our peril. This excellent book reminds us of the lessons we have identified, but to address the threat posed by increasingly complex sea mines today and in the future, they have to become lessons learnt.

RAdm Paddy McAlpine CBE, RN
Oerias, Portugal

Acknowledgements

Brilliant maritime and aviation artist Richard DeRosset has created another stunning book cover. The dazzle paint-clad ship is the USS *Richard Bulkeley*, a trawler leased from Britain and crewed by American sailors to assist in mine clearance in the North Sea. She was flying the Stars and Stripes when blown up with loss of ship and men killed. DeRosset is a prolific artist, having produced over 900 paintings and murals to date. His genius derives from heredity, his grandmother was an illustrator for Walt Disney, and much time spent at sea. After serving in the U.S. Navy, he worked aboard commercial fishing vessels, and later was master of the small cargo ship MV *Pacific Trojan*.

This book would not have been possible without much assistance and expertise lent by Dwight Messimer, George Duddy, and co-author Rob Hoole. Messimer is a former university lecturer, and acclaimed military historian and author. A specialist on the German Navy and U-boats, he has written nearly a dozen books on this subject and on naval aviation covering the period 1925-1942. His work has also appeared in many periodicals, including *The American Neptune*, *The Quarterly Journal of Military History*, *War Revolution and Peace*, and *Naval History*. In addition to generously sharing source materials, he critically reviewed the manuscript, and was kind enough to pen a foreword.

Canadian George Duddy is a retired professional engineer with a keen interest in maritime subjects, particularly those relating to the maritime history of western Canada and the arctic. He has published several articles on these subjects on the Nauticapedia Project website mentioned later in this document. He has deep family roots in the British Isles particularly to the geographical area of this book. His father as a schoolboy took photographs of surrendered German battleships in the Firth of Forth; his great grandfather was a pioneering Leith steamship owner and his great great grandfather as Master in both sail and steam ended his career as marine superintendent for the Leith, Hull & Hamburg Steam Packet Co. One of his other relatives, Midshipman Percival George, fell to his death from the mast of a Royal Navy ship during the age of sail. Duddy lent his critical eye and keen mind during technical review and editing of the manuscript, and made many suggestions for improvements.

Rob Hoole is a former Royal Navy mine clearance diving officer and commanding officer of HMS *Berkeley* (M40)—a *Hunt*-class mine countermeasures vessel. An acknowledged expert on mine warfare, he is a long-standing member of the Ton Class Association and a regular contributor to its publications. Hoole is also founding Vice Chairman and Webmaster of the Royal Naval Minewarfare & Clearance Diving Officers' Association, and holds key positions in related organisations.

Within the American mine warfare community, George Pollitt and Christopher C. Wright provided materials and assistance. Pollitt is a former technical director for the U.S. Navy Mine Warfare Command, and currently serves as the mine warfare subject matter expert for the John Hopkin's Applied Physics Laboratory. Wright is the editor of the journal *Warship International.*

Rear Adm. Paddy A. McAlpine, CBE, RN, and Rear Adm. Paul J. Ryan, USN (Retired), added much richness to the book by providing in their respective forewords, unique perspective borne of senior command experience at sea and ashore. McAlpine is the Royal Navy's senior member of the Mine Warfare and Clearance Diver Officer community. In addition to his operational acumen, Ryan brought technical expertise and knowledge of marine engineering and repair to the U.S. Navy Mine Warfare community.

Rear Admiral McAlpine commanded the frigate HMS *Somerset* and the destroyer HMS *Daring.* Following operational and training command assignments of increased responsibility, and promotion to commodore, he flew his pennant from the Fleet Flagship, HMS *Bulwark*, as Commander United Kingdom Task Group during both the 2012 (Mediterranean) and 2013 (Gulf) COUGAR deployments and was then appointed in Command of the Portsmouth Flotilla in 2014. He was appointed as Deputy Commander Naval Striking and Support Forces NATO in 2015.

Rear Admiral Ryan, a nuclear engineer and career submariner, commanded the attack submarine USS *Philadelphia* and the submarine tender USS *L. Y. Spear.* Ashore, he served in a variety of assignments while assigned to the Navy and Joint Staffs in the Pentagon, and on the staff of Commander in Chief, U.S. Atlantic Fleet. In February 2002 he assumed command of Mine Warfare Command in Corpus Christi, Texas, where he was responsible for the deployment of mine warfare forces in support of Operation Iraqi Freedom in the Persian Gulf. He retired in December 2003.

Individuals not directly involved with the book, but whose work helped shape it, include John McFarlane, John Blatherwick, Gordon Smith, Don Kindell, and Iain Cameron. McFarlane is a former Royal Canadian naval officer, a Fellow of the Royal Geographical Society, a retired Director of the Maritime Museum of British Columbia, and founder of the Nauticapedia Project (www.nauticapedia.ca/index.php).

This site features articles on western Canadian and arctic maritime subjects and contains extensive databases on related ships and maritime personalities.

Blatherwick served as the Chief Medical Health Officer in Vancouver, British Columbia from 1984 to 2007, and concurrently in the Canadian Forces reserves. His keen interest in military medals and decorations led him to publish a landmark guide to Canadian Medals and Decorations, and make available related information at: www.blatherwick.net

Gordon Smith, the creator of Naval-History.Net recently passed away on 16 December 2016. He started the site with information from his books on the Royal and Dominion Navies of World War II, and expanded it to include a wide range of naval history research. I am also indebted to Don Kindell, an American who has researched the Royal Navy for decades, who worked with Smith, and who has contributed much material to Naval-History.net.

Retired mechanical engineer and native Scot, Iain Cameron, who worked on oil & gas production platforms in the North Sea and Indonesia provided geographical and engineering data as well as a photo of his great grandfather. See Chapter 10. His great grandfather and his grandfather were both Herring Drifter fishermen who are honored in this book. Both served on the Dover Patrol.

My son Michael Bruhn created many of the maps in the book, by starting with digital maps in the public domain and tailoring them to include specific ports and other features described in the text.

Lynn Marie Tosello was the final editor of this text. In addition to the style, eloquence, and proper syntax she lent to the work, she also kept Rob and me on our toes, by gently reminding us that some readers might not be familiar with terminology common to sailors and seamen. In the process, she added to her increasing knowledge of the naval history of Britain, Canada, and the United States.

Preface

It is doubtful if we could have defeated the Germans, at any rate as quickly as we did defeat them, if it had not been for the assistance which the Royal Navy received from the fishing community.

—Assertion by Adm. Sir Reginald Bacon, RN, KCB, KCVO, DSO. This sentiment was shared by Lord John Rushworth Jellicoe, who declared that the Royal Navy had saved the Empire, but it was fishermen in their boats who had saved the Royal Navy. The RNR (Royal Naval Reserve) of fishermen was "a Navy within the Navy," one that swept mines, escorted convoys, hunted U-boats, and carried out countless other dangerous duties.[1]

The dominance of the seas by allied navies that allowed the blockade of German ports to foodstuffs and vital war materiel was a key factor in finally bringing the German nation to its knees in World War I. Huge minefields planted in the English Channel and the North Sea were vital to this enterprise. Nearly one hundred years have passed since World War I ended at the 11th hour on the 11th day of the 11th month of 1918. At 0500 that morning, Germany, bereft of manpower and supplies and faced with imminent invasion, signed an armistice agreement with the Allies in a railroad car at Le Francport, outside Compiégne in northern France.

World War I was known as the "war to end all wars" because of the great slaughter and destruction it caused, leaving nine million soldiers dead and 21 million wounded, with Germany, Russia, Austria-Hungary, France, and Great Britain each losing nearly a million or more lives. Exactly five years after the assassination of Archduke Franz Ferdinand, the heir to the Austro-Hungarian empire—an event that is widely regarded as sparking the outbreak of World War I—the Treaty of Versailles formally ended the state of war between Germany and the Allied Powers. It was signed on 28 June 1919, amidst great hope for the future. Unfortunately, the treaty levied punitive terms on Germany that would destabilise Europe and lay the groundwork for World War II.

In the autumn of 1914, the officers and men of the Royal Navy, including its mine warfare branch, weren't much concerned about the distant future. Pressed into action when Great Britain declared war on Germany, they were focused on the immediate threat posed by the Imperial Navy's High Seas Fleet and its "stilettoes of the sea" (submarines). Despite being part of the Triple Entente (an alliance formed in 1907 with France and Russia) and having previously promised to defend Belgium under the Treaty of London of 1839, Britain was not committed to going to war in 1914. In the end, however, she refused to ignore the events of 4 August, when Germany attacked France through Belgium. Within hours, Britain declared war on Germany, and in a few days, Britain, France and Russia (the Allies) were all at war with Germany and Austria-Hungary (the Central Powers).[2]

COMPARISON OF BRITISH AND GERMAN NAVIES

As the conflict stretched on, and stalemated land forces suffered ever increasing casualties, the British and German navies each tried to help end the war through the attrition of one another's merchant shipping. In the early 1900s, following a period of expansion, the Imperial German Navy was second in strength only to the British Royal Navy.[3]

British and German Navies in 1914
Numbers of Major Combatant Ships

British Royal Navy		Imperial German Navy	
Pre-dreadnought Battleships	40	Pre-dreadnought Battleships	22
Dreadnought Battleships (13 under construction)	22	Dreadnought Battleships (5 under construction)	15
Battle Cruisers (1 under construction)	9	Battle Cruisers (3 under construction)	5
Cruisers	121	Cruisers	40
Destroyers	221	Destroyers	90
Submarines	73	Submarines	31
Total	486	Total	203[4]

The two nations had been locked in a naval race since 1898 when Germany embarked on the construction of a blue water navy that Britain viewed as a very significant threat to her well-being. Being an island nation, dependent on imports for food, fuel, and other vital supplies and materiel, Britain had to rule the waves. Should she find herself at war with Germany, defeat at sea could lead to blockade, possible starvation, and surrender.[5]

To avoid this possibility Britain pursued building greater numbers of, and more powerful, warships than Germany. By 1914, the Royal

Navy was the largest in the world, and the German Navy, though quite powerful, was numerically inferior to the British. When World War I broke out, Britain had over twice as many battleships, and other types of large combatant ships and submarines as did Germany.

While the Royal Navy hoped for a general fleet engagement at sea to help bring a rapid end to World War I, capital ships of the German High Seas Fleet remained in port. Frustration on the part of the British may have been what caused Winston Churchill, the First Lord of the Admiralty, to declare in 1915 that the British fleet would "dig the Germans out of their holes like rats." With superior naval forces, the British were able to rid the seas of German merchant ships by early 1915, effectively blocking Germany's trade routes. The Deutschland's increasingly desperate need for food and other supplies led to the German Navy's adoption of unrestricted submarine warfare and the mining of British waters in an effort to get Britain to capitulate.[6]

GERMANY'S U-BOAT FORCE

From the very start, Germany employed its small submarine force—which grew into a large force—aggressively. On 6 August 1914, only two days after Britain entered the war, a group of ten submarines—*U-5*, *U-7*, *U-8*, *U-9*, *U-13*, *U-14*, *U-15*, *U-16*, *U-17*, and *U-18*—sailed from Heligoland to attack Royal Navy warships in the North Sea. Their departure from a base in the small German archipelago in the southeastern corner of the North Sea, marked the first submarine war patrol in history. The operation was a failure. Following an encounter with the 1st Light Cruiser Squadron, only eight boats returned to port. However, it caused the Royal Navy some uneasiness, disproving earlier estimates as to the U-boats' range and leaving the security of the Grand Fleet's unprotected anchorage at Scapa Flow open to question.[7]

Another first occurred on 20 October 1914, when the SS *Glitra* became the first British merchant vessel to be sunk by a German submarine in World War I. She was bound from Grangemouth to Stavanger, Norway, with a cargo of coal when stopped by *U-17*, under the command of Kptlt. Johannes Feldkirchner. After ordering her crew into lifeboats, a boarding party opened the seacocks, sending the ship to the bottom west-southwest of Skudesnes, Norway (today, part of the municipalities of Bokn and Karmøy).[8]

This type of gentlemanly behavior was short-lived. The British, after having established a naval blockade of Germany at the outbreak of war in August 1914, declared the North Sea to be a war zone in early November, with any ships entering it doing so at their own risk.

The Germans regarded this as a blatant attempt to starve its people into submission and wanted to retaliate in kind.[9]

The only way available to counter the superior Royal Navy was to impose a similar blockade on Britain through the use of U-boats. On 4 February 1915, Vizeadmiral Hugo von Pohl, the commander of the High Seas Fleet, published a warning in the *Deutscher Reichsanzeiger* (Imperial German Gazette):

> The waters around Great Britain and Ireland, including the whole of the English Channel, are hereby declared to be a War Zone. From February 18 onwards, every enemy merchant vessel encountered in this zone will be destroyed, nor will it always be possible to avert the danger thereby threatened to the crew and passengers.
>
> Neutral vessels also will run a risk in the War Zone, because in view of the hazards of sea warfare and the British authorisation of January 31 of the misuse of neutral flags, it may not always be possible to prevent attacks on enemy ships from harming neutral ships.
>
> Navigation to the north of the Shetlands, in the eastern parts of the North Sea and through a zone at least thirty nautical miles wide along the Dutch coast is not exposed to danger.[10]

On 7 May 1915, *U-20* (Kptlt. Walther Schwieger) operating off the coast of Ireland fired a torpedo into RMS *Lusitania*, causing the massive ocean liner to list precariously and then sink in just eighteen minutes. The attack killed 1,198 passengers and crew—including 128 Americans. Contrary to popular belief, this did not directly precipitate U.S. involvement in World War I, but did serve as a widespread propaganda tool and rallying cry once American troops began shipping out overseas two years later.[11]

Photo Preface-1

A German postcard depicting the *U-20* sinking RMS *Lusitania* on 7 May 1915 off a headland near Kinsale, County Cork, Ireland.

Germany would commission 375 U-boats of thirty-three separate classes belonging to seven general types, before the war's end in 1918. Additional submarines under construction were finished after the war, the last one being the *UB-133* in April 1919.

Ocean-going torpedo attack submarines (90)

Class	No.	Class	No.	Class	No.	Class	No.
U-19	4	*U-31*	11	*U-57*	12	*U-81*	6
U-23	4	*U-43*	8	*U-63*	3	*U-87*	6
U-27	4	*U-51*	6	large Ms.	4	*U-93*	22

Submarines built for export (6)				Kerosene-powered submarines (18)			
U-66	5	UA	1	*U-1*	1	*U-9*	4
				U-2	1	*U-13*	3
				U-3	2	*U-16*	1
				U-5	4	*U-17*	2

U-cruisers/Merchant U-boats (11)				UB coastal torpedo attack subs (136)			
U-139	3	*U-151*	7	*UB-1*	17	UB III	89
U-142	1			UB II	30		

UC coastal minelayers (95)				UE ocean minelayers (19)			
UC-1	15	UC III	16	UE I	10	UE II	9[12]
UC II	64						

Two hundred, twenty-six submarines were torpedo-attack boats; 90 of them ocean-going and the remaining 136 coastal submarines. While these U-boats went after shipping, coastal and ocean minelayers (collectively numbering 114) sowed fields around the U.K., intended to close British channels and harbours to vessels carrying vital cargos.

It is probably sufficient at this point to appreciate that Germany had large numbers of submarines. For readers desiring to glean the relationships between a particular class and the hull numbers of the boats within that class, an italicised designation in the table represents the first in a series of hull numbers associated with that class. For example, submarines *UC-1* through *UC-15* constituted the *UC-1* class. Conversely, the UC II and UC III classes are not italicised, so it is not possible from the information provided, to identify the hull numbers of their sixty-four and sixteen members, respectively. Regarding the UC III class, additional units were planned, but only sixteen minelayers entered service:

- UC-II class: *UC-16* to *UC-79* all entered service
- UC-III class: *UC-80* to *UC-192* planned, but only *UC-90* to *UC-105* entered service. *UC-105* was commissioned on 28 October 1918, seven days after a recall order was sent to all U-boats at sea on 21 October 1918. She was the sixteenth UC-III boat commissioned, but never left the Blohm Voss yard at Hamburg. UC-80 to UC-86 were not built; *UC-106* to *UC-192* were not completed before the war ended.[13]

U-BOAT ROUTES TO ALLIED SHIPPING LANES

Our experience in attempting to close the Strait has involved both blood and tears.

—Observation by a British naval officer regarding initial efforts to deny Dover Strait to transit by German submarines. Blood referred to the men lost laying mines and nets, and tears because the arduous work of weeks could be swept away in the storm of a single night. Ultimately, however, these challenges were overcome.[14]

Once extended to include action against Allied shipping, the U-boat campaign was highly destructive, resulting in the loss of nearly half of Britain's merchant fleet during the course of the war. To counter the submarine threat, the Allies implemented a number of new measures, which included assigning destroyers as escorts for ship convoys, and laying mine barrages across the routes that U-boats regularly traversed.

German submarines operated from bases at Ostend and Zeebrugge on the Belgian coast, Wilhelmshaven and Cuxhaven on the

German coast, and from the harbour of Kiel in the Baltic Sea. From all these points, their transit to the great shipping concentrations to the west and south of Ireland was long and difficult. In order to reach these rich hunting grounds, U-boats had either to pass through the Straits of Dover to the south, or through the expansive passage between the Shetland Islands and Norway, where the North Sea opened into the Atlantic, and thence sail around the northern coast of Ireland.[15]

Preface Map-1

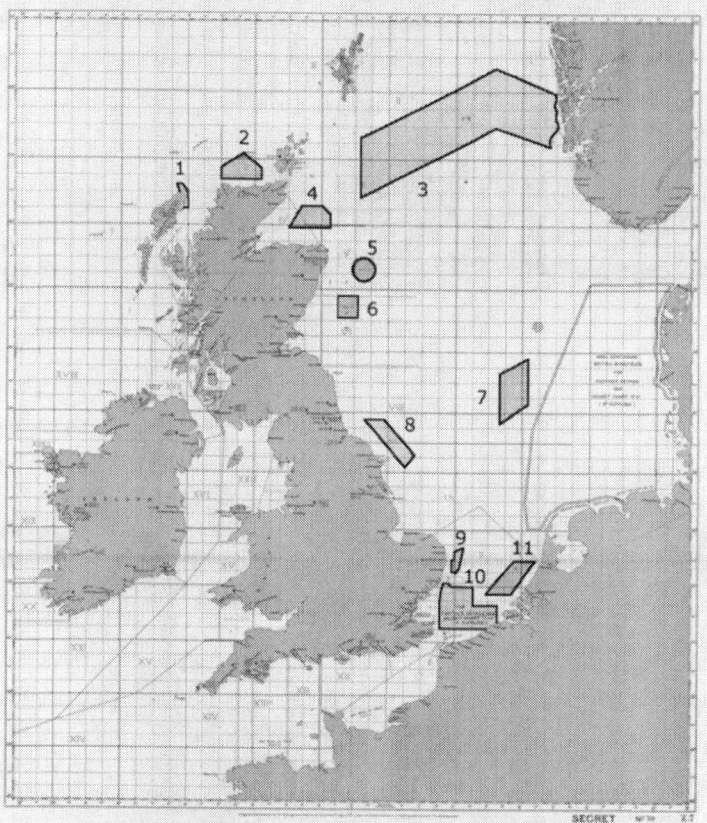

Approximate positions of minefields around the British Isles, 19 August 1918. William Rea Furlong map collection, Library of Congress.[16]

1. Butt of Lewis
2. West Orkney/Pentland Firth Barrage
3. North Sea (Northern) Mine Barrage
4. Firth of Moray Barrage
5. Long Forties Minefield
6. Stonehaven Minefield

7. Dogger Bank Minefield
8. Humber & Wash Minefield
9. Smith's Knoll Minefield
10. Dover Barrage
11. Flanders Barrage

Minelaying by British and later American ships was often carried out in darkness, particularly when nearer German than British waters, to lessen the chance of coming under attack. Thus, minelayers became known as "nightraiders." Theirs was a hazardous duty. In addition to the obvious dangers inherent in plying contested waters with cargos of high-explosives, they also faced the possibility of death by "stilettoes of the sea." Escort by British destroyers during minelaying operations helped to deter enemy warships that might contest them. However, nightraiders were fair game to German U-boats—both attack and minelaying types. Regarding the latter, the enemy was well aware that the British periodically sent out ships to replenish fields, replacing ordnance detonated by prey or carried away by strong seas. Accordingly, the Germans soon began despatching submarines to lay mines in adjacent areas—in the hopes of ambushing a minelayer. Such activity was not without risk. U-boats thus engaged infrequently fell victim to their own, or to Allied mines after stumbling into a British field, due to navigation error or some other miscalculation.

GERMANY'S NAVAL MINING CAMPAIGN

In addition to using its submarine force to offset the superiority of the Royal Navy, the Imperial Navy also pursued an aggressive mining campaign for the same purpose. Germany started laying operations almost as soon as war was declared, with the first minefield being sowed by the SS *Königin Luise*—a converted ferry—off Lowestoft on the east coast of England, on the night of 4 August 1914. The minelayer was sunk the next day by gunfire from HMS *Amphion*—the first German naval loss of the war. In a twist of fate, one of her mines sank the light cruiser the following day; the Royal Navy's first loss, with those killed being the first British casualties of the war.[17]

Over the course of the war, Germany laid more than 43,000 mines which claimed 497 merchant vessels. (One source cites 586 as the number of Allied merchant ship casualties.) The Royal Navy alone lost 46 warships and 225 auxiliaries to mines. The loss of the cruiser HMS *Hampshire* west of the Orkney Islands on 5 June 1916, was especially damaging as the casualties included the British Secretary of War, Lord Horatio Herbert Kitchener. There were only twelve survivors; Kitchener was among the 737 killed. *U-75*, commanded by Kptlt. Curt Beitzen, had sowed the 38 mines comprising the field that sank the warship.[18]

In addition to using conventional naval ships and submarines as minelayers, the Imperial German Navy also employed surface raiders, "wolves in sheep's clothing," in such roles. As year 1916 broke, the merchant raider *Möwe*—commanded by KKpt. Burggraf Graf Nikolaus zu Dohna-Schlodien—laid a large field of mines in the Pentland Firth near the main base of the British Home Fleet at Scapa Flow. On 6 January, as units of the fleet sailed from Scapa Flow for exercises, the pre-dreadnought battleship *King Edward VII* hit a mine and sank. The existence of *Möwe*, and others like her, resulted from a decision by Vizeadmiral von Pohl to implement an idea suggested by a relative junior officer, Lt. z. S. Theodor Wolff, in a paper.[19]

Pohl, an advocate of unrestricted submarine warfare, believed that the serviceable U-boats available to him at that time were too few to have the desired effect on shipping. He thus decided to try using innocuous looking freighters fitted with hidden weapons, as merchant raiders. In execution of this plan, he had ordered Dohna-Schlodien to find a ship suitable for fitting out as a minelayer. The latter individual searched through all the German ports for a suitable vessel, ideally a new one, meeting a particular set of criteria:

- Not too fast, so that coal could be conserved
- Cargo space sufficient for a large load of mines
- Decks sufficiently strong to bear the recoil and weight of 150mm guns
- Fast enough to overtake the average British tramp steamer[20]

Dohna-Schlodien found the 4,788-ton *Pungo* in Hamburg. Built to haul bananas from the Cameroons, the refrigerated ship could make 14 knots. During conversion, four 150mm guns (taken from a former battleship) were fitted forward, hidden behind false bulwarks, and disguised machinery above the after steering compartment housed a smaller 105mm gun. A torpedo tube was also added on each side abaft the foremast, and two others just before the mainmast. Lastly, 500 mines were loaded aboard. Disguised as a neutral cargo ship to enable her to get close to intended targets, *Möwe* would become the most successful commerce raider in either the First or Second World Wars, sinking thirty-nine ships.[21]

EXPANDED BRITISH MINESWEEPING FORCES

The Royal Navy's minesweeping forces in 1914 consisted of eighty-two trawlers of the Trawler Reserve and a handful of fleet sweepers (old torpedo boats). Faced with the German mine threat, construction was begun on *Flower-* and *Acadia*-class minesweepers to provide the Fleet with sufficient capability, while smaller paddle-wheelers and auxiliaries—mostly fishing trawlers from every port in Britain—swept home waters. By 1918, the British Minesweeping Service comprised 726 vessels of every description, supported by organisations in twenty-six ports at home and thirty-six ports abroad. The large numbers of minesweepers assigned to Royal Naval Reserve trawler units supported Lord Jellicoe's observation after the war, that the Royal Navy had saved the Empire, but it was fishermen in their boats who had saved the Royal Navy. In the below table, the acronym F.S.F. refers to Fast Sweeping Flotilla.[22]

British Minesweeping Units, at Home and Overseas in World War I

Fleet Sweepers	Galway Trawlers	Nore Paddlers
1st Sloop Flotilla	Granton Paddlers	Nore Trawlers
2nd F.S.F.	Granton Trawlers	North Sea (7th) F.S.F.
3rd F.S.F.	Grimsby Paddlers	Oban F.S.F.
4th F.S.F. (Scapa Trawlers)	Grimsby Trawlers	Peterhead Trawlers
5th F.S.F. (Stromness Trawlers)	Harwich (6th) F.S.F.	Plymouth (18th) F.S.F.
10th F.S.F.	Harwich Paddlers	Plymouth Trawlers
13th F.S.F. (gunboats)	Harwich Trawlers	Portland (17th) F.S.F.
Aegean Trawlers	Havre Trawlers	Portland Paddlers
Alexandria F.S.F.	Kingston Trawlers	Portland Trawlers
Androssan Trawlers	Kirkwall Trawlers	Portsmouth (9th) F.S.F.
Berehaven Trawlers	Larne Paddlers	Portsmouth Paddlers
Buncrana Trawlers	Larne Trawlers	Newhaven Trawlers
Cherbourg Trawlers	Lerwick Trawlers	Portsmouth Trawlers
Clyde F.S.F./Trawlers	Liverpool F.S.F.	Ragian Castle Flotilla
Cromarty Trawlers	Liverpool Paddlers	Queenstown (8th) F.S.F.
Devonport Trawlers	Liverpool Trawlers	Queenstown Trawlers
Dover Paddlers	Lough Swilly	Stornoway Paddlers
Dover M/S Tugs	Lowestoft Paddlers	Stornoway Trawlers
Dover Trawlers	Lowestoft Trawlers	Swansea (19th) F.S.F.
Dunkirk Paddlers	Malta F.S.F.	Swansea Paddlers
Egypt Trawlers	Malta Trawlers	Tyne Paddlers
Falmouth (15th) F.S.F.	Milford Haven	Tyne Trawlers
Falmouth Trawlers	Trawlers	White Sea Trawlers[23]

AMERICA ENTERS THE WAR

At this point, some readers may be wondering what role U.S. Mine Forces played in the prolonged, deadly battle between German submarines and Allied navies in the seas around the British Isles, the North Sea and the coast of France. It's interesting to note that preparations for mine warfare were already underway in the United States prior to her entry into the war. Following entry in April 1917, the U.S. Atlantic Fleet intensified its efforts in progress to acquire, equip and train a squadron of minelayers and their crews to send to Scotland. The squadron arrived there on 26 May 1918, and work was immediately begun, in conjunction with Royal Navy minelayers, to lay

a barrier stretching from the Orkney Islands to the coast of Norway—
a distance of some 230 nautical miles. This barrier represented a
remarkable piece of military engineering, mining waters 900 feet deep
in some places, while no previous minefield had been established in
waters more than 300 feet deep.

Preface Map-2

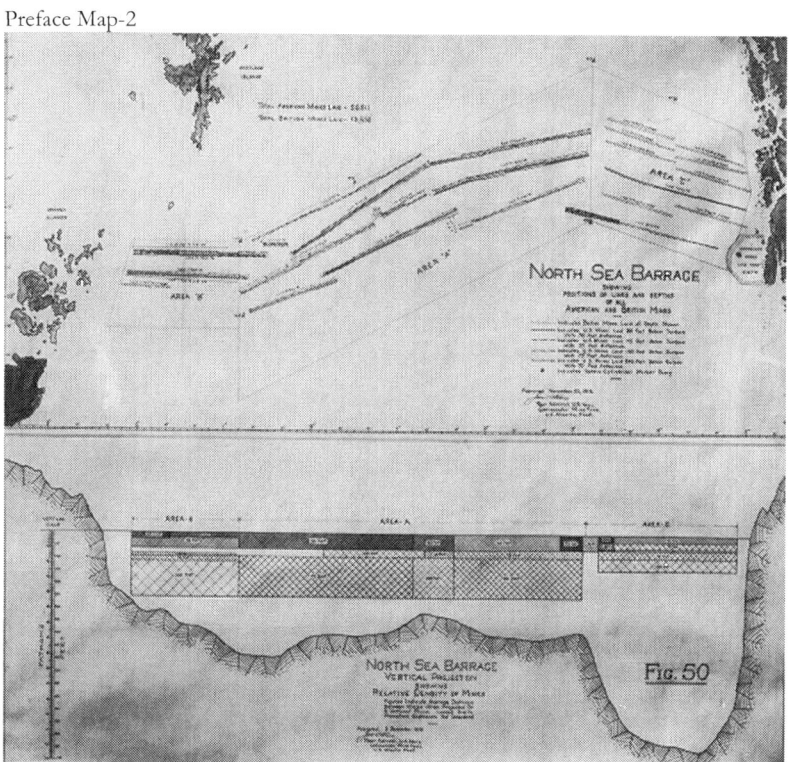

Chart of North Sea barrage, showing positions of lines and depths of American and
British mines, with a vertical projection displaying the relative density of mines.
The Northern Barrage and Other Mining Activities (Washington, DC, 1920)

The American portion of this barrier, which the U.S. Navy termed
the North Sea Mine Barrage, was seeded with 56,611 American-
designed and manufactured Mark VI mines. These mines were so new
that as sailors watched them roll along the track on the launching deck
to the jumping-off place at the stern and plunge over the side, they had
no idea how the "eggs" might be countered. In any case, it was up to
the Germans to figure out how to deal with these "nails in the coffin
of the Kaiser," as the men called these grim instruments.[24]

The British welcomed assistance from "the colonists" in battling U-boats, particularly since they had experienced many frustrations in regard to their minefields. In October 1914, in an effort to protect the passage of her troops across the English Channel, Britain had laid mines off the German naval base at Zeebrugge, Belgium. Mining was conducted in the German Bight in the summer of 1915 in an effort to restrict movements of the High Seas Fleet, and in 1916, Britain placed minefields and mine nets in the Dover Strait to deny passage to enemy submarines.   In addition to abiding hazards that accompanied minelaying—inclement weather, proximity to enemy forces, and the ordnance itself—the Royal Navy gradually became painfully aware that its mines rarely exploded, due to deficiencies in the two types in service until September 1917.[25]

These were the naval spherical mine and the "British Elia" mine, modified from an existing Italian version. Both types would fail to explode unless fairly violent contact was made with their firing arms or levers, and the mines turned out to be remarkably inefficient. But the process of developing and obtaining a new type in wartime proved slow, particularly due to the demands of the army on munition factories. In January 1917, the Royal Navy decided to use the much superior, standard German mine as a model, and its version, the Mark H2, became available in quantity in September 1917. Its use brought about vastly improved results against U-boats, and provided the British with reliable mines for their portion of the northern barrier.[26]

Despite herculean effort by U.S. and British minelayers in sowing 56,611 and 13,652 mines, respectively—and those of the British 14th Destroyer Flotilla and battleships of the Grand Fleet in providing protection while they did so—the barrier was only eighty-five percent completed when the war ended on 11 November 1918. The last minelaying took place on 26 October, after which bad weather and low visibility prevented further work. It did not matter, however. With the war drawing to a close, Kommodore Andreas Michelsen had issued orders on the 27th for U-boats at sea to return home.[27]

Following the war, the U.S. claimed four submarines sunk, two probable, and that many again damaged as a result of their attempted passage through the barrier. The Germans believe that five were likely destroyed and two damaged. Two critical shortcomings allowed U-boats relative safety. By August 1918, it had become apparent that submarine commanders were avoiding densely mined areas by steering through a ten-mile wide gap in the barrier off the Orkneys or around its east end, through unguarded Norwegian territorial waters. These conditions persisted to the end; the British did not want to restrict movements of the Grand Fleet by closing the gap, and Norway did not mine its waters until 7 October 1918.[28]

In total, Allied mines probably accounted for the destruction of fifty or more U-boats, with most losses occurring in the Dover Strait. Examination of Allied and German records after the war judged losses to be forty-some boats, but confirmed losses to "weapons that wait" have continued to rise, as present-day divers find the wreckage of submarines "still on patrol." In some cases, this is due to happenstance; more often dive operations follow purposeful location of targets by sonar scan. Inspection identifies shell-encrusted remains, and determines why individual boats rest in eerie solitude at particular locations on the sea floor.

MINE FORCES ORDERED TO CLEAR OWN MINES

On 31 October 1918, in recognition that victory was only weeks away, an Allied naval council met in London to consider what portions of mined waters should be cleared by each nation following the war. Understandably, the North Sea Mine Barrage, the Dover Barrage, and minefields in the Heligoland Bight off the North German coast were of highest priority. Exploratory minesweeping was to be undertaken in other specified areas to ensure they were clear of mines. Generally, the council allocated to nations the responsibility of clearing the waters bordering their individual seacoasts. America volunteered to remove all the mines she had laid in the North Sea Mine Barrage, and Great Britain similarly agreed to clear her portion of the barrier.[29]

The creation of the field stretching from the Orkneys to Bergen, Norway, had been a huge undertaking. Taking up the mines would be an even more daunting task, and ten-fold more dangerous because of the sensitivity and sophistication of the Mark VI's. During clearance operations between 29 April and 19 September 1919, when work by the American Mine Force was completed, several minesweepers suffered varying degrees of damage. Of these, *Bobolink* was completely disabled by a mine detonation on 14 May, and *Pelican* on 9 July. The bleakest day came on 12 July, when *Richard Bulkeley*—a British minesweeping trawler under lease and crewed by American sailors— was sunk with loss of life. Sub-chaser *SC-38* was disabled by a mine on 25 September and tragically, following all the dangerous toil, *SC-256* burned at sea on 1 November, due to a gasoline explosion on board.[30]

Photo Preface-2

USS *Pelican* being kept afloat by a pumping hose from sister ship USS *Eider*.
The Northern Barrage (Taking Up the Mines) (Washington, DC, 1920)

With this overview in their wake, readers may now stand out to sea (vicariously) a century ago, with sailors of the Royal and U.S. Navy Mine Forces. The only foray out of British home waters in coming pages is to describe a German submarine offensive off the North American Eastern Seaboard in 1918. Sending the group of U-boats across the Atlantic was apparently undertaken in the hope of alarming Americans sufficiently to demand the recall of U.S. Navy destroyers, then hunting U-boats in British waters, to defend the U.S. East Coast.

Since victims of U-boats operating off North America included both American and Canadian vessels, a short chapter introduces the Royal Canadian Navy, formed in 1910, and cites Canadian officers and ratings serving aboard Royal Navy ships in British home waters, the subject of this book. With apologies to the other British dominions (then Australia, New Zealand, Newfoundland, South Africa, and the Irish Free State) some, or all who may also have augmented the Royal Navy, there is not similar detail contained herein.

DIFFERENCES IN THE SPELLING OF WORDS

The British spelling of particular words are used throughout the text as a nod to the Royal Navy and the British people during World War I, to which a majority of the book is devoted. (They are also applicable to the Royal Canadian Navy and to Canadians generally.) The primary differences are the addition of the letter "u" in some words, and the use of "s" instead of "z" in others.

British	American
authorise	authorize
calibre	caliber
cheque	check
colour	color
defence	defense
despatch(es)	dispatch(es)
destabilise	destabilize
draught	draft
endeavour	endeavor
energise	energize
familiarise	familiarize
favourable	favorable
harbour	harbor
honour(s)	honor(s)
italicise	italicize
labour	labor
manoeuvre	maneuver
materiel	material
maximise	maximize
memorialise	memorialize
metre	meter
minimise	minimize
mobilisation	mobilization
organisation	organization
paralyse	paralyze
patronise	patronize
realise	realize
recognise	recognize
unfavourable	unfavorable
utilise	utilize
valour	valor
vigourous	vigorous
vulcanise	vulcanize

COMPARABLE NAVAL OFFICER RANK STRUCTURE

The United States and Royal Canadian navies were both patterned after the Royal Navy and, sharing a common language, utilised a similar officer rank structure. An RN sub lieutenant is the equivalent of a USN lieutenant (junior grade), and an RN midshipman the same as a USN ensign, because the Royal Navy does not use the latter rank. The rank of midshipman in the U.S. Navy and Imperial German Navy was below that of Ensign and Oberleutnant zur See, respectively.

Royal/Royal Canadian/U.S. Navy		Imperial German Navy	
Rank		**Rank**	
Admiral	Adm.	Admiral	Adm.
Vice Admiral	Vice Adm.	Vizeadmiral	VAdm.
Rear Admiral	Rear Adm.	Kontreadmiral	Kadm.
Captain	Capt.	Kapitän zur See	Kpt. z. S.
Commander	Comdr.	Fregattenkapitän	FKpt.
Lieutenant Commander	Lt. Comdr.	Korvettenkapitän	KKpt.
Lieutenant	Lt.	Kapitänleutnant	Kptlt.
Sub Lieutenant	Sub Lt. [RN]	Oberleutnant zur See	OLt. z. S.
Lieutenant, Junior Grade	Lt. (jg) [USN]	Oberleutnant zur See	OLt. z. S.
Ensign	Ens. [USN]	Leutnant zur See	Lt. z. S.
Midshipman	Mid. [RN]		
Midshipman	Mid. [USN]	Oberfähnrich zur See	Fähn. z. S.

A significant difference exists between references to officers in the Royal Navy and its dominions, and those of the United States Navy. Those of the former include "Sir," if knighted, following an individual's military rank, and reference to military awards earned after surname. A partial list of such awards follows; in order of precedence from top to bottom in the left column, followed by the right:

British Awards for Gallantry or Meritorious Service in WWI

Award	Full Title of Award	Award	Full Title of Award
VC	Victoria Cross	CGM	Conspicuous Gallantry Medal
DSO	Distinguished Service Order	DSM	Distinguished Service Medal
DSC	Distinguished Service Cross	MM	Military Medal
MC	Military Cross	DFM	Distinguished Flying Medal
DFC	Distinguished Flying Cross	AFM	Air Force Medal
AFC	Air Force Cross	MSM	Meritorious Service Medal
DCM	Distinguished Conduct Medal	MID	Mentioned in Despatches[31]

Over the course of their careers, officers advance in rank and may receive additional awards. Since it is difficult to associate the latter with the former at any given point in time, the convention is to denote the final rank of an officer, and all awards they received in the first reference to that officer. So, the first reference to fictional Lt. John Smith, RN, would include in parenthesis after his surname (later Vice Adm. Sir John Smith, VC, DSO, DSC, CGM). In order to make the text easier to follow, particularly for those without naval backgrounds, this information is provided after the individuals' names in the index.

NAUTICAL/NAVAL TERMS

Some readers may find one of more of the following definitions useful as they progress through the book:

- Bearing drift: A description of the relative motion of another vessel, or of a fixed object, in relationship to one's own vessel.
- Carley raft/float: An early life raft consisting of a large oval ring of copper tubing covered with kapok and waterproof canvas.
- Collier: A bulk cargo ship designed to carry coal, especially for naval use by coal-fired warships.
- Gunlayer(s): Member(s) of a gun crew responsible for manually aiming a gun at land, surface, or air targets by "training" it in the horizontal plane and "elevating" it in the vertical plane.
- Jackstay: A rope, bar, or batten placed along a ship's yard to bend the head of a square sail to. A line secured at both ends to serve as a support.
- LWOS: Low Water Ordinary Springs is a tidal datum based on low water of ordinary spring tides.
- Mole: A massive structure, usually of stone or concrete, used as a pier, breakwater, or a causeway between places separated by water. The mole's defining feature is that water cannot freely flow underneath it, unlike a true pier.
- Pulling cutter: A boat carried by ships for work in fairly sheltered water in which load-carrying capacity was needed, with propulsion provided by double-banked oars (two oarsmen on each thwart).
- Scuttle: To cause a vessel to sink by opening the seacocks or making holes in the bottom of its hull.
- Skiff: Small flat-bottomed open boat with a pointed bow and a flat stern originally developed for use by inshore fishermen.
- Slipped their moorings: Crewmen singling up and casting off (abandoning) their vessel's mooring lines, in lieu of the normal use of line-handlers ashore, and by this action, slip out of port undetected.

- Smack: Traditional fishing boat used off the coast of Britain and the Atlantic coast of America for most of the 19th century and, in small numbers, up to World War II.
- Steaming party: Minimum crew required to man a ship on passage.
- Stoker: An engineering rating responsible for feeding coal into the firebox of a boiler providing steam to propulsion turbine. "Stoker" survives as an unofficial term for a marine engineering mechanic in the Royal Navy to this day.
- Viaduct: A high bridge that carries a road or railroad over an area that is difficult to cross.

Photo 1-1

They Opened the Seaways by Richard DeRosset portrays a mine detonation off the port quarter of USS *Richard Bulkeley*. The wooden-hulled minesweeping trawler was sunk with loss of life while participating in post-World War I clearance of the North Sea Mine Barrage stretching from the Scottish Orkney Islands to Bergen, Norway.

1

A Dark Day

For exceptional meritorious service in a duty of great responsibility as commander of a division of trawlers, engaged in the difficult and hazardous operation of sweeping for and removing mines in the North Sea Barrage; and especially for his heroic conduct on the occasion of the destruction by mine explosion of his flagship, the Richard Bulkeley, *of which he was also the commanding officer. Although stunned by the explosion, he made every effort to save the lives of and to rescue men entrapped by steam in the fire-room. The rapid sinking of the vessel prevented his success in the undertaking. Finding the ship about to sink, he proceeded to the bridge, where he took his station, and went down with the ship.*

—Citation for the Navy Distinguished Service Medal awarded posthumously to Comdr. Frank Ragan King, USN, who perished on 12 July 1919 while trying to save his ship— the USS *Richard Bulkeley*, a minesweeping trawler leased from the Royal Navy—and crew.[1]

Photo 1-2

Kirkwall Harbour, Orkney Islands, circa mid-1919, while serving as a base for the North Sea minesweeping detachment.
Naval History and Heritage Command photograph #NH 45256

Map 1-1

Scotland

On 12 July 1919, a group of U.S. Navy minesweepers operating from Kirkwall—a seaport and the capital city of Scotland's Orkney Islands—were plying their dangerous vocation in the North Sea. They were assisted by sub-chasers, following astern; whose job was to destroy with gunfire, the deadly mines rising to the surface after the moorings tethering them in place were cut. World War I was over, Germany having signed an armistice with the Allies on 11 November 1918. While almost all American soldiers, sailors, and Marines were home from the war, enjoying hard-won peace, it was not so for the crews of the minesweepers and their counterparts aboard similar type ships of the Royal Navy. Grave danger continued to abound for ships in passage between Scotland and Norway, and along shores visited by mines torn from their moorings by fierce wind and wave, until Royal and U.S. Navy minesweeping forces cleared 70,263 mines (56,611 American and 13,652 British).[2]

The weather in the North Sea was notoriously bad throughout the year, and particularly so in the winter months. Dirty seas and the few short hours of daylight, made operations, including the sweeping, practically impossible for seven months of the year. It was important that the barrage be completely removed in the summer of 1919. Every possible moment and vessel available therefore had to be utilised. Five months had been required to lay the mines, but the task of bringing profuse numbers of "ship killers" up from the depths and rendering them safe was, by known practice, infinitely more difficult and exacting.[3]

Photo 1-3

USS *Sanderling*, a *Lapwing*-class minesweeper, in heavy seas during North Sea Mine Barrage clearance operations, circa mid-1919.
Naval History and Heritage Command photograph #NH 107317

A "MIXED BAG" OF SHIPS

The minesweepers and assisting ships had sailed from Kirkwall on 7 July. They were engaged on 12 July in the fourth of seven operations conducted by the American force between 29 April and 30 September 1919, when the barrage was finally cleared. Making up the forty-three ships assigned to this operation were groups of 187-foot steel-hulled *Lapwing*-class minesweepers (including *Curlew, Flamingo, Lapwing, Oriole, Pelican, Penguin,* and *Rail*), and wooden-hulled submarine chasers and minesweeping trawlers. Among the latter were sub-chaser *SC-46*, and trawlers *Richard Bulkeley* and *William Darnold* on lease from the Royal Navy. The fleet tug *Patapsco* was also present. Nine of these ten ships had been, or would be, damaged by mines between 7 and 17 July. Tragically, the tenth, *Richard Bulkeley*, was sunk with loss of life.[4]

But for the efforts of three of her sister ships operating in close enough proximity to provide assistance, *Pelican* would have been lost as well. Six mines exploded either close aboard or under her, rupturing her hull. As she filled with water and began to sink, *Auk* and *Eider* made up on either side, and *Teal* took the three ships in tow. After many hours of ceaseless pumping and labour of a dozen volunteers brave enough to remain aboard her, the group finally reached the shelter of Tresness Bay, on the southeast coast of Sanday in Orkney. From there, *Pelican* was taken to the Royal Navy base at Scapa Flow, where she was docked for temporary repairs to enable her to be towed south to Newcastle-on-Tyne in northeast England, where complete repairs could be undertaken.[5]

DIFFICULTIES POSED BY AMERICAN SEA MINES

Of the American and British mines that made up the North Sea Barrage, eighty percent had been laid by the United States Navy. Aside from the huge number, the American Mk VI mine presented almost insurmountable difficulties to planned clearance efforts on account of its novel design and sensitive firing device. The American mines, tens of thousands of large metal spheres packed with TNT, waited passively, suspended in the water column, held in place by tethers to anchors (resembling square metal boxes) on the bottom. Stretching upward from each mine body toward the surface was an antenna, seeking detection of a vessel passing close enough to detonate the explosives.[6]

Great Britain had gained extensive experience during the war in sweeping the types of mines which she had laid; she possessed minesweeping vessels with very shallow draughts, specially constructed for work of this nature; further, the work to be done was within close proximity to her coasts and operating bases. In addition to her portion of the North Sea Mine Barrage, Britain had other minefields to clear. There was also the Dover Barrage (a vast minefield laid between the coast of Belgium and Dover, designed to prevent the access of U-boats through the English Channel at its narrowest point) and miscellaneous minefields in the Heligoland Bight. The latter was a bay which formed the southern part of the German Bight, itself a bay of the North Sea, located at the mouth of the Elbe River.[7]

While methods of sweeping the British mines were understood, there was no known method of sweeping the mines which the United States had laid. With the uppermost end of an antenna at an average of 8 to 10 feet below the surface of the water, it was impossible for a steel-hulled ship to pass nearby without detonating the ordnance. A small piece of iron or steel no larger than a nail was sufficient to trigger the delicate firing mechanism. Consequently, it appeared that only wooden vessels would be safe in such a field, and then only provided that no metal projections, however small, were exposed on the hull of the ships.[8]

Photo 1-4

An American Mk VI mine, complete with anchor, recovered in the North Sea.
Naval History and Heritage Command photograph #NH 2507

The most feasible idea appeared to be the use of wooden vessels (with their propellers guarded from contact with the mines) to explode mines near the surface using a sweep wire to make contact with the antenna. After all the surface mines had thus been destroyed, larger, steel-hulled *Lapwing*-class minesweepers could then sweep the mines planted at lower levels. For the first phase of the work, wooden, steam-powered minesweeping trawlers were chartered from the British Admiralty, manned with U.S. Navy crews. For crewing the vessels, 400 trained petty officers and seamen were taken from the American minelayers that had planted the barrage (before the ships' departure for America). They were transferred to bases in Scotland prior to assignment to the trawlers; the idea being to have experienced men serve as the nucleus of each crew.[9]

A solution was found subsequently, that partially alleviated the danger that mines posed to the steel *Lapwing*s. Ens. Dudley A. Nichols, USN Reserve Force, came up with the concept of a protective device that would use electricity to prevent mines from exploding when struck by a ship. Following experimentation, specifications were drawn up for its manufacture and subsequent installation aboard the American minesweepers. Unfortunately, nothing could eliminate the possibility of a mine exploded by contact with a sweep wire setting off others nearby. In such cases, the protective device would be useless.[10]

Photo 1-5

The first American mine swept up in the North Sea Barrage, exploding after it touched a sweep wire.
Naval History and Heritage Command #NH 109652

BRITISH TRAWLERS PRESSED INTO DUTY

Requiring additional vessels for the impending minesweeping work, Rear Adm. Joseph Strauss, USN, the Mine Force commander, asked that thirty of the New England deep-sea trawlers acquired by the U.S. Navy during the war for patrol vessels, be sent to him for work in the North Sea. This did not occur as shortly after he made this request, the British Admiralty offered to provide, on charter, any number of newly built steam trawlers, if the Americans could furnish crews to man them. Being the most expedient solution, permission was obtained from the Navy Department to take over twenty trawlers, comprised of three different classes of vessels. The monthly rate of hire, respectively, for the 150-foot *Mersey*-class ships and for the smaller *Castle* and *Strath* types, was £240, £225 and £160. In the case of loss or damage, the United States would be responsible for the liabilities incurred.[11]

Lt. Comdr. E. N. Parker, USNRF (United States Naval Reserve Force), and Lt. T. D. Warner, USN, were sent to Falmouth, where eleven of these vessels were placed in commission with the assistance of the crew of cruiser USS *Chattanooga* and the British authorities. Parker and the *Chattanooga* later proceeded to Grimsby, England, where the nine remaining trawlers were turned over and commissioned before sailing for Kirkwall. Acquiring the vessels proved considerably easier than obtaining personnel to man them. Orders had just been received to begin the release of men who had enlisted for the duration of the war; and the mine force was, accordingly, undermanned. Both in officers and men, crews were at a premium.[12]

By 2 June 1919, all of the trawlers had arrived at Kirkwall. Although they had been built expressly for minesweeping, it proved impossible to fit them with the electrical protective device. Thus, it was decided to use them at the rear of the *Lapwings* to cover their swept paths and catch any mines which might have been missed.[13]

LOSS OF TRAWLER *RICHARD BULKELEY*

The relatively new, ill-fated *Richard Bulkeley*, a *Mersey*-class trawler, had been launched on 21 August 1917 by Cochrane & Sons (a riverfront yard at Selby in Yorkshire, England), as a patrol and antisubmarine vessel for the Royal Navy. She was acquired 31 May 1919 and commissioned the same day. The trawler served thereafter as flagship of Comdr. Frank R. King, USN; the commander of one of the four divisions of trawlers.[14]

Photo 1-6

Minesweeping trawler USS *Richard Bulkeley* photographed by T. M. Trimble aboard the submarine chaser USS *SC-182*, date unknown.
Sweeping the North Sea Mine Barrage, U.S. Navy North Sea Minesweeping Detachment

Rapidly constructed for war service, she, like the *Castle* and *Strath* trawlers, was both economical to build and to operate. Powered by a single coal-fed boiler—providing steam to a 3-cylinder triple expansion engine, driving a single shaft and propeller—she could make a modest 11 knots. Her armament was equally austere. A single 12-pound gun on the bow had likely afforded only a measure of comfort to her British crew during the earlier hostilities.[15]

Diagram 1-2

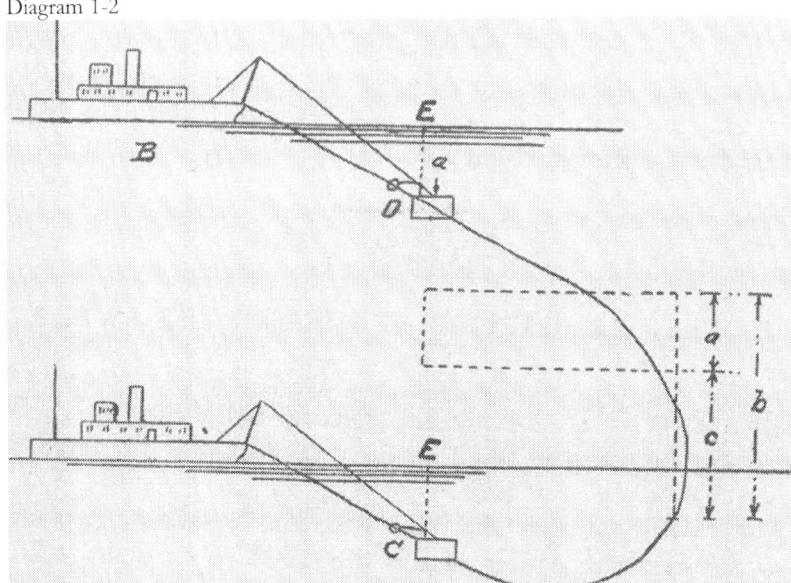

Diagram of two minesweepers streaming abreast of one another, at a distance apart about equal in yards to the number of fathoms of sweep wire out. The bight formed in the shared sweep wire, upon encountering the mooring cable of a mine in its path, either dragged the mine along with its anchor or, by seesawing, cut the mine's cable, letting the mine float to the surface, where it could be destroyed with gunfire. It was also possible that the sweep wire itself might explode the mine.
Source: *Mine Sweeping Manual United States Navy 1917.*[17]

Shortly before sunset on 12 July, *Richard Bulkeley* was sunk by the explosion of a mine fouled in the "kite" of her sweep gear. The Mine Force was using Type 7 plunger kites obtained from the British, a device which resembled a section of the wing of an airplane, except that it rode upside down in order to fly downward instead of upward. Although innovative at the time, the sweep gear was by the standards of WWII, rudimentary. There were no buoys to keep sweeps from striking the bottom, nor cutters affixed to sweep wires to sever the moorings of mines. Pairs of *Lapwings* operated together to clear the mines. Steaming abreast, with one end of a heavy wire made fast to each ship. Formed into a U-shaped catenary pulled down by a kite astern of each ship, the minesweepers employed the sweep wire to part (saw through) the wire cable moorings of tethered mines. Since this was done by friction, sweep wires regularly parted, necessitating frequent replacement of sweep gear.[16]

Photo 1-7

Minesweep detail aboard the USS *Tanager* handling a "kite," circa 1918-1919.
Naval History and Heritage Command photograph #NH 107321

Of greater significance, a sweep wire could inadvertently contact a mine casing often resulting in an enormous detonation and associated shock wave, which could then countermine (set off) other nearby mines. If one or more of these exploding spheres of TNT were close enough to a minesweeper, severe damage could occur to the vessels as well as injury and death to the crews.

Detailed information about the activities of trawlers in trail behind pairs of *Lapwing*s through the field is scarce. Generally, in addition to sweeping, trawlers were employed to mark the boundaries of minefields, and to participate in the destruction of mines bobbing to the surface, once severed from their moorings. On the day she was sunk, *Richard Bulkeley* was likely sweeping in concert with another trawler (perhaps the *George Clarke*), before she had occasion to recover her sweep wire and fouled kite.

Men assigned to recover the gear had sighted the mine a few feet below the surface while bringing in the sweep wire. In an attempt to reduce the danger, the wire was immediately veered (payed out) in order to get the kite-gripped mine farther astern. For some unknown reason it exploded, breaching the after hull and allowing the trawler to fill and sink within seven minutes. Vessels of the Mine Force in the vicinity rushed to her assistance, but before they could arrive she had disappeared into the deep of the frigid North Sea.[18]

The trawler USS *George Clarke*, under the command of Lt. (jg) Edwin V. Wilder, USN, was approximately 400 yards from the *Bulkeley* when the mine detonated. She steamed to the rescue, but was still over one-quarter that distance away when the stricken ship went down. She was able to retrieve twelve survivors and returned them to Kirkwall.[19]

Comdr. Ellis Lando, USN, the commander of Trawler Division 4 leapt overboard from his flagship USS *William Johnson*, into the rough, cold waters, to rescue Seaman First Class Antino Perfidio who was unconscious at the time. Although Perfidio died, Lando received the Distinguished Service Medal for his unselfish act of heroism.

Through the efforts of trawlers *George Clarke* and *William Johnson* and perhaps other vessels, all of *Richard Bulkeley*'s crew was recovered except for one officer and six men (who drowned, were carried down with their ship, or perished following rescue) identified below.

- Comdr. Frank Ragan King
- Engineman 1st Class Floyd Harman
- Fireman 1st Class George M. Sowers
- Fireman 2nd Class George P. Rezab
- Ship's Cook 1st Class Antino Perfidio
- Seaman 2nd Class Homer Perdue
- Seaman 2nd Class John V. Mallon[20]

Photo 1-8

Survivors of the USS *Richard Bulkeley*, sunk by a mine caught in her sweep gear while conducting clearance operations in the North Sea.
Naval History and Heritage Command photograph #NH 121110

Comdr. Frank Ragan King was last seen on the bridge of *Richard Bulkeley*, after searching for members of his crew that might be trapped aboard as the trawler settled lower and lower in the water. When a sailor struggled to the deck half stunned by the shock of the explosion which had blown off his life preserver, King had taken off his own lifebelt, buckled it around the man, and helped him to get clear of the vessel before it plunged, stern first, beneath the surface.[21]

Photo 1-9

Portrait of Frank Ragan King, USN, taken while a lieutenant prior to WWI. Naval History and Heritage Command photograph #NH 843-A

King was awarded the Navy Distinguished Service Medal (posthumously) for extraordinary heroism, as was also Seaman Second Class John V. Mallon, USN. At the time of the mine explosion, Mallon was on duty as signalman of the watch and remained at his post on the bridge and went down with the ship. Although his citation does not detail his actions, Mallon was likely signaling vessels steaming toward the trawler in fading light, the locations of shipmates in the water, perhaps injured, struggling to stay afloat in the frigid sea.[22]

AFTERMATH

At a conference aboard the *George Clarke* the following day, Rear Admiral Strauss decided that the hulls of the trawlers were not strong enough to withstand the shock of mine detonations close aboard. The wooden vessels had been assigned to follow the initial sweeps of the more heavily built, steel-hulled *Lapwing*s, but even this had proven too much for ships of their design when confronted with exploding mines—more of which were left for follow-up sweeps than had been estimated.[23]

Such danger would continue to exist, so Strauss opted to return the majority of the trawlers to the Admiralty, retaining only six to be used for miscellaneous purposes, transporting stores from Inverness, in the Scottish Highlands, to Kirkwall and carrying minesweeping gear and provisions to vessels in the minefield. In the case of *George Clarke*, preparations for her return to Admiralty custody began in mid-July at Kirkwall and were completed with her transfer to the Royal Navy, at Brightlingsea, England, on 16 August 1919.[24]

A few months later, in commemoration of the gallantry of Frank Ragan King, the Secretary of the Navy named a new ship, USS *King* (DD-242), in his honour. His namesake, a *Clemson*-class destroyer was commissioned on 16 December 1920.[25]

2

Mines, Minelaying and Minesweeping

The ex-pleasure steamers, in particular, were very lightly built, and practically fell to pieces when struck by a mine. There was rarely any hope of saving them. They had to be abandoned just as fast as the survivors could leave them. The unostentatious heroism of those who continued to work in these ships after once having been blown up, or having seen their friends blown up, can hardly be exaggerated. They had none of the excitement of battle against a visible foe – nothing of the supreme satisfaction of being able to hit back. The work was entirely one-sided – 'Heads you win. Tails I lose."

—Capt. Henry Taprell Dorling, RN, in *Swept Channels*.[1]

A total of 235,983 mines were laid in all parts of the world in World War I. Those planted by Britain (130,402), America (56,611), and Germany (43,636) accounted for 98 percent of this number. Britain concentrated her efforts in three locations: the Heligoland Bight off Germany (42,899), the eastern part of the English Channel (40,286), and the North Sea Barrage (13,652). The American mines (56,611) made up the other portion of the North Sea Barrage, which the British termed the Northern Barrier. Germany laid 43,636 mines, primarily in the North Sea and around the British Isles. Germany possessed superior mines and, except for a few defensive fields around her coastal areas, employed them offensively. Britain concentrated largely on large-scale defensive mining, in an effort to keep enemy ships and submarines from entering and attacking Allied shipping in home waters. She did eventually mine the Heligoland Bight, directed against the German High Seas Fleet, which traversed the bay when leaving and returning to home port.[2]

Forty-six Royal Navy ships were lost to German mines. An official British report issued in 1919, cited two fewer ships, but later information indicated that the losses of two torpedo-boats attributed to submarines were, in fact, destroyed by mines. The total number of Royal Navy and British vessels believed lost to mines was a staggering 807, a figure that would have been much higher but for the efforts of minesweepers—which lost 214 of their own while plying their dangerous trade. Moreover, without the minesweepers, it is likely that Britain, instead of Germany would have had to capitulate, owing to overwhelming losses of merchant shipping delivering critical food, supplies, and materiel to the British Isles. As it was, German U-boats and mines came very close to cutting off food supplies from overseas.[3]

The following statistics, from Capt. Henry Taprell Dorling's book *Swept Channels*, do not reflect the total number of sailors killed by mines, only those serving in British merchant ships and fishing vessels. Also, while merchant ship/fishing vessel losses are divided into those sunk and those damaged, the data for the other vessel categories is combined. For example, the 214 minesweepers lost include both those sunk, and those damaged sufficiently to cause their removal from service.

Royal Navy Ships, Auxiliaries, Merchant Ships, Fishing Vessels, and Minesweepers Lost to Sea Mines in WWI

Vessel Category	Lost/ Sunk	Damaged	Personnel Losses
HM Ships (Royal Navy)	46		
Auxiliaries employed on Admiralty Service	225		
Merchant Ships (259), Fishing Vessels (63)	322	84	1,889
Minesweepers[4]	214		

At the time of the Armistice, the British Minesweeping Service was comprised of 726 vessels. Of these, 110 were regular naval vessels (mostly built during the war), allocated among twenty fast-sweeping flotillas to sweep ahead of the Royal Navy's fleets and Allied merchant convoys. Performing the daily work of clearing enemy mines from Britain's waters were: (1) 52 paddle-steamers, (2) 412 fishing trawlers, (3) 142 drifters, and (4) 10 "tunnel" minesweepers of the *Dance*-class.[5]

Because hired fishing vessels (trawlers and drifters) fitted with sweep gear comprised three-quarters of the Minesweeping Service, a majority of the sweepers lost to mines were fishing vessels. The Admiralty was well aware of the contributions and sacrifices of their crews, as witnessed by Admiral Jellicoe's assertion after the war that "the Royal Navy had saved the Empire, but it was fishermen in their boats who had saved the Royal Navy." Clearance of mines allowed the Royal Navy freedom of movement necessary for command of the seas. Being the stronger sea power, Britain was able to maintain the blockade against Germany and confine her capital ships to port, which eventually brought her to her knees.[6]

Mine warfare has always been very dangerous work. The next few pages provide readers an introduction to naval mines and the methods of employing and removing them including use of minelayers, and minesweepers. The Allied navies and the Imperial German Navy employed various types of mines and mine-countermeasures during the war. Only representative types and methods are discussed. United States mines, minelaying, and minesweeping are covered later in the book, in chapters devoted to America's participation in the war.

MOORED MINES AND MINELAYING

Germany employed both surface ships and submarines to lay mines. Crewmen aboard naval and merchant vessels fitted with rails on their decks for this purpose, pushed mines along the rails and over the stern into the sea. Mines carried aboard submarines were stored in isolated inclined tubes in their hulls, sloping aft, from which they could be dropped. The Allies employed mainly large, fast surface vessels for their minelaying, some converted military and other requisitioned commercial with large storage capacity. Like Germany, Britain also used submarines to lay mines but they only accounted for two percent of the mines planted.

In German minelaying, whether launched from a ship or submarine, a mine and sinker (anchor), weighing roughly half-a-ton, went straight to the bottom. Each mine was equipped with a timer attached to a latching mechanism on a mooring cable reel. After a predetermined short interval to allow the laying vessel to get clear, the mine would start to rise under its own buoyancy, unreeling the mooring wire as it rose. German mines employed hydrostatic pressure sensing devices for setting the mines to a predetermined depth below the surface. On each mine the sensor was coupled to a set of jaws through which the mooring cable was run. The jaws locked the cable at the desired depth when the correct pressure was measured.[7]

The diagrams of German moored mines on the following page (from a 1918 U.S. Office of Naval Intelligence publication) illustrate the deployment of a mine. The diagram on the left shows the sinker of a Carbonit mine on the bottom with the mine body beginning to rise to the set depth. The one on the right shows the final position of a Type I mine once deployed. Its mooring wire ran from the sinker through a set of jaws on the mine and back to a drum on the sinker. The disadvantage of this system was that the mine body had to support double the weight of wire when moored. The Carbonit mine utilised a 220-lb TNT charge, while the buoyant body of the latter type could support only 160 lbs. of explosives.[8]

The detonation of a German mine was caused by a target vessel striking one of Herz-horns protruding from the top of the mine.

Invented in 1868 by Dr. Herz of the German Mine Defence Committee, this innovation enabled mines to work reliably even after being in the sea for several years.   Each Herz (chemical) horn contained the components of an electrical battery.   These were a carbon plate, a zinc plate, and a bichromate solution, the latter was contained inside a sealed glass tube in each lead horn.   When a ship bumped against the mine and bent a horn, the glass tube inside fractured allowing the liquid to come into contact with the two plates.   This completed the battery, producing about 1.8 volts, sufficient to fire an electric detonator, which detonated the main charge through a primer or dry guncotton.[9]

Diagram 2-1

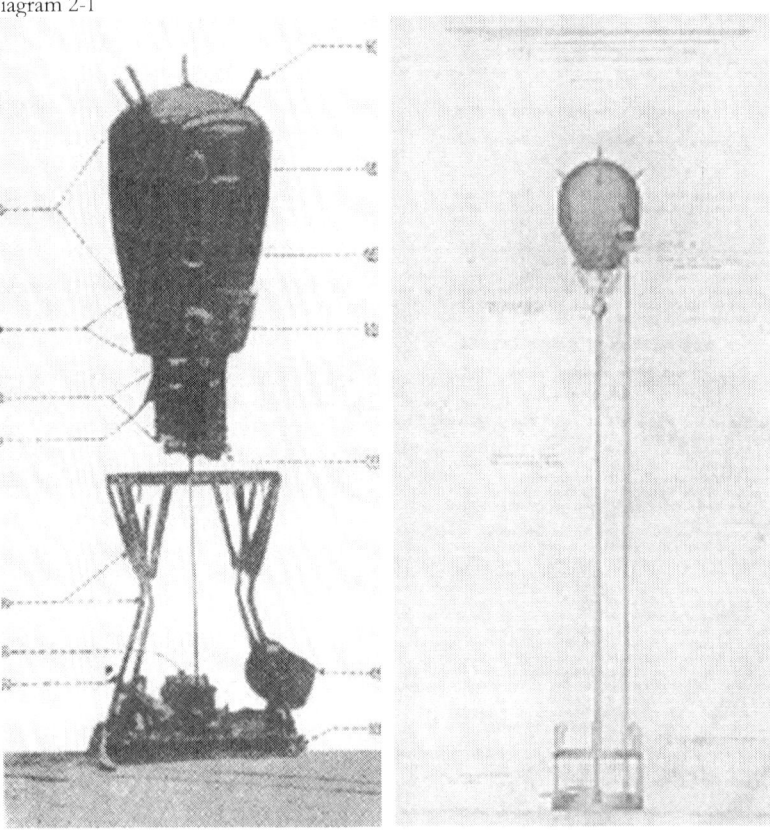

German Carbonit moored mine.   German Type I moored mine.
Source: *Antisubmarine Information O. N. I. Compilation No. 14 – 1918*

In British minelaying, the mine detached from its sinker the moment it went over the stern of a ship or was released from a submarine. The mine case would float for a few seconds while the heavy sinker plummeted toward the sea bottom, the mooring wire spooling from its drum on the sinker as it travelled downward. Below the sinker was a small weight known as a "plummet," attached by a chain to the sinker. When the plummet hit the bottom, the slacking of its chain locked the drum on the sinker, preventing any additional wire from running out. The sinker, upon reaching the bottom, pulled the mine case down to its predetermined depth below the surface.[10]

BRITISH MINELAYERS

No country had ships designed and built specifically as minelayers. Each relied on the adaptation or conversion of merchant vessels, small craft, and naval ships, including in some cases submarines. Over the course of the war, the British employed 9 converted merchant vessels, 32 warships, 6 submarines, and a host of light craft (trawlers, motor launches, lighters, and coastal motor boats) to lay mines. The bulk of such work was performed by nine large merchant ships and passenger liners pressed into these duties.

Converted Merchant Ships and Passenger Liners (68,687 mines/53%)

Ship	#Mines	Ship	#Mines
Angora	14,729	*Perdita*	1,332
Biarritz	5,673	*Princess Irene*, destroyed	723
Gazelle	243	*Princess Margaret*	25,242
Orvieto	3,131	*Wahine*	11,378
Paris	6,236		

Battleship (2,640 mines/2%)

London	2,640

Cruisers (14,964 mines/11%)

Ship	#Mines	Ship	#Mines
Amphitrite	5,053	*Iphigenia*, sunk as blockship	640
Andromache	1,425	*Latona*	2,499
Apollo	1,600	*Naiad*	800
Ariadne, sunk by *UC-65*	708	*Thetis*, sunk as blockship	800
Intrepid, sunk as blockship	1,439		

Light Cruisers (4,280 mines/3%)

Aurora, Bellona, Blanche, Boadicea, Galatea, Inconstant, Penelope, Phaeton, Royalist

Flotilla Leaders and Destroyers (23,136 mines/18%)

Ship	#Mines	Ship	#Mines
Abdiel	6,293	*Tarpon*	1,425
Ariel, sunk	1,237	*Telemachus*	1,898
Ferret	1,875	*Vanoc*	965
Gabriel	850	*Vanquisher*	1,859
Legion	2,033	*Vehement*, sunk by enemy mine	554
Meteor	1,082	*Venturous*	1,823
Sandfly	1,242		

Light Craft (14,226 mines/11%)		
Coastal motor boats (55)	Trawlers (9,345)	Motor launches and lighters (4,826)
Submarines (2,469 mines/2%)		
E-24	20	E-45	640
E-34	478	E-46	240
E-41	591	E-51	500[11]

Six minelayers were lost in the war; two due to enemy action, one as a result of an explosion on board while loading mines, and three which were purposefully sunk as blockships during British raids on Zeebrugge. The obliteration of HMS *Princess Irene* and associated deaths of hundreds of crewmen killed in the explosion, and of the heroic actions of the crews of *Intrepid*, *Iphigenia*, and *Thetis*, who scuttled their ships while under enemy fire, are discussed in later chapters.

MINESWEEPING GEAR/TECHNIQUES

The wire cable connecting a mine body to its sinker ranged from about $1\frac{1}{4}$ to $1\frac{1}{2}$ inches in circumference. In British minesweeping trawlers, the wire used to cut a mine's mooring was about the same diameter. Two trawlers working together to sever a mine from its mooring, often ended up dragging the mine about with its sinker pounding the bottom. As useful as trawlers were, their speed of 6 to 7 knots when sweeping was often insufficient to develop the necessary momentum to sever a mooring. In such cases it was necessary for the vessels to drag the mine into shallow water, to enable it to be exploded with gunfire. Towing a high explosive astern was obviously a dangerous manoeuvre. This practice changed in 1916, with the introduction of serrated sweep wire. Unlike wire laid in the ordinary way, one of the strands was irregular which, when under strain, exercised a sawing action on the mooring, severing it and releasing the mine to come to the surface where it could be destroyed with rifle fire.[12]

Various forms of minesweeping were tried and evolved during the war. The sweep employed for the bulk of the clearance work, was the British 'A' sweep. It proved to be efficient in all weathers, with the added merit of simplicity, as it could be easily handled by trawlermen drafted to sweep mines. After many years of experience on the fishing grounds, they were well accustomed to working aboard such vessels dealing with taut wires and steam winches in the bitter cold, gales, and heavy seas of winter. Others also became proficient in the use of the sweep, including officers and seamen of the Royal and Merchant navies, and thousands of landsmen from every walk of life who served in minesweepers.[13]

A general drawing of a Type A sweep (Diagram 1-2) performed by a pair of minesweepers, is provided in Chapter 1. One showing detail how it was rigged, follows.

Diagram 2-2

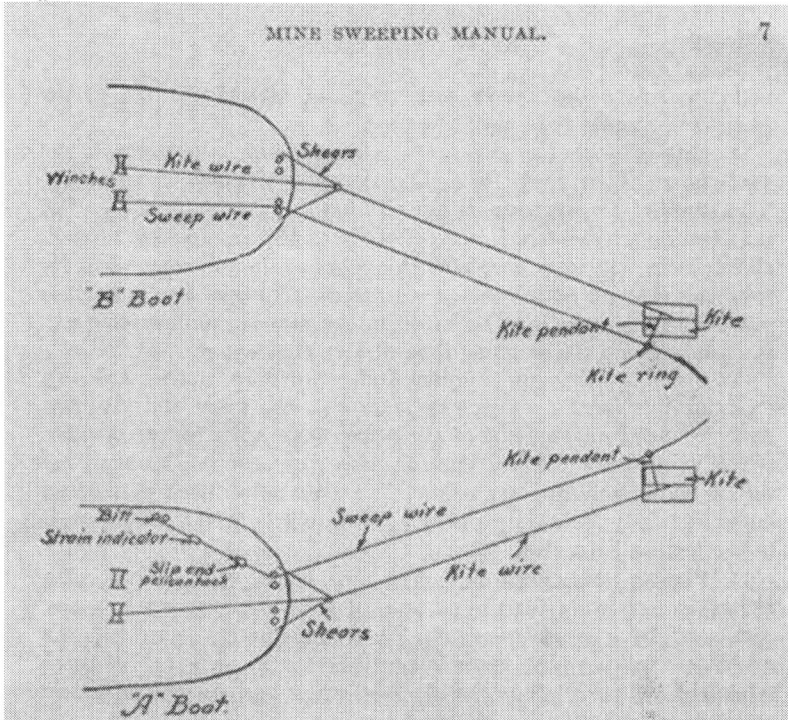

British 'A' type sweep. This sketch erroneously omitted the section of wire at the catenary (bend) of the sweep wire or, it was meant to depict the gear each vessel would have to recover when the sweep wire broke—a common occurrence when sawing through the mooring cables of enemy mines.
Source: *Mine Sweeping Manual, United States Navy, 1917*

With the sweep wire reeled on a steam winch aboard one of the vessels, the other vessel would manoeuvre alongside the first one, so close as to be nearly touching. The free end of the wire was then passed to the second vessel and secured to a bit on its stern. Once this had occurred, the two vessels would separate out from one another, to a predetermined distance, which they would maintain while sweeping. The sweeping distance at which two minesweepers could work apart (generally 300-500 yards) was dependent on their speed, towing capacity, and the state of the weather.[14]

Each vessel, in addition to dragging its end of the sweep wire, towed a kite attached to its own dedicated wire from a second steam winch. A "kite" was a heavy apparatus designed to be dragged under water when towed, an action similar to an ordinary kite rising in the air because of wind deflection. Each kite was attached to the sweep wire by a kite pendant. Its weight took the sweep wire down to the prescribed depth, based on how much wire was eased out and the towing speed. The kites of the two ships separated from each other, similar to the manner in which "otter boards" used by fishing trawlers, swim out laterally under water to keep the mouth of trawl nets open.[15]

There were other British developments in minesweeping during the war, but they played little or no part in overall clearance efforts. One of these was the *Actaeon* sweep, named after the parent ship of the Sheerness torpedo school where it was developed. Designed for use by a single ship, it consisted of a light wire, a depth float, a small kite, and an explosive grapnel. One of these sweeps was towed off each quarter of a minesweeper; upon encountering a mine, the grapnel blew up and parted its mooring. This type sweep was useful for locating new fields, but not for clearing them.[16]

The most noteworthy development was the *Oropesa* Mk 1 sweep, which would come into prominence in World War II. Named after the trawler involved in its trial, the wire sweep could be employed by a single vessel but was not formally accepted into service until 1919. The *Oropesa* sweep was kept at the required depth by a multi-vane kite otter. Its end was diverted laterally by another kite on its side, or by an otter board, suspended beneath a streamlined float. A V-cutter at the end of the sweep severed the mooring of any mine left intact by the serrated wire.[17]

BOTTOM SWEEPING

Moored mines which had failed to release from their sinkers when laid, or mines that had sunk without exploding, had to be removed as part of the clearance of each field. The process was known as "Bottom Sweeping" and was performed after a minefield was cleared of moored mines. It was a labourious job involving two trawlers towing a sweep wire and two short lengths of chain between them. The chain scoured the seafloor to break loose, any mines remaining on their sinkers, in order that they float to the surface to be destroyed. Such dangerous work was carried out by trawlers in fair or foul weather, whenever possible. Swirling tides, fierce gales, heavy seas, and frequent fog in any but calm seas, made the operation very difficult. Add to that the constant wetness, bitter cold of winter, and threat posed by submarines and mines, and one begins to appreciate the strength, fortitude, and endurance required of the men who manned the minesweeping trawlers.[18]

USE OF DRIFT NETS FOR MINESWEEPING

Early in the war, the British tried to clear located German-laid minefields by the employment of long drift nets then in use by herring fisherman. These nets buoyed on their tops and weighted on their bottoms hung down vertically from the surface. Employed in fishing they were not towed, but allowed to drift until being recovered. It was possible to allow them to drift down on a field with the tide to ensnare the mines, but the result often caused the loss of life and vessels. Often the mines were snared in the nets without exploding, posing extreme danger to those charged with buoying and slipping the nets. Moreover, if not dealt with properly, clumps of mines left alone to await further action, presented extreme danger to shipping.[19]

Despite the drawbacks associated with using nets to collect mines, the practice was not totally discarded. After the war, each country was required to clear any remaining mines it had laid. Fortunately for the Royal Navy, the British mines had been made in accordance with the Hague Convention, whereby they were safe on the surface after having been cut from their moorings. While trying to find ways to dispose of floating mines, Lt. George E. Blackmore, RN, executive officer aboard the minesweeping sloop HMS *Cupar*, devised a special net:

> My scheme simply consisted of a large net, floated and kept open by otter boards like the mouth of a trawl. At the cod-end was an E.C. [electro-contact] mine electrically connected, and when about twenty mines had been collected we veered the contraption to a safe distance astern, fired the E.C. mine, and destroyed the whole bunch by detonation…. I believe the idea was later improved by the net, with several E.C. mines attached to it, being towed with a drifter [fishing vessel] at each end.[20]

EMPLOYMENT OF MINESWEEPERS

Trawlers requisitioned from the fishing fleet comprised the bulk of the initial vessels employed for minesweeping, and remained so throughout the war. They had many shortcomings, chiefly they were too slow to work with the fleet, and their deep draughts put both vessel and crew at great risk when sweeping mines lying just below the surface of the sea. However, against these defects, they had many advantages. They were available in large numbers, were very seaworthy, and were economical in coal consumption, allowing them to remain at sea for long periods.

They were therefore best utilised carrying out the routine of sweeping coastwise shipping lanes.[21]

Later, paddle-sweepers joined the British Minesweeping Service. With their lesser draughts and higher speeds, they performed the bulk of the clearance work after a minefield had been located. As necessary, their efforts were augmented by those of fleet gunboat-sweepers and/or trawlers. The first paddle-sweepers were ordinary paddle-steamers of the type patronised by excursionists. While not suited for extreme bad weather, they were moderately fast and, drew comparatively little water. The converted paddle-steamers were later augmented by *Ascot*-class Admiralty-built paddle-sweepers.[22]

Much faster fleet minesweepers primarily supported fleet units and merchant convoys by sweeping ahead of them. The first fleet minesweepers were ex-torpedo-gunboats, which were joined later in the war by purposefully built *Flower*- and *Hunt*-class minesweeping sloops. There were also ten *Dance*-class minesweepers built as shallow-draught twin-screw tunnel tugs, which did little fleet duty due to their slow speeds. With their light draught, they proved useful sweeping the coast of Flanders, but could not operate in anything approaching bad weather. Four *Dance*-class ships were completed after the war, bringing the total number to fourteen.[23]

USE OF PARAVANES FOR SHIP SELF-PROTECTION

Because Royal Navy warships and merchant vessels had to venture outside coastal shipping channels, which were swept daily, some form of self-protection was desirable. (At any particular time, there might also be newly-laid mines in a swept channel.) This requirement led to the development of the Burney paravane, so named after its inventor Lt. Charles Denniston Burney, Royal Navy. The torpedo-shaped device was about twelve feet long and non-explosive. It was successfully tested in 1916, and by year's end had been supplied to 180 of HM ships over twelve feet in draught. Ultimately, 2,740 merchant vessels were also fitted with this device as a defence against moored mines.[24]

A pair of paravanes was towed in a v-shaped configuration from the point on a ship where its stem met the keel. Each of the devices was streamed on its wire at about a 50-degree angle off the respective ship's side. The ship's motion and the paravanes shape caused them to stand out at a considerable lateral distance from the ship's sides, thus preventing a mine strike on its hull. When the mooring of a mine was encountered, it slid along the paravane tow wire, and entered a pair of jaws on the paravane, which immediately cut it. A modified form of the paravane (called an "otter") was utilised by merchant ships.[25]

Photo 2-1

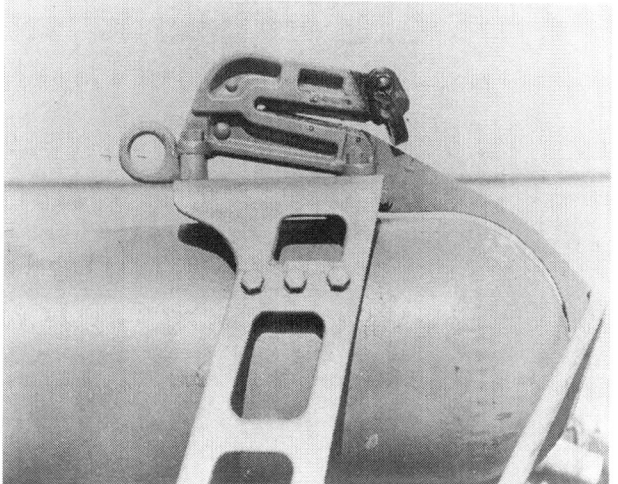

Cutting jaws of a paravane, used for minesweeping in World War I.
Naval History and Heritage Command photograph #NH 60758

Photo 2-2

A paravane, shaped somewhat like a torpedo, was dragged through the water by a
ship. The sharp v-knife at the top was used for cutting the moor holding a mine
in place. The mine then floated to the surface and was exploded by rifle fire.
Naval History and Heritage Command photograph #NH 124026

In his book *Swept Channels*, Dorling cites 55 mine moorings cut by
warships during the war, and between 40 and 50 by merchant vessels.
Like the *Oropesa* sweep, the use of paravanes has endured to the present
time. The Burney paravane was designed for any class of vessel. When

used to sweep ahead of the fleet at high speed for search purposes, it was referred to as the High Speed Minesweep. Although it could be used at a higher speed than any other form of minesweep, there was no method to ensure that the paravanes were working accurately once they were towed. Thus, it was deemed unsuitable for clearing a minefield.[26]

HIGH-SPEED SUBMARINE SWEEP

Britain also developed an anti-submarine paravane, referred to as the "high speed submarine sweep." It consisted of two explosive paravanes towed from the quarters of a destroyer. (Their usage is discussed here to highlight that they were not associated with mine sweeping, as some sources erroneously imply.) Ships' commanding officers thoroughly disliked these devices. Capt. Henry Taprell Dorling, who commanded the destroyer HMS *Murray*, explained their disdain in *Swept Channels*.

> We hated the contrivance, which was difficult to use, and always going wrong. Moreover, the ship had to ease down [slow] when the sweep was being got in or out, which was always a risk if a submarine was in the vicinity. Added to this, no commanding officer really felt happy with two explosive objects towing from his stern. There was the chance that they might be forgotten in a sudden emergency. For instance, if the ship had to go astern to avoid a collision, the paravane wires might quite easily be wrapped up round the propellers, and the explosive fish bob up alongside.[27]

Dorling noted in *Swept Channels* that, "so far as it is possible to discover, only two U-boats were destroyed by this particular method of attack." The idea behind the high speed submarine sweep was that the paravanes could be set at any depth, enabling a destroyer to attack a submarine whose position was only approximately known.[28]

3

Disposition of British Naval
Forces in Home Waters

There was no question of seeking out the enemy, for normally his fleet lay behind his base defences where it was inaccessible. All our own fleet could do was to take the most suitable position for confining him to port or bringing him to action if he put to sea. There was always the hope that the pressure so exercised would sooner or later force him to offer battle. But until an opportunity for decisive action arose, it was by patient and alert vigil it sought to attain its ultimate object – that is, primarily to cover the squadrons and flotillas which formed our floating defence against invasion, and secondarily to cover those which operated in the home terminals of our trade routes for the protection of our own commerce and the disturbance of that of the enemy, so far as geographical conditions permitted of both duties being performed simultaneously.

Over and above the burden that lay on our sea-going ships there remained the task of protecting our own shores from attack by lightly escorted raiding forces. To this function were assigned all the destroyer flotillas except the first four which were attached to the Grand Fleet, and the 5th which was in the Mediterranean. They were organised in "Patrol" and "Local Defence" Flotillas.

—Julian S. Corbett in *History of the Great War,
Naval Operations Vol. I, To the Battle of
the Falklands December 1914.*[1]

The Royal Navy recognised well before Britain's entry into war with Germany, it would be confronted with challenges different than those encountered during its long history of dominance at sea. Almost without exception, Britain had previously contended only with enemies that lay to the south. Not since the Dutch wars of the seventeenth century had she had to deal with a first class naval power based northward of the Dover defile (a narrow part of the English Channel). Germany had easy access to the North Sea bordering Britain's north and east coasts, via two widely separate points linked together by an inland waterway, the Kaiser Wilhelm (Kiel) Canal. Moreover, the enemy would face a long stretch of British coast dotted with vulnerable commercial ports, unlike England's southern seaboard, which had many well-disposed naval ports. There was not a single major Fleet base along the east coast except for Chatham on the Thames, which owing to navigational difficulties, was disadvantaged.[2]

In acknowledgement of these shortcomings, the Admiralty began to consider changing the disposition of its forces. On Britain's east coast, only Harwich offered a "war anchorage." Admittedly, there were several defended commercial ports including the Humber, the Tees, Hartlepool, the Tyne, the Tay, and Aberdeen, which would serve the same purpose. But all were cramped river ports and, owing to tidal conditions, they did not offer freedom of access to the Channel and North Sea at all times. Moreover, beyond these drawbacks, none of these ports were far enough north to satisfy the fundamental need to control the approach to the North Sea. The best locations from which the British Grand Fleet could accomplish this were in Scottish waters; at Rosyth on the Firth of Forth and Cromarty in the Moray Firth in the north of Scotland, and even farther north at Scapa Flow in the Orkney Islands.[3]

Map 3-1

Scotland

Although Rosyth was designated as the headquarters and principal base for the Grand Fleet, Scapa was regarded as the best station. Because Germany's whole Battle Fleet was concentrated in the North Sea, the fleet anchorage at Scapa Flow would provide the Royal Navy an ideal location to counter-concentrate the bulk of its forces; except for those needed to secure the Straits of Dover. The latter forces were expected to be mainly torpedo boats and their supporting cruisers and minor battleships.[4]

Photo 3-1

Boom at Scapa Flow intended to deny enemy vessels access to the Fleet anchorage. Naval History and Heritage Command photograph #NH 110539

PATROL AND LOCAL DEFENCE FLOTILLAS

Beyond the Royal Navy's duty to counter Germany's High Seas Fleet, there remained the task of protecting Britain's shores from attack by lightly escorted raiding forces. To this function were assigned all the destroyer flotillas, except the four assigned to the Grand Fleet (the 1st, 2nd, 3rd, and 4th) and the 5th Flotilla in the Mediterranean. The 6th, 7th, 8th, and 9th Destroyer Flotillas—and their attached light cruisers— were organised in "Patrol Flotillas" under a special officer designated "Admiral of Patrols." This post was initially held by Commodore George A. Ballard, RN, appointed to that position on 1 May 1914. The Local "Defence Flotillas" were comprised of older destroyers and torpedo boats, which were attached to the naval ports they were to protect.[5]

The Royal Navy's opinion was that no raid would likely be attempted on the east coast except across the North Sea, therefore the Patrol Flotillas were distributed along the east coast. The 6th Flotilla, known as the Dover Patrol, was assigned the defence of the Straits; the 7th was based on the Humber, the 8th on the Tyne, and the 9th on the Firth of Forth at Rosyth.[6]

Royal Navy's Patrol Flotillas

Base-Flotilla	Light Cruisers	Destroyers	Torpedo Boats
Dover Patrol – 6th Flotilla	2	22	
Humber – 7th Flotilla	1	22	12
Tyne – 8th Flotilla	1	8	12
Forth- 9th Flotilla	1	18	

It was judged that north of the Firth of Forth Area, the Scottish Coast would be sufficiently safeguarded by the Grand Fleet bases at Cromarty and at Scapa, to which a special Defence Flotilla of two destroyer divisions was assigned. The East Anglian Coast between the Dover and Humber Patrols would be equally well protected by the active forces based at Harwich. These included Commodore Reginald Tyrwhitt's 1st and 3rd Destroyer Flotillas and their attached light cruisers, and the 8th Flotilla of submarines under Commodore Roger Keyes. Should the enemy make an attack before declaration of war, the first function of the Harwich Destroyer Flotillas would be to provide a patrol for the defence of the Thames Estuary. But, as soon as the Nore Defence Flotilla was ready to take over this duty, the Harwich Flotillas would assume their real place in the war plan, offensive operations against Germany's destroyers and minelayers operating in the southern part of the North Sea.[7]

Under Keyes were also the five oldest flotillas of submarines, which were distributed amongst the Patrol Flotillas and formed part of the patrol organisation under Ballard. The oldest boats of all were attached to the local defence flotillas.[8]

PRELUDE TO WAR

As far as the Royal Navy was concerned, in the early months of 1914, everything was in a state of war readiness, the Home Fleets beyond what the war plans dictated. In March, Parliament announced (following Admiralty advisement) that instead of the usual summer fleet manoeuvres a test mobilisation would be conducted. It was to begin about mid-July, and, after carrying out exercises at sea, the various fleets and flotillas would disperse on the 23rd. It was in no sense a real war mobilisation, for the Reserves were invited, not ordered to participate. Moreover, the officers were appointed to vessels and stations convenient to their homes, and not to their true war stations. Further, the composition of cruiser squadrons differed in some cases from that of the War Organisation.[9]

Operation orders were issued on 10 July for the ships to assemble at Portland, Dorset, under the command of Adm. George Callaghan, commander-in-chief of the Home Fleets. His First, Second, and Third Fleets were in progressive states of readiness for war, with the First Fleet the most advanced. Intended to become the "Grand Fleet" and to occupy the North Sea at the outbreak of war, the First Fleet was kept in full commission ready for immediate action. The Third Fleet was in essence a reserve fleet, comprised of old battleships and cruisers still on the active list, but not in commission. Groups of these ships were assigned to various ports, manned by "care and maintenance" parties; for full crews, they had to rely on the Reserves.[10]

In total, including fleet auxiliaries, not less than 460 vessels were under Callaghan's command. They included the whole of the Home Fleets, with the exception of the 4th Destroyer Flotilla which, owing to an unhappy state of affairs in Ulster, was engaged in police duty in the Irish Sea. The response of the Reserves was satisfactory, and by 16 July the whole of the Home Fleet was mobilised. The Grand Fleet would be formed in August 1914 from the First Fleet and elements of the Second Fleet; commanded by Adm. John Jellicoe. Jellicoe was eventually succeeded in December 1916 by Adm. David Beatty.[11]

On 28 July, with war drawing nearer, even with the British Foreign office still hopeful that a peaceful solution was possible, the War Office proceeded to complete all its preparations; and ordered the Admiralty to take even more drastic steps. The patrol and local defence flotillas— first for service—were ordered to take action to obtain full crews, short of recalling men from leave or disturbing the general mobilisation arrangements. Orders were issued that evening, at 1700, for the First Fleet to proceed the next morning to its preliminary war station at Scapa. A report, that the German High Seas Fleet was off the coast of

Norway, raised concerns that it might strike preemptively. Accordingly, First Fleet was to steer out into the middle of the English Channel and proceed eastward so as to pass the Dover Strait by night without lights.[12]

Map 3-2

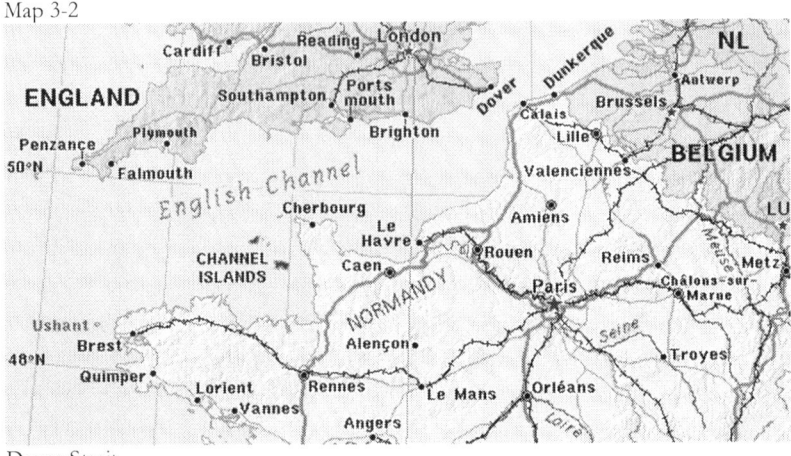

Dover Strait

As ordered, the First Fleet put to sea at 0700 on the 29th. This was a day that would witness relations among opposing governments, already strained, dramatically worsen. The Austrians bombarded Belgrade, Serbia; Russia continued to mobilise her southern forces; and Germany threatened to complete her mobilisation, unless all preparations for war were discontinued in Russia. Since it was unlikely this demand would be met, it appeared that only a miracle could now avert war. Late that day, the Admiralty telegraphed orders that all officers and men on leave be recalled. Six days later, on 4 August 1914, Britain declared war on Germany, as she had failed to comply with an ultimatum by the British foreign secretary, Sir Edward Grey, demanding the withdrawal of German troops from neutral Belgium.[13]

HUMBLE BEGINNINGS OF THE MINE FORCE

The strongest fleet was paralysed in its offensive by the menace of the mine and the torpedo.

—Winston Churchill, in his book, *The World Crisis 1915*.[14]

At the onset of World War I, there was little appreciation or advocacy within the British Admiralty for the use of sea mines, either offensively or defensively. The First Sea Lord, Adm. John ("Jackie") Fisher had earlier abandoned their use for the defence of harbours and, moreover, while a squadron of old second-class protected cruisers had been converted to minelayers, the Royal Navy had no reliable mines. The term "protected" referred to a type of cruiser of the late 19th century, whose armoured deck offered protection for vital machine spaces from fragments caused by exploding shells above. Protected cruisers were less shielded than heavier "armoured cruisers," which also had a belt of armour along their sides.[15]

Former *Apollo*-class Cruisers
(314 feet, 4,700 tons, 19 knots)

Ship	Built	Fate
Andromache	Dec 1891	broken up in 1920
Apollo	Apr 1892	broken up in 1920
Intrepid	Nov 1892	expended as blockship in 1918
Iphigenia	May 1893	expended as blockship in 1918
Latona	Apr 1891	broken up in 1920
Naiad	Jan 1892	broken up in 1922
Thetis	Apr 1892	expended as blockship in 1918

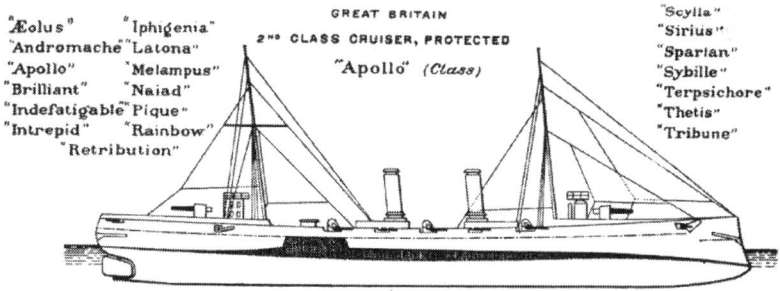

Apollo-class of twenty-one protected cruisers built in the late 19th Century. *Brassey's Naval Annual*, 1897

On 5 August 1914, seventeen ships comprised the Royal Navy's entire mine force. In addition to the seven members of the minelaying squadron at Sheerness, there were also ten minesweepers, former *Sharpshooter-* and *Alarm*-class torpedo gunboats converted in 1909.[16]

Former *Alarm*-class Torpedo Gunboats
(230 feet, 810 tons, 19 knots)

Name	Launched	Builder	Disposition
Circle	14 June 1892	Sheerness	Sold 30 Jul 1920 to H. Auten
Jason	14 May 1892	Vickers	Mined 7 Apr 1917 west of Scotland
Leda	13 Sep 1892	Sheerness	Sold 14 Jul 1920 to Cardiff Marine Stores; *BU 1922* in Germany
Niger	17 Dec 1892	Vickers	Sunk 11-12 Nov 1914 off Deal
Speedy	15 May 1893	Thornycroft	Mined 3 Sep 1914 off the Humber

Former *Sharpshooter*-Class Torpedo Gunboats
(230 feet, 735 tons, 20 knots)

Name	Launched	Builder	Disposition
Gossamer	9 Jan 1890	Sheerness	Sold 20 Mar 1920 to Cornish Salvage Co, Ilfracombe
Seagull	31 May 1889	Chatham	Sunk 30 Sep 1918 in collision with SS *Corrib* in Clyde
Skipjack	30 Apr 1889	Chatham	Sold 23 Feb 1920 to Hammond Lane Foundry, Dublin
Spanker	27 Feb 1889	Devonport	Sold 20 Mar 1920 to Cornish Salvage Co, Ilfracombe
Speedwell	15 Mar 1889	Devonport	Sold 20 Mar 1920 to Cornish Salvage Co, Ilfracombe[17]

Photo 3-2

Portside view of torpedo-gunboat HMS *Spanker*, date photograph taken is unknown. Naval History and Heritage Command photograph #NH 54862

Lending support to the ten Royal Navy minesweepers was an auxiliary minesweeping service of hired trawlers, whose organisation had begun in 1911. These vessels were manned by a special section of the RNR (Royal Naval Reserve), known as the Trawler Section. Its members were recruited from ordinary fishing crews, under an officer designated "Inspecting Captain of Minesweepers." Operating under the Admiral of Patrols, the minesweepers were assigned to Trawler Stations at Cromarty, the Forth, the Humber, Harwich, the Nore (a sandbar at the mouth of the Thames Estuary), Dover, Portsmouth, Portland and Devonport.[18]

Progress was such that by 3 December 1913, Capt. Thomas P. Bonham, RN (Inspecting Captain of Minesweepers) anticipated that in the event of war, eighty-two trawlers would be immediately available. The work of training and organising the Trawler Section was entrusted to the torpedo-gunboats employed on Fishery Protection duties in the North Sea. The Senior Naval Officer, Comdr. Alfred A. Ellison of HMS *Halcyon*, operated under the supervision of Capt. Bonham. (On 22 January 1916, Bonham was appointed captain of the armoured cruiser *Black Prince*. He was killed along with his entire crew when she was destroyed in night fighting at the Battle of Jutland.)[19]

Map 3-3

Lowestoft on England's east coast

Following a decision by the Admiralty on 7 August 1914 to form a flotilla of eighty trawlers to ensure a clear channel from the Downs to the Outer Dowsing, Ellison was ordered to take charge of the flotilla and organise it at Lowestoft. Ten days later, on 17 August, orders were given for a number of the trawlers at Lowestoft to be fitted with an early form of an explosive sweep. The trawlers so fitted were formed into a Northern Flotilla to operate against submarines in the waters of the Grand Fleet bases. (Ellison was assigned additional duties as Captain-in-Charge, Naval Base Lowestoft, in March of the following year.)[20]

By 13 August, it was estimated that 100 trawlers were available for minesweeping service. On 1 September 1914, Rear Adm. Edward Charlton, RN, was appointed as Admiral-in-Charge of Minesweeping (AMS), responsible for supervising and coordinating the work of minesweepers on the east coast of England. Well before year's end, auxiliary vessels would far outnumber those on the Navy List. Numbers of armed merchant cruisers rapidly multiplied; trawlers, drifters and yachts were taken up in scores for minesweeping and anti-submarine patrols, and steam vessels of all kinds for the Examination Service, which controlled the flow of trade in home waters.[21]

HMS VERNON

Responsibility for fielding a reliable mine was the task of HMS Vernon, the home of the Royal Navy's Torpedo Branch at Portsmouth, but it was hampered by a lack of funds. Details of the Russian mines were known to British authorities, and ones left over from the Russo-Japanese War were available. The simple and effective mine was adopted by the Germans with conspicuous success, but at a cost of some £200 each, the British had to be content with a cheaper one. This was the naval spherical mine and at the outbreak of the war, there were 4,000 available.[22]

Non-British readers may infer that HMS (His Majesty's Ship) Vernon was a ship, but it was actually a collection of hulks used as a floating naval base. Even Royal Navy shore bases and air stations, known as 'stone frigates', are prefixed HMS and retain all the customs and traditions of life on board a warship including the practice of 'going ashore' for leave or duty. In the case of HMS Vernon, and other hulks (such as the naval training school HMS Conway, located on the Mersey near Liverpool), the British had found a way to keep formerly beloved ships in use. Comprising HMS Vernon were, Vernon II (the hulk of the old three-decker *Marlborough*) connected by bridges to *Actaeon* (Vernon IV) and the old *Donegal* (Vernon I). Vernon III was the former ironclad

Warrior, which served as a floating workshop, power plant and wireless telegraphy school.[23]

Photo 3-3

HMS *Donegal* (Vernon I) in Portchester Creek. Photo is from an album dated 1923. Courtesy of Rob Hoole

During the war, work at HMS Vernon concentrated on torpedo trials and training; research and development of anti-submarine devices and related training in their use; as well as mines and ships' electrics. After the war, on 1 October 1923, HMS Vernon (or "The Vernon" as it came to be known) was established ashore at Portsmouth. At the site of the old Gunwharf Quays, Mining, Torpedo, and Electrical departments were formed in the relocated establishment.[24]

Despite the paucity of the Royal Navy's minelaying program, war preparations included plans to sow mines in the southern part of the North Sea. Even though notices to mariners and neutrals were prepared for release, it was found the mines in stock were defective; their firing mechanisms were too sensitive and their mooring-wires too weak. It was decided that sowing would be delayed. Additionally, the older admirals were not in favor of mining these waters, believing that the British should keep the sea open for use by their own ships.[25]

Photo 3-4

HMS *Marlborough* (Vernon II); from an album dated 1923.
Courtesy of Rob Hoole

Photo 3-5

HMS *Warrior* (Vernon III); from an album dated 1923.
Courtesy of Rob Hoole

LOSS OF SMS *KÖNIGIN LUISE* AND HMS *AMPHION*

In the opening movements of the war, the Southern Force was at sea, carrying out a sweep of the lower part of the North Sea. Based at Harwich, the force consisted of the 1st and 3rd Destroyer Flotillas under Commodore Tyrwhitt, and the submarines of the 8th Flotilla under Commodore Keyes; with support from some of the 7th Cruiser Squadron under Rear Admiral Campbell.[26]

Tyrwhitt, embarked in the cruiser *Amethyst*, left Harwich at dawn on 5 August, with the cruisers *Bacchante*, *Aboukir* and *Euryalus* and two submarines supporting his destroyers to look into the Heligoland Bight. While the 1st Destroyer Flotilla swept up the Dutch coast, Capt. Cecil H. Fox in the cruiser *Amphion* followed with the 3rd Flotilla. He had not gone far before he encountered the first sign that Germany was pursuing a mining campaign. A stray fishing trawler informed him there was a suspicious vessel in the vicinity "throwing things overboard twenty miles northeast of the Outer Gabbard."[27]

Map 3-4

Jade Bight and Heligoland Bight, small bays off the German Bight (Bay).

While the flotilla spread out in search, destroyers *Lance* and *Landrail* were sent ahead to investigate the area. About 1100, they sighted the *Königin Luise*, which had left Borkum (the largest of the seven East Frisian Islands in northwestern Germany), the previous night. The *Königin Luise* was a steam ferry, taken by the Kaiserliche Marine for use as an auxiliary minelayer capable of carrying two hundred mines. A chase by the two destroyers ensued in which *Amphion* joined; by noon they had sunk the minelayer with gunfire, drawing first blood on the second day of naval warfare with Germany.[28]

Kaiserliche Marine (Imperial German Navy)

| War Ensign (1903–1918) | Navy Jack (1903–1918) |

The Kaiserliche Marine (Imperial German Navy) had been created in 1871 concurrent with the formation of the German Empire. Growing out of the small Prussian Navy (from 1867, the North German Federal Navy), the Kaiserliche Marine would exist until 1919. The names of Imperial Navy ships were prefaced with SMS, for Seiner Majestät Schiff (His Majesty's Ship).

The crew of the *Königin Luise* was taken aboard the *Amphion* and the sweep continued without further incident, until the return passage. In the early hours of 6 August, *Amphion* changed her course so as to avoid the minefield the enemy had been laying. But at 0630, just when she believed she was clear, a violent explosion shattered the dawn, gravely damaging her. Abandon ship was ordered, but she struck another mine and went down so quickly that it was impossible to save all the crew. One officer and 150 men perished, as well as most of the prisoners from the German minelayer.[29]

The minefield had been laid about thirty miles off Orfordness—right in the fairway, regardless of the presence of neutral shipping, and in violation of the time-honoured customs of the sea—apparently for the express purpose of sinking any British forces proceeding from Harwich toward Germany. The incident "opened the eyes of the British" regarding the type of war Germany intended to wage, yet as inhuman as the practice appeared, there was no immediate thought of retaliation in kind. The flotillas were ordered back to Harwich, and the cruisers to the Downs, while immediate steps were taken to clear the suspected area. The Admiralty also directed the Admiral of Patrols to patrol the coast day and night to prevent further enemy minelaying operations.[30]

ABOUKIR, *CRESSY*, AND *HOGUE* SUNK BY U-BOAT

I had been going ahead partly submerged, with about five feet of my periscope showing. Almost immediately I caught sight of the first cruiser and two others.... I could see their grey-black sides riding high over the water.... Then I loosed one of my torpedoes at the middle ship... and discovered that the shot had gone straight and true, striking the ship, which I later learned was the Aboukir, *under one of her magazines, which in exploding helped the torpedo's work of destruction.... I submerged at once. But I had stayed on top long enough to see the other cruisers, which I learned were the* Cressy *and the* Hogue, *turn and steam full speed to their dying sister, whose plight they could not understand, unless it had been due to an accident....*

As I reached my torpedo depth I sent a second charge at the nearest of the oncoming vessels, which was the Hogue.... *The attack on the* Hogue *went true. But this time I did not have the advantageous aid of having the torpedo detonate under the magazine, so for twenty minutes the* Hogue *lay wounded and helpless on the surface before she heaved, half turned over and sank....*

When I got within suitable range I sent away my third attack [on the Cressy]. *This time I sent a second torpedo after the first to make the strike doubly certain.... My luck was with me again, for the enemy was made useless and at once began sinking by her head. Then she careened far over, but all the while her men stayed at the guns looking for their invisible foe. They were brave and true to their country's sea traditions. Then she eventually suffered a boiler explosion and completely turned turtle. With her keel uppermost she floated until the air got out from under her and then she sank with a loud sound, as if from a creature in pain.*

The whole affair had taken less than one hour from the time of shooting off the first torpedo until the Cressy *went to the bottom. Not one of the three had been able to use any of its big guns.*

—Otto Weddigen, commander of German submarine *U-9*.[31]

The sinking of three British cruisers—the *Aboukir*, *Cressy* and *Hogue*—northwest of the Hook of Holland by a single German submarine, *U-9*, on 22 September 1914, startled the Royal Navy. The loss of three ships to a U-boat and one to sea mines in the early days of the war, gave notice of the prominent role these weapons were to play, and a decision was finally made by the British to lay mines in the North Sea. The first line of 1,264 mines was planted on 2 October 1914, ten miles north of the Belgian coastal city Ostend. In November, mines were reintroduced for the defence of British harbours. By the end of 1914 some 2,000 mines had been laid in the southern part of the North Sea, which forced neutral shipping to pass through the Downs—the passage, strictly speaking, an anchorage between the Goodwin Sands (a 10-mile long sandbank in the English Channel) and the coast of Kent—where every ship en route to or from Dutch or Scandinavian ports could be examined. For a time, this deterred U-boats from approaching the English Channel.[32]

4

Britain Lays Minefield to Counter U-boats/Protect Troops

The loss of life was consequently very great. In all 60 officers and 777 men were saved, which meant that as many officers and nearly 1,400 men were drowned. To give the last touch of bitterness, the old cruisers, being amongst the latest to mobilise, were manned mainly by Royal Naval Reserve ratings, most of whom were married men with families. Yet in spite of the rawness of the crews and the appalling nature of the disaster, by every testimony the discipline displayed was admirable and the conduct of the men beyond all praise both before and after the ships went down.

—Julian S. Corbett describing in *History of the Great War, Naval Operations Vol. I, To the Battle of the Falklands*, the devastating loss of the cruisers *Aboukir, Cressy,* and *Hogue*—to the German submarine *U-9*, on 22 September 1914.[1]

By the end of August 1914, the Admiralty had become aware that Germany was utilising a form of attack which, at the Hague Conference of 1907, in the name of humanity, it had solemnly deprecated. Mines had been used extensively during the Russo-Japanese War (1904–05), resulting in considerable costs to the naval fleets of both belligerents. Much damage was also done to commercial shipping, both during and after the war, due to their unrestricted use. As a result, many of the dominant naval powers sought a ban on sea mines, particularly unanchored ones.[2]

This proposition was opposed by emerging naval powers that wanted to preserve the ability of their ships to deploy mines to hamper pursuit and to institute blockades. The resulting treaty—the Convention of 1907 Relative to the Laying of Automatic Submarine Mines (Hague VIII)—reflected a compromise agreement founded on different competing claims. The stronger of two opposing fleets, in its desire to seek out and destroy the enemy, wanted a clean sea. A weaker navy might wish to negate numerical and/or technological advantages of its adversary, by using mines to attrite the other's warships and to sink merchant vessels conveying food and ammunitions.[3]

German minefields discovered off the Tyne and the Humber early in the hostilities (rivers that empty into the North Sea along England's east coast) were at first believed by the Admiralty to have been laid surreptitiously by trawlers in the employment of Germany under neutral colours. The Germans, however, wasted no time in declaring that the mines had been laid by ships of the Imperial Navy. Illegitimate or not (as the Admiralty believed this action was, judging by past agreements and the traditions of naval warfare), it was clear these weapons posed a threat to the British Home Fleets.[4]

THE FIRST NIGHTRAIDERS

Photo 4-1

German cruiser-minelayer SMS *Nautilus* passing under the Levensau Bridge of the Kaiser Wilhelm (Kiel) Canal in 1907, soon after entering service on 19 March 1907. Naval History and Heritage Command photograph #NH 46829

The forces that laid the Tyne and Humber minefields consisted of two groups of vessels. They had sailed from Heligoland (a small German archipelago in the North Sea) in early morning on 25 August, bound for the east coast of England. The minelayer SMS *Albatros*, escorted by the light cruiser *Stuttgart* and a half-flotilla of torpedo boats from Heligoland, headed for the Tyne; while sistership *Nautilus*, accompanied by *Mainz* and another half flotilla of torpedo boats (this group from the Ems River in northwestern Germany) set a course for the Humber. Arriving in their respective areas, the "nightraiders" laid their contact mines under the cloak of darkness, in thick weather. The laying of the Tyne field was begun about 0030 on the 26th. It was to have been about five miles off the estuary, but ended up nearer thirty miles offshore as a consequence of heavy fog at the time. The sinking of a Danish/Icelandic fishing vessel that evening gave notice of its existence.[5]

Map 4-1

Tyne River and Humber River on England's northeast coast

The Humber field, started earlier at 2300 on 25 August, stretched from Flamborough Head down to Outer Dowsing about thirty miles offshore. Upon its completion (around 0150 on the 26th), the force set a course for home. Both German forces sank trawlers while on the fishing grounds; the Tyne force a total of six, and the Humber group, seven or ten (accounts differ). Boarding parties took the crews off (as the minelayers continued their missions), then sank their boats with explosives. Later that day, a mine from the Humber field detonated in the nets of the fishing trawler *City of Bristol*.[6]

TYNE FIELD CLAIMS TWO ADMIRALTY TRAWLERS

When word of the shipping casualties off the Tyne River reached shore, the four minesweepers based at Tynemouth (a village at the mouth of the Tyne) were despatched at 0745 on 27 August. The flotilla under the command of a retired naval officer, Comdr. Robert W. Dalgety, consisted of HM trawlers *Thomas W. Irvin* (61), *Island Prince* (62), *Agnes H. Hastie* (105) and *Crathie* (106). They were all recently leased Royal Navy fishing trawlers. They, and hundreds of others of their ilk acquired for naval service, were referred to by a variety of terms. These included: HM trawler (His Majesty's trawler) or simply HMT, followed by the minesweeper's name while in service as a fishing vessel and the newly acquired Admiralty number, or perhaps only "trawler" and this number.[7]

The four trawlers rendezvoused with torpedo boat *24* at 1030, and clearance efforts began immediately. The torpedo boat was originally of the *Cricket* destroyer-class, which, owing to their small dimensions (186 feet in length), had proved unsuitable for performing ocean escort work. They had been reclassified as 1st class torpedo boats shortly after trials of the first two ships of this class.[8]

That afternoon, tragedy struck the minesweeping flotilla twice. The first casualty was the *Thomas W. Irvin* hired only that month as an unarmed minesweeper. Her skipper was a reservist, Henry Charles Thompson, RNR. At 1625 after seven mines had been swept up and destroyed, one detonated near her, and she broke up and sank quickly at 55°01'N, 01°22'45"W. Three crewmen (ratings) were lost.[9]

Less than an hour later, a second trawler the *Crathie* was lost. Herbert Henry Cook, RNR, was her skipper. Formerly of Caledonian Steam Trawling, Aberdeen, she also had been hired in August for service as an unarmed minesweeper (Admiralty No. 106). Two mines had snagged in her sweep wires that afternoon without incident, but at 1706 a third one exploded under her. She sank rapidly at 55°01'N, 01°22'W, with two ratings lost in the explosion.[10]

Trawler *Agnes H. Hastie* picked up survivors, as did torpedo boat *24*, which rescued men in the water and returned to harbour. *Agnes H. Hastie* then towed the remaining trawler, *Island Prince* (which had earlier fouled her propeller) back to port.[11]

The diary of the commanding officer of the patrol-destroyer HMS *Stour*, Lt. Basil Owen, RN, provides perspective on the ignorance of many senior officers regarding the deadly threat posed by German mines. *Stour* and the *Kale* had sailed to relieve another division, and while searching for one of its members, the *Eden*, had come upon TBs *22* and *24* with four minesweeping trawlers. Owen intercepted a W/T (wireless telegraph) transmission to *Kale* from Captain D (destroyers) ordering the two ships to close the torpedo boats and mine trawlers and assist them to clear the minefield. Having witnessed the detonations immediately prior to *Crathie*'s destruction, his recorded opinion on their capability of assistance was merely in finding mines by running onto them.[12]

In addition to the challenges posed by the primitive minesweeping gear and techniques then in use (which were employed by seamen whose prey earlier had been fish), the minesweeping trawlers were getting little assistance from "on high." Commodore Ballard as Admiral of Patrols was in overall charge of trawler-sweeper operations, with Senior Naval Officers (SNOs) of ports locally responsible. He was also responsible for temporarily ordering minesweeping craft away from defended naval ports, as required. However, when called upon to act on such needs, he advised the Admiralty that local SNOs should deal with their own areas. As an example cited, he indicated he had only two trawlers at hand at Humber. If they were detailed to other duties, the Humber (which was important not only as a battle cruiser base, but also as an oil fuel depot) could not be swept. It was in this light that a decision to create the Lowestoft Flotilla was taken (based around HMS *Halcyon*, a *Dryad*-class torpedo gunboat converted to minesweeper in 1914). The unit was responsible for a coastal channel between the South Goodwin Sands in Kent and the Outer Dowsing off the mouth of the Humber.[13]

BATTLE OF HELIGOLAND BIGHT

Everybody [is] quite mad with delight at the success of our first naval venture.

—Observation made by Vice Adm. David Beatty, commander
1st Battle Cruiser Squadron, in a letter to his wife,
following the Battle of Heligoland Bight.

Photo 4-2

King George V, and Admiral Sir David Beatty aboard the battleship
HMS *Queen Elizabeth*, date unknown.
Naval History and Heritage Command photograph #NH 120592

During the early days of the war, the German High Seas Fleet stood
ready in its North Sea harbours, but none of its capital ships had been
met by the British at sea. On 28 August 1914, the first major naval battle
between British and German ships broke out near the northern coast of
Germany. The battle took place in the Heligoland Bight, a partially
enclosed body of water which offered shelter to several bases of the
German High Seas Fleet and was a starting-off point for attacks against
the British Isles. Over the three-and-a half weeks since Britain entered
the war, the German fleet rarely ventured far from port. In an effort to
bring it to action, Commodore Reginald Tyrwhitt was given the task of
leading a small force of British ships, including the light cruisers HMS
Fearless and *Arethusa*, and a number of destroyers, into the bight in an
effort to lure the enemy to chase them out to sea, where a larger British
force, commanded by Vice Adm. Sir David Beatty, would be waiting to
confront them.[14]

Around 0700 on the morning of 28 August, Tyrwhitt's squadron
began the operation by sinking two German torpedo boats. But the
British attack had not caught the German fleet entirely by surprise, and
Tyrwhitt soon found himself outgunned by a force, including six light

cruisers. They used thick fog hanging over the bight as concealment as they fired unexpectedly on the British ships. At 1125, Tyrwhitt called on Beatty for immediate assistance, and the 1st Battle Cruiser Squadron rushed to his aid from well offshore, reaching the bight at 1240. The powerful British squadron subsequently sank three German cruisers (including the minelayer *Mainz*) and damaged three others, resulting in 1,200 casualties. Britain lost only thirty-five sailors, and no ships, although the light cruiser *Arethusa* and destroyers *Goshawk*, *Laurel*, *Liberty*, and *Laertes* were damaged.[15]

Photo 4-3

Rear Adm. Reginald Y. Tyrwhitt, RN, aboard his flagship, the light cruiser HMS *Curacoa*, at Harwich, England, in November 1918. Naval History and Heritage Command photograph #NH 42495

The one-sided British victory, however, had some unanticipated consequences. As a result of this overwhelming German defeat at the very onset of the war, Kaiser Wilhelm II concluded that his capital ships should be kept off the open seas, with their best use being as a deterrent serving as a "fleet in waiting." As the war continued, Germany's greatest naval weapon would not be its warships, but its lethal submarines. Used with great effect against both Allied and neutral shipping, the success of the U-boats would help spur one previously neutral great power, the United States, to entering World War I against Germany.[16]

Photo 4-4

German Kaiser Wilhelm II discussing war plans with field marshal Paul von Hindenburg (left) and General Erich Ludendorff (right), in January 1917.
National Archives Description photograph #165-GB-1000

THREE MINESWEEPERS LOST TO HUMBER FIELD

Lessons learned from the Tyne field sweeping experience challenged the accepted wisdom of the Admiralty's torpedo school that "...the discovery of mines is the important matter; once discovered they may be avoided and destroyed at leisure." New urgency to rapidly define the limits of the Humber field resulted in the use of drifters as minesweepers. This came about as a consequence of suggestions put forth by both naval officers and vessel owners, and the shortage of trawlers—in spite of the absence of any training, or even trials, in their use.[17]

Photo 4-5

HMS *Donegal* (Vernon I) Torpedo Lecture Room.
Courtesy of Rob Hoole

TRAWLERS AND DRIFTERS

The Admiralty had already obtained thirty drifters by 15 August, to serve
as patrol craft. A drifter was a fishing boat designed to catch herring in
a long drift net and, outfitted to tow heavy trawls, they were easily
adapted to pull sweep gear. The crew and the layout were already suited
to the task, and drifters, like trawlers, were robust boats built to work in
most weather conditions. However, they were without armament, and
had no means to pass information other than verbally to a destroyer or
by landing near a Coast Guard Station.[18]

There were, however, significant differences between trawlers and
drifters. A drifter was smaller, and usually built of wood, though a few
were of steel; and, unlike a steam trawler, she relied very much on her
mizzen, not for speed, but for sea-keeping ability in bad weather and for
riding to her nets. Her engine speed was rarely more than 9 knots, and
she put to sea for only a few days at a time, returning to port to land her
fish and take aboard coal and water before going out again. A drifter's
crew was small, usually numbering not more than eight or nine all told;
and more often than not manned by members of one family. Frequently
the skipper was the father or father-in-law of the mate. The engineman
was as likely as not the latter's cousin, and the rest of the crew, if not
having some sort of relationship to the skipper, came from the same

fishing-village. To have split up the tightly knit group would have impaired the efficiency of the ship. Consequently, when the Admiralty took over drifters it usually accepted the crews en masse, and the men served in most cases till the end of the war.[19]

Under orders from *Halcyon*, the minesweeping torpedo-gunboat HMS *Speedy* sailed on 31 August with ten steam-propelled drifters; the drifters initially shot their nets on September 1st. Converted from an *Alarm*-class torpedo gunboat to minesweeper in 1909, *Speedy* had retained her guns and been fitted with a quarterdeck kite winch and gallows for new duties. The following morning, the drifter *Eyrie* (unarmed minesweeper No. 214)—struck a mine while operating in company with similar vessels and HMS *Speedy* near the Outer Dowsing shoal. *Eyrie* snagged a mine at 0920 off Cley next the Sea (a village on the River Glaven), which exploded, blowing apart her stern. She sank rapidly, taking Thomas Scarll, RNR, and five ratings with her. Her last noted position was 53°40'5"N, 01°01'5"E.[20]

Photo 4-6

HMS *Donegal* (Vernon I) Upper Parting Room.
Courtesy of Rob Hoole

The same field, laid near the *Outer Dowsing* light vessel, claimed two more minesweepers the following day. Drifter *Lindsell* (No. 224) was plying her new trade with *Speedy*, *Wishful*, and *Achievable*, when she struck a mine at 1100, and disappeared in a few minutes. Stern blown off and bow up-ended, she slid into the deep. Her skipper, Charles Woodgate RNR, mate, engineer and two deckhands perished. *Speedy*, operating nearby, lowered boats to pick up survivors.[21]

Intending to sweep under the previously shot nets, one end of a sweep wire had been made fast aboard the gunboat *Speedy*, and the other aboard *Lindsell*. The other two drifters, *Wishful* and *Achievable*, were providing *Lindsell* extra power by towing her. Lt. Comdr. Edward Miller Rutherford, *Speedy*'s commanding officer, rescued *Lindsell*'s survivors, but shortly after lost his own ship. A mine blew her after works apart, including rudder and propellers, and she flooded and sank an hour later, thirty miles off the Humber (53°34'N, 00°10'E). One rating was lost.[22]

While the behaviour of some of the drifters was laudable, a number anchored about four miles away refused to close when ordered; they merely launched their pulling boats. Five skippers were censured. For this Humber minefield clearing operation, apart from the vessel losses, twelve men were killed, and at least three injured (two badly). The minesweeping-gunboat HMS *Spanker*, in the vicinity, transported the wounded to Grimsby.[23]

The findings by HMS *Speedy*'s Court of Enquiry effected changes regarding vessels used for minesweeping. With draughts of twelve feet and ship's companies of ninety-four, gunboats were deemed unsuitable for clearing minefields (as were larger warships and torpedo-boats). North Sea deep-hulled trawlers drawing 15 to 17 feet, and drifters 13 feet were also not ideal, but had small crews. A proposal was made to use paddle-steamers (which only drew 7 ½ feet), and two of these craft were already in the process of conversion.[24]

After these ship losses, the Admiralty directed that the minefields off the Tyne and Humber were to be left in place with sweeping operations confined to clearing a navigational channel along the coast. Surprisingly, the mined areas soon proved to be a blessing in disguise. The main reason the German minelayers had been able to plant the field at the start of hostilities undetected, was that local patrol flotillas had been kept concentrated, ready to deal with any enemy attempts to raid the coast. Since the Germans themselves had barred the approaches to the Tyne and Humber areas to such an extent, it was now possible to use these flotillas to extend the system of continuous coastwise patrol. Eventually the fields were actually reinforced by British minelayers.[25]

RECOGNITION OF THREAT U-BOATS AND MINES POSE TO BRITAIN

At the start of the war, Germany's use of sea mines, in itself, was not particularly unsettling to the Royal Navy because of relatively few inflicted losses. The British had lost only minor warships to mines—an old gunboat converted to a minesweeper, and four Admiralty vessels (two trawlers and two drifters) serving the same purpose. But, losses were amplified by ever-increasing activity on the part of the enemy's submarines. In both methods of attack, the Royal Navy lacked experience in counter-measures, and each could only be met by small craft specially improvised for the work.[26]

By 1 September, besides the regular flotillas and minesweepers, there were in commission some 250 trawlers, drifters and similar craft, devoted to meeting the submarine and mine threat. Warfare by means of the mine, and by means of the submarine, differed little. The objective in each case was to sink the target ship by a violent explosion without the victim having so much as a chance of escaping. The only difference between the torpedo and the mine was that the former went to meet the ship, and the latter waited for the ship's coming. The result in the two cases was the same.[27]

The duties of the several classes of these craft were to sweep for mines, to guard the resultant swept channels, to patrol for sightings of submarines, and to examine seemingly harmless vessels to ensure they were not functioning as submarine tenders or minelayers. Even so, their numbers were proving inadequate. Efforts were proceeding to rapidly increase their numbers, but the vessels were provided little supportive organisation. For a long time they were unequal to their tasking.[28]

Nothing in the opening weeks of conflict had so emphatically demonstrated the changes in which future naval warfare would be conducted, as had the losses sustained to U-boats and mines—and never, perhaps, had so great a result been obtained by means so small. Occurring when it did, the effect of the loss of the three cruisers was deep and widespread.[29]

REQUIREMENT TO TRANSPORT TROOPS CROSS-CHANNEL PROMPTS ADMIRALTY'S USE OF MINES

On the European continent, the German Army was carrying out the Schlieffen Plan, a plan for war against France and Britain first proposed by the chief of staff Alfred von Schlieffen in 1905. General Helmuth von Moltke replaced von Schlieffen on 1 January 1906, and brought with him the same view, but with a different emphasis. The very real danger of a powerful French Army striking into southern Germany (and operating against the German flank that was invading Belgium), brought about changes in the Schlieffen plan including cutting down the German right wing to the point where it was insufficient for its purpose. Moltke held fast to his "modified" western solution, and plans for an attack on the East (Russia) were given no further consideration."[30]

In order to accomplish his objectives, the immediate defeat of France was necessary. Schlieffen believed that the easiest way to do this would be to attack France through another country, rather than the heavily fortified Franco-German border. Switzerland, with its high mountains and narrow passages, was essentially geographically invasion-proof; leaving neutral Belgium as the remaining option. Schlieffen had considered the role that Britain's protection of Belgian neutrality might imply, but quickly dismissed its threat. He was confident that Belgium would be defeated well before British troops could cross the Channel and supply reinforcement to the Belgian forces. Thus, the plan was set. The German Army would quickly pass through Belgium, and then defeat France.[31]

The so-called "swinging door" manoeuvre, called for the German right wing to swing through Belgium, using the left wing as the pivot. Moltke modified the plan by reducing the weight of the right wing and strengthening the left wing. The result was that the German line was shortened by pulling in the end of the right wing. The modified plan was implemented in October 1914, when the Germans mounted a major assault on Antwerp. This was a situation that called for immediate reinforcement of the Entente left wing by Entente forces to deal with a looming disaster. (Entente refers to France, Britain and Russia, the initial countries which opposed the Central Powers in the First World War.) French attempts to turn the Germans' right flank, with resultant efforts by the Germans to extend this flank to block them, became known as "the race to the sea."[32]

This "stretching-out of the battle front" toward the North Sea coast alarmed Winston Churchill, the First Lord of the Admiralty, who went to Antwerp to personally evaluate the situation. After his assessment, he immediately wired to London for reinforcements to be sent across the Channel to Zeebrugge, Ostend, and Dunkirk. The Belgian Government had recognised from the first week in September the impossibility of Antwerp resisting a formal attack by German forces. Accordingly, it had been asking the Allies for 25,000 troops to secure the retreat of its field army by way of St. Nicolas, Ghent, Bruges and Ostend. By month's end, the British 7th Division and the 3rd Cavalry Division were ready to take the field. Assuming the Navy was prepared to transport them, they could be landed at Dunkirk or Ostend. (Ultimately, the British War Office asked that the troops be taken to Zeebrugge.)[33]

Map 4-2

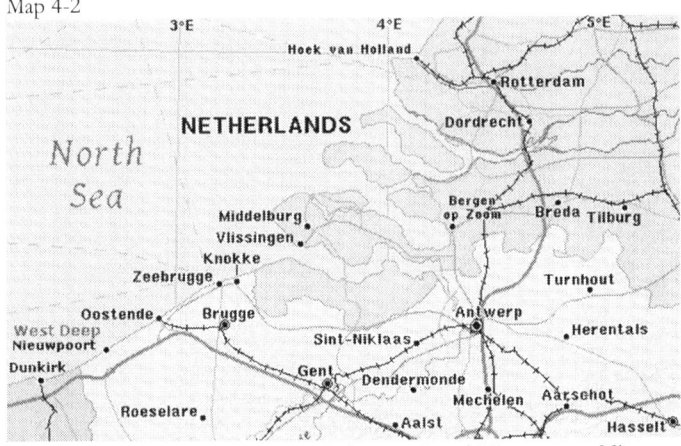

Belgian coast; Oostende is also spelled Ostend, and Nieuwpoort, Nieuport

In view of the critical military situation the sudden insecurity of the cross-channel lines of passage was intolerable. Action needed to be taken to curtail the threat posed by U-boats and mines, and nothing seemed feasible but a policy of extensive mining. This idea began to be pressed upon the Admiralty, which was unwilling to adopt the distasteful expedient and, in doing so, restrict the freedom of the Grand Fleet. The proposal was referred to Admiral Jellicoe, who was asked whether he objected to the scheme; and, if not, whether he would apply it to the Heligoland Bight or confine it to the narrow waters of the Southern Area. Jellicoe replied that (though generally opposed to any attempt to mine the Bight or the entrances of the German ports, since the risk would be great and the effect merely temporary, for minefields in those localities could not be watched) he regarded the mining of the Southern Area as desirable.[34]

His decision was implemented on 2 October, and orders to lay the field were issued. The mined area was to be in the shape of a parallelogram, whose southern base stretched from the middle of the Goodwin Sands to just north of Ostend. A line running eastwards from the Kentish Knock (a shoal east of the Thames Estuary in southeast England) formed the northern limit. Before the minelayers could begin their work on the morning of 2 October, submarine *B3*—of the Dover Patrol 4th Flotilla—was attacked unsuccessful by an enemy submarine (perhaps the *U-18*) off the southern end of the Goodwins. The torpedo missed, but served notice that the minelayers could only safely work at night and under destroyer protection.[35]

Photo 4-7

British cruiser HMS *Iphigenia* in 1891, prior to her conversion to minelayer. Naval History and Heritage Command photograph #NH 60124

That night, the cruisers *Andromache*, *Apollo*, *Intrepid*, and *Iphigenia* laid mines off the Belgian coastal city of Ostend. On the two succeeding nights they laid additional mines off Ostend and to the northeast of the Goodwin Sands (a 10-mile long sandbank in the English Channel). Britain was, however, not prepared to follow the example of Germany, by keeping the field secret—as advantageous as this might be. The enemy's practice to date had been a direct breach of Article 3 of the Hague Mine Convention, which directed that, "When anchored automatic contact mines are employed every possible precaution must be taken for the security of peaceful navigation." The Admiralty accordingly announced the existence of the minefield, and issued official notification of the limits of the danger area.[36]

The completed minefield was intended to protect the passage of transports to Dunkirk, in northern France, by blocking the approaches to Zeebrugge Harbour (located to the northeast, midway up the Belgian coast). When the combat situation ashore changed, the Navy was asked to take the troops to Zeebrugge, which would involve sweeping a channel through the field just laid. In the early hours of 5 October, orders went out to the two southern groups of minesweepers—then working between the Kentish Knock and the North Foreland (a chalk headland on the Kent coast)—to sweep the necessary channel, and forbade ships of convoys to proceed beyond Dover without orders.[37]

TRAWLERS *PRINCESS BEATRICE* AND *DRUMOAK* DISAPPEAR WHILE SWEEPING OFF ZEEBRUGGE

The weather was very bad for sweeping work, but an attempt was made to clear a passage off Zeebrugge with disastrous results. Two Admiralty trawlers, *Princess Beatrice* and *Drumoak*, sweeping in company near the *North Hinder* light vessel off the Belgian coast, disappeared with all hands. There were no witnesses to their loss, but ships in the area reported an explosion at 1930, followed fifteen minutes later by a second one, perhaps when the surviving sweeper went to the assistance of the first.[38]

The 208-ton *Drumoak*, recently obtained in August from North of Scotland Steam Fishing, had been built in 1902. The slightly larger and newer *Princess Beatrice* (212 tons, 1912) was a unit of the Dover Patrol. They, as was the convention for fishing vessels taken by the Admiralty for their type work, were designated minesweeper, unarmed.

Name	Skipper	Date Hired/ Admiralty No.	Casualties
Drumoak	Robert Smith Ellington RNR	August 1914 No. 342	Skipper and nine ratings
Princess Beatrice	Alexander Hall RNR	August 1914 No. 287	Skipper and ten ratings[39]

The Royal Navy finally landed the 7th Infantry Division in Zeebrugge and the 3rd Cavalry Division at Ostend in early October 1914, but they were too little and too late to change the outcome of the German invasion. The fall of Antwerp on 8 October freed-up large numbers of German infantry and artillery to flood down the coast to seize Bruges, Zeebrugge, Ostend, and Dunkirk. They fell short of taking Dunkirk, but by the 1st of November, Bruges, Zeebrugge, and Ostend were firmly under German control. The latter three cities would become active U-boat and torpedo boat bases on 27 March 1916 with the arrival of the *UB-10*, the same date KKpt. Karl Bartenbach took command of the Flanders U-Flotilla (discussed later in the book).[40]

5

German Raid on Britain and East Coast Minesweeping

If command of the sea meant the power to move fleets, troops and trade freely where we would, then our command was not undisputed, and indeed it seemed to be growing gradually more precarious, as the mining activities of the enemy extended to our western coasts and their submarines with increasing power and range spread further and further afield…

With sure instinct it was to the old well-spring of our sea power we went to renew our youth for the anxious contest. The fleet would no longer suffice, but behind it were still the deep-sea fisherman and the great seafaring population to whom nothing afloat came amiss…. In all tradition it had been a constant duty of the Grand Fleet to protect our fishing fleets; now it was the fishing fleets that must protect the Grand Fleet.

—Julian Corbett describing in *History of the Great War Naval Operations Vol. II* that, although over 150 trawlers and drifters had been taken up in the first few months of the war, and as practical were being fitted with guns and explosive sweeps, the Royal Navy required many additional fishing vessels to counter mines and U-boats.[1]

Beginning on the first day of the war when the *Königin Luise* laid her mines off the Suffolk coast, German ships and submarines embarked on a campaign that would deposit over 25,000 mines in the North Sea; most of them in defiance of the Hague Convention. Initially expecting a short war, Commodore Tyrwhitt had observed, "It will be months before the North Sea is safe for yachting." Lacking a sufficient number of minesweepers, the Admiralty soon learned that the most efficient way to deal with mines was to sink the minelayers. Such occurrences were rare, but one did occur on 17 October 1914 when the light cruiser *Undaunted* and four destroyers of Tyrwhitt's Harwich Force—*Lance, Lennox, Loyal* and *Legion*—encountered four German 206-foot torpedo boats headed west across the southern North Sea.[2]

The four members of the German 7th Half-Flotilla—*S-115, S-117, S-118,* and *S-119*—each with twelve mines, had left their base on the

Ems River at 0330, bound for the mouth of the Thames. The large (ocean-going) torpedo boats—known in German as Grosse (Hochsee) Torpedoboote—had been built in 1902-03 at the F. Schichau Elbing Shipyard. (Elbing is the German name of Elbląg, a city in northern Poland which until 1945 was a German city in the province of East Prussia.) Stretching 206 feet in length, with a 23-foot beam and an 8.8-foot draught, they had a top speed of 27 knots. Upon encountering the British naval force at 1330, they turned and ran, trying to escape. Pursued by faster, more heavily armed British warships, two of the torpedo-boats were sunk by mid-afternoon. The remaining two, which had turned back to help, were also sunk. The German survivors numbered only thirty officers and men.[3]

In addition to destroying four German minelayers, in a stroke of luck, the Royal Navy gained a much bigger prize. Before *S-119* (the flotilla leader) went under, her captain had properly placed his secret documents in a lead-lined chest and dropped it over the side. The chest remained on the seafloor until 30 November, when a British fishing trawler brought it up in its nets. Inside were charts of the North Sea, marked with an operational grid used to plot the location of friendly and enemy warships, and a code book new to the British. The code book, or Verkehrsbuch (VB) as it was known in German, was intended primarily for coding cable communications with warships overseas, and with naval attachés or embassies.[4]

The British called the chance recovery of the VB the "Miraculous Draught of Fishes." Also early in the war, they came into possession of two other code books used by the German Navy throughout the war; the Handelsverkehrsbuch (HVB), taken from the German freighter, SS *Hobart* off Port of Philip Head, Melbourne, Australia, on 11 August 1914, and the Signalbuch der Kaiserlichen Marine (SKM), which the Russians took from the wreck of the light cruiser SMS *Magdeburg* at Odensholm Island, off the east coast of Russian Estonia, in late August 1914. By the end of the first four months of the war, British Intelligence (Room 40) had all three code books. The acquisition of the code books was as important as the British breaking of the Enigma Code in WWII, and was likewise kept a secret.[5]

DREADNOUGHT HMS *AUDACIOUS* SUNK BY MINE

In late October, the German naval staff decided to mine the approaches to the large commercial harbour at Glasgow, and therefore despatched the North German Lloyd liner *Berlin* to the Firth of Clyde to perform this task. The reasons for employing her thus were twofold. If she were seen on an Atlantic shipping route she would not excite much suspicion, for she looked what she was, an Atlantic liner. Additionally, she had ample capacity to carry many hundreds of mines, and a long after-deck from which to lay them.[6]

Off the northern Irish coast, her captain decided to, instead, lay his mines off Tory Island, northwest of Lough Swilly (then serving as a Grand Fleet anchorage.) The Tory Island field claimed its first victim on 26 October when British merchant ship *Manchester Commerce* struck a mine and sank. The following day, a mine sank the dreadnought battleship *Audacious*. This event shocked the Admiralty—which had not yet received word about the loss of the merchantman, and therefore had not warned the fleet about the minefield. These sinkings provided Britain an excuse for a dramatic escalation of the war at sea.[7]

Map 5-1

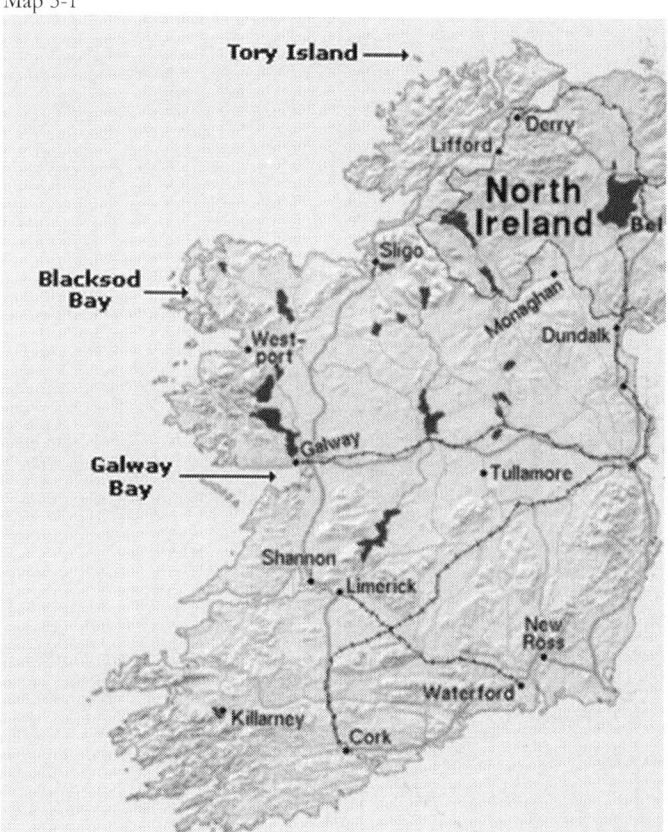

Ireland

On 2 November 1914, the British government issued a proclamation which, in effect, stated that the whole of the North Sea was out of bounds to world shipping without the express permission of the Royal Navy. Naturally this announcement brought a storm of anger and protest from the Germans. Vizeadmiral Reinhard Scheer (commander of the 2nd Battle Squadron of the High Seas Fleet), believing that the blockade was intended to starve Germany, declared that "success would be achieved gradually and silently, which meant the ruin of Germany as surely as the approach of winter meant the fall of the leaves from the trees."[8]

JELLICOE BELIEVES GRAND FLEET SAFER AT SEA

The Grand Fleet seemed to have chosen a very desolate and depressing place for a home. The Flow is a deep water anchorage at the southern end of the Orkneys, measuring roughly seven miles east and west, and four miles north and south. On the north side lies the mainland of the Orkneys, and on the south, east, and west sides lie islands, all hilly, bleak, and inhospitable. It is a dreary and depressing spot in winter.

—From G. H. P. Muhlhauser's *Small Craft*, published in London in 1920. This description refers to a visit by Rear Adm. Edward S. Fitzherbert (A.M.S., Admiral Commanding East Coast Minesweepers) to Scapa Flow aboard the auxiliary patrol vessel (hired yacht) *Sagitta*. Upon his return from visiting the flagship, HMS *Iron Duke*, he said that he had been congratulated on having chosen his weather so well, being told, "It is true that it is raining, but it is not blowing." As it was difficult to stand on the deck on account of the strength of the wind, some listeners likely wondered what it must be like when it was really blowing.[9]

German submarines and mines posed great danger to Royal Navy ships at sea, and no safe haven awaited the Grand Fleet when it returned from operations to its base at Scapa Flow. Upon the fleet's initial arrival at Scapa Flow on 2 August, Admiral Jellicoe had found the main war anchorage wholly undefended against enemy surface attack and, similarly, no manmade barriers to prevent penetration by submarines existed. The fleet's other northern bases—at Rosyth on the Firth of Forth, and Cromarty Firth, near Inverness—were scarcely better protected. Thus, during the early months of the war, Jellicoe felt more secure at sea. Between August and December 1914, the Grand Fleet steamed 16,800 miles.[10]

Photo 5-1

U.S. Navy 3rd and 6th Battle Squadrons following the battleship HMS *Queen Elizabeth* out of port at Rosyth, Scotland, late in the war.
Naval History and Heritage Command photograph #NH 110535

To reduce the number of channels leading into Scapa Flow, twelve "blockships" were used to close three of the seven entrances, leaving, besides the main southern entrance, one channel on the west side and two on the east. For these vulnerable entry points, anti-submarine defences (tried successfully at Cromarty) were being prepared, but they had not arrived when the defences were first employed. Until the anti-submarine devices were in position, the Grand Fleet had to rely on the destroyers and Auxiliary Patrol vessels for security. On 8 December, a submarine almost succeeded in gaining access to the upper eastern entrance to the anchorage. She was detected by HMS *Garry*, the destroyer on guard, which engaged her with gunfire. The submarine fired a torpedo and escaped seaward. It missed and no harm was done to the *Garry*.[11]

In addition to protecting his fleet base, Jellicoe also sought more elbow room at sea by clearing threatening minefields. This required improving his mine clearance capabilities. As useful as the

minesweeping trawlers were, their speed was insufficient to allow them
to work far enough afield. To address this deficiency until purposefully
built vessels became available, the Admiralty drafted eight fast railway
packets from the mercantile marine and commissioned them as "Fleet
Minesweepers." These were the HMS *Reindeer*, *Roebuck*, *Lynn*, and
Gazelle of the Great Western Railway; HMS *Folkstone* and *Hythe* of the
South-Eastern and Chatham Railway; and HMS *Clacton* and *Newmarket*
of the Great Eastern Railway.[12]

Efforts to improve the defence of Scapa Flow would continue, and
on 18 February 1915, they were completed, except for one of the booms
at the entrance to Hoy Sound. All the entrances to the Flow were then
blocked by sunken ships, wire hawsers, or booms, with a defensive
minefield between Hunda and South Ronaldsay. Gates admitted vessels
entering Scapa Flow through Hoxa Sound and Hoy Sound. At Loch
Ewe (in the northwest Highlands of Scotland, about eighty miles west
of Inverness), however, installation of the planned system of booms and
gates had not yet commenced.[13]

EXPANSION/FORMALISATION OF PATROL AREAS

Twelve destroyers had been lent to aid in the protection of Scapa Flow,
and the call for their return to their normal patrol duties in the south
was becoming more urgent. This was because the growing activity of
German submarines in the Channel required increased protection for
transports to France. The increasing numbers of anti-submarine craft
had outgrown the original organisation, and calls for further protection
from all quarters could only be met by a comprehensive system covering
the whole of Britain's coasts. To counter the submarine menace, the
Admiralty reorganised the whole system of patrols as shown in the
following table.

British Home Waters' Patrol Areas and Associated Bases

No.	Patrol Area	Base
I	Hebrides and the Minch	Lock Ewe and Stornoway
II	Shetland Islands	Longhope
III	Orkney Islands	Longhope
IV	Moray Firth	Cromarty
V	Off Rattray Head	Peterhead
VI	Forth to Rattray Head	Rosyth
VII	Seaward of the Forth	Granton (today a part of Edinburgh)
VIII	Tyne	Tyne
IX	Humber	Grimsby
X	Off East Anglian coast	Yarmouth and Harwich

XI	Dover Straits	Dover
XII	East Channel	Portsmouth
XIII	Mid-Channel	Portland
XIV	Western Approach	Devonport
XV	St. George's and Bristol Channel	Milford (sub-base Rosslare)
XVI	Irish Channel	Liverpool, Kingstown, Belfast
XVII	North Coast of Ireland	Lough Larne
XVIII	Northwest Coast Ireland	Lough Swilly
XIX	West Coast Ireland	Blacksod Bay
XX	West Coast Ireland	Galway Bay
XXI	South and Southwest Coast Ireland	Queenstown, Berehaven
	Special area of the Clyde	
	Special area of the Nore[14]	

As a part of this reorganisation, the post of "Captain Supervising Modified Sweeps" was abolished on 8 December, and replaced by a Submarine Attack Committee. Headed by Capt. Leonard Donaldson, RN, its role was to develop and organise the various methods of attack which at that time were ramming, gunfire, sweeps, and indicator nets. This type of net (then in an early experimental stage) was designed to detach from a larger anti-submarine net, after an enemy submarine collided with it. The idea was that the net would then envelope the submarine and indicate its presence by means of an attached buoy moving along the surface of the sea.[15]

Under the new organisation, patrol duties were to act against submarines, to prevent minelaying and to prevent espionage. (A separate organisation retained responsibility for the actual sweeping of mines.) An estimated seventy-four yachts and 462 trawlers and drifters would be required, besides motor boats for inshore work whenever such waters required protection. Soon after the system was implemented on 20 December 1914, necessary craft were being obtained in large numbers and armed under great urgency. However, it took some time before plan requirements were met.[16]

GERMAN RAID ON BRITAIN'S YORKSHIRE COAST

After the German defeat in the Battle of Heligoland Bight on 28 August, Admiral Friedrich von Ingenohl (commander-in-chief of the High Seas Fleet) fretted about the inaction of his fleet, imposed upon it by the Kaiser and his military advisors. Observing the spirit of the men under his command deteriorating, he begged to be given greater latitude. As it was counter to the policy to keep the fleet intact, the Naval Staff rebuffed his request. They saw a greater need to preserve their naval command of the Baltic, and to release the coast defence troops for service with the active army, which was possible with naval forces in port. Their response read:

> The fleet must therefore be held back and avoid action which might lead to heavy losses. This does not, however, prevent favourable opportunities being used to damage the enemy. Employment of the fleet outside the Bight, which the enemy tries to bring about by his movements in the Skagerrak [a strait between the southeast coast of Norway, the southwest coast of Sweden, and the Jutland Peninsula of Denmark], is not mentioned in the orders for operations as being one of such favourable opportunities. There is nothing to be said against an attempt of the big cruisers in the North Sea to damage the enemy.[17]

Inferring that this guidance tacitly allowed the use of his cruisers, von Ingenohl quickly devised a plan for a raid on the British coast that would restore the spirit of the fleet and might tempt a detachment of the Grand Fleet to venture within his reach. His plans did not come as a surprise to the Royal Navy. Using captured German code books, cryptanalysts in Room 40 of Naval Intelligence were able to read enemy radio communications shortly after they were transmitted. By 14 December, the Admiralty had received advanced warning of the operation.[18]

Map 5-2

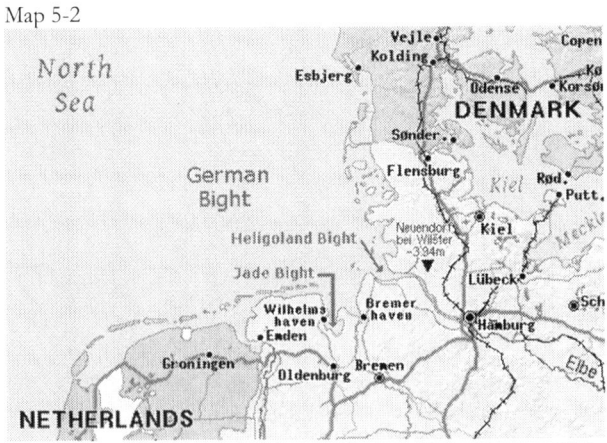

Jade Bight and Heligoland Bight, small bays off the German Bight

Forewarned an action was imminent, the British squadrons despatched to deal with the raid were already well out to sea by the time the German naval force began to cross the North Sea. However, the British did not know the enemy's objectives, nor were they aware the battleships of the High Seas Fleet had left their sanctuary at Wilhelmshaven in the Jade Bight (a bay on the North Sea coast of Germany) to cover the raid.[19]

Ensuing engagements between the German and British naval forces fell into three separate phases. In the first, the High Seas Fleet and the British squadrons came close to a confrontation, before the Germans turned back. In the second, German battle cruisers reached the east coast, shelled Scarborough, Hartlepool and Whitby, and then turned to make their escape. In the third, the British squadrons came close to catching the battle cruisers, but a combination of bad luck, poor signals and low visibility helped the Germans escape.[21]

Map 5-3

Scarborough, Hartlepool and Whitby, on England's northeast coast

The collective mood in Britain following the raid on Scarborough was one of anger about Germany's breach of the rules of civilised warfare in bombarding an open seaside resort, and a crowded seaport with minimal defences; and to a much lesser degree, toward the Royal Navy that had let them get away with it. Fortunately the public did not know that the fleet had received advance warning of the German raid or their anger against the Navy would have been much greater. At Scarborough, Scarborough Castle, the prominent Grand Hotel, three churches and various other properties were hit. The shelling of a coastguard station in nearby Whitby inflicted co-lateral damage on Whitby Abbey and other buildings in the town. Hartlepool, a much more significant target than the resort town of Scarborough, was defended by naval guns on the seafront. Gun rounds fired at the town by two battle cruisers and a slightly smaller armoured cruiser struck the steelworks, gasworks, railways, seven churches and hundreds of houses, resulting in large numbers of casualties. Both the shore guns and local naval forces were ineffective against the German warships.[22]

Photo 5-2

Line engraving of the Castle and Town of Scarborough from the *Lady's Magazine*, April 1789.
Naval History and Heritage Command photograph #NH 64018

The ease with which the enemy naval force had reached the east coast did nothing to dispel public concern about the possibility of a small scale invasion. As a result, Beatty's battle cruisers were relocated from Cromarty to Rosyth, halving the distance they would have to travel to reach the Yorkshire coast. Although much anguish was felt by the

British over the large number of casualties (137 killed and 592 injured), the greatest harm done by the raid was yet to come. While the coastal communities were under attack, the German cruiser *Kolberg* had laid a new minefield, beginning off Flamborough Head and extending ten miles out to sea.[23]

EXTENSION OF THE EXISTING WAR CHANNEL

The new minefield hindered coastwise shipping traffic and increased the burden of the already hard-worked North Sea minesweepers. These vessels had to keep a previously swept channel clear from the Downs, off the coast of Kent, to Flamborough Head, the largest promontory on England's northeast coast. This channel lay shoreward of the minefields the Germans had laid early in the war off the eastern counties, and the Humber, and which the British had purposefully left intact.[24]

Photo 5-3

British recruiting poster following the raid.

Following SMS *Königin Luise*'s laying of mines off Southwold (a small town south of Lowestoft) on 5 August 1914, the Admiralty had recognised the necessity for a definite and restricted transit route for men-of-war and important vessels, which could be patrolled and swept regularly. It directed buoying of a channel from the Downs to the Outer Dowsing, and printing of special track charts showing the routes to be followed for ships drawing over twelve feet of water. By 11 August, all the buoys had been laid, and arrangements made for the channel to be patrolled continuously by thirty drifters hired for that purpose. The channel was considered secret, and the charts drawn by warships and certain auxiliaries before proceeding up or down the east coast were returned at the end of each passage.[25]

By 3 September, the buoyed channel had been extended from the *Outer Dowsing* light vessel to Flamborough Head, but in view of the Humber minefield, this route was considered dangerous and was soon abandoned in favor of one closer inshore. This route ran from the *Haisborough* light vessel to the *Inner Dowsing* light vessel, and thence to Flamborough Head. After being swept and buoyed, it was substituted for the outer route on 12 September. The revised war channel remained unchanged until 18 December when, as a result of the Scarborough field, it was decided to continue the buoyed channel to a position off Hartlepool.[26]

GERMAN-LAID MINEFIELD OFF SCARBOROUGH

After the laying of the new German minefield, a safe channel had to be established northward past Scarborough, and until it was swept, shipping between the Tyne and Flamborough could not proceed. The minefield proved particularly difficult to locate, and it only became known by the loss of passing coasters (shallow-hulled coastal trading vessels). The actual minesweeping commenced on 19 December, carried out by groups of trawlers from Grimsby; the minesweeping gunboats HMS *Skipjack, Gossamer,* and *Jason,* sent to assist the trawlers; the paddle-steamer *Brighton Queen*; and from Lowestoft, eight drifters to assist in keeping merchant vessels out of the minefield.[27]

In order to ascertain how the mines lay, it was necessary to sweep at all states of the tide. Probably no one except those who plied their trade off this inhospitable coast during the few daylight hours of a December day can appreciate the anxieties and difficulties of the task. Gales sprang up at short warning, and the harbours at Bridlington and Scarborough could not be entered at all states of the tide. The nearest port was at Grimsby, involving a long passage for small craft along an unlighted coast. The minesweeping trawlers were able to remain at sea in almost any weather, but their deep draughts, particularly aft, put them in peril of falling victim to the hidden mines.[28]

HMS *Skipjack*, *Gossamer*, and *Jason* (under the command of Comdr. Lionel Preston, RN, of the *Skipjack*) began their work on 19 December, three days after the raid, sweeping north-northwest from Flamborough Head. Nothing was found until they were in waters off Scarborough, when two mines were caught in the sweep between *Skipjack* and *Gossamar*.[29]

The principal British method of clearing mines throughout the war was by the use of the 'A' sweep, which consisted of a single 2 ½-inch wire towed between two ships steaming 500 yards apart. The depth of the sweep was regulated by a "kite" twelve feet long and weighing a ton. When rigging the gear before commencement of sweeping, the (bitter) end of the wire had to be passed from one vessel to another. To do this rapidly under fire required sailors with exceptional training, skill and courage. In the case of fast sweepers, the momentum of the wire was sufficient to cut the mooring of a mine, but slow vessels (such as converted fishing trawlers) had to take their sweeps into shallow water where an entangled mine(s) could be seen and sunk by rifle fire.[30]

Photo 5-4

British torpedo gunboat *Skipjack*; date photo take unknown.
Naval History and Heritage Command photograph #NH 54855

As *Skipjack* made for the harbour, she came upon some minesweeping trawlers working southeast of the bay. The flotilla was operating out of patrol base Pekin at Grimsby, under the command of Lt. Godfrey Craik Parsons, RN; skipper of the *Passing*, one of the trawlers. Over the course of that day, the trawlers would explode eight mines, and bring to the surface six more—while suffering the loss of one of their members and damage to two others.[31]

HMT *Orianda* (99) was blown up close aboard Preston's ship by an exploding mine, and HMT *Passing* (58) and HMT *Star of Britain* (465) were damaged in the span of about ten minutes after his arrival. Although *Orianda* was lost, Lt. Hubert Boothby was able to get all his crew safely away except one (deckhand James Wilson, RNR, who had been killed by the explosion). Boothby, who was nearing his 40s, only managed to escape from the wheelhouse window, with many bruises, just before his vessel went under. Preston immediately anchored and began to destroy mines with gunfire as the remaining undamaged trawlers cut them loose.[32]

Three violent explosions under the stern of the *Star of Britain* had breached her hull. As she began to sink, Lt. Charles V. Crossley, RNR, had crawled into a confined space near the screw shaft to locate the source of the flooding. He was able to reduce the inflow of water sufficiently for the pumps to keep pace and save his ship. Crossley received the Distinguished Service Cross for this action and Engineman Robert A. Gray, the Distinguished Service Medal.[33]

Parson's own ship the *Passing* was also damaged. Although much more severely than the *Star of Britain*, she was also saved. Badly holed, down by the bow, aflame, and with steam emitting from a severed pipe, she was initially assisted by her sweeping partner and then towed stern-first across Cayton Bay by the paddle minesweeper *Brighton Queen* (Comdr. Richard H. Walters, RN). Beached on Scarborough Sands, with no lives lost, she was subsequently taken to Grimsby, repaired and put back into service. An account by Parsons of the last few minutes aboard her (as related by Preston in Henry Taprell Dorling's seminal book, *Swept Channels*) follows:

> The ship was rapidly going down. Little of the bows was left and nothing at all of the poor fellow who was there when the ship struck the mine. I gave the order to abandon ship and then found what wonderful fellows I commanded. The situation was of course utterly novel to them. Our consort, also mined, appeared a little distance away in a similar predicament. Our ship was likely to sink in a matter of minutes, if not seconds. Yet not a voice was raised, nor was there any sign of fear.

The Engineer reported quite calmly that he had stopped the engines and regretted that he had done so without orders. I apologised for the oversight, which I explained was due to the telegraph and voice-pipe from the wheelhouse both being blown away. Most of the crew by this time were in the boat. They were bailing her out with their caps, as she was leaking badly. But cookie was anxious not to waste his precious tea. I noticed him drawing jorums from an enormous teapot and passing them over the side of the boat.[34] [The British use the plural "bows," versus "bow" when describing the front part of a vessel.]

The gallant Lieutenant Parsons was awarded the DSC, as well. He went on to command the sweeping sloop HMS *Dahlia* from October 1915, and in May 1917 was appointed Minesweeping Officer at Dover, in the rank of Lieutenant Commander. Parsons was released in the rank of Commander (Emergency List) in November 1918.[35]

Lieutenant Boothby, who saved the survivors of the *Orianda*, was awarded the Distinguished Service Order—second only to the Victoria Cross in order of precedence for awards for heroism. His ship had gone down with her engines at full ahead, and the tip of her masthead the last part to disappear. Boothby would be blown up on 6 January 1915, once again in a trawler in the Scarborough field, this time aboard *The Banyers* (450), and once again he would survive.[36]

MINE CLEARANCE EFFORTS CONTINUE

Under Comdr. Richard Walters in HMS *Brighton Queen*, the sweeping continued until the end of 1914. When the first paddle-sweepers had come churning up the muddy Humber and made up at Grimsby Docks alongside the steel trawlers, many seamen had likely wondered, what good does the Navy expect to find in a former excursion paddle-steamer? Yet these vessels, drawing only about seven and a half feet, proved to be splendid minesweepers. They could go into a field with half the risk of a deep-draught trawler, and could make good speed. The result was that two or three pairs could soon clear up any suspected area and set merchant ships, which had been held up, free to proceed to their destinations. The first paddle-sweepers acquired by the Admiralty were the *Brighton Queen* and *Devonia*, which were sent round from Bristol to Devonport for fitting out, before taking up new duties.[37]

To assist him, Walters was given *Halcyon* and eight drifters from Lowestoft, totaling fourteen trawlers and twelves drifters in all. He reported the waters heavily mined, and day after day the dangerous work continued, broken only by even more hazardous rescue efforts. On the 20th and 25th of December, two more trawlers were mined and sunk in the North Sea. *Garmo*, a patrol vessel, was sunk off Scarborough, with the loss of an officer and five men. On Christmas morning, while sweeping south from Whitby, the trawler *Night Hawk* struck a mine and sank about five-and-a-half miles east of Scarborough. Only seven of her crew of thirteen survived, including the commanding officer, Sub-Lieutenant W. A. Senior, RNR.[38]

In the following summary, the initials RFR refer to the Royal Fleet Reserve and "trimmer" to members of the "black gang" (engineers). In the Trawler Section of the RNR, trimmers did the same job as stokers (who were generally assigned to warships of the fleet), that is, transporting and shoveling coal into the boiler furnaces.

Garmo Casualties

Thomas W. Berry, RFR	Able Seaman
Thaddeus Gilbert, RNR	Skipper
John R. Hare, RNR	Cook
Thomas G. Harris, RFR	Able Seaman
Walter R. Sparrow, RNR	Deck Hand
Joseph W. Thorton, RNR	Deck Hand

Night Hawk Casualties

Alfred W. J. Chapple, RNR	Engineman
Joseph Church, RNR	Trimmer
Arthur H. Hearne, RNR	Trimmer
George H. Hubbard, RNR	Deckhand
William H. Rowbotham, RNR	Engineman
Thomas H. Shearsmith, RNR	Cook[39]

The swept channel was completed to Scarborough by Christmas Eve 1914, and shipping was able to pass through during daylight. By the end of the year, work had begun to buoy the extended channel to mark the area of safe passage. While this was in progress, the losses of trawlers and vessels continued well into January 1915.[40]

SWEEPING ELSEWHERE ALONG THE EAST COAST

During this first autumn no seamen more thoroughly earned the gratitude of their nation than those of the busy minesweepers, whose work was never finished. From each East Coast port, day after day, six of them steamed out in line ahead just before dawn to their stations; and then they would get sweeps out and go rolling down the North Sea until relieved a few days later by another six; all the time they offered an easy target for the enemy's submarines, and were equally liable to be blown up on an unseen mine.

—From Archibald Hurd's book, *The Merchant Navy, Vol. I, 1914 to Spring 1915.*[41]

Once the buoying was finished, unceasing work still remained for the minesweepers and patrols, keeping the now 500 mile long East Channel open in all types of weather. Farther south, and particularly around the Straits of Dover—where heavy winter weather and strong tides were continuously tearing both British and German mines from their moorings and setting them adrift—the work was particularly arduous. (A British minefield laid across the Dover Straits to prevent U-boats from entering the channel and sinking shipping, had actually proved of little practical or moral effect, for the reason that most of the mines drifted away.) By year's end in 1914, enemy surface ships had laid a total of 1,004 mines in six separate fields.[42]

German Minefields Laid in British Waters in 1914

Date	Minelayer	Area	Mines
5 Aug 1914	*Königin Luise*	Southwold, S. of Lowestoft	180
26 Aug 1914	*Nautilus*	off the Humber River	200
26 Aug 1914	*Albatross*	off the Tyne River	194
26 Oct 1914	*Berlin*	Tory Island, Ireland	200
3 Nov 1914	*Kolberg*	Smith's Knoll, E. of Yarmouth	130
16 Dec 1914	*Kolberg*	Scarborough, North Yorkshire	100[43]

Moreover, the Irish minefield which the *Berlin* had laid off Tory Island was still uncleared. Persistently, as the weather permitted, six minesweeping trawlers under Lt. James H. Domville, RN, which had come down from Scapa Flow, worked at their tasks, and many mines were destroyed. Yet, on 19 December 1914 the liner *Tritonia* was sunk within a few miles of where the loss of the *Manchester Commerce* had first revealed the existence of these ship killers.[44]

The Admiralty acquired by the end of 1914, a total of 750 yachts, patrol trawlers, minesweeping trawlers, drifters, paddle-sweepers, motor-drifters, and motorboats. Serving aboard these vessels were 190 officers of the Royal Navy (RN) and Royal Naval Reserve (RNR), and 250 officers of the Royal Naval Volunteer Reserve (RNVR).[45]

AWARDS FOR VALOUR

Distinguished Service Order (DSO)

Date	Recipient	Minesweeper
19 Dec 1914	Lt. Hubert Boothby, RNR	trawler *Orianda* (99)

Distinguished Service Cross (DSC)

19 Dec 1914	Lt. Godfrey Craik Parsons, RN	trawler *Passing* (58)
19 Dec 1914	Lt. Charles V. Crossley, RNR	trawler *Star of Britain* (465)
25 Dec 1914	Skipper T. W. Trendall, RNR(T)	trawler *Solon* (55)
25 Dec 1914	Skipper Ernest V. Snowline, RNR(T)	drifter *Hilda and Ernest* (201)

Distinguished Service Medal (DSM)

19 Dec 1914	Robert A. Gray, Engineman, RNR	trawler *Star of Britain* (465)
6 Jan 1915	William A. Lewis, PO 1st Class	trawler *The Banyers* (450)
6 Jan 1915	Christopher Briggs, Engineman, RNR	trawler *The Banyers* (450)
6 Jan 1915	William Gladding, Cook, RNR	trawler *The Banyers* (450)
	Robert Frost, Second Hand, RNR	trawler *Escallonia* (43)

The above individuals all received awards of valour for East Coast Minesweeping. In addition to heroic actions by individuals previously discussed, Skipper T. Trendall, RNRT (Royal Naval Reserve, Trawler Section), took the trawler *Solon*, on his own initiative, to assist the British steamship SS *Gallier*. This action on the night of 25 December was particularly dangerous as it was low water, making any ship entering the Scarborough field more vulnerable to a mine strike. Complicating the situation, *Gallier*—which had just struck a mine—was showing no lights, and so had to be located in the field.[46]

Ernest V. Snowline, skipper of the drifter *Hilda and Ernest*, received the DSC for his actions while commodore of the Flotilla of Lowestoft drifters, and for keeping his station in heavy weather, while standing by the *Gallier* after she was damaged by the mine.[47]

Briggs, Lewis, and Gladding were crewmembers of *The Banyers*, a hired trawler, lost on 6 January 1915. Their actions (and those of Frost aboard trawler *Escallonia*) when their ships were in great peril, warranted Distinguished Service Medals.[48]

6

Battle of Dogger Bank

For the second time, when already in the jaws of destruction, the German Battle Cruiser Squadron escaped.

—Winston Churchill, First Lord of the Admiralty[1]

The disappointment of that day is more than I can bear to think of. Everybody thinks it was a great success, when in reality it was a terrible failure. I had made up my mind that we were going to get four, the lot, and four we ought to have got.

—Adm. David Beatty, RN, commander British Grand Fleet, in correspondence to Commodore Rodger Keyes, RN.[2]

As 1915 dawned, Konteradmiral Franz Hipper (the commander of the 1st Scouting Group of the High Seas Fleet) was restless. He disliked keeping his men and ships at a high state of readiness, while at the same time restricting them to port. Moreover, in addition to the German defeat in the Heligoland Bight, previous unsuccessful raids by his cruisers against the English east coast galled him.[3]

IMPETUS FOR THE RAID ON DOGGER BANK

On 3 October 1914, Admirals Hugo von Pohl, chief of the Naval Staff, and Friedrich von Ingenohl, commander-in-chief of the High Seas Fleet, had met onboard the fleet flagship (battleship *Friedrich der Grosse*) to discuss the Kaiser's decision to maintain a "fleet in being." Concluding that offensive minelaying off the British coast would be permissible, four torpedo-boats were sent to lay mines off the mouth of the Thames. When all four were sunk, without laying a single mine, Ingenohl had decided to take advantage of the caveat, "the battle fleet must avoid heavy losses, but there is nothing to be said about the battle cruisers trying to damage the enemy." Ingenohl judged that, if they were fortunate, battle cruiser raids against England's shore would entice units of the Grand Fleet to steam south, possibly into German-laid minefields and across a line of U-boats.[4]

Photo 6-1

Konteradmiral Franz Ritter von Hipper, Imperial German Navy.
Naval History and Heritage Command photograph #NH 120642

Map 6-1

Dogger Bank in the North Sea

RAIDS AGAINST YARMOUTH AND SCARBOROUGH ACHIEVE LITTLE

I don't want to go to the bottom so ingloriously. To run on mines and sink off the English coast is hardly what I'm out for.

—Konteradmiral Franz Hipper expressing concern about a possible encounter with British mines. He did not expect any opposition from British warships during the first raid by his battle cruisers against England, because he expected to surprise the enemy.[5]

At dawn on 3 November 1914, the minesweeping gunboat HMS *Halcyon* (Comdr. George N. Ballard) stood out of port at Yarmouth into the drifting mist off the Norfolk coast. The 262-foot former gunboat had once been described as "perhaps the smallest and least formidable vessel that ever crept into the Navy List." Commissioned in 1895, she had served until May 1901, then was paid off at Devonport and placed in the Fleet reserve. Brought out "of mothballs" to serve as a minesweeper, and recommissioned at Sheerness on 5 July 1913, she was the flagship of the Senior Naval Officer North Sea Fisheries. In trail behind her were the destroyers *Lively* and *Leopard*, preparing to take up their own routine offshore patrols. These three ships along with four other old destroyers, constituted Yarmouth's defence.[6]

Map 6-2

Yarmouth on England's east coast

The nearest heavy warships were old pre-dreadnaughts at Sheerness, a hundred miles down the coast. Beatty's battle cruisers were 300 miles to the north at Cromarty, and most of Jellicoe's battleships twice that distance at Lough Swilly—an inlet from the Atlantic in northwest Ireland.[7]

As *Halcyon* steered northeast toward the *Cross Sand* light vessel (with the intention of sweeping the channel which ran from it to Smith's Knoll), two unknown four-funneled cruisers appeared in the early morning light, five miles to the north. Later it was learned they were a part of Hipper's battle cruiser squadron. The minesweeper flashed a challenge by signal-light. The response was splashes near her from small-calibre naval guns, followed by towering waterspouts created by large 11-inch rounds. *Lively*, two miles astern, hurried to the scene and laid down a smoke screen between the minesweeper and the enemy.[8]

Photo 6-2

British torpedo-gunboat HMS *Halcyon*, date unknown.
Naval History and Heritage Command photograph #NH 75949

Although under the concentrated fire of three battle cruisers, at a range of 7,000-8,000 yards, *Halcyon* only sustained slight damage and was already entering the Yarmouth Roads, covered by the destroyers, when, at 0730, the enemy hauled off to the east-southeast allowing *Halcyon* to escape. So eager were the German gun crews, their nearly continuous fire had created a curtain of splashes that made accurate spotting (visual observation of where rounds land, to correct aim-point) impossible. Their exuberance probably saved *Halcyon*. However, she was hit on the bridge, which damaged her radio room and wounded three crewmen. Able Seaman Harry Scotney later died of his wounds.[9]

Hipper realised that he was wasting his time fighting the two remaining destroyers, and that a continued pursuit of them southward could take his force into a known minefield. He thus ceased fire and turned the squadron seaward. Departing the area, his battle cruisers flung a few rounds toward Yarmouth, but only hit the beach. During the earlier activity, the light cruiser *Stralsund* had been busy laying a line of mines, five miles long, between the Smith's Knoll and the *Cross Sand* light vessel.[10]

The Imperial German Navy's first major surface offensive into the North Sea was a failure, and the Scouting Group subsequently lost both a ship and a majority of her officers and men before its conclusion. Upon return to German waters the night of 3 November, the group found heavy fog covering the Heligoland Bight. Considering it unsafe to proceed, Ingenohl ordered all ships to anchor overnight in Schillig Roads. The following morning conditions had not improved, but the armoured cruiser *Yorck* was given permission to proceed into Wilhelmshaven to receive repairs necessary to replenish her fresh water tanks.[11]

While trying, in the murk, to find the entrance to a double row of mines that guarded the southern side of Schillig Roads, she was set by current toward the wrong side of the swept channel. In trying to extract herself from this difficulty, *Yorck* turned using too much rudder, and overcorrected for her error. Carried south by the current and her momentum, she struck a mine, and a minute later, hit another. Fatally damaged by the explosions, the armoured cruiser capsized and began sinking. Many in the crew saved themselves by clinging to the protruding keel of the overturned, still afloat ship. Two hundred thirty-five men were lost; some were trapped inside the cruiser, and others drowned in the icy sea while attempting to swim to safety.[12]

The only success achieved by the raid was that of the laying of the minefield by *Stralsund* in Smith's Knoll, which subsequently claimed a British submarine leaving port and several fishing boats. (It was not known whether the submarine HMS *D-5* was lost to a drifting mine or one of *Stralsund*'s.) Three of the other victims were sail fishing vessels all sunk by contacting mines: the *Speculator* on 10 November with five lives lost; the *Seymolicus* eight days later with nine men killed, including the skipper; and *Lord Carnarvon* on 20 November with her skipper and nine other men.[13]

The field also claimed one of the minesweepers sent to clear it. The trawler *Mary* (No. 361) was sunk on 5 November 1914, while sweeping the Yarmouth field near Smith's Knoll Buoy with trawlers *Columbia* and *Driver*. Following a mine detonation just after 1000 which destroyed the after part of the vessel, the forward part settled and sank within two minutes. The skipper, William Stephen Greenaway RNR, and seven ratings were lost. The remaining six survivors were rescued by the other two trawlers.[14]

INACTIVITY OF BRITISH NAVAL FORCES

Several hours of tension passed; and then gradually it became clear that the German battle cruisers were returning home at full speed and that nothing else was apparently happening; and the incredible conclusion forced itself upon us that the German Admiralty had had no other purpose than this silly demonstration off Yarmouth beach.

—Winston Churchill, First Lord of the Admiralty, describing his shock, followed by relief, that the German raid had done Britain no harm. Churchill was the political head of the Board of the Admiralty, charged with overseeing the Naval Service. The Board's other members were four Sea Lords, and a Civil Lord, with a Parliamentary and a Permanent Secretary.[15]

Although Room 40 (Naval Intelligence) had been monitoring German signals since 0700 that morning, the Admiralty had not ordered any ships or squadrons to sea. Churchill later explained the basis for this apparent oversight:

Early in the morning of November 3…heavy shells were reported to be bursting in the water and on the beach near Yarmouth…. The question was what did it mean?… Obviously, this was a demonstration to divert the British Fleet from something else which was going to happen—was perhaps already happening…. We had no means of judging. The last thing it seemed possible to believe was that first-class units of the German Fleet would have been sent across the North Sea simply in order to disturb the fisher-folk of Yarmouth…. Meanwhile, nothing to be done but put everyone on guard.[16]

HIPPER WANTS TO ELIMINATE FISHING VESSELS HE BELIEVES ARE ALERTING BRITISH FORCES

First Lord, those fellows are coming out again. When? Tonight. We have just got time to get Beatty there.

—Conversation between First Lord Winston Churchill and Adm. Sir Arthur Wilson, an advisor to Churchill.[17]

Konteradmiral Hipper believed that his lack of success (the Scouting Group's frustrated approach to Yarmouth, and its close escape after Scarborough) was because the British had known in advance about his plans. How they knew, he was uncertain, but he believed that some of the fishing vessels working on the outskirts of the Bight and on the Dogger Bank (a rich fishing ground between Heligoland and the coast of England) were there mainly for observation and espionage.[18]

To eliminate these "scouts," Hipper proposed an operation in which his force would clear the Dogger of British fishing vessels and suspicious neutral craft, and also attack any light British warships patrolling the bank. He envisioned involving only the German battle cruisers and their escorting light cruisers and destroyers, with their withdrawal covered by the High Seas Fleet. Ingenohl authorised the operation with a signal sent to Hipper the morning of 23 January: "Scouting Forces are to reconnoiter Dogger Bank. Leave tonight at twilight, return tomorrow at darkness." However, at a meeting aboard the flagship before sailing, the fleet commander denied Hipper's request for High Seas Fleet support. Acknowledging that there would be no covering force, Hipper promised Ingenohl that if there was a chance a stronger British force might cut him off from the Bight, he would immediately turn and run for home.[19]

Constituting Hipper's force were four light cruisers—*Stralsund*, *Rostock*, *Kolberg*, and *Graudenz*—and a strong destroyer flotilla, supported by the battle cruisers *Seydlitz*, *Moltke*, and *Derfflinger*, and a smaller armoured cruiser *Blücher*.[20]

The British Admiralty learned from an intercepted message that the German battle cruisers were putting to sea that evening for a reconnaissance in force as far as the Dogger Bank, but considered that another raid on the English coast was possible. This information was sent out at a little past noon to Admiral Jellicoe at Scapa, to Admiral Beatty and Admiral Bradford (commanding the 8th Battle Squadron) at Rosyth, on the Firth of Forth, and to Commodore Tyrwhitt at Harwich. Charts and a clock at the Admiralty indicated that there was just enough time for Beatty, coming from the Forth, and Tyrwhitt from Harwich, to rendezvous at daylight near the northeast part of the Dogger, and intercept Hipper.[21]

Following additional discussion and concurrence from the First Sea Lord, Adm. John "Jackie" Fisher, the plan was set. Beatty's five battle cruisers and Commodore William Goodenough's light cruisers, coming down from the north, would join forces at dawn with Tyrwhitt's three light cruisers and thirty-five destroyers proceeding northward. Vice Adm. Edward Bradford was to take the 3rd Battle Squadron (whose eight pre-dreadnaught members were known as "The Wobbly Eight") and the 3rd Cruiser Squadron northwest of Beatty's forces, to intercept Hipper if he turned north. Jellicoe was to proceed with the *Dreadnaught* fleet, and his three cruiser squadrons (1st, 2nd, and 6th) from Scapa Flow and cruise farther to the north to oppose the High Seas Fleet, should it put to sea. Movement to sea of the various components of the Grand Fleet went smoothly, except that, owing to fog, the Harwich destroyer flotillas were a little late.[22]

Beatty and Goodenough arrived at the rendezvous point a little after 0700. Ten minutes later a sighting was made of the light cruiser *Arethusa*, Tyrwhitt's flagship, and seven fast M-class destroyers he had brought up from Harwich. At 0720 a signal from the light cruiser *Aurora*, leading one of Tyrwhitt's slower destroyer flotillas, reported: "Am in action with the High Seas Fleet." Beatty immediately ordered the battle cruisers to turn in the direction of the gun flashes, and they steamed southeast at 22 knots. *Aurora* had actually encountered the *Kolberg* (a minelayer) and four destroyers. Believing the three-funneled light cruiser was likely the *Arethusa*, she closed to 8,000 yards before giving the challenge. The unknown ship (*Kolberg*) opened fire and *Aurora*, hit slightly three times, began to return fire. After a round struck *Kolberg* below her forebridge and exploded, the German ships turned away to the east. *Aurora* (who'd received only slight damage) and her escorted destroyers continued on to the rendezvous.[23]

At about the same time, Goodenough, aboard the *Southampton*, sighted a group of ships to the south, and another to the east. Those to the south were *Aurora* and the Harwich Force. To the east, he could make out in the distance, two light cruisers (*Stralsund* and *Graudenz*) and, at 0730, the German battle cruisers. Hipper's ships were steaming northwest at a leisurely 15 knots, spread across a broad front to search for fishing vessels and, if lucky, to encounter light patrol forces. After receiving a report from *Kolberg* of her encounter with the British cruiser and destroyers, Hipper turned his battle cruisers south toward *Kolberg*'s position. Perhaps, the ships that had accosted her would prove to be the forces he had come to mop up.[24]

As Hipper approached, *Kolberg* warned that she had sighted smoke to the southwest, and *Stralsund* reported she was also seeing thick smoke, but to the northwest. The armoured cruiser *Blücher* provided an amplifying report of seven British light cruisers, and more than twenty destroyers to the northwest—steering a parallel course out of gun range. Hipper now knew this was no mere patrol force and the presence of so many cruisers and destroyers suggested the possibility of more powerful ships nearby. *Stralsund* then signaled that there were at least eight large ships under the cloud of smoke to the northwest.[25]

Concerned that this group might be one of the Grand Fleet's battleship squadrons, and knowing that if so, his own force was weaker than either it or Beatty's battle cruisers (which he believed must be nearby) individually, Hipper signaled his force at 0735 to turn southeast and retire at 20 knots. Hipper was leading in the *Seydlitz*, with *Derfflinger* second, *Moltke* third, and *Blücher* last, with his light cruisers and the destroyer flotilla ahead.[26]

BATTLE IS JOINED

The ships to the northwest were in fact, Beatty's five battle cruisers. By 0800, the chase was on with the British steering a converging, but parallel course as they tried desperately to catch the four German battle cruisers. Beatty employed this tactic partially because of concern the retreating enemy might drop mines in their wake. More importantly, with his battle cruisers closing the starboard quarter of the German force from downwind, they could fire unimpeded by smoke from their own guns and funnels. The key to success, however, was speed. Hipper's head start in the race across the North Sea to German waters had him 7,000 yards beyond the effective range of the British guns.[27]

Aboard *Lion*, his flagship, Beatty expressed this urgency to Percy Green, the chief engineer, "Tell your stokers all depends on them." "They know that, sir," Green replied. What followed were herculean efforts by the "black gangs" in every one of the battle cruisers. By 0830, *Lion* was doing 26 knots and the admiral called for 27. The *Indomitable* (whose trial speed was only just over 25) was keeping up, and the flagship, in admiration, signaled "Well steamed, *Indomitable*." A midshipman aboard her later graphically described the flurry of activity in one of the firerooms:

> The furnaces devoured coal as fast as a man could feed them. Black, begrimed and sweating men working in the ship's side dug the coal out and loaded it into skids which were then dragged along the steel deck and emptied on the floor plates in front of each boiler.... Watching the pressure gauges for any fall in steam pressure, the Chief Stoker walked to and fro, encouraging his men. Now and then the telegraph from the engine room would clang and the finger on the dial move round to the section marked "More Steam." The chief would press the reply gong with an oath, "What do the bastards think we're doing? Come on boys, shake it up, get going," and the sweating men would redouble their efforts, throw open the furnace doors and shovel still more coal into the blazing inferno.[28]

As Beatty called for ever more speed, the distance between his ships and those of the enemy gradually lessened. At 0852, he signaled for 29 knots, well knowing that his two rear ships would fall astern; but this action was necessary to catch the rear of the flying enemy. At the same time, with the distance to the *Blücher* now at 20,000, the upper B turret on *Lion*'s bow fired a single 13.5-inch ranging shot at her. It fell short, gun elevation was adjusted, and the next two more shots were over, straddling her. At 0905, Beatty signaled to the squadron: "Open fire and engage the enemy." The guns of *Lion* and those of *Tiger* (close behind her) erupted with salvos of armour-piercing rounds. Soon, *Princess Royal* joined in. At 0918, *Lion* shifted her fire to the third enemy ship in line, the battle cruiser *Moltke*. As the Germans began firing back, the sea boiled with tall columns. Not surprisingly, *Blücher* was receiving the most punishment.[29]

By 0935, *New Zealand* had closed the range to *Blücher* sufficiently, and opened fire. *Blücher*'s position at the rear of the enemy column (placed thus because she was Hipper's slowest ship) sealed her fate. Every overtaking British battle cruiser fired at her first, before shifting to larger German ships farther up the line. Badly damaged, on fire and listing, *Blücher* fell out of line and sheered away to port. At 1048, Beatty ordered his rearmost battle cruiser, *Indomitable*, to: "Attack the enemy breaking away to northward."[30]

FALSE REPORT OF SUBMARINE, AND CONFUSED SIGNALS FROM FLAGSHIP SAVE HIPPER

During this action, Beatty's ships were taking punishment as well, but up to this point he had conducted the battle well. At 1054, a report of submarines on *Lion*'s starboard bow changed everything. To negate the danger that one or more submarines would present, Beatty signaled for eight points together to port (a ninety-degree turn). This action sent his ships north, at a right angle across the wake of the fleeing Germans. Realising the turn had been unnecessarily wide, he signaled four minutes later, "Course North East," to resume the pursuit of Hipper's battle cruisers. (After the battle, Beatty reported to the Admiralty that he had personally observed the wash of a periscope on the bow.)[31]

However, this setback was compounded by a subsequent signal Beatty ordered sent by *Lion*. Heavily damaged, the flagship (*Lion*) was falling astern of the other ships. Before they pulled away out of visual range, he ordered the signal: "Attack the rear of the enemy" hoisted aloft. Beatty meant for his ships to attack Hipper's battle cruisers drawing away to the southeast, but confusion resulted because the previous signal, "Course North East," was still flying. Thus, his captains incorrectly inferred that he was directing them to "attack the rear of the enemy, northeast." The four British battle cruisers gave up their pursuit of Hipper's ships and steered for the battered, yet still afloat *Blücher*. With *Lion* able to direct the squadron only by flag hoist signals, and having fallen too far astern for the other ships to see them, command of the battle cruisers automatically passed to Rear Adm. Archibald Moore aboard *New Zealand*.[32]

Blücher was exchanging fire with Goodenough's four light cruisers (who were 14,000 yards distant) when, at 1120, Tyrwhitt in *Arethusa* accompanied by four M-class destroyers arrived. *Meteor* came in close enough to *Blücher* to launch her torpedoes, before a hit from one of the enemy's guns knocked her out of action. The other three destroyers also fired their torpedoes, and believed they scored five hits. *Arethusa* then came in, firing her 6-inch guns as the range closed to 2,500 yards, before launching two torpedoes as she turned away. Both of the "fish" hit *Blücher*, knocking out her electrical power. As *Tiger*, *Princess Royal*, *New Zealand*, and *Indomitable* arrived on the scene, the massacre began in earnest. Hit continuously by 13.5 and 12-inch gun rounds, the helpless *Blücher* was soon a mass of fire and smoke. At 1207, she heeled over, floated for a few minutes overturned, and then sank.[33]

Arethusa and her destroyers lowered boats, and began picking up survivors from the water. Of the 1,200 officers and men in the crew, only 234 were saved. FKpt. Alexander Erdmann (who fought his ship so valiantly) survived, but later died of pneumonia as a prisoner of war in England. During over three hours of naval combat, in which she was hit by seventy gun rounds and seven torpedoes, *Blücher* had fought to the end. As noted by the official British history, "As an example of discipline, courage and fighting spirit, her last hours have seldom been surpassed."[34]

WHY DIDN'T YOU GET THE LOT?

Photo 6-3

Admiral Lord John ("Jackie") Fisher, Royal Navy, date unknown
Naval History and Heritage Command photograph #NH 120570

The battle of Dogger Bank was a British victory, but it did not achieve the total annihilation of the enemy that the Royal Navy and the public so eagerly desired. After receiving a letter from Adm. "Jackie" Fisher, the First Sea Lord, inquiring how it was the action had been broken off, Beatty sent a lieutenant assigned to the *Lion* (who knew Lord Fisher personally) to carry to London a response he'd penned. Upon his arrival at the Admiralty, Filson Young was taken to meet with Lord Fisher. Following minimal pleasantries, the 74 year old admiral got right to the point:

He shook hands…and turning his hard, wise old eye on me, he said, "Well, tell me about it. How was it they got away? What's the explanation? Why didn't you get the lot?[35]

After making inquiries into how so strong a Royal Navy force had sunk but a single ship, Churchill and Fisher "wanted to have the blood of someone" and settled on Rear Admiral Moore. They were furious that he'd failed to send a portion of his battle cruisers to dispose of the crippled, fleeing enemy ships, and had instead focused solely on *Blücher*. Near the end of February, Moore was reassigned to command a cruiser squadron in the Canary Islands, where the possibility of an encounter with German warships seemed remote.[36]

AWARDS FOR VALOUR

The *London Gazette* No. 9088, of 2 March 1915, cited the below individuals for gallantry during the Battle of Dogger Bank. (Because many honours and gallantry awards lists published in the *Gazette* did not associate ships or battles/campaigns with those decorated, this list and others in the book, may be incomplete.)   Most of those cited for gallantry at Dogger Bank were engineers (ratings), whose herculean efforts in feeding the furnaces of Beatty's cruisers enabled them to close Kontreadmiral Franz Hipper's force and to engage it in combat.

Companion of the Order of the Bath (GCB)

Awardee	Position
Capt. Osmond de Beauvoir Brock, RN	Captain of the *Princess Royal* at the Battle of Heligoland Bight and the Battle of Dogger Bank; also promoted to Rear Admiral

Distinguished Service Order (DSO)

Awardee	Position
Lt. Frederick Thornton Peters, RN	First Lieutenant, destroyer HMS *Meteor*

Distinguished Service Medal (DSM)

Awardee and Title/Rating	Awardee and Title/Rating
Surgeon Probationer James Alexander Stirling, RNVR	Chief Stoker Alfred Wm. Ferris
Gunner (T) Joseph H. Burton	Chief Stoker John Ernest James
Chief Carpenter Frederick E. Dailey	Chief Stoker Walter E. James
Petty Officer John William Kemmett	Chief Stoker James Keating, RFR
Able Seaman Henry Davis	Stoker Petty Officer Michael Flood, RFR
Able Seaman Hubert F. Griffin	Stoker Petty Officer Thomas Wm. Hardy
Able Seaman Peter Stanley Livingstone	Stoker Petty Officer Albert John Sims

Able Seaman Herbert Robison	Stoker Petty Officer Samuel Westaway, RFR
Able Seaman George Henry le Seilleur	Acting Leading Stoker John Blackburn
Boy, 1st Class, Francis G. H. Bamford	Stoker, 1st Class, Alan H. Bennet
Boy, 1st Class, Julius F. Rogers	Stoker, 2nd Class, Harold Turner
Chief Engine-Room Artificer, 1st Class, Evan Richard Hughes	Leading Carpenter's Crew, Emmanuel Omega Bradley
Chief Engine-Room Artificer, 2nd Class, Win. Beaty Dand	Leading Carpenter's Crew, Elisha Currie
Chief Engine-Room Artificer W. Gillespie	Sick Berth Attendant Charles S. Hutchinson
Mechanician Alexander James Cannon	Chief Writer Samuel G. White
Mechanician Edward Charles Ephgrave	Third Writer Herbert C. Green
Chief Stoker Patrick Callaghan	Officers' Steward, 3rd Class, Fred W. Kearley

CANADIAN RECEIVES SECOND HIGHEST AWARD

Lt. Frederick Thornton Peters, RN, a Canadian serving aboard the destroyer HMS *Meteor* as first lieutenant/torpedo officer, received the Distinguished Service Order. He had joined the Royal Navy as a 16-year-old cadet in January 1905, following completion of his schooling in Prince Rupert, British Columbia. While still a midshipman, Peters was awarded the Silver Messina Earthquake medal in 1908 by the Italian government in recognition of his service in leading rescue parties during the evacuation of citizens in danger from the erupting Mount Messina. In 1909, he was commissioned as a Sub-Lieutenant, and operated gunboats on "The China Station" prior to World War I. By the end of the war, Peters would also earn a Distinguished Service Cross and a Mention in Despatches—in addition to his DSO.[37]

Although his career is not within the scope of this book, perhaps readers will permit a few more paragraphs devoted to Capt. Frederick Peters, as he was perhaps Canada's bravest naval officer. Peters was promoted to commander at the beginning of World War II, and given command of a flotilla of small boats credited with sinking two U-boats. He was awarded a bar to his Distinguished Service Cross in 1940, and was later promoted to captain and appointed to serve as an instructor at a British "Spy School" (perhaps the Special Operations Executive training establishment in Beaulieu, Hampshire).[38]

Returning to sea duty, Captain Peters was sent to Gibraltar to plan an attack on the harbour at Oran, protected by the Vichy French. Deemed a suicide mission, the senior officer (who was now in his early

50s) personally took command of the cutters HMS *Hartland* and HMS *Walney* and led it. For his heroic actions, Peters was awarded the Victoria Cross. The medal citation reads:

> Captain Peters was in the 'suicide charge' by two little cutters at Oran. *Walney* and *Hartland* were two ex-American coast guard cutters which were lost in a gallant attempt to force the boom defences in the harbour of Oran during the landings on the North African Coast. Captain Peters led his force through the boom in the face of point-blank fire from shore batteries, a destroyer and cruiser – a feat which was described as one of the great episodes of naval history. The *Walney* reached the jetty disabled and ablaze, and went down with her colours flying. Blinded in one eye, Captain Peters was the only survivor of the seventeen men on the bridge of the *Walney*. He was taken prisoner but was later released when Oran was captured. On being liberated from gaol, he was carried through the streets where the citizens hailed him with flowers.[39]

Tragically, Peters died in an aircraft accident on 13 November 1942. An RAF Sunderland Flying Boat, in which he was a passenger, was approaching Plymouth in heavy fog when it crashed into the sea near the breakwater off the English harbour.[40]

As a tribute to the estimated 3,000 Canadians who served in the Royal Navy in World War I, a short introductory chapter about the small Royal Canadian Navy formed in 1910, follows. A later chapter takes readers to the eastern seaboard of North America, where Germany sent seven U-boats from February to September 1918 to conduct an offensive. (The last two boats did not reach their patrol area before the German Navy issued a general recall.) This action was apparently an effort to panic Americans sufficiently for public sentiment to bring about the return to the East Coast of U.S. Navy destroyers hunting U-boats in European waters. During their stint off North America, the subs sank many vessels with guns, mines, and scuttling charges. Measures enacted by the U.S. and Canadian navies to combat the threat helped to develop expertise in antisubmarine warfare and mine countermeasures that would be vital in World War II. Of course, their involvement with the Royal Navy greatly facilitated the development of these proficiencies.

7

Royal Canadian Navy
"Ready Aye Ready"

The wholesome sea is at her gates, her gates both east and west.

—Words inscribed above the four doors to the entrance
of Canada's Parliament Buildings in Ottawa.

*That in the opinion of this House, in view of her great and varied resources, of her
geographical position and national environments, and of that spirit of self-help and
self-respect which alone befits a strong and growing people, Canada should no
longer delay in assuming her proper share of the responsibility and financial burden
incident to the suitable protection of her exposed coast line and great seaports.*

—Resolution by Sir George E. Foster presented to Parliament on 29
March 1909, calling on the Canadian government to take more
concrete action on the "naval issue." Foster put forward two
alternatives to the ongoing debate—a Canadian Navy or
direct financial funding to the Mother Country, Britain.[1]

Canada was formally created by an act of the British Parliament on 1
July 1867, but many currently believe by an act emblazoned in the hearts
of its citizens, she came into practical being when the Canadian Corps,
finally under the command of its own officers, drove the Germans off
the Vimy Ridge in April 1917. (This military engagement was fought
primarily as part of the Battle of Arras, in the Nord-Pas-de-Calais region
of France.) Her contribution and other members of the British Empire
and Commonwealth to the land war were huge. Canada's casualties of
the war at nearly 57,000 (Australia and India even higher) exceeded
those of the United States. Her naval contribution was far less extensive
and poorly documented; but was significant. As discussed in the
following pages, the Royal Canadian Navy was still in its formative stage
during the war, so most of her volunteer force served with units of the
Royal Navy.[2]

The Canadian Navy came into being on 4 May 1910—following intense Parliamentary debate—when the Naval Service Act of Canada received royal assent. It became the Royal Canadian Navy (RCN) on 29 August 1911. The debate had revolved around two possible policies; a contribution of money or ships to the British Admiralty, or assumption by Canadians of the defence of their own ports and coasts. The Liberal government of the day of Sir Wilfrid Laurier favoured a Canadian navy, built and manned by Canadians. The opposition Conservatives under Robert Borden opposed a Canadian navy, favouring instead Canada's financial support of the Royal Navy, which would, in turn, defend Canadian waters. The Laurier government intended that a fleet of five cruisers and six torpedo-boat destroyers be built in Canada.[3]

The Naval Service Act created a Department of Naval Service under the Minister of Marine and Fisheries, who would now be the Minister of the Naval Service as well. The Commander in Chief of the naval forces was "to continue to be vested in the [British] King." Under Conditions of Service, Section 23 of the Act read:

> In case of an emergency the Governor in Council may place at the disposal of his Majesty, for general service in the Royal Navy, the Naval Service or any part thereof, any ships or vessels of the Naval Service, and the officers and seamen serving in such ships or vessels, or any officers or seamen belonging to the Naval Service.[4]

The Act authorised a Naval Reserve Force and a Naval Volunteer Force, which could be called to active service in an emergency. The British Naval Discipline Act of 1866, and the King's Regulations and Admiralty Instructions—where applicable, and except to the extent that they might be inconsistent with the Naval Service Act, or regulations made under it—were to apply. Regulations for the entry of officers and men into the Navy Service were issued; a naval college was established in Halifax; and two cruisers were purchased from the Admiralty. The smaller of the two, HMCS *Rainbow*, was intended for the west coast; with the other, HMCS *Niobe*—a heavily armed, protected cruiser of the *Diadem*-class—to be based at Halifax. (*Rainbow* was one of the *Apollo*-class cruisers described in Chapter 2. As noted, many of her sisters were converted to RN minelayers).[5]

For several months after the arrival of the ships in Canada, such recruits as offered themselves on board the cruisers were accepted if they met the physical and education requirements. In February 1911, recruiting posters were exhibited in principal cities and towns, and local postmasters were authorised to act as recruiting agents. Seamen were entered between the ages of 15 and 23, stokers (engineers) from 18 to

23, and boys from 14 to 16 years. The Admiralty allowed Pensioners and Fleet Reserve men of the Royal Navy to enlist in the Canadian Service, and many did so, providing welcomed experience and expertise.[6]

Photo 7-1

British cruiser HMS *Niobe*, built in 1899, before her acquisition by the newly constituted Royal Canadian Navy.
Naval History and Heritage Command photograph #NH 58647

CHANGE IN GOVERNMENT DECIMATES NEW NAVY

Sixteen months after the establishment of the Canadian Navy, the federal election in September 1911 was won by Conservatives who had vowed, if elected, to repeal the Naval Service Act. As debate on the "naval question" continued into 1913, reductions in funding forced the RCN to lay up *Rainbow* and *Niobe*. Moreover, while the Naval Service Act was not repealed, plans for an all-Canadian fleet were cancelled. Earlier, in June 1911, a lieutenant, two midshipmen, and thirty-five ratings had represented the Royal Canadian Navy at the coronation of King George V. By the end of the year, with no contracts for new ships and the expressed intention of the Borden government to ask for the repeal of the Naval Service Act, there was no inducement for young men to seek a career in the naval service.[7]

This malaise continued to exist until the entry of Canada into war, alongside Britain, in early August 1914. In his annual report for the year ending 31 March 1912, the deputy minister of the Naval Service stated that no special efforts had been made to obtain recruits. In February 1913, he highlighted that the training cruisers had only about half their full complements on board, and were confined to harbour and almost reduced to the condition of hulks. In the year preceding 31 March 1914, no recruiting was done and a majority of the officers and men on loan from the Admiralty, having completed their service, were returned to Great Britain without being replaced.[8]

With no actions taken or plans to obtain warships, recruitment of officers, ratings, and cadets decreased dramatically, as the following table indicates:

Year	No. of Cadets Entering	No. of RCN Officers and Ratings	Naval Expenditures
1910-11	28	704	$1,790,017
1911-12	10	695	1,233,456
1912-13	9	592	1,085,660
1913-14	4	330	597, 566[9]

NEWS OF WAR, AND A CALL TO ARMS

It was 11 o'clock at night—12 by German time—when the ultimatum expired. The windows of the Admiralty were thrown wide open in the warm night air. Under the roof from which Nelson had received his orders were gathered a small group of Admirals and Captains and a cluster of clerks, pencils in hand, waiting. Along the Mall from the direction of the Palace the sound of an immense concourse singing 'God save the King' floated in. On this deep wave there broke the chimes of Big Ben; and, as the first stroke of the hour boomed out, a rustle of movement swept across the room. The war telegraph, which meant 'Commence hostilities against Germany', was flashed to the ships and establishments under the White Ensign all over the world.

—Winston Churchill describing in *The World Crisis* the scene at the Admiralty, immediately prior to and during issuance of orders to ships and shore stations, to commence war with Germany.

When Canada entered the war, alongside Britain on 4 August 1914, less than 350 men and two old ships, HMCS *Rainbow* and HMCS *Niobe*, constituted her Navy. Nonetheless, available actions were taken to gain a war footing: (1) the two cruisers were placed at the disposal of His

Majesty for service in the Royal Navy; (2) CGS *Canada* and CGS *Margaret* were transferred from the Department of Customs to the Naval Service; and (3) the naval and naval volunteer forces were called to active duty. Beginning in 1912, *Canada* and other fisheries protection vessels had begun to carry out minesweeping exercises and ship examination duties at Halifax, in conjunction with militia mobilisation exercises at the port's forts.[10]

Photo 7-2

Postcard photograph of the Canadian Government Ship CGS *Canada*, taken sometime before 1908; she was drafted for war service in 1914 as HMCS *Canada*.
Naval History and Heritage Command photograph #NH 94933

Recognising that Canada could not assume its own naval defence, Britain called on her dominion to contribute servicemen to the war in Europe (soldiers were most needed), leaving to the Royal Navy the defence of shipping in Canadian waters and the North Atlantic. Called upon to serve, regular and reserve Canadian naval officers and sailors reported for active duty in both the RCN and RN.[11]

ACQUISION OF SUBMARINES *CC-1* and *CC-2*

The most innovative action in the mobilisation process occurred on 4 August 1914, albeit not by the Canadian government. On that day, Sir Richard McBride, Premier of British Columbia, put into motion a daring plan. It involved spiriting away two newly constructed submarines built for Chile, under the cover of darkness, from the Seattle Dry Dock &

Construction Company. This effort was aided by the president of the yard.[12]

Photo 7-3

Canadian World War I recruiting poster.

The 144-foot-long *Iquique* and 152-foot *Antofagasta* had been built by the Seattle Shipyard under contract to the Electric Boat Company of New Jersey, for the Chilean Navy. Both submarines had a beam of 15 feet, and were designed to have a displacement of 313 tons surfaced, and 412 submerged. Their design speed was 13 knots surfaced and a little over 10 knots submerged. *Iquique* would later, as *CC-1*, achieve a speed of 15.1 knots on 2 November 1914, during a trial over a measured mile. *Iquique* had five torpedo tubes, and *Antofagasta* three, with each having one tube mounted in the stern. Neither submarine carried any gun armament.[13]

Chile had paid $714,000 of the agreed upon price of $818,000 for the two boats. However, the Chilean Navy rejected the submarines because they failed to meet construction specifications, and the balance of payments fell into arrears. With a declaration of war less than a week away, fate intervened. James Venn Paterson, president of the Seattle Shipyard, was in Victoria on business. At Victoria's Union Club, he mentioned the two submarines just completed and the troubles he was having with the Chilean government over payment.[14]

Map 7-1

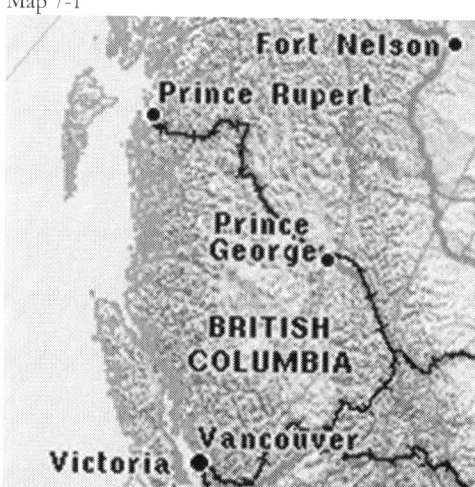

West coast of Canada

McBride soon learned of this predicament, and took immediate action to acquire the submarines for the defence of British Columbia. He had become concerned about the increased likelihood of war in Europe, and this anxiety had increased when Britain recalled its Pacific Fleet to England, leaving his province vulnerable to German raiders. Canada's fledgling navy did not have any ships to guard her west coast; and there had been reports of German warships harassing shipping traffic near Mexico. British Columbia's fishing fleets, as well as the cities of Vancouver and Victoria, might become potential targets. The Royal Navy had committed all of its available resources to defending the Atlantic shipping lanes, trusting Britain's ally Japan to keep an eye on Canada's west coast.[15]

McBride initiated an avalanche of telegram communications with Victoria, Ottawa, and London, but little could be done in the few days remaining before the imminent outbreak of war and a resulting American embargo on the provision of war materiel to combatants. Receiving no assistance from official channels, McBride decided to use provincial funds to get possession of the much-needed submarines before it was too late. On his own initiative, he decided to advance the $1,150,000 demanded by Paterson. This enormous sum was twice the annual budget for the RCN for 1913-1914, and his action constituted a violation of U.S. neutrality.[16]

Paterson had offered the sale to the British Columbia government on the condition that payment was cash on delivery. Also, the deal had to be done quickly, lest American neutrality laws block the sale. At 2200 on 4 August 1914 (by which time Britain had already been at war for some eight hours), the two submarines slipped their moorings, and running on electric motors, they quietly left the harbour under the cover of darkness and fog. Once clear, they started their diesel engines and headed north to a rendezvous point five miles from Trial Island, off the southeastern tip of Vancouver Island, British Columbia.[17]

They were met by the steamer *Salvor*, carrying Lt. Comdr. Bertram Edward Jones, RN, a qualified submariner, and Lt. Reginald Henry Wood, RN, Chief Engineer at the Esquimalt Dockyard. While inspection of the boats was in progress, Paterson, who had been aboard one of the submarines on their journey from Seattle, paced the deck. Upon completion of a four-hour examination, he was handed a cheque for $1.15 million, and the submarines proceeded at speed toward Esquimalt.[18]

As Canadian provinces were not allowed to maintain militaries, the submarines were quickly transferred by order to the federal government, which handed them off to the Royal Canadian Navy. The province was reimbursed by Ottawa, and the former *Iquique* and *Antofagasta* were commissioned into the RCN as HMCS *CC-1* and *CC-2*, respectively, under the white ensign. The Navy was now faced with recruiting and training submariners, and finding torpedoes for the boats since they sailed without any on board. The Senior Naval Officer at Esquimalt wanted to name Canada's first two submarines Paterson and McBride, but approval for such action was not forthcoming.[19]

Canadian Naval Ensign 1911-1922

SERVICE IN THE ROYAL NAVY

At the end of July, 1914, the total manpower of the Royal Canadian Navy did not exceed 350 officers and ratings, and an even smaller number of officers and ratings comprised the Royal Naval Canadian Volunteer Reserve (RNCVR), established earlier in the year. The latter 250 men were members of one company in Victoria, British Columbia. The figures for total enrollment of officers and ratings during the war are shown below. Highlighted in Gilbert Tucker's *The Naval Service of Canada, Vol. I, Origins and Early Years* these sums are round numbers only, and even in that form most are offered diffidently.

Royal Canadian Navy (RCN)		1,000
Royal Navy and Royal Naval Reserve (RN and RNR)		600
Royal Naval Canadian Volunteer Reserve (RNCVR)		8,000
Atlantic Subdivision	4,300	
Pacific Subdivision	2,000	
Overseas Division	1,700	
Total:		9,600[20]

A large, but unknown number of Canadians enlisted and served in the Royal Navy; which presumably is the basis for an often cited estimate that 3,000 Canadians served overseas with the Royal Navy (1,700 in Overseas Division and an estimated 1,300 enlisted members). A majority of these officers and ratings likely served aboard Royal Navy ships in British home waters, the focus of this book. (The 600 RN and RNR members listed in the table were assigned by the Admiralty to the Canadian Naval Service.)[21]

Photo 7-4

Royal Hospital School Greenwich at which officer candidates trained.
Courtesy of John MacFarlane

Four such individuals were Fred MacFarlane, Peter Leslie, George Bunt, and John H. Cates, who in July 1916 travelled to Britain aboard the Allan line Royal Mail steamer SS *Grampion*. The men trained at the Royal Hospital School Greenwich with hundreds of others (mainly British but some from the Dominions and colonies) as officer candidates. They wore sailor uniforms and were rated as Ordinary Seamen. Those who "washed out" of the training/commissioning process were simply transferred, in grade, to an operational unit and remained as part of the "lower deck" until the end of the war. Those who succeeded were commissioned as Temporary Sub–Lieutenants, RNVR.[22]

Photo 7-5

Newly commissioned Temporary Sub–Lieutenants, RNVR; front (left to right) Fred R. MacFarlane, John H. Cates; back (l-r) Peter L. Leslie, George D. Bunt. Photo courtesy of John MacFarlane

Because of the shape of the officer's gold braid on their uniform sleeves, reserve officers rapidly commissioned for war service were often referred to by RN officers as the "Wavy Navy." This derisive term likely stemmed from the much longer route to a commission endured by officers in the Royal Navy, who went to sea as boys and spent years as midshipmen before becoming officers. Despite these differences in training and development, reserve officers contributed much to the war effort, before returning home to their civilian lives. Of the Canadians pictured, Bunt was lost at sea; the other three became well-known British Columbia ship masters after the war.[23]

EXPANSION OF THE CANADIAN NAVAL SERVICE

Each degree of Latitude
Strung about Creation
Seeth one (or more) of us...

—Reference to the trawlers and drifters that comprised the auxiliary fleet of the Canadian Naval Service. Built for antisubmarine patrol, minesweeping, and (ship) examination duties, they had the status of warships and flew the white ensign.[24]

Because Britain's greatest need was for augmentation of her army by Canadian servicemen, and no significant naval threat existed off Canada's coasts, the Canadian Naval Service initially grew at a relatively slow pace. On 31 January 1917, the German government announced to the world that shipping found in the Mediterranean and northeastern Atlantic would be sunk on sight. Although this assertion did not directly apply to Canadian and Newfoundland waters, it increased the potential danger, spurring the Admiralty to devote more resources to the protection of Canada's east coast. Britain asked the Canadian government to arrange for and supervise the building of 36 trawlers and 100 drifters. The vessels were to be paid for by Britain, and built in Canada for antisubmarine patrol, minesweeping, and examination duties.[25]

Examination services were maintained at Canada's principal ports in order to prevent hostile ships from entering. The Canadian Naval Service was also responsible for naval control of the ports, which included controlling the movement of shipping inward and outward;

giving routing and other instructions to merchant ships about ready to sail; and organising and directing the sailing of convoys.[26]

Photo 7-6

Mexican patrol vessel *Vera Cruz* photographed in 1942. She was formerly a Canadian *Castle*-class trawler (*TR-1*) built in 1918.
Naval History and Heritage Command photograph #NH 45361

U-BOAT ATTACKS OFF THE EASTERN SEABOARD SPUR URGENCY IN VESSEL CONSTRUCTION

Photo 7-7

Two RCN drifters flanked by a 110-foot American sub-chaser, the USS *SC-240*, and HMCS *TR-11*, a larger Canadian-built *Castle*-class minesweeping trawler.
Courtesy of John MacFarlane

In 1918, Germany sent a small group of U-boats across the Atlantic to attack shipping off the North American eastern seaboard, which increased the sense of urgency. The last summer of the war witnessed a great increase in the size of the Canadian Navy, as newly built trawlers and drifters became available after the St. Lawrence opened in the spring. The construction of these vessels had been slower than anticipated. Nevertheless, soon after the river thawed, nearly fifty patrol ships were available, and by early October the auxiliary fleet consisted of 116 vessels. Eighty-seven belonged to the Admiralty and the other twenty-nine to the Canadian Naval Service, but all except those assigned to Halifax were under the command of the RN's Captain of Patrols. The twelve new trawlers of the Canadian Naval Service (modeled on North Sea fishing vessels) were 136-ton seaworthy craft, capable of a speed of 10 knots. Each cost $191,000 to build and boasted one 12-pounder gun and depth charges. The smaller drifters had a 6-pounder and depth charges as well.[27]

Map 7-2

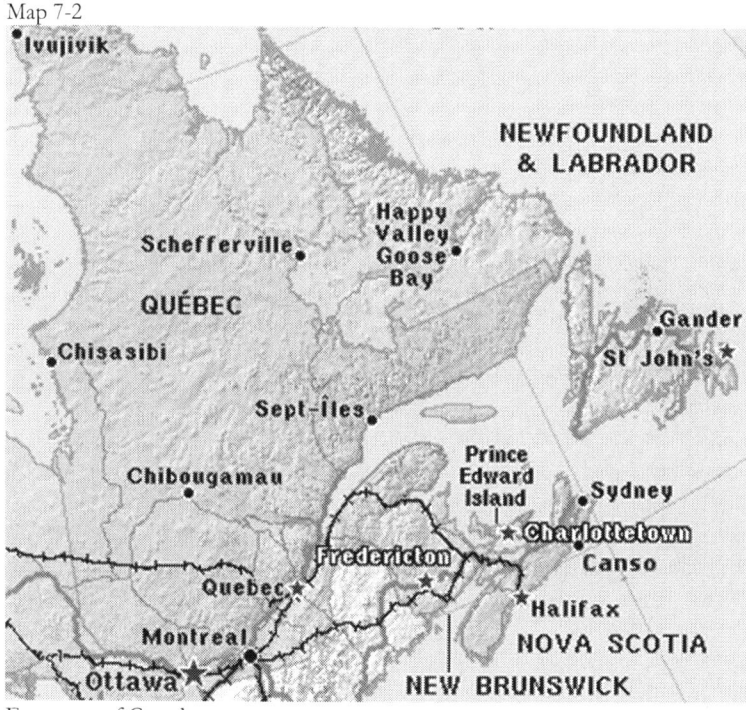

East coast of Canada

AUXILIARY FLOTILLA AT WAR'S END

The flotilla was prolific of precedents: it was the first fleet to be commanded by an officer of the Royal Canadian Navy; it contained the first ships built expressly for the Naval Service; and it faced the, first direct naval attack in the history of the Dominion.

—Gilbert Norman Tucker, *The Naval Service of Canada, Vol. I, Origins and Early Years.*[28]

Royal Canadian Navy Badge

Finding adequate numbers of personnel to operate vessels of the Canadian Naval Service proved difficult, as practically all the trained personnel in Canada were already serving. Nonetheless, by the end of the war, there were nearly two thousand officers and ratings aboard the east coast patrol vessels. Although this organisation was never called upon to deal with any sustained or serious attack, the east coast patrols were a necessary precaution, and may have been a deterrent as well.[29]

The most important contribution of the Auxiliary Flotilla may have been in helping to build a large foundation of experience on which Canada's campaign against U-boats in World War II was based. Adopted at some point in its now rich history, the Canadian Navy's motto today is: Parati vero parati (READY AYE READY).[30]

8

Germany and Britain Mine
Additional Waters in 1915

The German submarines now infest the English Channel, and are so unchecked in their roamings that our heavy ships are shut up in those few harbours that are submarine-proof, and our transport of troops to France greatly endangered.

—First Sea Lord Adm. John Fisher, RN, in
a memorandum dated 17 January 1915.[1]

The action off Dogger Bank on 24 January 1915 was the third of Admiral Friedrich von Ingenohl's battle cruiser raids against the English east coast. As a result of the disastrous results, Ingenohl ceded command of the High Seas Fleet to Admiral von Pohl on 2 February. The balance of gain and loss in these raids was sufficiently adverse that Pohl declined to repeat them. Although the High Seas Fleet would occasionally sortie from its safe bastions in coming months, the battle squadrons only briefly interrupted the prevailing, incessant warfare of submarine and anti-submarine minelaying and minesweeping.[2]

The Royal Navy possessed an overwhelming advantage as a result of being able to read the enemy's signals, coupled with their free use of wireless telegraphy. German submarines advertised their movements much less freely than the High Seas Fleet, and the minelayers were the stealthiest of the German forces. The latter fact was amplified by the unsettling discovery in mid-1915, of submarine minelayers, whose possible existence had previously been discredited.[3]

BRITAIN DECIDES TO LAY OTHER MINEFIELDS
The Admiralty had in early December 1914, called upon the Commanders-in-Chief afloat and ashore, Commodore of Submarines, the Admirals of Patrols, and of the Dover Patrol for reports on the methods they had used, and proposals for active attack on enemy submarines. Most of the replies were related to attacking a submarine located in an area occupied by British forces. On the offensive side,

several senior officers, including Admiral Beatty, advocated mining Heligoland Bight. Beatty wrote:

> Hitherto the menace has only been met by ultra-defensive measures on the part of the coastal patrols. These measures have met with so little success that the large numbers of vessels so employed have not justified their existence....
>
> To act offensively against enemy submarines one is limited to two places: (a) His point of departure; (b) The area in which he is likely to operate.
>
> Taking the point of departure—he can be attacked only through the medium of mines laid at varying depths, and in large quantities.
>
> For this form of attack there is much to be said. If carried out thoroughly and effectively, it would necessitate large sweeping operations on the part of the enemy which would provide an object for attack by our small craft, as such operations can only take place in daylight. This would necessitate covering action on the part of the enemy, which might easily lead up to an offensive operation on a large scale....[4]

NEW BRITISH MINEFIELD EAST OF DOVER STRAIT

After highlighting the threat that German submarines posed, Admiral Fisher advocated further mining of the Dover Strait, explaining:

> This is obligatory for another important reason beyond deterring submarines, and that is our Southern Force is necessarily weak, and, owing to lack of berthing accommodation in any submarine-proof anchorage, it cannot be concentrated, and so the great point is to deny the Dover Straits to the passage of German ships.[5]

The Chief of Staff, the First Lord, and Sir Arthur Wilson were all doubtful about the benefits of more British minefields. The defensive mines already laid had a bad habit of breaking adrift. Moreover, since passage by the Downs (between the Goodwin Sands and the coast of Kent) was very congested, and not safe at low water, the new field would effectively close the Straits to battleships and other heavy draught vessels at certain stages of the tide. Despite these valid concerns, Fisher pressed his proposal and it was adopted.[6]

Since the area selected for the minefield lay along the sea route between the ports of Nieuport, Belgium, and Calais, France, a passage from Dunkirk to Nieuport was left open. As an additional defensive measure, the lights along the French coast between Dieppe and Calais were reduced to a range of ten miles. The barrage was to consist of seventeen lines of mines, which tidal conditions would permit laying only at slack water half-flood in the daytime, or on exceptionally bright moonlit nights.[7]

Map 8-1

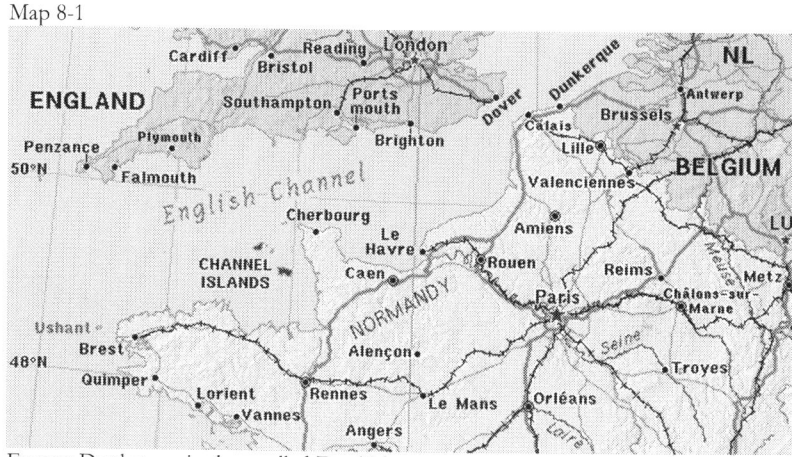

France; Dunkerque is also spelled Dunkirk

HMS *Paris* was chosen to lay the mines. She was a former steam packet of the London, Brighton and South Coast Railway, previously employed making cross-channel runs between Newhaven, England, and Dieppe, France. When acquired by the Admiralty at the end of 1914, *Paris* was then the only small merchant ship in the world capable of a speed of over 25 knots. She was fitted out at "Blackwall" (a shipyard on the Thames at Blackwall, London) as a minelayer. In addition to necessary modifications to carry 140 Elia Mk VI mines on her upper deck, she also received armament of one 4-inch, one 12-pounder, and one 6-pounder HA gun. The smaller-calibre high-angle gun was for use against enemy aircraft. Following these changes, and particularly with a deck-load of mines, her speed was greatly reduced. HMS *Paris* was commissioned on 14 January 1915.[8]

Paris (Comdr. Lockhart Leith, RN) commenced the Dover Strait minelaying operation on 4 February, escorted by HMS *Miranda* and six other *M*-class destroyers for protection. The field was completed on 16 February, with 3,390 mines having been laid. The barrage was intended particularly for use against vessels on the surface; no mining action was taken against submarines traveling submerged. In an effort to thwart clearance work by enemy minesweepers, an obstruction was placed in front of every tenth mine in the northern lines. Each obstruction consisted of a ton of pig-iron connected by a span to a 560-lb anchor, both joined by a 3 ½-inch mooring cable buoyed by an empty 76-lb mine case, adjusted to six feet below LWOS. (Low Water Ordinary Springs is a tidal datum based on low water of ordinary spring tides.) Below the mine case was affixed a jagged iron claw intended to catch and sever a sweeping wire.[9]

Even before the field was completed, mines began to detonate spontaneously and break adrift. From 10 February 1915, mine explosions were heard from the lines nearest the coast, and were duly reported by Rear Adm. Horace Hood, RN (commander of the Dover Patrol), in whose area this was occurring.[10]

GERMAN SURFACE SHIPS LAY OFFENSIVE AND DEFENSIVE MINEFIELDS THROUGH AUTUMN 1915

While the British Admiralty deliberated about laying a mine barrage across the Dover Strait, the German Navy continued its own minelaying campaign. Much effort was devoted to offensive mining in British waters. However, it also employed mines defensively to (1) help protect its forces in German waters against attacks from the sea, and (2) to hinder units of the Royal Navy which had been carrying out periodic shore bombardment against German troops on the Belgian coast. The latter operations began on 19 October 1914, but the Germans did not mine the West Deep (the area used by bombardment ships) until January 1915.[11]

Map 8-2

The West Deep was a coastal area off Nieuwpoort (Nieuport), from which Royal Navy vessels conducted bombardment of German positions ashore

The other surface ship-laid fields identified in the following table were offensive in nature. Those sown by SMS *Meteor* and *Möwe* were aimed specifically at the Grand Fleet operating from Scapa Flow. By autumn 1915, Royal Navy defensive actions compelled the German Navy to abandon its use of surface ships to lay mines in British waters and accordingly, the Germans had to turn to submarine minelayers. The mines laid by SMS *Möwe* on the first day of 1916, was an aberration to this practice, as this action was a collateral duty in carrying out tasking as a commerce raider.[12]

German Minefields Laid by Surface Vessels in 1915

Date/#Mines	Minelayer(s)	Minefield/Area
January 1915	Surface vessels	West Deep off Nieuport, Belgium
4 Apr 1915 (360 mines)	Surface vessels	Humber River approach
18 Apr 1915 (240 mines)	SMS *Stralsund*, *Strassburg*	Swarte Bank in the southern North Sea
17-18 May 1915 (480 mines)	SMS *Graudenz*, *Pillau*, *Rostock*, *Stralsund*, *Strassburg*	Eastern Dogger Bank in the central North Sea off the east coast of England
7-8 Aug 1915 (380 mines)	SMS *Meteor*	Moray Firth in the north of Scotland
11-12 Sep 1915	SMS *Graudenz*, *Pillau*, *Regensburg*, *Rostock*, *Stralsund*, *Strassburg*	Swarte Bank in the southern North Sea
1 Jan 1916 (252 mines)	SMS *Möwe*	Whiten Head Bank, west of Orkney Islands[13]

ENEMY MINES IN THE WEST DEEP OFF BELGIUM

Soldiers,

For two months and more you have been fighting for the most just of causes: your homes and national independence.

You have held the enemy's armies, sustained three sieges, executed several sorties, and successfully carried out a long retreat through a narrow defile.

So far, you have been alone in this tremendous struggle. Now you are at the side of the valiant French and British Armies.

It is your duty to uphold the reputation of our arms with that spirit of tenacity and bravery of which you have given so many proofs. Our national honour is at stake.

—Portion of an Order of the Day issued by King Albert I (who led the
Belgian Army in World War I) on the eve of the Battle of the Yser
(16 October-10 November 1914), to inspire his men to hold the
line in the last area of unoccupied Belgium
against the German Army.[14]

Only days after Rear Admiral Hood had assumed command of the
Dover Patrol on 13 October 1914, the Battle of the Yser (fought
between Allied and German forces along a long stretch of the Yser River
and Ypres canal in Belgium) began. From 14 October, Belgian troops
began to dig in a defensive line at the Yser River sector, and the French
Fusiliers Marins brigade at Dixmude. The defensive line stretched for
twenty-two miles from the sea at Nieuport to the village of Zuydschoote
about eight miles north of Ypres. Two French territorial divisions (the
87th and 89th) arrived in the area and moved into position between
Dixmude and Boesinghe, where the Ypres Canal joined the Yser Canal.
In October, Hood's force provided artillery support from the sea which,
in the opinion of Colonel Bridges (a British General Staff Officer
attached to the Belgian Headquarters) "undoubtedly saved the Belgian
left flank." A large Belgian force was able to hold the front line, halting
the German advance in a costly defensive battle.[15]

However, the German Army would hold occupied territory along
the Belgian coast from Zeebrugge to Nieuport from October 1914 to
October 1918. During this period the Germans fortified the sandy
coastline. As the most northerly part of Imperial Germany's Western
Front, they had to protect this right flank against the possibility of an
Allied invasion from the sea, and to defend it against British Royal Navy
bombardments and bombing by Allied aircraft.[16]

As a part of this effort, the German Navy mined the West Deep,
from which Hood's ships had conducted shore bombardment. This
stretch of deep water (some seven miles long, running parallel to and
some two-and-one-half miles off shore) was the only position from
which effective bombardment of the coast could be carried out. North
of the Deep lay the shallow waters of the Small Bank and Nieuport
Bank. The only access into the Deep from the North Sea was through
the Zuidcoote Pass (which lay between the Hills and Traepegeer Banks),
a narrow channel reported to have a low-water depth of only twelve
feet.[17]

Toward the end of January 1915, as the French gained ground near
Lombartzyde (located a short distance northeast of Nieuport), news that
German reinforcements had begun arriving at Middelkerke and
Westende Bains, prompted fears that a counterattack could occur at any

time. French General Dimitry, seeing Royal Navy gunboats and destroyers to seaward, sent a request through Colonel Bridges that they immediately begin laying down a barrage of fire to the east of a line formed by Westende Bains-Westende. In response to this request, Hood explained that the ships were there to guard the coast at night and were unsuitable for bombarding. Moreover, the West Deep was full of mines, making it impractical for bombardment vessels to work there. Previously, the French had been asked to maintain a patrol there, and to keep it swept, but had failed to do so.[18]

The French now took steps to sweep the West Deep, but their gear (a sort of toothed rake towed by the sweeping vessel) was not well suited for use in shoal water. Despite this handicap, their minesweepers destroyed thirteen mines on 1-2 February 1915. There were apparently about 100 mines in the area east of the bell buoy, and work progressed slowly. The French swept only during the day because good light was necessary to see cut mines bobbing on the surface that had to be destroyed by rifle fire. In mid-afternoon on 20 February, the French minesweeper *Marie* struck a mine about a mile and a half east of the entrance to Zuidcoote, her boiler exploded and she sank. Sadly, despite the hardship and danger endured by the French sweepers (imposed by the mines and exposure to enemy fire), there was no guarantee that an area supposedly cleared by day, would not be mined by German vessels overnight. Because the French did not maintain a nighttime patrol to keep watch over the area, there was no way of knowing.[19]

The British Admiralty had furnished the French with a copy of the Royal Navy's "Instructions for Minesweeping," which contained a complete description of the British methods. Nevertheless, the presence of the minefield and the difficulties that prevented efficient sweeping put an end to any effective support from Hood's Dover Patrol to the Allied armies on shore. It also made Royal Naval Air Service raids on German naval bases on the Belgian coast more hazardous for pilots. In these early days of aviation, a plane's engine might stop for no apparent reason. It might also stop due to enemy inflicted-damage. In either case, the "machine" and pilot would then fall into the sea, and the mined West Deep occupied much of the water flown over.[20]

ROYAL NAVAL AIR SERVICE (RNAS) RAIDS ON THE BELGIAN COAST

During the last twenty-four hours, combined aeroplane and seaplane operations have been carried out by the Naval Wing in the Bruges, Zeebrugge, Blankenberghe and Ostend districts, with a view to preventing the development of submarine bases and establishments.

Thirty-four naval aeroplanes and seaplanes took part. Great damage is reported to have been done to Ostend Railway Station, which, according to present information, has probably been burnt to the ground. The railway station at Blankenberghe was damaged and railway lines were torn up in many places. Bombs were dropped on gun positions at Middelkerke, also on the power station and German minesweeping vessels at Zeebrugge, but the damage done is unknown.

During the attack the machines encountered heavy banks of snow. No submarines were seen. Flight Commander Grahame-White fell into the sea off Nieuport and was rescued by a French vessel.

Although exposed to heavy gun-fire from rifles, anti-aircraft guns, mitrailleuses, etc., all pilots are safe. Two machines were damaged. The seaplanes and aeroplanes were under the command of Wing Commander Samson, assisted by Wing Commander Longmore and Squadron Commanders Porte, Courtney, and Rathbone.

—British Admiralty's official account of a Royal Naval Air Service raid in early February 1915 against the Belgian coast.[21]

The Royal Naval Air Service was the air arm of the Royal Navy from its inception on 1 July 1914 to 1 April 1918, when it was merged with the British Army's Royal Flying Corps to form the Royal Air Force. The primary roles of land and sea-based RNAS aircraft were fleet reconnaissance, patrolling coasts for enemy ships and submarines, and attacking enemy coastal territory. However, RNAS pilots flew many diverse missions, including ones in support of the British Army.[22]

In January 1915, the RNAS began carrying out bombing raids on German U-boat bases at Ostend and Zeebrugge. For one such mission on 23 January 1915, squadron commander Richard Bell Davies and Flight Lieutenant Richard Edmund Charles Peirse were awarded the Distinguished Service Order. The association medal citation follows:

Squadron Commander Richard Bell Davies
Flight Lieutenant Richard Edmund Charles Peirse

These Officers have repeatedly attacked the German submarine station at Ostend and Zeebrugge, being subjected on each occasion to heavy and accurate fire, their machines being frequently hit. In particular, on 23rd January, they each discharged eight bombs in an attack upon submarines alongside the mole at Zeebrugge, flying down to close range. At the outset of this flight Lieutenant Davies was severely wounded by a bullet in the thigh, but nevertheless he accomplished his task, handling his machine for an hour with great skill in spite of pain and loss of blood.[23]

After an air raid on 11 February 1915, flight commander Claude Grahame-White, who had taken part in it, crashed his aeroplane into the West Deep. He was rescued by the French minesweeper *Bustard*. The following day, another flying officer who also crashed was saved by another French minesweeper, the *Excellent*. Grahame-White was an English pioneer of aviation, and had been the first to make a night flight, during the Daily Mail-sponsored London to Manchester race in 1910.[24]

GERMAN-LAID SWARTE BANK MINEFIELD

*Great ships and mighty captains—to these their
    meed of praise*
*For patience, skill and daring and loud victorious
    days;*
To every man his portion, as is both right and fair,
*But oh! forget not the small craft, for they have done
    their share.*

Small craft—small craft, from Scapa Flow to Dover,
Small craft—small craft, all the wide world over,
*At risk of war and shipwreck, torpedo, mine and
    shell,*
*All honour be to small craft, for oh, they've earned
    it well!*

C. F. S.

—From G. H. P. Muhlhauser's book *Small Craft*.[25]

At the end of April 1915 after being carefully swept, the area off Scarborough was declared free of mines. The clearing-up had been a long and arduous task, but the passage of this Yorkshire coast was at last freed from the mine peril. Almost simultaneously with the elimination of this minefield it became known that another had been laid in the Swarte Bank area, in the southern North Sea. This discovery was made by the steam trawler *Sutterton*, which brought up a mine in her nets.[26]

Photo 8-1

German light cruiser SMS *Strassburg*, circa 1914 to 1916.
Naval History and Heritage Command photograph #NH 92716

The field had been laid by German light cruisers SMS *Stralsund* and *Strassburg*. Leaving the Jade Bight (a bay on the North Sea coast of Germany) at 1130 on 17 April 1915, the two ships had transited Norderney Passage by mid-afternoon of that day. Each carried 120 mines to sow that night; but should British forces be encountered, the operation was to be abandoned. This possibility did not occur, and the "nightraiders" successfully laid their mines off the Swarte Bank between midnight and 0100 on 18 April. As far as the Germans could ascertain, the operation was unobserved by any British vessel. The 240 mines, spaced 250 yards apart, formed a line 30 miles long. They were set to lie at a depth of 13-16 feet below the surface at low water, and 23 feet at high water.[27]

Upon discovering the Swarte minefield, the Royal Navy sent out large numbers of auxiliary craft to ascertain its boundaries, while merchant shipping traffic between Britain and the Netherlands was suspended. Soon it became known that lines of mines were oriented in an easterly direction from a starting point at 53°26'N, 2°25'E. By the end of the first week in May, most of the mines along the first seventeen miles of the thirty mile-long field had been destroyed. Tragically, three British fishing trawlers performing their normal fishing operations were lost to mines. On 3 May, *Uxbridge* caught a mine in her trawl, which exploded and sank her. Three days later, *Don* was mined with seven lives lost, and on 8 May, *Hellenic* similarly mined with three lives lost.[28]

Apparently the German Naval Command believed that the area it had mined was used by the Grand Fleet, or at least by Commodore Tyrwhitt's Harwich Force as a shortcut when bound north and, accordingly, the mines were planted at a greater depth than was usual. This allowed merchant ships which were accustomed to pass along this route in considerable numbers, to steam over them in safety without revealing the lurking threat to larger naval vessels. Thus it was hoped, from the enemy's point of view, nothing should happen which would cause the new field to be prematurely revealed.[29]

SAGITTA RECOVERS NEW TYPE OF GERMAN MINE

In preparation for a British naval bombardment of the Belgian coast by monitors, the patrol vessel HMS *Sagitta* and four Grimsby paddle-steamers had been sent to sweep mines in the West Deep from 26 to 28 April 1915. On their return transit across the North Sea they worked the Swarte Bank area. The *Sagitta* was a Camper & Nicholson-built 750-ton hired yacht, which had previously belonged to a French Duke. A fine sea boat, fast for a yacht (15 knots), and very luxurious, she now served as a minesweeper and flagship of Rear Adm. Edward S. Fitzherbert, AMS (Admiral of Minesweepers). She had a wireless radio, and also two 12-pounder guns, and would later receive a 6-pounder high-angle gun.[30]

Almost all of the officers and men making up her crew had previously served together aboard the steam yacht *Zarefah*. They had changed ships after Fitzherbert decided the 129-foot *Zarefah* was too small for operations in the North Sea in winter. Lt. George H. P. Muhlhauser, RNR (one of the ship's officers who served aboard both hired yachts) later described the original crew of the *Zarefah* in his book *Small Craft*, a memoir of his war experiences published in 1920:

> There was nothing remarkable about the ship, but she carried, perhaps, the most remarkable crew that put to sea during the war, as all the deckhands were Cambridge graduates or undergraduates.

Though not seamen they were all watermen, and amongst them were some famous oars, including [C.] R. Leblanc Smith, captain of the boats; K. [G.] Garnett, who rowed in the 'Varsity boat in 1914; [Alfred] A. Swann, twice winner of the Goblets, and one of the crew which beat the Germans in the final for the Stewards Cup in 1914, and who had other wins to his credit, and who has since rowed in the Cambridge crew for 1920; while the rest were mostly well to the fore in the athletic world.[31]

Included among the Cambridge graduates and undergraduates and other kindred spirits who had joined up in the RNVS was a magistrate, a Commissioner of Oaths (a person with power to administer oaths or take affidavits), two sons of millionaires, and a gentleman of means who was found smoking his own special brand of cigars on watch. Many of these men, who started out as able bodied seamen, later obtained commissions. They rendered excellent service in minesweepers. It appears though, that some of these gentlemen did not initially take the war too seriously.[32]

On one occasion, while the flagship *Zarefah* was waiting to enter Harwich for the first time, one of the amateur signalmen amused himself by sending signals in German to the station ashore. Suspicion that she might be a spy ship resulted in her being brought into harbour under arrest. A senior naval officer boarding the yacht to investigate found a young relative among the crew and matters were explained. Presumably, the admiral had not been aboard, and upon learning of the incident was not particularly pleased.[33]

All but six of the men that had comprised *Zarefah*'s original crew transferred to the *Sagitta*. The exceptions were an engineer, a stoker, and four of the Cambridge men. Of the latter, one had previously left to join the Naval Division and three to take Army commissions. By this point, Leblanc Smith had been killed serving in the British Army, to the great grief of all who had been privileged to know him.[34]

On a beautiful day in April 1915, operations in the Swarte Bank field commenced. Although a slight haze lay along the horizon, the sun shone brightly and the sea was smooth but for a slight swell. Suddenly, two mines exploded in a large report in the sweep between *Sagitta* and her partner, the paddle-minesweeper *Westward Ho*, and a mound of water was hurled into the air. Prior to the two mines exploding, it was hard to imagine that beneath the surface of the undisturbed water, there might be lurking mines powerful enough to blow a hole in the hull of the largest warship—or completely destroy a minesweeper of a few hundred tons. Yet the hidden explosives were there, ready to tear apart any vessel striking them in passing.[35]

A few seconds later another mine, cut by the same sweep, rose to the surface. Complete silence had followed the earlier explosion, as all the vessels immediately stopped, rolling slightly to the disturbance caused by the bursting mines. After verifying that no harm had been done, *Sagitta's* commanding officer, Lt. Comdr. William H. Stuart Garnett, RNR, declared "We will pick up that mine." He knew that it should be recovered for examination by British naval experts.[36]

Garnett was a Cambridge "wrangler," and a keen yachtsman. (A wrangler was a student who gained first-class honours in the third year of the university's undergraduate degree in mathematics.) At the start of the war, Garnett had volunteered and received a commission and, on his own initiative, he also obtained the loan of the steam yacht *Zarefah* (ex-*Maretanza V*) from Mr. Steane Price of Hampstead. The enterprising officer then recruited some Cambridge graduates and undergraduates to crew the vessel, before offering her services to the Admiralty, which assigned the yacht to the Minesweeping Service.[37]

Photo 8-2

British paddle-sweeper picking up German mine, identity and date unknown. Naval History and Heritage Command photograph #NH 110571

The end of the sweep wire aboard *Sagitta* was slipped, a boat was lowered, and off went Garnett, and two hands, while the rest of the crew looked on, and wondered what would happen. Lt. George H. P. Muhlhauser described the recovery and disassembly of the mine:

The boat circled round the black, sinister looking mine, bobbing about so innocently in the sea, and then the C.O. [commanding officer] jumped into the water, swam up to the mine, and cut the two outside wires leading up to the detonator…. The mine was then towed alongside, a derrick swung out, the mine hooked on, hoisted out, and lowered on deck after the detonator had been pulled out. We breathed freely once more.

The next job was to pick it to pieces, and this was successfully done. It was found to be surprisingly well made, and all the inside parts were highly finished. In fact they could hardly have been bettered if intended for an exhibit. Considering that it was destined in the ordinary way to be blown to bits it seems strange that so much care should have been bestowed on polishing and machining the works.

One of the parts bore a quite recent date, proving that the mines had not been laid long. In fact in one way and another quite a lot of information was gleaned from this mine, which was sent to the Admiralty when we returned to harbour.[38]

The recovery of this mine and a second one later by a rating, Alfred Evans, was significant. They turned out to be the latest German mines, and HMS Vernon's Mine Design Section drew up designs for a British copy, known as the H mine. It was a great improvement over even the latest Mk IV version of the Service mechanical mine, and was put into production in 1917 as the H2 (the first such mines were laid in the Heligoland Bight on 24 September 1917.) For his courageous act the Admiralty sent the ship's captain an expression of appreciation.[39]

Regrettably, some months later Lieutenant Commander Garnett, having in the meantime transferred to the Royal Flying Corps, met his death in a flying accident. *Sagitta* received Battle Honours BELGIAN COAST 1915. *Zarefah* was mined on 8 May 1917 off Mull Head (the cliffs of Deerness), Orkney Islands, and sank with sixteen officers and men killed. A list of all Royal Navy mine warfare ships which received Battle Honours during the war may be found in Appendix A.[40]

BRITAIN MINES THE GERMAN DEEP

In addition to the Admiralty's earlier decision to lay additional mines in home waters as a deterrent to German U-boats and surface vessels, it had also adopted a philosophy of mining the enemy's waters, preferring to not consume all available mining materiel on defensive fields. However, this policy had been held in abeyance after the mining of Amrum Bank in January 1915. At that time, as the Royal Navy had no fast minelayers, they had to use old *Edgar*-class cruisers. Their maximum speed of 15 knots and use in close proximity to enemy forces, had made the mining operation, conducted only some 65 miles from Heligoland, an extremely hazardous project.[41]

Map 8-3

Amrum Bank, Dogger Bank, Swarte Bank, and Horn Reefs

Once three fast minelayers—HMS *Princess Margaret*, *Princess Irene*, and *Orvieto* (all former passenger liners)—became available, the Admiralty decided to mine the German Bight, a bay of the North Sea at the mouth of the Elbe River. The plan for the operation (codenamed Q) was to lay two minefields simultaneously; one fifteen miles north of the *Borkum Riff* light vessel, and the other a few miles north of the Amrum Bank. The two Princesses were to lay the Borkum Field, while *Orvieto* laid the Amrum Field. *Orvieto*, a former Orient liner of 12,130 tons, had been fitted out in March as a minelayer to carry 600 Service mines on her decks, and a similar amount in her hold. When the plan was developed, she was at Scapa Flow, attached to the Grand Fleet. Descriptions of *Princess Margaret* and *Princess Irene* follow in a subsequent chapter.[42]

On 8 May 1915, the *Princess Margaret* and *Princess Irene* left Sheerness at 0730, escorted by the light cruiser HMS *Aurora* and two divisions of destroyers of the 10th Flotilla. Keeping as far westward as possible to avoid detection, they followed a route which took them between British and German minefields to the North Hinder, and reached the ordered position. Mining commenced at 2330 and when completed, the minelayers and their escorts returned to Sheerness.[43]

Orvieto's first mission was unsuccessful. She had left Scapa Flow at 1230 on 6 April, escorted by the destroyer tender HMS *Broke* and eight destroyers of the 2nd Flotilla. The group soon encountered dense fog, conditions which resulted in a collision between two destroyers. One, HMS *Nemesis*, was seriously damaged. Fearing that the fog delay would prevent the possibility of success, the commander-in-chief of the Grand Fleet recalled the force.[44]

Map 8-4

Jade Bight and Heligoland Bight, small bays off the German Bight (Bay)

Orvieto started out again on 9 April with a similar escort. Horn Reefs light was sighted at 2000 the following day, and shortly thereafter some vessels, which may have been German patrols, were seen. Two hours later, *Orvieto*'s commanding officer, Capt. Harry H. Smyth, observed a searchlight beam probing the darkness. To avoid detection, he begin laying the field at once, although he was still some miles northwest of the position indicated in his orders. Proceeding southwest from this point (54°49'N, 7°21'E), *Orvieto* laid 577 mines over a distance of thirteen miles, in an operation believed unseen by the enemy.[45]

This belief proved to be false as far as the presence of the ships were concerned, but not as to the presence and location of the mines sown. A German submarine, *U-39*, sighted the Scapa Flow-bound squadron at 0600 on 10 April, seventy miles northwest of the Horn Reefs. She attempted an attack on the *Orvieto*, but was unsuccessful owing to the great range and high speed of the liner. However, Kptlt. Walter Forstmann guessed the *Orvieto*'s mission and at 0650, he sent a signal reporting that he had seen four British destroyers proceeding north in company with a very large steamer, probably a minelayer. A division of minesweepers was sent out to search the channel off Germany's Schleswig-Holstein coast and along the sea routes to List (located on the North Sea island of Sylt) which, however, was not where the mines had been laid.[46]

Photo 8-3

Austrian submarine, ex-German *U-39*, on 12 August 1917 with damage to her conning tower and deck gun. The depot ship GAA is in the background.
Naval History and Heritage Command photograph #NH 87766

EASTERN DOGGER BANK MINEFIELD

While efforts were in progress by the Royal Navy to clear new German fields, other areas at the same time required constant attention to detect any new minelaying. The Northern Dogger Bank area was checked and found to be clear of mines; but a very large suspicious area was found in the middle of the North Sea, later known as the Eastern Dogger Bank Minefield. Bounded by points 54°40' and 56°N, and 2°30' and 5°E, the four-sided, 6,000-square-mile area lay near where the British Grand Fleet must have passed in making an earlier sweep down the North Sea toward Heligoland. Had the German High Seas Fleet come out as far as the southern boundary of this area, refused action, and enticed the Grand Fleet to take up a pursuit, a minefield here would likely cause heavy losses to the British.[47]

The Eastern Dogger Bank Minefield was placed as a strategy by the High Seas Fleet Command to cripple the Grand Fleet, should rumors of an impending British attack on the German Bight or the battleship SMS *Schleswig-Holstein* be true. In anticipation of such a possibility, the light cruisers of the 4th Scouting Group were recalled by the Command on 13 May from the Baltic to serve as minelayers. Admiral von Pohl had directed that the field be laid where the meridian of 4°E crossed the Dogger Bank.[48]

In early evening on 17 May, the battleships and the battle cruisers of the High Seas Fleet proceeded from the Jade, well screened by destroyers. The light cruisers had gone on ahead, accompanied by two half-flotillas of destroyers as defence against submarines. The 480 mines were laid by midnight and the light cruisers turned back to join the main body. During the ensuing passage of the combined force, two of the destroyers, *V-150* and *V-157*, collided in the dark; *V-150* sank with the loss of sixty lives. At 0818, the light cruiser *Danzig*, which was steering a southeast course ten miles ahead of the main body, struck one of the mines *Orvieto* had laid on 10 April. *Danzig* did not sink, but required towing to Bremerhaven for repairs. The High Seas Fleet anchored that evening at Wilhelmshaven.[49]

The Germans located one end of the British minefield (revealed by the mining of the *Danzig*) on 21 May. Some of the mines were almost awash at low water, and it was found that airships could see others underwater. Thereafter, whenever the weather was favourable, Zeppelins added mineseeking to their already numerous and varied duties. Despite knowing the field's location, clearance efforts proved difficult due to its distance from the German minesweeping base.[50]

The German Navy was extremely fortunate that the British did not acquire reliable mines until late 1917. Until this happened, few U-boats and other craft were sunk by striking mines. Postwar comments by former Royal Navy officers highlighted their frustrations regarding the terrible performance of their mines throughout much of the war:

> German submarines could carry these ineffective engines on their bows [mines struck, or torn from their moorings] and shake them or bump against them with impunity. Many German warships had as a souvenir a British mine mounted on a stand.

Our deficiency was clearly shown in trials in which one of our submarines was run against a number of our mines with the result that only one-third of the mines fitted with small charges [for purposes of the trials] exploded. The Germans were well aware that our mines were not very effective against U-boats.

Had we been in possession of a reliable mine and mooring in adequate numbers, we could have strangled the submarine menace within the first few months. The British minefields that existed in the Eastern English Channel approaches were negligible and inefficient. Our mines were unsatisfactory and the moorings were weak. The result was that practically every mine got adrift and was either sunk by our own flotillas or made its way across the North Sea. Some washed up on the Dutch coast and were turned into flowerpots.[51]

BRITISH CLEARANCE EFFORTS IN THE EASTERN DOGGER BANK MINEFIELD

While the German Navy was dealing with the British-laid minefield in the Bight, Royal Navy minesweepers were plying their trade in the Eastern Dogger Bank Minefield. Large numbers of enemy mines were located. Early on, forty-one mines were swept up and exploded. In addition, the fishing vessel *Reverto* brought up a newly-painted mine in her nets on 18 May 1915. The gear was cut away and the mine sank back into the depths without exploding. On 21 May, the Norwegian tanker S.S. *Maricopa* struck a mine in the field and suffered damage. HMS *Sagitta* and her group proceeded to sweep the area where *Maricopa* had been mined, and promptly destroyed forty-three mines. This was on 23 May, and the following day ten more mines were accounted for. Two were brought into port by *Sagitta*, having been found floating awash, nearly full of water.[52]

Minesweeping gunboats, which also were engaged in the work, destroyed a number of mines. The yacht *Sagitta* and her paddler-wheelers continued to search the field, escorted by destroyers and supported by light cruisers. The destroyers were of great service in examining and warning passing vessels. By the end of May, eighty-six mines (which had been laid in lines just inside the 20-fathom curve) had been swept up.[53]

BRITISH WORLD WAR I MINESWEEPERS

Britain's best bulwarks are her wooden walls.

—Thomas Augustine Arne, English musician and composer (1710-1778), relating Britain's security to her fleets of wooden ships. In similar fashion, a common adage among World War I sailors was that *Flower*-class minesweeping sloops helped to create and maintain "herbaceous borders."

Photo 8-4

British sloop HMS *Foxglove* lying at anchor in Hong Kong, BCC, in October 1920. Naval History and Heritage Command #NH 83025

As the Germany Navy continued to mine British waters, the Royal Navy kept acquiring ever-greater numbers of minesweepers. By the summer of 1915, five separate classes of minesweepers were in service including a new class known as sloops:

- Fleet sweepers, including the old gunboats *Skipjack* and *Jason*
- Eight auxiliary sweepers chartered from the railway companies for the Grand Fleet
- Paddle-steamers employed for rapid sweeping near the coast
- Minesweeping trawlers/drifters
- A new class bearing the old historic designation of "sloop"[54]

This chapter concludes with an introduction of the *Flower*-class minesweeping sloops that would join the Royal Navy in 1915-1916. Comprising the seventy-two *Flowers* were three sub-classes of *Acacia*- (24), *Azalea*- (12), and *Arabis*-class sloops (36).

Flower-class Minesweeping Sloops

Acacia-class Sloops (250 feet, 1,200 tons, 17 knots, 77 man crew)

Ship	Launched	Ship	Launched
Acacia	15 Apr 1915	*Laburnum*	10 June 1915
Anemone	13 May 1915	*Larkspur*	11 May 1915
Aster (mined)	1 May 1915	*Lavender* (sunk)	12 Jun 1915
Bluebell	24 Jul 1915	*Lilac*	2 Apr 1915
Daffodil	17 Aug 1915	*Lily*	16 Jun 1915
Dahlia	21 Apr 1915	*Magnolia*	26 Jun 1915
Daphne	19 May 1915	*Mallow*	13 Jul 1915
Foxglove	30 Mar 1915	*Marigold*	27 May 1915
Hollyhock	1 May 1915	*Mimosa*	16 Jul 1915
Honeysuckle	29 Apr 1915	*Primrose*	29 Jun 1915
Iris	2 Jun 1915	*Sunflower*	28 May 1915
Jonquil	12 May 1915	*Veronica*	27 May 1915

Azalea-class Sloops (255-feet, 1,250 tons, 17 knots, 79 man crew)

Ship	Launched	Ship	Launched
Azalea	10 Sep 1915	*Jessamine*	9 Sep 1915
Begonia (sunk)	26 Aug 1915	*Myrtle* (mined)	11 Oct 1915
Camellia	25 Sep 1915	*Narcissus*	22 Sep 1915
Carnation	6 Sep 1915	*Peony*	27 Oct 1915
Clematis	29 Jul 1915	*Snowdrop*	7 Oct 1915
Heliotrope	10 Sep 1915	*Zinnia*	12 Aug 1915

Arabis-class Sloops (255-feet, 1,250 tons, 17 knots, 79 man crew)

Ship	Launched	Ship	Launched
Alyssum (mined)	5 Nov 1915	*Lobelia*	7 Mar 1916
Amaryllis	9 Dec 1915	*Lupin*	31 May 1916
Arabis (sunk)	6 Nov 1915	*Marguerite*	23 Nov 1915
Asphodel	21 Dec 1915	*Mignonette*	17 Mar 1917
Berberis	18 Mar 1917	*Myosotis*	4 Apr 1916
Buttercup	24 Oct 1915	*Nasturtium* (mined)	21 Dec 1915
Campanula	25 Dec 1915	*Nigella*	10 Dec 1915
Celandine	19 Feb 1916	*Pansy*	12 Jan 1920
Cornflower	30 Mar 1916	*Pentstemon*	5 Feb 1916
Crocus	24 Dec 1915	*Petunia*	3 Apr 1916
Cyclamen	22 Feb 1916	*Poppy*	9 Nov 1915
Delphinium	23 Dec 1915	*Primula* (sunk)	6 Dec 1915
Genista (sunk)	26 Feb 1916	*Rosemary*	22 Nov 1915
Gentian (mined)	23 Dec 1915	*Snapdragon*	21 Dec 1915
Geranium	8 Nov 1915	*Valerian*	21 Feb 1916
Gladiolus	25 Oct 1915	*Verbena*	9 Nov 1915
Godetia	8 Jan 1916	*Wallflower*	8 Nov 1915
Hydrangea	2 Mar 1916	*Wistaria*	7 Dec 1915[55]

Ten of the sloops would be lost during, or immediately following the war, owing to enemy action, mines or, in one case, collision with a U-boat.

Losses of *Flower*-class Minesweeping Sloops

Date	Ship	Cause
10 Feb 1916	*Arabis*	Sunk by German torpedo boats off the Dogger Bank
29 Feb 1916	*Primula*	Sunk (torpedoed) by *U-35* near Cerigo Island in the Mediterranean
27 Apr 1916	*Nasturtium*	Mined near Malta
23 Oct 1916	*Genista*	Sunk by *U-57* in the Atlantic
18 Mar 1917	*Alyssum*	Mined southwest of Ireland
5 May 1917	*Lavender*	Sunk (torpedoed) by *UC-75* off Ireland south of Mine Head
4 Jul 1917	*Aster*	Mined in the Mediterranean
2 Oct 1917	*Begonia*	As Q-ship S.S. *Dolcis Jessop*, sunk in collision with *U-151* off Casablanca
16 Jul 1919	*Gentian*	Mined in the Gulf of Finland
16 Jul 1919	*Myrtle*	Mined in the Gulf of Finland[56]

Other classes of minesweepers would later join the Royal Navy, including: (1) *Strath-*, *Castle-*, and *Mersey*-class trawlers; (2) *Ascot*-class ("racecourse") paddle sweepers; (3) *Hunt*-class screw minesweepers; and (4) *Dance*-class shallow-draught tunnel minesweepers. By 1918, the Minesweeping Service would comprise 726 ships of every description.[57]

9

British Minelaying Force

Thursday night. H.M. Auxiliary Ship Princess Irene *was accidentally blown up in Sheerness Harbour this morning. So far as it is yet known, only one survivor Stoker David Wills was picked up. Wills has sustained burns from the explosion. Three men Able Seaman W. J. Paice, Signalman J. T. Sutton and Chief Steward J. Thompson were not on board at time of the disaster. 76 Dockyard workmen are reported to have been on board the* Princess Irene *this morning and must have perished. Several men belonging to vessels lying close to the* Princess Irene *were wounded by falling splinters.*

273 persons on board H.M. Ship Princess Irene *who, in the absence of evidence to the contrary must be regarded to have lost their lives. Of this number 30 were officers, 243 petty officers, non-commissioned officers and men including mercantile crew ratings, chiefly firemen and five ratings serving in steam launch* No. 263 *which was alongside at the time of the accident.*

—Statements from the British Admiralty regarding the destruction
of HMS *Princess Irene*, while loading mines on 27 May 1915 in
Saltpan Reach, on the Medway Estuary between Port Victoria
and Sheerness, Kent, England. Over 350 lives were lost
when the ship blew up; obliterating everything but the
keel, lower keel, lower hull, and lower decks—and
everyone aboard her but for a single sailor.[1]

BRITISH MINELAYING EFFORTS IN 1915

By early 1915, it had become clear to the Admiralty that it should be committed to an extensive minelaying campaign. Not only were the activities of U-boats causing concern, Admiral Jellicoe had advocated laying mines in the Heligoland Bight to counter the movement of German surface forces, and had asked for a supply of Swedish-designed Leon mines for use by destroyers operating with the Grand Fleet. Additional British naval spherical mines ("Service mines") were ordered, and also a small number of Leon mines, of which Messrs. Beardmore held the British manufacturing rights.[2]

The Leon was an oscillating mine. When it was laid it sank to a position just below the set depth. A hydrostatic value then closed, and completed the circuit from a battery to a small electric motor driving a propeller at the lower end of the cylindrical mine. The action propelled the mine back toward the surface until just above the set depth, when the valve again operated, the electric motor stopped and the mine began to sink again. This cycle of events was repeated until the battery was dead or switched off by a timing device. The mine was detonated by an inertia pistol.[3]

The chief obstacle to an expanded British minelaying program was a shortage of minelayers. The old converted cruisers of the *Apollo*-class were slow and poorly armed, rendering them unsuitable for operating in enemy waters. HMS *Apollo*, *Iphigenia*, *Latona*, and *Naiad* had laid the first British minefield in the Heligoland Bight (off Amrum Bank) in January 1915. The ships were twenty-five years old, were armed with 4.7-inch guns of an obsolete type, and incapable of exceeding a speed of 15 knots. It had therefore been decided to obtain and convert six merchant ships to perform minelaying duties.[4]

Photo 9-1

British cruiser HMS *Naiad*, location and date unknown.
Naval History and Heritage Command photograph #NH 58637

In the table, Characteristics refers to vessel length in feet, tons displacement, and speed in knots. Quantities of mines carried are also provided, as are the identities of commanding officers and their dates of appointment or periods in command, if known. "A/" refers to "Acting" or temporary rank.

Ship	Characteristics	Mines	Commanding Officer(s)
HMS *Princess Irene*	395/5,440/21	500	Capt. Mervyn H. Cobbe, 9 Mar-27 May 1915; died when ship exploded and sank on 27 May while loading mines
HMS *Princess Margaret*	395/5,440/21	500	Capt. Frederick S. Litchfield-Speer, before 15 Aug 1915; Comdr. Lockhart Leith, 2 Jan 1916; Capt. Harry H. Smyth, 3 Jan 1918-9 Nov 1919
HMS *Orvieto*	528/12,130/18	600	Capt. Harry H. Smyth, 8 Mar 1915-25 May 1916
HMS *Paris*	293/2,030/21	80	Comdr. Lockhart Leith, 14 Dec 1914; A/Comdr. John May, 2 Jan 1916
HMS *Angora*	390/4,299/16.5	320	Capt. Walter R. G. Petre, 11 May 1915-4 April 1918
HMS *Biarritz*	341/2,700/21	305	A/Capt. Edgar R. Morant, 11 Mar 1915; Comdr. Richard H. O. Lane-Poole, 14 Aug 1918[5]

HMS *Princess Margaret* and HMS *Princess Irene* were products of William Denny and Brothers Ltd. (a shipyard on the River Leven at Dumbarton, Scotland, often referred to simply as "Denny"), as were the other minelayers, with the exception of *Orvieto*. The Royal Navy was desperate for fast minelayers to operate off the German coast. The sister ships (laid down as coastal liners for the Canadian Pacific Railway's British Columbia Coast Service for use on the "Triangle Route" of Seattle-Victoria-Vancouver) were well suited for such duty, each being able to make 21 knots. Additionally, spanning 395 feet in length with a 54-foot beam, they could carry a large load of mines. The two Princesses joined the Minelayer Squadron in March 1915.

HMS *Angora* had been built by "Denny" for the British India Steam Navigation Company Ltd. at a cost of £117,753 and delivered on 24 February 1911. In the early part of World War I, *Angora* had served as an Indian Expeditionary Force transport. Her duties included carrying 1,200 Gurkhas and 100 mules from Bombay, India, to Marseilles, France, in September 1914. The accommodation was described as overcrowded.[7]

Taken over by the Royal Navy on 27 February 1915, *Angora* was fitted with three 4.7-inch and two 6-pounder guns along with 320 mines. Most of her war service was in the North Sea. Surprised on one occasion by two German cruisers, she made her escape at over 20 knots by screwing down her boiler safety valves, earning her Chief Engineer the Distinguished Service Order. Following the war, *Angora* resumed Calcutta/Rangoon mail service in May 1920.[8]

The William Denny and Brothers yard built all types of vessels, but was particularly well known as producers of fine cross-channel steamships and ferries. The channel steamer *Paris*, completed in 1913, was acquired by the Admiralty on 14 November 1914 and converted to a minelayer. HMS *Paris* was listed as a new member of the Minelayer Squadron in December 1914. She returned to civilian service after the war, before being called upon in 1939 for duty as Hospital Carrier No. 32. HMHS *Paris* was bombed on 2 June 1940 while serving as a hospital ship in the evacuation of British troops from Dunkirk, and sank the next day.[9]

HMS *Biarritz*, a former passenger ferry completed by William Denny and Brothers in March 1915, would serve as a minelayer until 1919 before taking up more mundane duties for Southern Railway, London. She too was later at Dunkirk, serving as a trooper for the evacuation. In 1942, *Biarritz* was converted from a military transport into a Mercantile Infantry Landing Ship. The versatile ship was later pressed into MOWT (Ministry of War Transport) duties, carrying troops for the British Army of the Rhine. Following thirty-four years of military and civilian duties, *Biarritz* was withdrawn from service in August 1949, and laid up at Dover.[10]

HMS *Orvieto* was a former Orient Steam Navigation Company liner built by Workman Clark & Company, Belfast, Ireland. Following delivery to the Orient Line on 6 November 1909, *Orvieto* began service as a passenger cruiser on the London to Brisbane mail run. While in Australia, shortly after the start of the war, she was requisitioned by the Commonwealth Government of Australia. After two months in the Sydney dockyard being fitted out as a troop transport, she sailed for Egypt with the officers and men of the Australian Imperial Force, as part of a convoy escorted by Royal Navy and Japanese cruisers.[11]

While at Colombo, Ceylon (today, Sri Lanka), on 15 November 1914, the *Orvieto* took aboard a number of prisoners from the famous German commerce raider, the light cruiser SMS *Emden*—which had grounded after being disabled in battle with the Australian light cruiser HMAS *Sydney*. The prisoners included the FKpt. Karl von Müller, the ship's commanding officer, and her torpedo officer, Prince Franz Josef von Hohenzollern. The Australian troops and German POWs were disembarked upon the troop ship's arrival at Suez, after which *Orvieto* proceeded to London, arriving in January 1915.[12]

Thereafter, the Admiralty requisitioned her as an armed merchant cruiser and she was fitted out at Millwall (an area in London, on the southwestern side of the Isle of Dogs), being armed with eight 6-inch guns. On 8 March 1915 she was commissioned HMS *Orvieto*, Capt. Harry H. Smyth, RN, in command. A two-day drydocking at Tilbury preceded her departure for Scapa Flow. After arriving at the Fleet base on 21 March, she spent little time at sea, and on 8 June departed for Immingham. Situated on the southwest bank of the Humber Estuary, six miles northwest of Grimsby, it would be her base for the next ten months. *Orvieto*'s duties as a minelayer took her all along the coast between Sheerness and Rosyth, often accompanied by *Princess Margaret*.[13]

On 18 February 1916, *Orvieto* suffered slight damage in a collision with the Swedish cargo ship SS *Abisko* at Immingham and, adding insult to injury, went aground for a time off Sheerness a month later. The *Orvieto*'s first commission came to an end on 25 May 1916 at the Royal Albert Docks in London, where the ship's company was paid off. Following overhaul and assembly of a new crew, she returned to service, but not as a minelayer.[14]

BRITISH MINELAYING FORCE STRENGTHENED, BUT DEFICIENCIES IN MINES EMPLOYED PERSIST

Of these six ships, the *Princess Margaret*, *Biarritz* and *Paris* were originally fitted to carry Elia mines, and the remainder to carry Service mines. The "British Elia" was a modified mine of Italian origin, which differed from the original Elia chiefly in the design of the firing pistol. Because the glass vial used in the Hertz horn on the Italian mine was sensitive to the shock of other mines in a field going off, the British utilised a mechanical device to actuate it rather than an electrical one. The Royal Navy preferred a long arm with a float on the end to operate the mine. The rod safety sleeve and connector were held suspended in the water by a cork float, which acted as a fin on the rod. If the mine was bumped, an induced rotary motion operated the detonator. This alternation did not prove successful.[15]

Another shortcoming was that a different arrangement of mine rails was required for the Service and Elia types, which reduced the flexibility of the minelaying force. The Royal Navy's minelaying capabilities were greatly strengthened by the acquisition of ships much newer, and more capable than the old protected cruisers available at war's commencement. Regrettably, the quality of British mines lagged the new minelaying force. In June, following the loss of HMS *Princess Irene* due to the defective British Elia mine, minelaying ceased for a time. Still, fifteen minefields were laid in the narrows in 1915, chiefly between the Goodwin Sands and the Belgian coast.[16]

PRINCESS IRENE DESTROYED, ALMOST ENTIRE CREW KILLED BY MINE EXPLOSIONS ON BOARD

Soon after *Princess Irene* was launched on 20 October 1914, and before her fitting out was completed, she was requisitioned by the Admiralty, and taken to Sheerness (forty miles east of London at the mouth of the River Medway) for conversion to a minelayer. The former liner entered the Royal Navy Dockyard on Sheerness Peninsula, where workers removed her main deck to provide space for 400 mines and tracks, and cut minelaying ports into her stern. For armament, she received two 4.6-inch guns, and four smaller gun mounts.[17]

By 25 May 1915, *Princess Irene*, now the commissioned HMS *Princess Irene*, had participated in two minelaying operations, and was at Sheerness undergoing a refit, when the mines arrived for her third trip. She was moored at buoy 28, off Victoria Pier in Salt Pan Reach, near the Isle of Grain three miles southwest of Sheerness. Aboard *Irene* was her full crew of 225 officers and men, except for three officers who were ashore. Also on board was a party of eighty-eight petty officers and ratings from Chatham, in addition to seventy-eight dockyard workers there to complete work still remaining to be done, including strengthening her improvised gun decks prior to the minelayer's planned departure on the 29th.[18]

Photo 9-2

British minelayer HMS *Princess Irene*, location and date unknown.
Source: www.clydeships.co.uk

Wednesday, 26 May, began with crewmen priming the first fifty mines loaded onboard. This involved fitting a detonator and primer, known as a "pistol." By day's end, work was almost completed, with all of the remaining mines scheduled to be primed the following day. Dockyard workers began boarding the ship at 0700 the next morning, 27 May, to finish their work, as priming of the remaining mines continued. At 1108, there was a terrific flash and a huge column of flame. Seconds later, another column of flame erupted, both reaching over 300 feet into the sky. At 1114, an enormous explosion lifted *Irene* out of the water, leaving nothing but debris and a mushroom plume of white smoke rising miles up into the sky.[19]

Princess Irene's destruction was shocking, sudden and complete. She did not sink into the waters of the Salt Pan Reach off the Isle of Grain, as one might expect, but instead seemed to be hurled into the air a mile high in 10,000 fragments. The force of the explosion, which could be clearly heard more than twelves miles away, was terrific, and her remains, and those of the men aboard her, were distributed over many miles. A part of one of *Irene*'s boilers landed on a collier, half a mile away, a 10-ton section of the ship landed on the Isle of Grain, and smaller pieces of wreckage were flung up to twenty miles away. The bodies of victims able to be recovered were buried at Woodlands Road Cemetery, in Gillingham. A memorial service for the deceased was held at the Dockyard Church, Sheerness on 1 June 1915. The victims from *Princess Irene* are commemorated on the Naval Memorial at Southsea and at the Dockyard Church at Sheerness.[20]

INVESTIGATION OF DISASTER IS INCONCLUSIVE

A Court of Inquiry (whose members were a rear admiral, a captain, and a commander from HMS Pembroke (a shore establishment), HMS *Conquest*, and HMS *Angora*, respectively) was convened to investigate the circumstances attending the loss of the minelayer. Although a conclusive cause for the disaster was not ascertained, the Court did offer some speculative findings in its report:

> ... It appears that a premature explosion might be caused by faulty construction of a pistol if the striker projected into the primer holder so that it could penetrate the detonator when the primer was being screwed on. A faulty pistol in which the striker projected more than one sixteenth of an inch as supplied to HMS *Angora* was produced to the Court.

> A second possible cause of explosion might be if when fitting a pistol the tumbler levers did not properly engage under the dropper ring; it has been shown that they will hold with only one under or with all three bearing against but not under the dropper ring. In such

a case, if the pistol were being fitted into the mine, any jar might release the striker and explode the detonator.

A third possible cause of explosion would be if the indiarubber washer was left out of the top of the primer leaving the detonator free to be thrown against the striker, but this could only occur if the striker projected too far as in the first case.[21]

While the Court did not attribute blame for the accident, it noted that, "no plea of haste should ever allow of these pistols being fitted by other than fully qualified men and further that a slight mechanical device should be fitted to the pistols to ensure that the pistol could not fire until it is properly placed with the other safety devices in the mine."[22]

Whether due to deficiencies in the mines themselves, or in their handling, this tragedy seemed to suggest that arming these type mines could be fraught with danger. Following the loss of *Irene*, *Princess Margaret* became flagship of the squadron.

10

Minelaying Subs increase British Minesweepers' Toil

To navigate among the shoals and swirls of the East Coast of England in a U.C. boat whose maximum speed was 6 ½ knots on the surface, and less below it, seems in itself sufficiently difficult; but, in addition to that, to cross continually waters known to be mined and to penetrate through a patrol keenly alert and ready with nets, guns and bombs, calls for a special degree of courage. Yet, in spite of all the opposition and danger they knew they could expect, the U.C. boats had fouled with their mines all the parts of the swept channel within their reach; and even in Boulogne Harbour itself had destroyed some ships.

—Tribute paid by official Royal Navy history to the commanding officers of Germany's small coastal minelaying submarines.[1]

The Royal Navy Minesweeping Service likely felt a measure of comfort as the first of the new *Flower*-class sloops joined its gunboats, paddle-wheelers, and trawlers working tirelessly to keep Britain's channels and harbour approaches swept clear of mines so that fighting ships and merchantmen might pass in safety. In 1914, German surface ships had laid 840 mines off the coasts of Britain, upwards of fifty merchant vessels or fishing craft had been mined, and 300 mines had been swept up or rendered harmless by other means.[2]

By April, 1915, about 238 vessels were engaged sweeping British home waters. In the table, the quantities of minesweepers associated with particular locations represent trawlers, unless otherwise noted:

Location	# Minesweepers	Location	# Minesweepers
Grand Fleet	6 gunboats, 1 new sloop, 10 trawlers	The Nore (for Thames Estuary)	25
Peterhead	8	Dover	12
Cromarty	18	Portsmouth	9
Granton	21	Portland	8
North Shields	12	Devonport	7
Grimsby	30 and 6 hired paddlers	Milford Haven	4
Lowestoft	47	The Clyde River	6 hired paddlers[3]
Harwich	8		

The full number of personnel assigned to the Minesweeping Service around this time is difficult to ascertain. By the end of 1914, it included 100 officers of the RN and RNR, together with 250 of the Royal Naval Volunteer Reserve, which had been established in 1903. Following the war, the RNVR administered the Mine Clearance Service (MCS), created in 1919 to clear all sea mines. MCS members came from all branches of the Royal Navy. The RNVR was eventually merged with the Royal Naval Reserve in 1958.[4]

Photo 10-1

Lt. Draper L. Kauffman, RNVR, September 1940-November 1941. The Royal Naval Volunteer Service was called the "Wavy Navy," after the 3/8-inch wavy sleeve 'rings' that its officers wore to differentiate them from RN/RNR officers. Kauffman retired in the rank of Rear Admiral, USN.
Naval History and Heritage Command photograph #NH 95549

AB Alexander Cameron, a Scottish fisherman who served in minesweepers on the Dover Patrol in World War I, attired in his Royal Navy uniform. An Able Seaman (AB) was a Naval rating of the deck department of a merchant ship.
Photograph courtesy of Iain Cameron

Persistently over the course of the war, in fair weather or foul, minesweepers went about their vital business. The sweepers fell into three main categories, realising the groupings were somewhat flexible, as it was often the case of "all hands to the job." Fast sweepers, however, rarely left the Grand Fleet.

- Fast Sweepers: Converted gunboats and minesweepers built during the war (including the *Flower*-class sloops) which swept ahead of fleets and convoys, and searched the approaches to Fleet bases and Convoy ports
- Routine Sweepers: Trawlers and drifters (assisted by motor launches) which carried out daily searches of the War Channels and the approaches to harbours
- Clearance Sweepers: Shallow-draught paddle-steamers which cleared minefields when located

When weather permitted, motor launches were also useful for clearance work.[5]

If there was a belief that the work of the minesweeping forces would lessen, and that fewer ships would be lost to mines as a result of *Flower*-class sloops entering the fleet, this optimism was short-lived. The advent of German minelaying submarines in 1915 imposed a tremendous strain on Britain's minesweeping resources. While the minesweepers toiled without reprieve in an effort to lessen vessel losses to enemy mines, German submarines breached British defensive minefields almost with impunity. The presence of the more powerful Royal Navy induced the High Seas Fleet to remain in port, but German U-boats continued to have freedom of movement, and Allied shipping losses to enemy torpedoes and mines continued to mount.[6]

BRITAIN REINFORCES DOVER STRAIT MINEFIELD

From 20 October 1914, when Britain had laid its first minefield, 7,438 mines had been placed in the hope of preventing U-boats from entering the English Channel through the Dover Strait. Britain had mined the northern entrance to Dover Strait in February 1915. It had been done rapidly, on an emergency basis with the materiel available, and the mines quickly began to break adrift.[7]

By the end of May 1915, the field had deteriorated to such extent that Admiral Jellicoe proposed that it be re-laid. This necessitated minesweepers clearing the remaining mines before minelayers could safely enter the field. Following a determination that an insufficient number of minesweepers were available for this task, it was decided that four minelayers would lay new lines, to the northward of the existing field. The minelayers tasked to carry out the operation were converted merchant vessels from a newly formed squadron based at Sheerness.

This was the first time that ships from the squadron operated together. HMS *Orvieto* and three other unidentified minelayers, from among those listed in the table, carried out the operation.[8]

British Minelayers (Converted Merchant Ships and Ocean Liners)

Ship	Built	Fitted Out	Mines	Service
Angora	1911	Blackwell	320	27 Feb 1915-15 Nov 1919
Biarritz	1915	Denny	180	8 Mar 1915-6 May 1920
Gazelle	1889		50	May-Nov 1915, later minesweeper
Orvieto	1909	Blackwell	600	6 Jan 1915, over six operations laid 3,000 mines; after 27 May 1916, armed merchant cruiser
Paris	1913	Blackwell	140	14 Nov 1914-5 Nov 1919
Perdita	1910	Mudros	100	7 Aug 1915-21 Aug 1919
Princess Irene	1914	Denny	500	20 Jan 1915, destroyed 27 May 1915 by mine explosion on board
Princess Margaret	1914	Denny	500	26 Dec 1914-14 Jun 1919
Wahine[9]	1913	Blackwell	180	22 Jul 1916-17 Feb 1920

On 9 July 1915, *Orvieto* and the three other minelayers, proceeding abreast, and under escort by eight destroyers, laid four lines of mines strengthening the existing Straits of Dover Minefield. The mines were sown between the North Falls and North Hinder Shoals in an area previously identified as dangerous in an Admiralty Notice to Mariners. All HM ships and bases were notified of the new field. In 1915, no additional mines were laid in this area.[10]

GERMANY BEGINS USING U-BOATS TO LAY MINES

Up until late May 1915, surface ships had been responsible for laying all the German minefields. This practice changed on 2 June 1915, with the discovery of mines off the South Foreland. This proved to be the work of the German Flanders U-Flotilla. Minefields planted by *UC-1*, *2*, *3*, and *11* were found off Harwich and Dover on 18 June. On 30 June, the old destroyer HMS *Lightning* (launched in 1895) was sunk by a mine off the *Kentish Knock* light vessel, although it may not have been one laid by a submarine.[11]

Following her sinking, thirteen other vessels were lost in July, August, and September 1915 attributed to mines laid by UC boats in the Dover, Harwich, and Yarmouth areas. In the following table, the initials AP denote "Auxiliary Patrol" and MS "Minesweeper."

British Vessels Lost to German UC Boat-laid Mines
July-August 1915

Date	Vessels Sunk by Mines	Location/UC Boat
15 Jul 1915	hired trawler MS *Agamemnon II* (9 killed)	off Shipwash/*UC-1*
20 Jul 1915	hired yacht *Rhiannon* (5 killed)	off Longsand/*UC-3*
21 Jul 1915	hired trawler *Briton* (11 killed)	off Longsand/*UC-3*
6 Aug 1915	hired trawler MS *Leandros* (7 killed)	off N. Knock/*UC-5*
8 Aug 1915	hired trawler MS *Ben Ardna* (2 killed)	off Elbow Buoy/*UC-1*
14 Aug 1915	hired trawler AP *Worsley* (1 killed)	off Aldeburgh/*UC-6*
16 Aug 1915	hired trawler MS *Japan* (5 killed)	off Shipwash/*UC-6*
23 Aug 1915	hired trawler *Miura* (11 killed)	off Yarmouth/*UB-2*
28 Aug 1915	hired trawler AP *Dane* (5 killed)	off Aldeburgh/*UC-6*
1 Sep 1915	hired trawler MS *Nadine* (9 killed)	off N. Shipwash Buoy/*UC-7*
1 Sep 1915	hired trawler AP *Malta* (7 killed)	off N. Shipwash Buoy/*UC-7*
3 Sep 1915	collier *Churston* (4 killed)	off Orfordness/*UC-7*
18 Sep 1915	hired trawler MS *Lydian* (8 killed)	off S. Foreland/*UC-6*[12]

Photo 10-2

British destroyer HMS *Lightning*, date unknown.
Naval History and Heritage Command photograph #NH 59901

GERMAN UC MINELAYING SUBMARINES

The coastal minelaying submarines accounting for such vast early destruction had been hurriedly built after being ordered in November 1914. They were both small and economical: 112 feet in length, 168-ton surface displacement, with a top speed of 6.2 knots on the surface or 5.2 submerged. The UC boats had neither torpedo tubes, nor a deck gun. When operating on the surface, their only defence was a machine gun which was normally stored inside the submarine, and brought topside when needed.

Much of the space inside the fore section of the submarine was taken up by twelve mines, stored in six inclined tubes. When released, each mine and its 350 pounds of TNT explosive dropped from its tube, and was carried to the bottom by a sinker. Each mine had a timer that would permit it to sit on the bottom until a sufficient amount of time had passed for the submarine to get clear. The timer consisted of a soluble plug which would dissolve and release the mine, causing it to rise by its internal buoyancy assisted by the release of inertia from a compressed starting spring. It then rose in the water column to a location near the surface, as determined by the length of its mooring cable, to await any unsuspecting vessel.[13]

Photo 10-3

German minelaying submarine SMS *UC-5*, date unknown.
Naval History and Heritage Command photograph #NH 111094

The Admiralty first learned about the capabilities of the UC boats after the British coaster SS *Cottingham* accidentally ran down and sank *UC-2* off Yarmouth on 2 July 1915. Divers sent down (by Capt. Alfred A. Ellison, RN, commanding the Yarmouth area) to investigate the wreckage found the sunken UC boat in two parts. The after section contained nothing of particular interest, but inside the fore part were six inclined mine tubes, each three-and-a-half feet in diameter and eighteen feet long. Three of the forward tubes still contained mines. They were removed by the divers, in a process of great danger. Ellison suggested that the fore part of the submarine be raised for investigatory purposes. The Admiralty instead, in the face of risks involved, ignored his advice and decided to dispose of the wreck with explosives.[14]

Photo 10-4

German mines aboard the destroyer tender USS *Melville*, recovered by divers from the submarine *UC-44*, which had been destroyed by her own mines in 1917. U.S. Naval History and Heritage Command photograph #NH 85

LOCATIONS OF UC SUBMARINE-LAID MINEFIELDS

After the South Foreland discovery previously described, the first minefield found in July, was located at the north end of the Longsand Shoal in the approaches to the Thames Estuary. The field had been laid by *UC-3*, which came over from Flanders on the 5th. Its presence was soon evident. At 1000 that morning, the Norwegian cargo ship SS *Peik*, in passage up the East Coast war channel, blew up and sank one mile northwest of the *Longsand* light vessel. The area was immediately swept but strangely no mines were found.[15]

On 20 July the armed yacht *Rhiannon* struck a mine and sank near the wreck of the *Peik*. Four paddle-sweepers from Grimsby and two minesweeping gunboats from the Grand Fleet—*Seagull* and *Spanker*—were immediately ordered to Harwich. While the paddlers were temporary, the gunboats were to help deal with this particular field, and then remain at Harwich and sweep ahead of the Harwich Force whenever it put to sea. The following day, on 21 July, the trawler *Briton* was blown up near Longsand Head.[16]

After the war, it was learned from German records that the first field laid by the Flanders U-Flotilla had been one by *UC-11* off the South Foreland on the last day of May. In the coming weeks, UC boats laid fields near the *Sunk* light vessel and *Kentish Knock* light vessel in the Thames Estuary, and the *South Goodwin* light vessel and *Gull* light vessel in the Dover area. The UCs also mined other areas near Dover, Nore, and Yarmouth; and for good measure off the French coast, at Calais and Dunkirk, and near the *Dyck* light vessel at Boulogne.

Minefields Laid by UC Boats (31 May-18 August 1915)

Date	Boat	Position Mined	Area
31 May 1915	*UC-11*	S. Foreland	Dover
8 Jun 1915	*UC-11*	*Sunk* light vessel	Yarmouth
30 Jun 1915	*UC-1*	*Kentish Knock* light vessel	Yarmouth
2 Jul 1915	*UC-2*	Stanford Channel	Yarmouth
5 Jul 1915	*UC-3*	*Longsand* light vessel	Yarmouth
10 Jul 1915	*UC-11*	*S. Goodwin* light vessel	Dover
11 Jul 1915	*UC-1*	W. of *Shipwash* light vessel	Yarmouth
11 Jul 1915	*UC-3*	Calais, France	French
17 Jul 1915	*UC-3*	*Dyck* light vessel, Boulogne	French
27 Jul 1915	*UC-1*	*Gull* light vessel	Dover
31 Jul 1915	*UC-1* or *3*	Gull Buoy	Dover
3 Aug 1915	*UC-5*	*Kentish Knock* light vessel	Yarmouth
4 Aug 1915	*UC-1*	Elbow Buoy	Nore
5 Aug 1915	*UC-6*	W. of *Sunk* light vessel	Yarmouth
12 Aug 1915		Aldborough Ridge	Yarmouth
12 Aug 1915	*UC-5*	*Corton* light vessel	Yarmouth
12 Aug 1915	*UC-5*	Stanford Channel	Yarmouth
	UC-1	NW of Elbow Buoy	Nore
18 Aug 1915	*UC-1*	Dunkirk, France	French[17]

Operations of UC minelaying submarines in July were aided by UB torpedo attack boats from Flanders, which reconnoitered in advance the positions to be mined. On one occasion, *UB-10* visited the Downs, entering by the north and proceeding as far as the Gull Buoy, thereby obtaining knowledge of the active patrol maintained by trawlers and destroyers. (A description of UB boats and information about their activities is provided following the UC-related section.)

As indicated by the quoted material at the chapter's head, the slow, small, unarmed UC minelayers faced great danger in carrying out their missions. Not surprisingly, their 14-man crews paid a huge price for such work. Of the six boats listed below, only one survived the war. The coastal minelayers *UC-1, 2, 3, 5,* and *6* were products of the Vulcan, Hamburg Shipyard and *UC-11* of the A. G. Weser, Bremen Shipyard.

All were newly commissioned in April through July 1915.

Vulcan, Hamburg Shipyard

Boat	Commis- Sioned	Commanding Officer	Disposition
UC-1 Sunk	5 Jul 1915	Oblt. Egon von Werner 7 May 1915-13 Apr 1916	Possibly mined 19 Jul 1917 off Nieuport; all hands lost
UC-2 Sunk	17 May 1915	Oblt. Karl Mey 17 May-30 Jun 1915	Destroyed by detonation of own mines 30 Jun 1915 off Yarmouth; all hands lost
UC-3 Sunk	1 Jun 1915	Kptlt. Erwin Weisbach 1 Jun-26 Sep 1915	Mined N. of Zeebrugge 27 May 1916; all hands lost
UC-5 Captured	19 Jun 1915	Oblt. Herbert Pustkuchen 19 Jun-18 Dec 1915	Captured by British after grounding 27 Apr 1916 on the Shipwash Shoal
UC-6 Sunk	24 Jun 1915	Oblt. Matthias Graf von Schmettow 24 Jun 1915-4 May 1916	Sunk in a mined net off North Foreland 27 Sep 1917; all hands lost

A. G. Weser, Bremen Shipyard

Boat	Commis- Sioned	Commanding Officer	Disposition
UC-11 Sunk	23 Apr 1915	Oblt. Walter Gottfried Schmidt 23 Apr 1915-11 Aug 1916	Hit a mine while submerged 26 Jun 1918 and blew up in Strait of Dover; 18 dead and 1 survivor[18]

Three of the commanding officers received the Knight's Cross with Swords of the Hohenzollern House Order; Pustkuchen survived the war, but von Schmettow and von Werner were killed. Matthias Graf von Schmettow received his medal for service in *UC-26*, following his command of *UC-6*.

Medal	Awardee	Date	Boat
	Herbert Pustkuchen	19 Nov 1915	UC-5
	Matthias Graf von Schmettow	22 Nov 1916	UC-26
	Egon von Werner[19]	29 Mar 1916	UC-1

The Knight's Cross with Swords of the Hohenzollern House Order was effectively the intermediate award for officers between the Iron Cross First Class and the Pour Le Mérite.

DIFFICULTIES ENCOUNTERED IN MINESWEEPING

Admiralty suspicions that small groups of mines found periodically near light vessels were the work of submarines were confirmed by a German signal intercepted on 12 July. Sent by a UC boat returning to Zeebrugge, the message reported "Mines laid as ordered." The Admiralty immediately warned the Senior Naval Officers from Dover to Lowestoft that submarines from Belgium were being used to lay mines, and extra protections should be taken as regards sweeping.[20]

The clearance of such mines outside the Thames Estuary proved challenging, because the difference in the rise and fall of the tide was only about twelve feet. Thus, sweeping in places where mines were known to be close to the surface, posed great risk to minesweeping trawlers drawing fifteen feet of water. The relatively slow trawlers also had difficulty severing the moorings of German mines. The French cutting sweep was tried and also proved inadequate. The solution appeared to be finding some paddle-steamers (which had greater speed and shallower draughts than hired fishing vessels) for minesweeping.[21]

Capt. Edward C. Villiers, RN, the officer in charge of the Nore Local Defence, requested assignment from the Admiralty of some light-draught sweepers. Suitable vessels being hard to find, "top brass" asked him to use London County Council steamers, which in peace plied from Westminster to Richmond. None, however, were available until October. Until then the Nore minesweeping service did its best with seventeen minesweeping trawlers. Of these, six were ordered to Malta, their places taken by six trawlers which had been prepared for minelaying, whose gear was now changed for minesweeping.[22]

FLAGSHIP AND ACCOMPANYING MINESWEEPERS

It seemed impossible that any living thing could survive that awful smash, but we presently saw men in the water among the wreckage floating about on the surface. The boats made towards them as fast as they could be driven through the water, picked up all they could see, and returned immediately bearing six living and five dead men.

—G. H. P. Muhlhauser describing in *Small Craft*, efforts made by the armed yacht *Sagitta* (the flagship of Rear Adm. Edward Fitzherbert) and accompanying paddle-minesweepers to save the survivors of the British cargo ship SS *Savona*, which had struck a mine near the *Shipwash* light vessel and sank.[23]

The last minefield laid by UCs during this period was not discovered until 1 September 1915, when a group of minesweepers witnessed the British cargo ship *Savona* blown up in it. Rear Adm. Fitzherbert aboard *Sagitta*, with three paddle-sweepers, had stood out of Yarmouth at 0430 that morning, and swept from the *Corton* light vessel to Aldborough Napes, located one-half mile outside the war channel. At 1253, he and others witnessed the 1,180-ton *Savona* explode a mine and sink within a few hundred yards of a line swept by the paddlers. As two armed trawlers proceeded to pick up the survivors, one of the would-be rescuers, the *Malta*, struck a mine. She sank in ten seconds with her screw still turning, leaving only seven survivors. These men, picked up by boat, were all suffering from shock, their faces had a bluish tinge, and they were shivering violently. A few hours later the armed trawler *Nadine* was sunk in the same area, with all but three of her crew killed.[24]

Two days later, on 3 September, *Sagitta* was coming with the same force down from the north, to sweep round the North Shipwash Buoy, when at 0838 a sighting was made of a large collier of about 3,000 tons. She was heading for the danger area, and was too far off to see any flag signals hoisted to warn her. The only way to stop her was to fire a warning shot in her direction. The *Churston* took no notice and continued on. Water, smoke and debris shooting into the air soon made known that she had struck a mine. Four men were killed by the explosion. The survivors abandoned in a boat, and were lying on their oars (had stopped rowing) a short distance away when a paddle-wheeler picked them up.[25]

Churston did not sink immediately. A boarding party from *Sagitta* went aboard and found that she was badly holed port side, amidships. With her engine room, stockhold and port tanks filled with water, it was only a matter of time before her aft bulkheads gave way. When this occurred she would sink rapidly. The collier disappeared into the deep before 1300—another victim of the *UC-7* field, laid 20 August.[26]

THE FIRST "Q-SHIPS": ARMED FISHING SMACKS

Four smacks have now been armed with 3-pdr. guns and will cruise to seaward of and near to the fishing fleet. It is hoped that success will attend this scheme, as from all reports the submarines engaged in this work are of small size, carry no guns, and always come close alongside the smacks they are going to sink.

—From a report by Capt. William Ruck-Keene, RN, regarding his
inquiry for the British Admiralty into reports of repeated raids
by enemy submarines on the Lowestoft fishing fleet.[27]

Photo 10-5

Fishing smack *Red Fern*, of Lowestoft, which was used by the U.S. mine force for
experiments in the North Sea Mine Barrage in 1918-1919.
Naval History and Heritage Command photograph #NH 63771

While the UC boats were busy laying mines, UB boats carried out raids
on the Lowestoft Fishing Fleet. *UB-6* conducted the first such on 12
July 1915, targeting a group of smacks fishing about twenty miles to the
east of Lowestoft. When the submarine came upon the fishing fleet,
there was scarcely any wind to fill their sails. As they were unable to
either resist or escape, *UB-6* systematically boarded and sank them.
After using rifle fire to make a smack hove to, and its crew to abandon,
three Germans would board the craft. One of the sailors obtained the
vessel's flag (presumably as proof of its destruction), while another
searched the cabin, and the remaining man placed a bomb in the
forecastle, activating its delayed-fuse before departure.[28]

For some reason *Emerald*, one of the vessels so attacked, did not
sink, while *Purple Heather*, *Merlin*, *Speedwell*, and *Woodbine* did so in
succession. Some of the fishermen were given bread and water by the
Germans before being allowed to depart in their pulling boats.
Following the destruction of *Woodbine*, fishermen on nearby smacks that
were not attacked observed that the submarine appeared to be in
distress as she was departing the area. This occurred at 2100 following
seven hours spent boarding, seizing and destroying the fishing boats.
The fishermen from vessels attacked were picked up by surviving

smacks.   The minesweeping gunboat HMS *Speedwell*, upon coming across the *Emerald* still afloat detailed some of her own crew to sail the fishing vessel into Lowestoft.[29]

The attacks on the fishing vessels continued. On 11 August, a UB boat sank *Humphrey* off Smith's Knoll and later that day *Leader*, on the same fishing grounds, the thirty-ninth and fortieth smack to be destroyed since 1 July. In fishing vessels, the UB boats had found their easiest and most defenceless prey.   Finally, in desperation, Captain Ellison took action to protect the Lowestoft fishing fleet.   He commissioned four smacks, with part RNVR crews, and armed each with a 3-pounder gun (disguised as much as possible). Ellison believed that if the UB boats continued to attack in the normal manner, coming alongside a smack with conning tower open, and three or four men on deck, the destruction of a submarine was a certainty.[30]

SMACK *INVERLYON* SINKS *UB-4* OFF YARMOUTH

One of the decoy smacks, the *Inverlyon*, was fishing off Smith's Knoll Buoy on 15 August when, at dusk, a small submarine came up to her. As the UB approached, the officer on her deck shouted something about a boat to the *Inverlyon*, obviously instructions for the smack's crew to abandon. The submarine closed to within about thirty yards and stopped. With an ideal target, the British crew aboard the smack sprang into action. As the White Ensign was hoisted aloft, Gunnery Warrant Officer Ernest M. Jehan, RN, fired his revolver at the captain of the submarine. (Jehan was from the minesweeper HMS *Dryad*, serving as the captain of the *Inverlyon*.)[31]

Jehan's action was the signal for the smack's 3-pounder gun to open fire. Only nine rounds were necessary to send the enemy on her last voyage. The first and third rounds pierced the submarine's conning tower and exploded inside, the second cleared away the after part of the conning tower and the flag above it. The officer topside fell overboard, and the submarine, carried by the tide, swept round the *Inverlyon*'s stern. Four additional hits were made on the conning tower and hull, and the critically hurt submarine plunged, bow down at a steep angle, into the depths. Three bodies came up with the swirl. Believing one to be alive, Jehan went over the side and swam out with a lifebuoy, but the German seaman slipped below before he could be reached.[32]

Toward the end of September, 1915, the armed smacks *Glory*, *Inverlyon*, *G and F*, and *Pet* were paid off. The UB boats no longer made extended voyages. Warrant Gunner Ernest Martin Jehan, RN, was awarded the DSC on 19 November 1915, and was promoted to lieutenant. The sum of £1,000 was divided among the crew for their part in the destruction of SMS *UB-4*. Jehan, who had enlisted in the Royal Navy on 8 February 1894, was ordered to the destroyer HMS *Sarpedon* to serve as executive officer. He commanded the patrol boat HMS *PC-55* from 1919 to 1920, before retiring on 29 October 1920.[33]

UB COASTAL TORPEDO ATTACK BOATS

The submarine was the *UB-4*, a 92-foot coastal torpedo attack boat, which had left Zeebrugge on Friday, the 13th of August. She and the other sixteen *UB-1* Type Coastal U-boats were fitted with two torpedo tubes forward (with no reloads). They carried no mines or a deck gun. Thus their crews (a single officer and thirteen men) had devised a means to destroy enemy vessels—at least defenceless ones. Induce a ship to hove to, and her crew to abandon using rifle fire, then send over some sailors, and one or more bombs in a boat, to blow her up. The two torpedoes the subs carried were reserved for ships which presented a threat. With a top speed of only 6.5 knots on the surface, 5.5 knots submerged, gaining a torpedo firing position against any but a slow moving target was challenging for a UB boat. Pursuit of one, unless crippled, was nearly impossible.[34]

Coastal torpedo attack boat *UB-4* (commissioned on 23 March 1915, with Oblt. Karl Grob in command) had operated in areas where slow coastal traffic had to pass, and later against stationary fishing smacks all alone, out on the fishing grounds. After first gaining experience in the North Hinder area of the approaches to Flushing (Vlissingen), Belgium, *UB-4* had begun to venture across the North Sea to British waters. During her short service, she put down four vessels, including the smack *Bona Fide*, before her own demise at the hands of a smack—albeit an armed one.

Vessels Sunk by *UB-4*

Date	Ship (Tons)	Nation	Area Where Sunk
10 Apr 1915	SS *Harpalyce* (5,940)	British	7 miles SE of the *North Hinder* light vessel
17 Apr 1915	SS *Ellispontos* (2,989)	Greek	*North Hinder* LV area
29 Jul 1915	SS *Princesse Marie Jose* (1,954)	Belgian	1.5 miles E of the *Shipwash* LV
14 Aug 1915	smack *Bona Fide* (59)	British	Sunk by scuttling charge 35 miles ENE of Lowestoft[35]

FLANDERS U-FLOTILLA

The U-boat flotilla, to which the UC and UB Boats were assigned, had been formed on 29 March 1915 at the port of Bruges in occupied Belgium. Its mission, under the command of KKpt. Paul Bartenbach, was a simple one: harass Allied cross-channel traffic and coastal shipping, directly by torpedo attacks and indirectly by sowing mine fields.[36]

Photo 10-6

German coastal torpedo attack boat of the *UB-1* class.
Naval History and Heritage Command photograph #NH 111086

The development and production of the *UB-1* type submarines was spurred by the German Army's offensive into the Low Countries in the summer of 1914. Seizure of the ports of Bruges and Ostend provided improved access to the North Sea and the English Channel. Recognising that British divisions opposing its army at the Front required a steady flow of ammunition and stores across the Channel, the German High Command had set plans in motion to disrupt Channel shipping as soon as possible. Judging that its large ocean-going submarines could not operate efficiently in the restrictive waters, a new, smaller submarine was needed: one that could be built rapidly and transported overland to operating bases in Flanders.[37]

The design of the resultant *UB-1*-class, 125-ton, single-hulled submarine was dictated by the maximum allowable width for rail transportation (3.15 metres) and a requirement for quick, simple construction devoid of compound curves and complex assemblies. The pressure hull was fabricated from cylindrical and truncated conical boiler plate sections. Because of the size constraint, a single propeller was used, driven by the Körting diesel engine used in large motor launches. A Siemens Schuckertwerke 120 shaft-horsepower electric motor pushed the boats through the water when submerged. Although possessing only modest speed, the boat's range was respectable: 1,600 nautical miles at 5 knots when on the surface, and ten hours submerged at 4 knots when running on batteries.[38]

The *UC-1* class coastal minelaying submarines were developed in parallel with the *UB-1* torpedo attack type, with both designed for rapid production to meet wartime needs. The construction time of the coastal submarines was incredibly short; *UB-1* was completed at Germaniawerft on 22 January 1915, only 109 days after the contracts were signed and 75 days after her keel was laid. The class construction program was totally completed by 21 April 1915. The more complex *UC-1* type minelayers, with their greater displacement, a six-cylinder diesel, and correspondingly larger electric motors and storage batteries, required only four months each to complete.[39]

Four of the UB boats (*10*, *12*, *16*, and *17*) were converted to minelayers in late 1916/early 1917. The length of these submarines was increased to 105 feet to accommodate four mine tubes (eight mines) in place of the two torpedo tubes. In contrast, the 112-foot *UC-1* type boats carried six tubes and twelve mines. The size of the converted UB boats was limited by their smaller propulsion plant.[40]

Flanders U-Flotilla Coastal Torpedo Attack Boats/UB Minelayers

Boat	Service	Disposition
UB-2	20 Feb 1915-30 Sep 1918	Surrendered at end of war
UB-4	23 Mar 1915-13 Aug 1915	Sunk by HM *Inverlyon* off Smith's Knoll
UB-5	25 Mar 1915-13 Sep 1918	Surrendered at end of war
UB-6	8 Apr 1915-12 Mar 1917	Interned in Netherlands after stranding
UB-10	15 Mar 1915-14 Sep 1918	Surrendered at end of war
UB-12	29 Mar 1915-19 Aug 1918	Lost at sea
UB-13	16 Apr 1915-23 Apr 1916	Sunk by mine off Walcheren, Netherlands
UB-16	12 May 1915-6 Dec 1916	Lost at sea
UB-17	4 May 1915-8 Sep 1917	Lost at sea[41]

11

Mining and Countermining Operations Continue

I submit that the operation of minelaying in the enemy's waters should be conducted with absolute secrecy, and that the minelayer or minelayers should, after dark, be entirely alone, on the principle that the smaller the number of ships, the less the chance of discovery.

Minelaying must be accepted as a dangerous operation, and should only be undertaken on the darkest nights of the months or during foggy or misty weather.

Given a dark night the risk of discovery is exceedingly small, especially as it is of necessity a surprise to the enemy, who neither know the locality it is proposed to lay the mines in, nor even that such an operation is in hand.

—Commodore Reginald Tyrwhitt, RN, expressing his views to the Admiralty, regarding the number and disposition of destroyers escorting minelayers in the future. The Admiral requested a statement following the abandonment of a minelaying operation after German torpedo craft torpedoed one of the seven destroyers screening the minelayer HMS *Princess Margaret*.[1]

Concurrent with its initial employment in mid-1915 of submarine-minelayers, the German Naval Staff decided to despatch SMS *Meteor*, a converted freighter, on a second minelaying mission. *Meteor* had recently returned from her successful maiden operation, which had been to attack Allied merchant ships transporting coal and other materiel to Russia, and to mine the entrance to the White Sea. Within that body of water (a southern inlet of the Barents Sea on the northwest coast of Russia) was the major port of Arkhangelsk (Archangel in English). Following this operation, the Staff chose a target nearer to home. The German Navy had long wanted to mine waters near one of the bases of the Grand Fleet. The area selected was Moray Firth, an inlet on Scotland's north coast near Cromarty and to the northeast of Inverness.[1]

Map 11-1

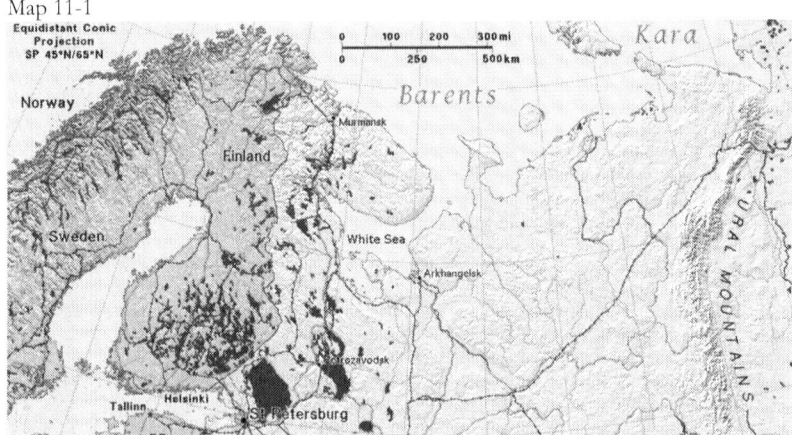

The port of Arkhangelsk is located in the White Sea, a southern inlet of the Barents Sea on the northwest coast of Russia.

Photo 11-1

Monitors entering the ice in the White Sea, date and location unknown.
Naval History and Heritage Command photograph #NH 110552

There were disadvantages to using *Meteor* to mine the Moray Firth, a mission which, unlike the one in the White Sea, would require her to operate in close proximity to the Grand Fleet. The most significant deficit was her slow speed of only 14 knots. On the plus side, being a former British ship, she might not arouse the suspicions of any patrols sighting her silhouette at night. The SS *Vienna* (a product of Ramage and Ferguson, Leith, Scotland) had been at Hamburg when war broke out, and was seized by the German government. Turned over to the German Navy, the 280-foot freighter had been renamed *Meteor* and fitted with two 88mm guns, two smaller 37mm guns, and two 45cm torpedo tubes. She had served as a minesweeper in the Baltic until May 1915.[2]

Her commanding officer, KKpt. Wolfram von Knorr, wrote to superiors that he could only hope for success "if he secured the cooperation of the fleet to such an extent that the operation would not from the beginning bear the stamp of complete futility." He wanted the assistance of a group of barrier breakers and of a submarine to precede him, sufficient air reconnaissance, and exclusive service of submarines operating off the Scottish coast. Von Knorr also demanded and received modifications to *Meteor*, which included the ability to carry mines concealed beneath her decks, and the installation of a powerful wireless radio and an additional gun aft.[3]

Map 11-2

Germany's North Sea coast

In response to these demands, von Knorr was provided the services of the submarine *U-17* and the airship *SL-3* (a naval Schütte-Lanz airship) as scouts. *U-17* left Heligoland Bight in the afternoon of 5 August 1915, preceding *Meteor*. (The kerosene-powered submarine had achieved notoriety in Britain earlier in the war, by being the first U-boat to sink a British merchant vessel. On 20 October 1914, she stopped the 866-ton SS *Glitra* off the Norwegian coast, searched her cargo, ordered her crew into lifeboats, and then scuttled her.) *Meteor* left port in early morning darkness, at 0300, on 6 August. The *SL-3*—based at Airship Port Seddin in German Pomerania (today a part of Poland)—rose at 0700. Flying conditions were unfavourable, forcing her to turn back forty-five miles west of the Horn Reefs.[4]

Map 11-3

North Sea

BRITISH CRUISERS SENT TO INTERCEPT *METEOR*

The Admiralty intercepted and decoded a German signal on 5 August, directing that one of the outer lights at the Jade Bight (on the North Sea coast of Germany) be lit from 0300-0430 the following morning. This action was taken to provide a navigational aid for the outward passage of *Meteor*. Identifying her as the *Meteor* and believing that she was responsible for the White Sea minefield, a message was immediately sent to Admiral Jellicoe at Scapa Flow advising him to watch for her off the Norwegian coast, as she might be off on another minelaying mission. The message also advised that interception be executed with something more powerful than armed trawlers. Unfamiliar with the ship, Jellicoe requested and received this description: "1,912 tons, 14 knots speed, two masts, one funnel, two searchlights on bridge, straight bow, two torpedo tubes on forecastle." The description warned that a neutral ship had reported she carried an unknown number of 4-inch guns. The Admiralty was unaware her armament was hidden, similar to that of British decoy ships.[5]

Map 11-4

Scotland

Jellicoe decided to send light cruisers to intercept the minelayer. HMS *Calliope, Phaeton,* and *Carysfort* of the 4th Light Cruiser Squadron, under Commodore Charles Edward Le Mesueier, sailed from Scapa at 1800 on 6 August to patrol off Norway. Their efforts were fruitless. However, the Admiralty learned of *Meteor*'s movements the evening of 8 August, via an intercepted signal. In it, von Knorr reported that he had laid his mines, had sunk the armed boarding steamer HMS *Ramsey* after saving her crew, and was now returning to Wilhelmshaven. Recognising that there was still time to intercept the minelayer, the Admiralty ordered two of the Rosyth light cruiser squadrons and all of the light cruisers with Commodore Tyrwhitt to raise steam. Tyrwhitt was to take his cruisers, steer toward Horn Reefs, and intercept the *Meteor,* while the Rosyth squadrons were to search along her track and hopefully overtake her.[6]

METEOR SENDS ANOTHER MESSAGE

Later that evening, 8 August, several listening stations intercepted another message sent by von Knorr, which was forwarded to the Admiralty and interpreted as follows:

> Southern minefield laid according to plan, northern not possible because of the watch [patrol], therefore sowed middle of bay and steamer track [shipping channel] favourable with mines. Although 72,059 (ship's name unknown) was observed, her character was not recognised; she laid mines unnoticed. Auxiliary cruiser crew of 98 perished, except 40 men and four officers, among them five severely wounded.[7]

The Admiralty informed the commander-in-chief High Seas Fleet about the mining of a shipping channel, possibly that between Rattray Head and Pentland Firth (a strait which separates the Orkney Islands from Caithness in the north of Scotland). Admiral Jellicoe was already aware of the two minefields laid to foul the approach to Cromarty and the Grand Fleet base at Invergordon. (Cromarty was a seaport and naval base on the southern shore of the mouth of Cromarty Firth, five miles seaward from Invergordon on the opposite coast.) A minesweeping trawler had discovered the mines the morning of 8 August, while making a routine sweep.[8]

LOSS OF HMS *RAMSEY*

HMS *Ramsey*, the ship sunk by the *Meteor* on 8 August southeast of Pentland Firth, was the former SS *Duke of Lancaster*. Built in 1895, she had been operated as a passenger ship by the Isle of Man Steam Packet Company immediately prior to the Admiralty requisitioning her for use as an armed boarding steamer. Fitted with two 12-pounder guns, the *Ramsey* was based at Scapa Flow under the command of Lt. Charles Raby, RNR. Many armed boarding steamers worked with cruiser squadrons and carried out examination duties at sea. Her duty involved night patrols, dangerous work directed by radio messages from headquarters, carried out with navigation lights extinguished, and guns manned throughout.[9]

Ramsey left the Orkneys at nightfall on 7 August to patrol to the eastward. In early morning, a sighting was made at 0400 of a merchant vessel, flying the Russian flag. *Ramsey* signaled the unknown ship to stop by hoisting the International Commercial Code Signal MN, and closed to about eighty yards to lower a boat, with the intention of boarding her. Without warning, *Meteor* fired a torpedo at *Ramsey*, swept her decks with machine gun fire, and fired 4-inch rounds into her engine room. Concurrently, she hoisted the German ensign and hauled down the Russian one. All of her guns and torpedo tubes had been concealed from view.[10]

The action was completely one-sided and over very quickly. Owing to the placement of *Ramsey's* two guns, she could only engage the *Meteor* with one of them. This gun was continuously under fire by the enemy, and all of the gun crew was killed. *Ramsey* sank in three minutes, with fifty-three men lost, including Raby. Owing to the starboard list of the sinking ship, only two boats got away. They had to clear her side quickly, and as a consequence most of her remaining crew took to the water. SMS *Meteor* recovered four British officers and thirty-nine men before shaping a course for Heligoland Bight.[11]

VON KNORR SCUTTLES SMS *METEOR*

At 0400 on 9 August, von Knorr used his wireless radio to report: (1) that he had sunk a Danish barque (the *Jason*); (2) to provide his position, course and speed; and (3) to request that a hospital ship be sent out to receive the British wounded. The Admiralty sent this intercept to Commodore Tyrwhitt. Tyrwhitt did not believe *Meteor's* position was accurate, based on the distance she could have travelled at 14 knots since her reported position at 1800 the previous day.[12]

Tyrwhitt based his search on *Meteor's* 1800 position, and followed a northeasterly course until noon. When about twelve miles from the *Horn Reefs* light vessel, he spread his cruisers in a line abreast on a course toward the Moray Fifth, taking the centre line himself in HMS *Arethusa*. Half an hour later, a ship was sighted ahead. As *Arethusa* and *Cleopatra* approached, the unknown ship appeared to be turning in a small circle. Drawing closer, they could see that she was settling by the stern and flew no flag. While still two miles distant, she sank rapidly.[13]

Only a few minutes earlier, *Cleopatra* had sighted a Swedish lugger, aboard which was apparently the crew of the sunken ship. Among the men on deck were some in British naval uniforms. When queried by the *Cleopatra*, "What ship is that?," the misleading reply had been, "*Ramsey*," upon which the light cruiser had ordered the lugger to steer southwest. Tyrwhitt, upon later receiving a report of this incident, turned back to rescue *Ramsey's* crew from the vessel. By 1530, they were all aboard the ships of his squadron, and he learned that the sinking ship had not been the *Ramsey*, but instead the one for which he had been searching. At 1638, Tyrwhitt reported to the Admiralty, "*Meteor* has been sunk."[14]

VON KNORR, OFFICERS AND CREW SLIP AWAY

As explained by Lt. Percy S. Atkins, RNR, the *Ramsey*'s senior surviving officer, von Knorr and the crew of *Meteor*, as well as the survivors from *Ramsey* and *Jason*, had been aboard the lugger with which *Cleopatra* had exchanged signals. Earlier, upon receiving a report from Zeppelin *L-7* that British cruisers were approaching the *Meteor*, von Knorr had decided to sink his ship rather than risk an action. When *Cleopatra* appeared on the horizon, he threw his code book overboard and hurriedly disembarked his crew and prisoners into a Swedish sailing vessel. He then opened *Meteor*'s seacocks and, as his final action, sent a message to the commander-in-chief High Seas Fleet, "Schiff wird versenkt" (ship sunk).[15]

Photo 11-2

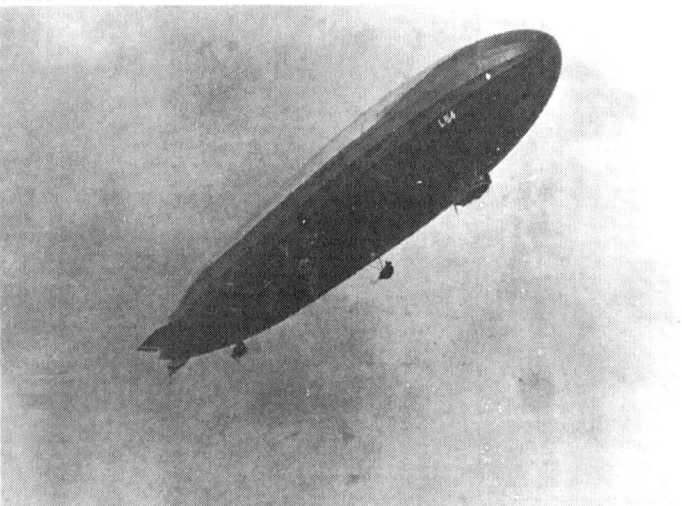

German Zeppelin *L-64*, which Britain acquired after the war.
Naval History and Heritage Command photograph #NH 60773

Atkins also explained why the British sailors were aboard a Norwegian lugger when ultimately rescued, and not the Swedish one in which the Germans had fled the scuttled *Meteor*. Aboard the Swedish vessel, there had been a dispute between the Germans and British about whether they should proceed southwest as directed. Von Knorr had allowed the British to sail her, and at some point they encountered a Norwegian lugger. Atkins proposed to Von Knorr that the British board her, allowing the Germans to proceed in the Swedish vessel. He agreed and as the *Ramsey* survivors were shifting into the other vessel, it occurred to von Knorr that they might need some money. He offered-up and insisted that Atkins should take £7, which, curiously, was in British banknotes.[16]

Photo 11-3

U-28 circa 28 April 1918 (then an Austrian submarine), with her periscope sheared off by a vessel ramming her as she was preparing to make a submerged torpedo attack. Naval History and Heritage Command photograph #NH 87758

Von Knorr and his crew reached the *Horn Reefs* light vessel near midnight on 9 August. There, they transferred the *Jason*'s crew to a Danish craft and continued their voyage in the lugger, subsisting on raw mackerel, biscuits, and potatoes. A submarine was sighted at 0600 the following morning. It proved to be the *U-28* which took the lugger in tow, and brought it into Lister Deep, a channel between the Horn Reefs and the Elbe River.[17]

BRITISH MINE CLEARANCE IN MORAY FIRTH

Much effort was required to clear the 380 mines laid by *Meteor* off the Moray Firth. On 18 August 1915, the minesweeping sloop *Lilac* located the easternmost field, when a mine blew off her bow and killed sixteen crewmen. Another minesweeping sloop, *Dahlia*, struck a mine on 4 September within a mile of the southern shore. She suffered four casualties. The whole mined area was defined by 10 September. A ten-mile wide channel was swept and maintained along the northern shore and a similar channel along the southern shore. The mines in the middle were left in place to form a defensive barrier.[18]

The fields offered no deterrence to movements of the Grand Fleet, and caught no large ships. While one or two trawlers and a couple of small coastal steamers were lost (in addition to the minesweeping sloops), it is unlikely the Germans considered this adequate compensation for the loss of *Meteor* and her potential to cause future damage to Allied shipping.[19]

ADMIRALTY DECIDES TO RE-MINE AMRUM BANK

As British minesweepers worked to clear the Moray Firth field, the Admiralty decided to mine Amrum Bank for a second time. Located in the North Sea, it lay about sixty-two miles from Heligoland. Orders were issued on 15 August 1915 for the operation. Only one minelayer, HMS *Princess Margaret* was to be employed, accompanied by two divisions of destroyers. As added protection, all available Harwich light cruisers and a third destroyer division were to cruise 30-50 miles to the westward of the minelayer while the operation was in progress—should the enemy make an attack, the destroyers were to keep contact with the minelayer, while maintaining a running fight.[20]

Princess Margaret left Sheerness in late afternoon on 16 August. The Captain-in-Charge of Minelayers, who was also her commanding officer, Frederick Litchfield-Speer, was in charge of the operation. He was met in Black Deep, a shipping route past the shoals in the North Sea and outer Thames Estuary, by two divisions of the 10th Flotilla. The squadron formed, then proceeded out G Channel into the North Sea. Speed was adjusted as necessary so as to pass Haisborough Light before it was extinguished at 0200, and to sight Horn Reefs light at night on 17 August.[21]

The passage of the minelayer and her escort was without incident until 1600 on 17 August, when German trawlers came into sight. As the squadron continued on its intended course, the number of trawlers sighted increased. Some flew no flags, and were considered to be German; while others were clearly Swedish or Danish. Litchfield-Speer believed that hidden among the fishing trawlers were some functioning as patrol vessels. Between 1800 and 1900, while still thirty miles from the *Horn Reefs* light vessel, he intercepted wireless signals in an unknown code. It seemed probable that these came from the trawlers. The light vessel was sighted twelve miles ahead at 2000, an hour after sunset. By this point, so many trawlers had seen the squadron and there had been so much signaling, Litchfield-Speer had little hope of being able to complete the operation unopposed.[22]

He was aware that a German destroyer flotilla was at sea and reconnoitering. The Admiralty had earlier learned from intercepted German signals that for unknown reasons the 2nd Torpedo Boat Flotilla was about to proceed to the north of Heligoland in the early afternoon on 17 August. (The ocean-going torpedo boats of the Imperial German Navy were in many ways the equivalent of the contemporary destroyers in other navies, and were often referred to as such.) Having fixed his position by the *Horn Reefs* light vessel, Litchfield-Speer proceeded at 15 knots on a southerly course toward the area he was to mine, hoping to escape notice in the dark. At 2025, he increased speed to 19 knots, the highest *Princess Margaret* could make. She led the squadron with the destroyers formed in columns, on her port and starboard quarter.[23]

ENEMY SIGHTED, GERMANS MAKE AN ATTACK

Unbeknownst to Litchfield-Speer, his squadron and the German torpedo boat flotilla he hoped to avoid were then approaching one another. The night sky was clear overhead with heavy clouds toward the east. Thus, the grey hulls of the German torpedo boats to the east (part of the 2nd Flotilla) were merged in overhanging thunderclouds, while the British showed up against the faintly illuminated western sky. At 2045, Litchfield-Speer sighted four torpedo boats a mile or so off to the southeast, three points (33-45 degrees) on the minelayer's port bow. He immediately came right to a northwest course, and increased to top speed, to put distance between *Princess Margaret* and the enemy. He assumed his escort had also seen the enemy and would engage them. While in the starboard turn, Litchfield-Speer heard a loud report astern, which he believed to be gunfire by one of his destroyers.[24]

In the German flotilla a few minutes earlier, the commander, KKpt. Heinrich Schuur in destroyer *B-98*, had sighted a large darkened ship

9,000 yards distant on his starboard beam. He altered course toward her at 21 knots, and soon sighted what he thought was a light cruiser and eight smaller ships in company with her. Realising that this was an enemy force, he decided to engage it using a running attack. At 2045, when a little more than 2,000 yards from the leading ship, he made a turn to port and fired two torpedoes.[25]

The first, aimed at the larger ship, missed. The second hit the leading destroyer, HMS *Mentor*, and exploded. The remaining British destroyers were manoeuvering, and no further attack was possible. None of the other German destroyers fired. The distance was too great, they were approaching at a large angle, and their view was obstructed by smoke from *B-98*'s funnels. Schuur made no attempt to follow up his initial success. Loud wireless signals which he heard immediately following the attack, suggested to him that strong British forces would soon be on the scene. Not wishing to hazard his flotilla against anything less than battleships, which he believed were unlikely to be approaching, he turned eastward and left the scene of action.[26]

HMS *MENTOR* TORPEDOED

The approaching Germans were seen by at least the destroyers HMS *Mentor* and *Morris*, the two division leaders, as well as by the *Princess Margaret*. But, glimpses of the enemy in the distance were so fleeting, an attack was not possible so long as the destroyers remained in contact with the minelayer. This they did, screening her after the German attack, per operation orders. Litchfield-Speer was unaware that *Mentor* had been torpedoed; believing that the explosion he had heard was either an exploding shell or gunfire. This seemed to be confirmed by a report from the officer-in-charge of *Princess Margaret*'s after guns that he believed *Mentor* had fired her forward gun.[27]

Thus, *Mentor* was unknowingly left behind by *Princess Margaret* and the other destroyers running at full speed, as she was taking on water from torpedo damage. At 1920, Litchfield-Speer made a turn to port, in preparation for commencing minelaying under the cover of a rain-squall. A few minutes later, he received a report from the *Morris* that she believed *Mentor* had been torpedoed. If this were true, it must mean that the enemy was aware of the presence of the squadron, and Litchfield-Speer decided to cancel the operation. He reported his action to Commodore Tyrwhitt (who was at sea in charge of the Harwich light cruisers and third Destroyer Division to the west) and set a return course for G Channel.[28]

Tyrwhitt, upon learning the *Mentor* had been torpedoed, proceeded to her last known position, calling for her at intervals on wireless telegraph. By 0703 on 18 August, having found no trace of her, and warned by the Admiralty that a superior German force had left the Jade Bight at 0400, he turned back in a rising wind and sea bound for Harwich. *Mentor* could not reply, the explosion having wrecked her communications equipment. She was badly damaged forward and settling by the bow, but Comdr. Edward T. Inman, by patching and shoring forward and flooding compartments aft, brought her to an even keel.[29]

Practically all navigational capabilities were gone, but Inman set a course westward, steaming first at 16 knots, later at 10 and then 8 as the seas increased. At 1530, off the entrance to G Channel, Inman sighted two British submarines, which reported her arrival to Harwich. *Mentor* reached harbour safely that same night, her only casualties were three men slightly injured.[30]

CONDUCT OF OPERATION QUESTIONED

The fact that German destroyers had been able to approach within a mile of the squadron, and torpedo a British destroyer without opposition, causing the abandonment of a carefully planned operation, prompted Admiralty interest. When queried, Tyrwhitt was critical of Litchfield-Speer's disposition of the destroyers in columns astern, and argued that their positioning should be at the discretion of the senior officer of destroyers present. The Admiralty did not agree, believing that disposition of escort ships should continue to remain in the hands of the Senior Officer under whom they were working.[31]

The Admiralty also asked Tyrwhitt for a statement regarding his views about the number and disposition of destroyers escorting minelayers in the future. His reply began with, "It is my opinion that the destroyers, whether stationed on the bow, beam, or quarter, could not have prevented the *Princess Margaret* from being attacked by enemy destroyers." An excerpt from his statement is provided in the quoted material at the chapter's head. Tyrwhitt believed that minelayers should only be sent out on the darkest nights, or during inclement weather; such operations should be conducted with the utmost secrecy; and "nightraiders" should carry out their work alone, so as to minimise the chance of discovery.[32]

THIRD ATTEMPT AT MINING AMRUM BANK

Three British minelayers—*Princess Margaret*, *Angora*, and *Orvieto*—sailed from the Humber at 0630 on 10 September, and proceeded toward Amrum Bank via H Channel. As in the previous month, a period of "moon darkness" was chosen; there had been a new moon the previous night. Each minelayer was escorted by two *M*-class destroyers at the disposal of Captain Litchfield-Speer, as he saw fit. In support, but not in contact, were the 5th Light Cruiser Squadron from Harwich and five destroyers of the 9th Flotilla, under Commodore Tyrwhitt embarked in the light cruiser *Cleopatra*.[33]

As the ships stood out to sea, it seemed, based on weather conditions, that the operation might be unusually hazardous. It was a brilliantly clear day with a cloudless sky, and it was followed by an extraordinarily light night considering there was only a sliver of a moon. It appeared to Litchfield-Speer that the minelayers could not escape being seen, if any German patrol vessels or airships were on the lookout. But no trawlers were sighted, nor Zeppelins. A further concern was *Orvieto*'s relatively slow speed, which reduced that of the squadron to 15½ knots. Based on these considerations, Litchfield-Speer decided to dispense with the destroyer escort, believing its absence would increase his odds of remaining undetected. At 1900, he sent them to join Tyrwhitt.[34]

In spite of the light night (Litchfield-Speer could easily recognise the features of sailors on the far side of the bridge of *Princess Margaret*), there was no indication that the minelayers had been observed either before or while laying the minefield. It was successfully sown between midnight and 0212 the following morning. The minefield consisted of 1,450 mines laid in three extremely irregular lines, which it was hoped would prove difficult for the Germans to locate and sweep. But subsequently, as was the case in other British minefields, some of the mines soon broke their moorings and came to the surface, revealing its presence.[35]

GERMANS CONCURRENTLY LAY ANOTHER FIELD OFF SWARTE BANK, SUPPORTED BY FLEET UNITS

As the British minelayers were executing their orders near Amrum Bank, two German light cruisers—SMS *Stralsund* and SMS *Regensburg*— were preparing to lay another minefield off Swarte Bank. Admiral von Pohl had decided to place another field in the North Sea, which might catch British forces en route to Heligoland Bight. The chosen site was to the northeast of Swarte Bank, where British forces were frequently reported, suggesting it was their favorite route to the Bight. As the loss of *Meteor* had shocked the Germans, and her loss hoped not to be repeated, Von Pohl involved the whole High Seas Fleet in the new minelaying operation, beginning with extensive reconnaissance.[36]

Air reconnaissance over the German Bight located several British submarines north of Tershelling Island, a member of the West Frisian

Island group in the northern Netherlands. On three occasions, bombs were dropped on them. In late morning on 11 September, an aircraft sighted a destroyer north of Ameland, another island in the West Frisian chain, and attacked it unsuccessfully. A preliminary defensive measure taken was the stationing of five submarines (including the newest boats *U-43* and *U-44*) roughly on the parallel of latitude 54 degrees, 30 minutes. Extending westward as far as the longitude of Swarte Bank, this line of U-boats was intended to serve as an extended screen on the northern flank of the fleet.[37]

Following reconnaissance and with the submarines in place, the German minelayers departed Wilhelmshaven, accompanied by the 2nd Scouting Group, in early evening on 11 September. They passed into the North Sea via a transit route between Norderney (an East Frisian Island) and the German coast. At 2030, Konteradmiral Hipper followed by the same route with the High Seas Fleet's battle cruisers and six destroyers, bound for his supporting position at 54°10'N, 4°30'E. An hour and a half later, Admiral von Pohl sortied with the battle fleet: 14 dreadnaughts, 7 older battleships, 6 light cruisers, and 37 destroyers. His station was twenty miles eastward of the battle cruisers.[38]

The two minelayers reached the specified area for the field in early morning darkness on 12 September. Working quickly between 0115 and 0224, *Stralsund* and *Regensburg* laid their mines in six groups. Each carried 140 mines, and as *Stralsund* completed the northern three groups, *Regensburg* took care of the others. A light cruiser preceded each minelayer, and for added protection each had an escort of three destroyers, positioned on its western side. By this means, the destroyers were free to attack any British ships sighted to the west, while the minelayers had open waters to the east should it be necessary for them to escape to their home ports.[39]

In returning to port, von Pohl took his force across the German Bight via Amrum Bank, because British submarines had been sighted many times outside the Norderney passage. At 0500, he steered for the *Amrum Bank* light vessel, completely unaware that his ships were headed for the British minefield laid the day before. Fortunately for the Germans, some of the mines had failed to maintain their depths and were visible. At 0900, the cruiser SMS *München*, scouting to the northeast of the fleet, sighted a mine ahead to starboard. Turning to port to avoid it, she found herself in a larger east-west oriented field. She directed a destroyer to sink the mine with gunfire and then reported the presence of the field.[40]

The message was not marked priority, and did not reach von Pohl until 0950, by which time the battle squadrons knew from reports made by destroyers screening northward of them that they were in mine-infested waters. Von Pohl altered course to clear the dangerous area, a move that steered his force toward the German minefield, which he intended to round. He shifted to a "single line ahead" formation, and then turned to the northeast to avoid the field. No sooner had the fleet steadied up on the new course than moored mines were sighted ahead.[41]

Von Pohl ordered a sharp turn to avoid them, but even when clear of the German field, and about to turn southward, the fleet had another narrow escape. *München* once again sighted mines, and the destroyer *G-196*, positioned 500 yards on the port beam of the battleship *Kaiser*, exploded one and nearly sank. Following the turn to the south, still more mines were sighted and it was obvious that the British had mined the area to the west of Amrum Bank. Yet, because some the mines had exposed themselves, the whole High Seas Fleet passed unscathed, with the exception of the one destroyer that was damaged.[42]

NEW GERMAN MINEFIELD CAUSES LITTLE HARM

The reports of sightings of British naval forces in the particular area, on which Von Pohl had based his selection of the site for the minefield laid on 12 September, proved to be inaccurate. British warships rarely traversed that area. Commodore Tyrwhitt in proceeding to and from Amrum Bank typically passed well north of the new field. Similarly, his usual course to Borkum (an island in northwestern Germany), led close to but clear of the southern end of the field. A month passed before any of the new German mines were evident. It was the fate of the Dutch fishing fleet to discover them. A mine exploded in a net on 8 October and again on the 13th. A Dutch lugger was also blown up on the 8th, but the position given for this event implied that the vessel had run into a mine from the southern of the two Dogger Bank fields. Mines reported from time to time associated with the new field, were assumed to belong to one of the existing fields, so no new danger area was identified by the Admiralty.[43]

UCs and a Raider, and British Ships Continue laying Mines

The best method of dealing with the whole question is to take Ostend and Zeebrugge, if the military authorities can be prevailed upon to cooperate.

—Vice Adm. Reginald Bacon, RN, commander of the Dover Patrol, expressing his belief that, following a series of setbacks in trying to deny German minelaying submarine access to British home waters, the best action would be to capture the German naval bases in occupied Belgium from which they operated.[1]

BRITISH LAY DEFENSIVE MINEFIELD OFF FLEET BASES AT SCAPA FLOW AND ROSYTH, SCOTLAND

In order to maintain dominance over the German High Seas Fleet, blockade German ports, and protect Allied shipping, the British Grand Fleet required freedom of movement. In an effort to deny Britain command of the seas—operating where it wanted, when it wanted—Germany desired to mine the approaches to the British Fleet bases at Scapa Flow and Rosyth. Such operations had little chance of success, except on the darkest nights when it might be possible for the ship(s) used to escape the attention of the Royal Navy.

The British, of course, well understood the enemy's intention. Thus, whenever the moon conditions made a German attempt at minelaying probable, the destroyer patrol to the southeast of Pentland Firth (the body of water separating the Orkneys from Caithness, Scotland) was sent out, with one or two cruisers in support, to intercept any German minelayers approaching Scapa Flow. Similar precautions were taken off Rosyth, Scotland.[2]

It was also determined that deep minefields should be laid off Rosyth where the British surface patrol might force enemy submarines to dive. On 2 October 1915, HMS *Paris* and *Biarritz* laid a single 2 ½-mile long row of mines (with the mine bodies 48 feet below the surface) east of Bass Rock, an island in the outer part of the Firth of Forth.

Known as the South Carr Minefield, its southern end lay a mile or so north of the South Carr headland. Five days later, the *Orvieto* laid 500 mines (at a 48-foot depth) near the North Carr at Fife. This was called the St. Andrew's Bay Field. (See Map 12-5, near chapter's end.)[3]

BRITISH MINE GERMAN BIGHT

In a separate action, *Paris* and *Biarritz* laid a shallow field (12-foot depth) of 259 mines in the German Bight on 13 October. This was done to try to prevent German naval forces from coming out of the Bight into the North Sea. The minelayers were escorted by the light cruiser HMS *Penelope* and four *M*-class destroyers, with the rest of the Harwich Force in support. The destroyers parted company with the minelayers after nightfall, and the light cruiser led *Paris* and *Biarritz* to a spot fifteen miles north of where the minelaying was to commence, and then left the minelayers to finish their work alone.[4]

Map 12-1

North Sea coast of Germany

The resultant minefield stretched between 54°3'N, 6°46'30"E, and 54°1'30"N, 6°22"E. It remained undiscovered by the Germans for a week, who mistakenly assumed it to be part of an earlier field.[5]

BRITISH MINE BORKUM AREA AGAIN

The Royal Navy soon undertook another expedition to mine the exits from the German Bight. The operation order tasked *Princess Margaret* and *Angora* to lay an east-west oriented zigzag minefield, about ten miles north of the field laid on 13 October. The two minelayers were to be escorted by six Harwich destroyers and a light cruiser to a point forty miles north of Borkum Island. The escort would then part company as the two ships continued on alone to where they were to commence minelaying, one working eastward and the other westward. Captain Litchfield-Speer was in charge of the minelayers and their escort. Previously titled Captain-in-Charge of Minelayers, his position was now denoted Captain (M).[6]

Map 12-2

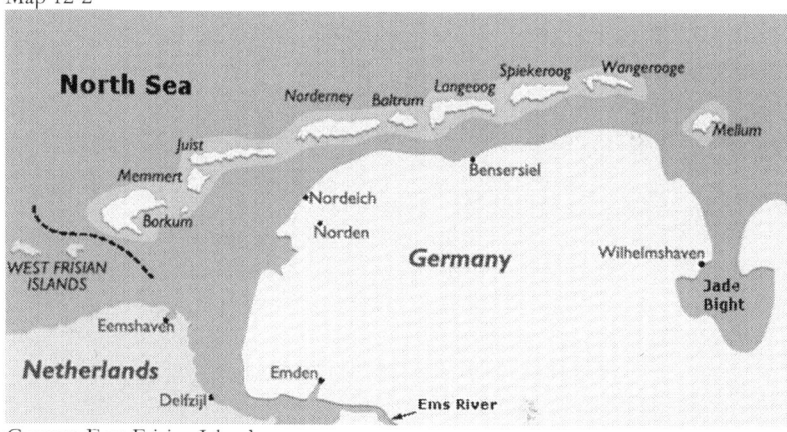

German East Frisian Islands

Litchfield-Speer left the Thames with the minelayers in heavy weather on 7 November 1915, and was joined by his escort (light cruiser HMS *Cleopatra* and six *L*-class destroyers) the next morning off the *Cross Sand* light vessel. While serving as the guide for the minelayers in darkness and drizzling rain, *Cleopatra* collided with a fishing vessel. She was undamaged, but stopping to lower a boat to provide assistance, *Princess Margaret* and *Angora* went on without her. The weather worsened and rain and seas breaking over *Angora*'s deck flooded her mining chamber and lifted a mine off the rails. Lt. Comdr. Malcolm Maxwell-Scott, RN, ordered the mine's firing levers removed, probably saving his ship from being blown up. The mine became jammed in the trap, but was got overboard with crowbars.[7]

Angora would lay 14,729 mines during her Royal Navy service. The British were critical of her slow speed and low drop point, which made minelaying in following seas difficult to impossible. However, she was well equipped to load mines, using her normal winches to lower them into her mining chamber through hatches.[8]

In spite of the adverse conditions, the two ships were able to lay a field of 850 mines, in a fifteen-mile long irregular line stretching from 54°10'N, 6°25'E to 54°12'N, 6°56'E. Fortunately, no German patrols appeared, and the greatest danger faced by *Princess Margaret* and *Angora* was from the mines they had just sown. Litchfield-Speer observed about the operation, "I do not think that mines could have been safely laid an hour or two later when the wind and sea increased."[9]

During the operation, Commodore Tyrwhitt had been cruising in support near Terschelling with the rest of the Harwich force. On account of the gale, he ordered the seven destroyers which had come out with him to return to port. One of these, HMS *Matchless*, was en route to Harwich on 9 November (via the swept channel off Orfordness) when at 1755, a mine exploded under her stern. She did not sink and was towed into port. The mine was one laid by German submarines in their attempts to sink vessels on the English coast.[10]

WORK OF GERMAN UC BOATS

During October 1915, seventeen vessels had struck mines laid by UC boats in the Dover and Nore areas, and the task of sweeping and directing ships clear of danger had become very arduous. The mines were the result of the activities of *UC-1, 3, 5, 6, 7,* and *9,* of which *UC-6* carried out five operations. Sixteen different locations were mined, including for the first time even the approaches to Portsmouth.[11]

One of the vessels mined was the paddler HMS *Brighton Queen*. The mine which exploded under her paddle box (while she was engaged in sweeping a passage for monitors bombarding Ostend) was part of a field laid by *UC-5* in the West Deep off Nieuport. (These Belgian coastal towns are also spelled Oostende and Nieuwpoort, as on the following map.) Vice Adm. Reginald Bacon, the commander of the Dover Patrol had been using his monitors to bombard the German-occupied Belgian coast whenever weather conditions were favourable. Bacon had replaced Rear Adm. Horace Hood in April 1915. Bombardments were continued on German batteries or positions of military value throughout autumn, but remarkably there was no special effort to concentrate on Zeebrugge, with the objective of curtailing the submarine minelaying campaign.[12]

Photo 12-1

British monitor HMS *Abercrombie*. Her 14-inch guns, manufactured in the United States, were originally intended for the Greek battle cruiser *Salamis*. The turrets could not be delivered, and the Royal Navy immediately purchased them and outfitted a class of monitors, designed for shore bombardment.
Naval History and Heritage Command photograph #NH 63153

Map 12-3

North Sea coast of Belgium

The UC boats did not emerge unscathed from their dangerous operations.   The most active of the diminutive submarines *UC-6* (commanded by Oblt. z. S. Paul Günther) had two accidents.   In early October 1915, she was rammed by a British destroyer but escaped with slight damage.   Mid-month she became entangled in a net northwest of Calais, France.   A section of the netting fouled her screw and, although she managed to free herself, with her mobility impaired, she had to return to port with her mines still on board.   Her luck ran out under similar circumstances later in the war.   She was sunk on 28 September 1917, in a mined net off the North Foreland (a chalk headland forming the eastern end of the Isle of Thanet, on the coast of southeast England) with the loss of all hands.   Another example of entanglement was *UC-7*.   On 20 October 1915, she was caught up in a net while off the Humber River.   Oblt. z. S. Franz *Wäger* managed to free his submarine, but also failed to lay mines.[13]

UC-9 (Oblt. z. S. Paul Schürmann) was lost at sea during this period, cause unknown.   After leaving Flanders on 20 October to lay a field south of the *Longsand* light vessel, she failed to return and all hands were assumed lost.   The body of her chief engineer washed ashore two weeks later on 12 November 1915.[14]

VIABILITY OF THE DOVER BARRAGE SUSPECT

Although most of the mines laid by German submarines (and resultant shipping losses) were in the Thames Estuary and elsewhere along England's east coast, some were laid westward of the Dover Straits.   The discovery of mines in this location raised doubts about the effectiveness of the Dover barrage.   The Folkestone-Gris Nez boom, intended to be an impassible barrier to prevent German submarines from the North Sea from attacking ports in southern England, proved impractical to maintain.   Laid between Folkestone (a port town in southeast England) and Cape Gris Nez in northern France, it consisted of weighted steel nets attached to heavy wire hawsers stretched between anchored buoys and floated between individual sections of timber each weighing four tons.   After three gales, only one section was left completely intact.   As corrective actions could not be pursued that winter because of weather and sea conditions, the commander of the Dover Patrol was summoned to the Admiralty for a conference on the situation.[15]

The general conclusions arrived at were: (1) cease efforts during the winter to maintain nets and floats, (2) salvage all floats and nets that were possible to recover, (3) maintain a mock defence of buoys connected by hawsers without nets in the hope of inducing submarines to come to the surface to avoid the fake barrier, and (4) reduce the plant and boom defence establishments at Boulogne in northern France, and at Folkestone.[16]

Admiral Bacon had also by this point begun to lose faith in the value of a drift net barrage. Previously when the primary threat had been German torpedo submarines operating by day, the nets and British destroyer patrols had formed a fairly efficient barrier across the channel, as the presence of the destroyers forced submarines to dive down into the nets. After the principal enemy became minelaying submarines operating on the surface at night, the conditions had changed. Moreover, it was not difficult for submarines to deduce the positions of the nets from the state of the tide, and the Germans had access to unnetted ship channels along the British and French coasts.[17]

UC BOATS LAY STILL MORE FIELDS IN NOVEMBER

The approach of winter conditions seemingly made little difference to the UC boats, which in November 1915 laid mines at eleven locations. Two areas were mined twice. All were in English waters, except for Havre, Bassure de Baas, and Boulogne, France.

UC Boat-Laid Minefields in November 1915

UC	Location	Mined	Commanding Officer
UC-1	Elbow Buoy	twice	Oblt. z. S. Egon von Werner
	off Margate	once	
UC-3	*Galloper* light vessel	twice	Oblt. z. S. Erwin Wabner
UC-5	*Sunk* light vessel	once	Oblt. z. S. Herbert Pustkuchen
	Dover	once	
	Bassure de Baas off Boulogne, France	once	
UC-6	Boulogne, France	once	Oblt. z. S. Matthias Graf von Schmettow
	Havre, France	once	
UC-7	Kentish Knock	once	Oblt. z. S. Franz Wäger
	Longsand Head	once	
	Covehithe	once[18]	

On the night of 6 November, a submarine passed within thirty yards of a group of drifters operating explosive nets placed to intercept UC boats transiting at night by the Ruytingen Buoy along the French coast. The submarine missed the nets, and because none of the drifters possessed guns, she was able to proceed unopposed on a southwesterly course. The following morning, two sightings were made near Ruytingen Bank of what may have been the same boat. On the other side of the channel, an armed trawler fired on a different UC twelve miles southwest of Folkestone Gate.[19]

UC-8 CAPTURED BY DUTCH AFTER GROUNDING

Against the vessel losses resulting from UC-boat laid mines, could be placed the loss to Germany of *UC-8* commanded by Oblt. z. S. Walter Gottfried Schmidt. On 4 November 1915, the submarine ran aground on the Dutch coast (52°23'N, 05°05'E) while on passage to Flanders. Although the Netherlands maintained a state of neutrality in WWI, Dutch vessels towed her in to port at Terschelling. *UC-8* was sold to the Netherlands and served as the Dutch submarine *M-1*. Her captain and crew were interned at Nieuwediep and Alkmaar, Netherlands.[20]

UC MINEFIELDS OF DECEMBER 1915

In December, UC boats laid seventeen fields, consisting of twelve mines each. Two were in the Nore area at the Kentish Knock (a shoal in the North Sea, east of the Thames Estuary), and several others were on the borders of the Nore and Lowestoft areas. The Dover command area was the most heavily mined, with six new fields: one at the *South Goodwin* light vessel; two at the buoy marking the Elbow shoal; one in Folkestone Gate (off the same named port town); and one each at Calais and Boulogne, on France's northern coast.[21]

Map 12-4

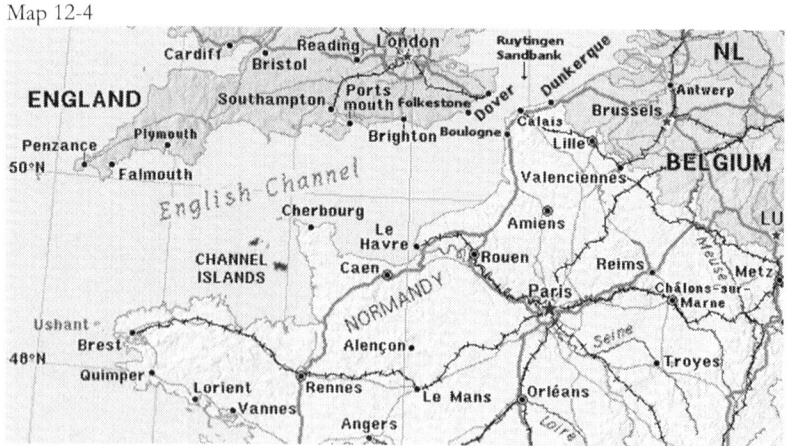

The Dover area, Dover Strait and adjacent coasts of England and France

Admiral Bacon believed that the UC minelayers were entering his area from the French coast, and not from his own swept channels, and he was able to convince the French to reorganise their minesweeping and drifter services similar to those at Dover. In sharing their duties, it was agreed the British would patrol northward from Boulogne to the Ruytingen buoy at the exit of the strait, and the French eastward from this buoy toward the French coast. It was decided that the British should sweep the cross channel routes to within three miles of Boulogne, and from Dunkirk (also spelled Dunkerque) around the *Dyck* light vessel, while the French, in turn, swept northeast from Dunkirk along the coast to the Whistle Buoy in the West Deep.[22]

When Bacon took over command of the Dover patrol in April 1915, he had appointed Capt. William Howard, RN, CTP (Captain, Trawler Patrol) and Lt. Comdr. Walter Rigg, the Port Minesweeping Officer, as his assistants. Howard's trawlers had the duty of minesweeping, as well as protection of the shipping routes and merchantmen in the Dover area from submarines. Of the trawlers in his command, some two dozen were on patrol for four-day shifts in all weather. They never left their assigned areas to take shelter. After completing their shifts, the next four days were theoretically spent in port "resting." In actuality, seventy-five present of the vessels supposed to be in harbour returned to sea with only a minimum rest period. They would actually be at sea for three days out of the four-day rest period. Their duties included escorting ships with particularly important cargos, cross-Channel steamers, cable-ships, Trinity House steamers and the like.[23]

Bacon's conviction that UC boats were not using swept channels proved incorrect. In December, *UC-6* succeeded in navigating the East Coast Swept Channel as far as the Humber and laying a field. This incident marked the first time one of these boats had managed to get as far as the command of Admiral Ballard. Ballard was newly appointed Rear-Admiral Commanding, East Coast of England, on 6 November 1915 after the former office, Admiral of Patrols, was abolished.[24]

BRITISH ENACT NEW MINESWEEPING PRACTICES

Trawlers owing to their low speed, usually tow the mines in their sweeps without parting the moorings. To make the mines show themselves they are towed on to a selected dumping ground where the water is shallow and the sweep is there slipped.

—Rear Adm. Edward Stafford Fitzherbert, RN, who on 6 December 1915 had relieved Rear Adm. Edward F. B. Charlton, RN, in command of the Minesweeping Service, describing the dangerous duty of hired minesweeping trawlers.[25]

On 2 January 1916, the British minesweeping trawler *Mediator* blew up about one mile from Spurn Lighthouse (located at the tip of the Spurn peninsula, which forms the north bank of the Humber Estuary), while bringing in a sweep wire—fortunately without loss of life. Four days later another trawler, the *Courtier*, was sunk with the loss of eleven of her crew. A witness to this tragedy wrote about the ship's loss, "There was just the explosion, a cloud of steam and nothing left but bits of wreckage."[26]

The loss of *Courtier* brought into question the practice of towing moored mines ensnared by sweep wires into shallow water, where the sweep wire could be slipped (released) along with the explosive affixed to it. The disadvantage of this practice was that mines slipped by trawlers (which required three fathoms of water in which to operate due to their deep draughts) were not always exposed so that they could be detonated by rifle fire. This meant they might remain intact to blow up the next minesweeper which came to the same dumping ground. This was likely the cause of the loss of *Courtier*, whereas *Mediator* was probably blown up by a mine caught in her sweep wire.[27]

A new technique was introduced to rid sweep wires of mines, in which a pair of minesweepers streaming a shared sweep wire would pass inside a second pair of minesweepers streaming the same type gear, approaching from the opposite direction. At least in theory, the sweep wires of each of the pairs of ships would cross, with the clean wire stripping away the mooring cable (and its associated mine) fouled in the other wire. (Presumably, the introduction of serrated sweep wire later that year ended this tenuous practice.)[28]

RAIDER SMS *MÖWE* MINES WHITEN HEAD BANK

Every one of them knows that the wilder the storm, the more certain we can be of escaping publicity. And everything depends on this; for if the enemy should get the slightest wind of what is happening here right under his nose, his minesweeping divisions would be at work the very next day, disinfecting the infected area after their own fashion. But, thank heaven, our dear cousins on their island have no suspicions.

—KKpt. Nikolaus zu Dohna-Schlodien, commanding officer of the German raider *Möwe*, describing the relief felt by his crew that strong wind and rain, followed by snow and hail, helped to shield their activities (laying mines to the west of the Orkney Islands) the night of 2-3 January 1916.[29]

The year 1916 opened in a period of very dark nights (the moon being new on 4 January), especially favourable to surface ship minelaying. Facing these conditions, Admiral Jellicoe issued orders for special patrols intended to intercept any German minelayers before they reached the entrances to his Grand Fleet bases. Between 2 and 10 January a pair of cruisers or flotilla leaders would continuously be on eastward patrol. Jellicoe further ordered a similar patrol to be carried out from Rosyth when weather permitted.[30]

The British patrols failed to detect the movements of the German raider SMS *Möwe*, which on the night of 2-3 January began laying a large field of 252 mines between Strathy Point and Cape Wrath (on Scotland's northern coastline).   *Möwe* was on her way into the Atlantic to commence her maiden cruise as a commerce raider. After sowing the first part of the field off the dangerous rocky coast, bad weather forced the minelayer to heave to, as heavy seas broke over her. For an entire week, the *Möwe* was hurled about, rolling and pitching wildly, with the efforts of her crew focused on keeping the bow of the ship into the sea. When the weather moderated a week and a half later, the German ship finished the field and then steamed away from the coast in bright sunshine. (The book's preface offers additional details about this "wolf in sheep's clothing.")[31]

LOSS OF THE BATTLESHIP HMS *KING EDWARD VII*

On 6 January, the battleship HMS *King Edward VII* left Scapa Flow on a voyage around the northern coast of Scotland to Belfast without an escort. Because of rough seas, destroyers could not keep up with her without the possibility of damage from hull pounding. *King Edward* was only thirty miles west of Pentland Firth, when in late morning there was a violent explosion under her starboard engine room. Capt. Crawford Maclachlan, RN, attributed it to a submarine-fired torpedo, and reported this in his damage report to Jellicoe. Jellicoe immediately sent flotilla leader HMS *Kempenfelt*, twelve destroyers, and all available tugs, out from Scapa to assist the battleship. Recognising that a mine might be responsible, he warned the ships en route to the scene of this possibility. (A mine was responsible, one laid by *Möwe*.)[33]

Map 12-5

Scotland's Pentland Firth

When they arrived, they found the battleship listed 8 degrees to starboard with both engine rooms flooded, because the door between them had been open at the time of the explosion. A tug and the *Kempenfelt* took her in tow, but half an hour later the tow line parted and fouled the *Kempenfelt*'s propeller. The beleaguered *King George VII* was now listing considerably, and was low in the water. The wind and sea were rising, and there was every chance she might sink that night before making port. Maclachlan decided to abandon her, and the crew disembarked into four destroyers. Three went into harbour, the fourth, aboard which Maclachlan was embarked, remained near the disabled ship until she rolled over and sank at 1950. Following loss of the battleship, Admiral Jellicoe observed that, "enemy minelaying is by far the most dangerous menace to Fleet or Mercantile Marine that we have to encounter."[33]

The area between Cape Wrath and longitude 3°40'W was at once proclaimed dangerous, and a route for colliers and store ships proceeding from the west of Scotland into Scapa Flow avoiding it was specified on 8 January 1916. Light draught vessels were instructed to hug the shore between Cape Wrath and the Orkneys. The day before the new routes were enacted, the Norwegian cargo ship SS *Bonheur* struck a mine near Stack Skerry, a remote volcanic island to the west of the Orkneys, so named because it rises 150 feet out of the sea. With her stern shipping water, *Bonheur* started to sink within a few minutes. The crew launched two open lifeboats and scrambled aboard. Each boat was equipped with four oars, as well as mast and sail, providing two means of propulsion. The northwesterly winds drove them toward the north coast of Scotland. Despite foul weather and nearly freezing temperatures (4°C that night), they landed in pounding surf, on a rocky shore near the village of Armadale (on the north coast of Scotland).[34]

Further evidence of a minefield was furnished by a German mine drifting ashore in Thurso Bay, on the north coast of Caithness, Scotland, on 14 January 1916. To locate the mines all available minesweeping sloops and gunboats left Scapa on 9 January, but because of weather and sea conditions were forced to take shelter until mid-month. It was not until 28 January that they found any of the mines laid by the *Möwe*. Once located, her minefield was treated in the same fashion as *Meteor*'s in the Moray Firth, by clearing a channel through it. This work was impeded by a series of gales, but seventy-one mines had been removed by May.[35]

UB ATTACKS ON FISHING SMACKS RESUME

In January 1916, attacks on the Lowestoft fishing fleet so prevalent the previous summer, resumed. On 17 January, the smack *Acacia* came into port and reported that she had been fired on by a submarine but had escaped. Her skipper, James Crooks had captained one of the smacks destroyed by UB boats in August 1915, and had made up his mind not to lose another fishing vessel.[36]

Crooks had been fishing when the submarine fired on *Acacia* at a range of about a mile. He left his gear down until the enemy had approached closer and stopped on the smack's windward quarter. Crooks then quickly cut the trawl rope and put her helm hard up. As the breeze filled her sails, the smack sprang ahead, straight for the submarine, which only had just time to submerge before being rammed. With no possibility of further action, Crooks sailed for Lowestoft and made his report; the holes in his sails and spars providing concrete proof of his story. The Admiralty expressed its appreciation of his conduct and awarded him £50 compensation for the damage his boat had suffered.[37]

Following the arrival of *Acacia* at Lowestoft, Capt. Alfred Ellison, RN, Senior Naval Officer, sent out two motor launches and two trawlers to search for the submarine. These efforts failed to prevent the destruction of three smacks around noon the following day, some thirty miles southeast of Lowestoft. The procedure was the same in each case. The submarine commander stopped the smack with rifle fire, made her crew bring the vessel's papers to him and then sank her with a bomb. The crews of each of the smacks noticed seeing a fish's head painted on the submarine's bow, with projections (gills) sticking out on each side. The submarine displayed no number, and did not appear to carry a deckgun.[38]

The Germans questioned British crewmen about whether any of the smacks in the fishing fleet were armed. They answered none were, as the previous decoy smacks had been paid off. With the resumption of attacks on sailing craft, Ellison took four smacks—*Fame*, *Foam Crest*, *Energic*, and *Telesia*—fitted them with 3-pounder guns, and manned them with suitable crews including four naval ratings. He also equipped two drifter-trawlers with trawl gear and a gun in each, with a petty officer and gunlayer in addition to the usual crew. The six decoy vessels were then sent out to fish with the smack fleet.[39]

Before they could provide any deterrence, the smack *Crystal* was destroyed by a submarine on 27 January, and four days later, four others on the same fishing grounds were similarly destroyed. These were the British *Arthur William*, *Hilda*, and *Radium*, and the Belgian *Marguerite*. On the first day in February, the armed drifter-trawler *Kentish Knock* arrived on the scene. That evening, an object fouled her trawl wire and a submarine surfaced fifteen yards away. The petty officer manning the gun aboard *Kentish Knock* got off three rounds, one exploded at the base of the conning tower of the submarine, which heeled over and disappeared in the darkness. *Kentish Knock* was awarded £100, but apparently no permanent harm was done the enemy. Postwar records do not reflect the loss of a UB boat around this period.[40]

The skippers of the *Radium* and the *Hilda*, who had skippered two of the smacks sunk the previous summer, reported that the submarine which had sunk their vessels appeared to be a different and larger class than their previous assailants. The UB I boats were ninety-two feet in length with a 14-man crew, while the later UB II boats were larger at 118 feet, and carried 23 men. Both classes carried only two torpedoes and had no deck gun. Much larger UB III boats were built from 1916-1919. At 181 feet, they were double the length of the UB I class, and had twice the crew complement with 34 men. Most importantly, these upgraded coastal attack boats carried 10 torpedoes (fired from 4 bow tubes or 1 stern tube) and was fitted with one 88mm deck gun.[41]

UC MINEFIELDS OF JANUARY-FEBRUARY 1916

Apart from the mines laid by the *Möwe*, all the enemy minefields put down in 1916 were from submarines. Their deadly cargos gradually appeared farther and farther afield as more and larger UC-boats were commissioned. Some of the boats still worked from Zeebrugge, while others attached to the High Seas Fleet operated from the Elbe River. The High Seas Fleet UC boats worked north of Flamborough Head; while the Flanders UC boats were responsible for the English east coast from Flamborough Head to Dover, as well as the English Channel, the Irish Sea, and the Irish coast as far west as Waterford.[42]

In January 1916, despite bad weather, the little boats *UC-1*, *3*, *5*, *7*, and *10* succeeded in laying thirteen minefields. *UC-3* was responsible for the one farthest west, which she laid in the first week in January off Boulogue; and *UC-7* for the one farthest north, placed off the mouth of the Humber at month's end.

Victims of Minefields laid by UC Boats in January 1916

Period	UC	Location	Victims
1st week in January	*UC-3*	off Boulogne (2 fields)	*Breslau*, damaged but made it into Boulogne
1st week in January	*UC-3*	South Goodwin	*Traquair*, sunk 12 January off Dover pier
middle of January	Believed *UC-1, 5*	near South Knock Buoy (2 fields)	4 ships damaged, 2 sunk 18-29 January. French *Leoville* and Dutch *Maasdijk* sunk. 1 British, 1 Norwegian, and 2 Dutch ships (including the liner *Rijndam*) damaged.
end of January	*UC-7*	off Humber River mouth	*Viking*, damaged on 29 January near Colbart, made it into Chatham[43]

The February fields were even more destructive than those laid in January. There were fifteen in all, comprising a total of 178 mines. It is believed that twenty-two vessels struck mines; an average of one ship to every eight mines, attesting to the effectiveness of the UC laid mine as a weapon. Partial data associated with vessel losses follows.

Minefields laid by UC Boats in February 1916

Date	UC	Location	Victims
10 February	*UC-6*	Folkestone	
10 February	*UC-7*	east of Harwich	*Arethusa* sunk on 11 February
20 February	*UC-6*	Folkestone	Liner *Maloja* sunk 2 miles from Dover Pier. Another merchant ship, two minesweepers (*Angelus* and *Weigelia*), and a patrol trawler also lost in field.
22 February	*UC-3*	Bassure de Baas	
27 February	*UC-4*	South Downs	
27 February	*UC-5*	Calais	
27 February	*UC-6*	Dover[44]	

Fortunately, despite the repeated mining of Folkestone in southeast England, and Boulogne in northern France, not a single ammunition or troop transport was lost during this period. In January and February 1916 over 150 military ships crossed from Newhaven and Folkestone to Boulogne.[45]

HMS *Firedrake* Captures German Submarine *UC-5*

One machine gun, usually unshipped; 12 mines placed in pairs, one above the other, in six slanting mine tubes forward; no torpedoes…. For surface running one 4-cycle Daimler motor [diesel engine] running at 550 revolutions; H.P. [horsepower] about 85.

—Technical details about *UC-5*, obtained during interrogation by the British Naval Intelligence Division of the crew of the captured minelaying submarine.[1]

A bright spot for the Royal Navy occurred on 27 April 1916, when the destroyer HMS *Firedrake* captured a German coastal submarine, *UC-5*, after it inadvertently ran aground on Shipwash Shoal, off Suffolk in the vicinity of Orfordness Lighthouse. The minelaying submarine, a product of the Vulcan Shipyard in Hamburg, was quite new, having been commissioned only ten months earlier on 19 June 1915. Upon leaving the builder's yard, she had joined the Flandern U-Flottille under the command of KKpt. Karl Bartenbach. The flotilla was a part of the Marinekorps Flandern (Flanders Naval Corps) under Adm. Ludwig von Schröder, who was commonly referred to as the Löwe von Flandern (Lion of Flanders). Schröder commanded all Flanders-assigned naval infantry, aircraft, coastal artillery, and the bases at Brugges, Zeebrugge, and Ostend, plus the Flanders Flotilla.[2]

UC-5 was part of a class of fifteen *UC-1* submarines built in 1914-1915 which were the first operational minelaying subs in the world. Powered by one Daimler-Motoren-Gesellschaft or Benz six-cylinder, four-stroke diesel engine, the diminutive 111-foot boats could make a maximum of 6.2 knots on the surface or 5.2 submerged. A glaring weakness of the small, economically built boats was the absence of either a deck gun or torpedo tubes for self-defence. This resulted from a decision by the vessels' architect to maximise space available to carry mines. With these type subs having but a single machine gun available when on the surface, it's not hard to imagine a crewmember of a boat preparing to leave on a mission, being advised by a friend to, "keep your head down, mate" (German equivalent of this British expression). Despite these shortcomings, *UC-5* had enjoyed much success since joining the flotilla. Her mines which she had laid in British waters had sent scores of Allied ships to the bottom. A few fortunate vessels were only damaged.[3]

OLt. z. S. Ulrich Mohrbutter was in command of the *UC-5* when she was captured. Since taking over the boat from Oblt. Herbert Pustkuchen (her first captain) on 18 December 1915, ten vessels had fallen victim to his mines. Four of these were British, three Dutch, and one each, Danish, French, and Norwegian. Seven of the ten vessels were sunk; one was able to beach after being hit, but was a total loss; and the remaining two were damaged. The most aggrieved victim was likely the 303-ton fishing trawler *Khartoum*. Nine persons aboard her were lost, including Able Seaman Fred Lindo.[4]

Vessels Sunk or Damaged by Oblt. Ulrich Mohrbutter

Date	Ship	Tons	Nat.	Fate
1 Feb 1916	SS *Prinses Juliana*	2,885	Dutch	Beached near Felixstowe, Suffolk, but a total loss
15 Feb 1916	SS *Bandoeng*	5,851	Dutch	Damaged 4 miles south of the *Kentish Knock* light vessel at Thames' mouth
20 Feb 1916	SS *Dingle*	593	British	Sunk 10 miles SW of the *Kentish Knock* light vessel
21 Feb 1916	tanker *La Flandre*	2,018	Dutch	Sunk near *Galloper* light vessel in a Thames' Estuary
24 Feb 1916	SS *Tummel*	531	British	Sunk 7 miles S of the *Kentish Knock* light vessel
26 Mar 1916	SS *Hebe*	1,494	French	Sunk 6 miles E of *Sunk* light vessel 51°53'N, 01°46'30"E
26 Mar 1916	FV *Khartoum*	303	British	Sunk 6 miles NE of the *Longstone* light vessel, Farne Islands, NE England
27 Mar 1916	SS *Harriet*	1,372	Danish	Sunk 5 miles E of *Sunk* light vessel 51°53'30"N 01°45'E
31 Mar 1916	SS *Clinton*	3,381	British	Damaged 4 miles SE of Lowestoft
31 Mar 1916	SS *Memento*	1,076	Norwegian	Sunk 1½ miles SE of the Pakefield Gateway Buoy, off Lowestoft

UC-5 had laid two rows of mines off the *Shipwash* light vessel on 17 January, and two weeks later off the *Sunk* light vessel. It was not until the SS *Prinses Juliana* struck one of the mines near the latter location that Harwich-based minesweepers located the field. In February, *UC-5* laid mines off the *Kentish Knock* light vessel, which damaged the SS *Bandoeng*, and sank SS *Dingle* and SS *Tummel*. The submarine revisited *Sunk* light vessel in mid-March, followed by (right on schedule) a visit two weeks later to the *Corton* light vessel area off Lowestoft. During January through March, *UC-5* mined areas near the British light vessels with such regularity, that it became possible to predict the dates of her visits with almost certainty.[5]

UC-5 DEPARTS ZEEBRUGGE ON FINAL MISSION

Minelaying submarine *UC-5* left her base at Zeebrugge (a very busy and important commercial harbour on the coast of Belgium) on 26 April to lay a field of twelve mines one mile east of the *Shipwash* light vessel (off Harwich in the North Sea) the following day. Harwich, a port town in Essex, England, lay at the junction of two estuaries forming one of Britain's major harbours. However, most freight shipping operated from Felixstowe, a short distance to the south, rather than from Harwich itself.[6]

Photo 13-1

Paddle-minesweepers HMS *Snowdon* and HMS *Bourne* off Harwich on 15 April 1918. Naval History and Heritage Command photograph #NH 110567

From the start, the mission was beset with problems. While running on the surface, outbound from the Belgian coast on 26 April, the *UC-5* encountered fog. Normal aids to navigation—the Thornton Bank Buoy and the *North-Hinder* light vessel—were not visible, and the *Galloper* light vessel had been moved. A sighting was made of an unidentified light vessel, which was not helpful as its position was uncertain. Further, although the presence of shipping traffic provided some indication as to the submarine's position, it offered no indication of the correct course to Shipwash Sands. Unable to get a navigational "fix," Mohrbutter proceeded on an estimated best course, which took into account the effect of the current.[7]

UC-5 was still running on the surface around midnight when she grounded. Mohrbutter believed they were then east of Shipwash. Unfortunately, the water was ebbing when the submarine grounded, which stranded instead of floating her free. The ebb tide continued, and three hours later, at low water, she was nearly "high and dry." Later, at about 0600 on 27 April, on the rising tide (and after lightening the boat by throwing all unnecessary weight overboard), the submarine came free by backing full astern. Wanting to be out of sight when the sun came up, Mohrbutter set a northeast course into deep water and dove. A periscope view of the water's surface at daybreak revealed hazy, intermittently foggy weather conditions, and calm seas.[8]

Although freed from the previous night's predicament, circumstances turned worse for the crew of *UC-5*, as Mohrbutter described in a postwar report to the German Admiralty (Admiralstab):

> A lightship was seen through the periscope. In order to identify the ship, and to gain information for navigating, we waited for slack water before approaching her. Our position soon became untenable, as dozens of patrol craft with search gear and flocks of destroyers were all around and over us. At 0915, we proceeded toward the Lightvessel submerged. The periscope was used sparingly due to the number of patrol boats. The Lightvessel had neither name nor insignia. We steered to escape the sea [evade shoal water], the searchers and to gain deep water. At 1015 we ran aground in 30 feet of water. We immediately blew the [ballast] tanks and went full astern. The boat remained stuck fast, the current pushed us farther into the sand, and the boat rolled onto her side.[9]

With *UC-5* heeled over on her port side, only a rising tide and one or more tugs could have freed her from the sandbar. Unable to back clear before she rolled over—despite having used Utmost Speed (575 revolutions)—Mohrbutter also could not wiggle off the bar, having but a single propulsion engine and propeller available to him. (The commander of a submarine with two engines and both a port and a starboard screw, could have went ahead on one engine and backed the other full, in an effort to twist free.) *UC-5* was stuck, in plain view of any passing warship, with only a single machine gun for self-protection. If this wasn't bad enough, her load of mines could kill everyone aboard, if detonated by enemy naval gunfire.[10]

Mohrbutter radioed Zeebrugge to report his situation and to seek assistance. Unfortunately for him, the British intercepted the message and ordered the destroyer HMS *Firedrake* to the scene. Upon sighting a warship racing toward his position, Bohrbutter ordered his crew to abandon, and to destroy the submarine with scuttling charges. For his part, the destroyer's captain, Comdr. Aubrey Tillard, RN, upon noticing that the entire crew of the submarine appeared to be on deck, brusquely invited the Germans to surrender.[11]

The war was over for Mohrbutter and the other seventeen men. But, moments before obeying orders to board the destroyer, a member of the crew still inside the submarine set off explosive charges. A time delay fuse allowed him, and the Germans already up on deck to leave safely. Mohrbutter's intention was to totally destroy the *UC-5*. To accomplish that, scuttling charges were placed so as to detonate the mines, but for reasons unknown, that did not happen. Instead, the only damage done was a hole blown in *UC-5*'s pressure hull, enabling the British to capture the submarine intact, after a diver rendered the mines safe. (The Germans contended that she was awash at high water, making her salvage rather easy.) As reported by *The Naval and Army Record of London* journal:

> It was an act of heroism on the part of a young officer that rendered the submarine capable of being brought in as a prize. The officer went down in a diving suit and made the mines safe by detaching the detonators, afterward securing them in such a position that the salvers could work in comparative safety.[12]

Earlier and in preparation for scuttling, with *UC-5* stuck fast on the sandbar and rolled onto her side, Mohrbutter had ordered the submarine rigged for destruction. The codebooks, machine gun, and rifles were thrown overboard, and charts with minefield locations annotated on them were burned. Machine manuals and signal books were also destroyed. At least one important item was overlooked. The British recovered her war log intact, and from it learned that U-boats were passing through the Dover Straits defences with ease. *UC-5*'s capture also gave the British the opportunity to closely examine the type mines the UC-boats were laying. The Germans were not pleased.[13]

Photo 13-2

German submarine *UC-5* with the British ensign flying over the German naval ensign, following her capture by HMS *Firedrake* and salvage operations on the scuttled U-boat. Naval History and Heritage Command photograph #NH 111091

UC-5 DISPLAYED IN BRITAIN AND AMERICA

Mohrbutter and all of his crew were taken by HMS *Firedrake* to Harwich and turned over to the naval authorities. Later *UC-5* was also brought to Harwich to enter dry dock for hull repairs. According to *The Times*, she arrived in London on 24 July 1916, lashed to the tug *Princess* and under tow by the tug *Bruno*. The captured U-boat was exhibited on the Thames at Temple Pier to generate funds for war loans and charities. Later she was shipped to America for similar purposes.[14]

To add insult to injury, *UC-5* also appeared on at least two British postcards. A sample of one is provided below. The original card had a scroll in the upper left corner, which proclaimed proudly:[15]

CAPTURED GERMAN
UC-5
MINE LAYING SUBMARINE
BY AUTHORITY OF THE ADMIRALTY
JULY 1916

Diagram 13-1

Cutaway drawing of German minelaying submarine *UC-5*.
Naval History and Heritage Command photograph #NH 111095

Comdr. Aubrey Tillard, RN, who had commanded the *Firedrake* since 5 January 1915, was mentioned in despatches for his part in the capture. (A service member mentioned in despatches was one whose name appeared in an official report written by a superior officer and sent to the high command, in which was described their gallant or meritorious action in the face of the enemy. Despatches were published in the *London Gazette*, an occurrence that became known as "being Gazetted.") Tillard was promoted to the rank of rear admiral on 16 October 1932, and placed on the Retired List the following day, but his maritime service to the Crown was not over. On 28 August 1939, he was appointed to SS *Malabar* as Convoy Commodore. Rear Admiral Tillard passed away on 12 December 1952.[16]

Oblt. Ulrich Mohrbutter was promoted to Kapitänleutnant on 17 May 1919. He continued what would be a 21-year naval career, and then became a German film producer. Mohrbutter died on 21 January 1971 at Birkenstein, Bavaria.[17]

British Minelaying Success
at Battle of Jutland

The present proportion of strength forbids us in the first place seeking a decisive battle with the concentrated forces of the English fleet. But our strategy must also prevent a decisive battle being forced on us by our opponents.

Systematic and steady pressure must be exerted on the enemy to force him out of his attitude of waiting, and compel him to send forces against us, which will offer us favourable possibilities of attack. On the other hand, we must not allow the enemy's feeling of superiority to grow so strong that he will not hesitate to bring us to action when he will.

—From a memorandum by German Admiral Reinhard Scheer, titled Guiding Principles for Sea Warfare in the North Sea, issued on his appointment as commander-in-chief High Seas Fleet in February 1916. His aims were to be obtained by: submarine warfare, mine warfare, war against trade in the north, and active employment of the High Seas Fleet in sorties.[1]

Following commencement of the war, until mid-1916 naval forces of Britain's Grand Fleet and Germany's High Seas Fleet had only engaged one another in skirmishes at Heligoland Bight and Dogger Bank. Two fleets with such power could inflict great damage, but both were aware that a decisive loss to the other would leave their respective nations vulnerable to attack.

The British navy in the North Sea was based at Rosyth, Cromarty and Scapa Flow, from which it could protect the central and northern areas of the North Sea and stop the German High Seas Fleet from getting into the Atlantic where it could attack Britain's merchant fleet. The British believed that German surface forces would not attempt to rush the English Channel and face the might of the British navy based in Portsmouth and Plymouth. Therefore, providing the Royal Navy retained its advantage, German surface warships could only operate in the North Sea.[2]

Taking advantage of her superior naval strength, Britain had, by 1916, achieved an effective blockade of Germany. Germany's northern coastline was very small, and restricting the maritime supply of goods to the Central Powers, which included Germany, Austria-Hungary and Turkey, was relatively easy. This was done by denying entry into German ports to ships carrying foodstuffs and military materiel. Admiral Reinhard Scheer, upon taking over command of the High Seas Fleet from Admiral von Pohl in January 1916, decided that the blockade was causing too much damage to Germany.[3]

To break the blockade, Scheer wanted to lure, out of their respective naval bases, components of the British fleet and, using a combination of submarines and surface ships, attack and destroy them. On the night of 24-25 April 1916, the German Navy attacked the coastal towns of Lowestoft and Yarmouth, seeking a response from the British fleet. In May, Scheer ordered Konteradmiral Franz Hipper to sea with forty ships to move along the Danish coast. The news of this movement soon reached Admiral Jellicoe in Rosyth. He viewed the movement of such a large force as threatening, and ordered the Grand Fleet to put to sea. The Battle of Jutland began on 31 May 1916.[4]

BATTLE OF JUTLAND

The bloodiest naval battle of the war pitted 151 British warships against 99 German ships, involving tens of thousands of sailors. Fought over two days from 31 May to 1 June 1916, it marked the first and only time the two battle fleets confronted each other, and was the only fleet action fought between dreadnoughts (modern battleships) until the latter stages of World War II.[5]

The Grand Fleet lost fourteen ships and 6,000 sailors, most of them aboard three large battle cruisers—HMS *Indefatigable*, *Invincible*, and *Queen Mary*—destroyed with few survivors. The High Seas Fleet suffered the loss of 2,500 sailors and eleven ships, including the heavy cruiser SMS *Lützow* and pre-dreadnought battleship *Pommern*. A wide range of warship types took part in the battle. (The Naval Order of Battle is provided in Appendix B.) The focus of this chapter is on the actions of HMS *Abdiel*, the only minelayer present.[6]

FIRST PHASE OF THE BATTLE

Locating the enemy proved to be a reasonably difficult task. Because the distance surveilled was too vast for reconnaissance aircraft, both fleets sent out fast cruisers to discover the location of their opponents. In late afternoon on 31 May, the scouting forces of Vice Admiral David Beatty and Konteradmiral Franz Hipper commenced a running artillery

duel at fifteen thousand yards in the Skagerrak (Jutland), just off
Denmark's North Sea coast. The opposing forces opened fire at one
another at a distance of about ten miles, and though they were a smaller
force, the initial advantage was with the Germans who were assisted by
the lay of the sun blinding the British gunners. The German ships took
a severe pounding but survived due to their superior honeycomb hull
construction. The British lost three battle cruisers due to lack of
antiflash protection in the gun turrets, which allowed fires started by
enemy shells to reach the powder magazines.[7]

Map 14-1

North Sea coast of Denmark

The British battle cruiser *Indefatigable* (Capt. Charles Sowerby) was hit by salvos fired by the German battle cruiser *Von der Tann*. The resultant explosion of *Indefatigable*'s magazines and her subsequent sinking brought about the loss of the lives of a thousand men. Less than thirty minutes later, the battle cruiser HMS *Queen Mary* (Capt. Cecil Irby Prowse) was destroyed. She sank after a gun round from the battle cruiser *Derfflinger* detonated one or both of her forward magazines. The explosion broke the *Queen Mary* in half near her foremast; of her crew, 1,266 were lost while only twenty were rescued.[8]

The position of the British became more difficult when Hipper's battle cruisers of the 1st Scouting Group were joined by Scheer's High Seas Fleet. Jellicoe's force was about fifteen miles from Beatty's force when the fleet battle started. As the two opposing fleets converged, the British suffered a third major loss when the battle cruiser HMS *Invincible* (Capt. Arthur Lindesay Cay) was sunk shortly after 1830. She was lost at the climax of the Battle of Jutland, along with all but six of her crew of 1,031. The actual engagement of the two battle fleets at Jutland lasted only a few minutes before the heavily outnumbered German High Seas Fleet retired. But during this action *Invincible* was the lead British ship. Taken under fire at the short range of 9,000 yards, she (just like the two other battle cruisers destroyed earlier in the battle) blew up in a massive conflagration, and sank in less than a minute, giving little chance for any of her crew to escape.[9]

MAIN BATTLE

Commenting, "There seems to be something wrong with our bloody ships today," Beatty, after this initial encounter, turned north and lured the Germans onto the Grand Fleet. The second phase of the battle started at 1915, when Admiral Jellicoe brought his ships into a single battle line and, gaining the advantage of the fading light, prevailed in the exchange of gunfire. Admiral Scheer's ships took seventy direct hits (while scoring but twenty against Jellicoe), and escaped certain annihilation only by turning away and running for German waters.[10]

JELLICOE ORDERS *ABDIEL* TO MINE WATERS IN PATH OF RETREATING GERMAN NAVAL FORCES

Soon after the main battle commenced, the minelayer HMS *Abdiel* took her station close to Jellicoe's flagship (the battleship *Iron Duke*). *Abdiel*, with a full load of mines, was effectively a floating magazine of high explosives which could easily have been detonated by a single enemy shell, whilst her own 4-inch guns did not have the range to participate in the fleet action. However, *Abdiel* remained unscathed and the main action was broken off at about 2100 when the outnumbered German fleet began to retire toward Wilhelmshaven.[11]

At about 2130, *Abdiel* (Comdr. Berwick Curtis, RN) received orders to proceed at high speed toward the German coast to extend a minefield the ship had previously sown off the Horn Reefs on 3-4 May 1916, and in the path of the retiring German fleet. To execute these orders' tasking, Commander Curtis would have to take *Abdiel* through the opposing squadrons and get ahead of the German fleet.[12]

HMS *ABDIEL* (G35)

Photo 14-1

British minelayer HMS *Abdiel*, circa 1916-1918.
Photograph SP 3155 from the collections of the Imperial War Museums

Abdiel was a bright and shiny new destroyer-minelayer, having been commissioned only weeks earlier on 26 March 1916. She had been laid down at the builder's yard (Cammell Laird in Birkenhead, on the west bank of the River Mersey, opposite the city of Liverpool) on 6 May 1915. One of seven *Marksman*-class flotilla leaders built during the war, *Abdiel* was 324 feet in length, with a 31-foot beam. Her three Parsons turbines (fed by four Yarrow boilers) producing 36,000 shaft-horsepower, were capable of propelling her through the water at a speed of 34 knots.[13]

Like other British flotilla leaders, the *Marksmen* were significantly larger than the typical destroyers of the day, in order to accommodate the flotilla commander ("Captain (D)" in Royal Navy parlance) and his staff, and their necessary signaling gear. All of the *Marksman*-class ships had four funnels, and were armed with four quick firing 4-inch guns and torpedo tubes. The guns were mounted one each on the forecastle, one each between the first three funnels and one on a bandstand on the quarterdeck. *Abdiel* and *Gabriel* were fitted as fast minelayers, for which purpose the after 4-inch guns and torpedo tubes were removed. The area freed up by these modifications accommodated a load of mines, hidden from view behind canvas panels from the fourth funnel to the stern.[14]

Photo 14-2

HMS *Abdiel* alongside the light cruiser HMS *Aurora*, both with a full load of mines. Imperial War Museum photograph

COMMANDING OFFICER'S ACCOUNT

Up until the opposing battle fleets met, the *Abdiel* was with the 4th Light Cruiser Squadron, stationed 5 miles ahead of the Battle Fleet and steaming in line abreast, ships a mile apart. When the fleets sighted each other and the deployment signal was made, the 4th LCS proceeded to its station ahead of the line. Comdr. Berwick Curtis described in a letter the actions of his ship as well as the British Fleet itself:

> *Abdiel* remained where she was until the fleet had nearly completed deploying, by which time the "overs" [gun rounds whose trajectories are too high to hit their intended targets] from the Germans, strafing two of our four-funneled cruisers about half a mile south-west of us and the three battle cruisers led by *Invincible* about half a mile to the south-east of us, came buzzing about and bursting round us.
>
> I, therefore, legged it round the head of our battle line, which had finished deploying, and managed to get through four lines of destroyers taking up their position ahead of the fleet, and finally got to my battle position half a mile or so on the disengaged beam of the *Iron Duke*. Here we remained until dusk. At about 9.30 pm I got orders to proceed to a position south of *Vyl* Lightship [off Esbjerg, Denmark] and lay a line of mines.
>
> We therefore went off at 32 knots, passing on our way several ships in the distance, and also a flotilla of sorts which were making a great deal of smoke, but as we were not making any smoke ourselves, we presumably were not seen. We reached our position about 1 a.m., and laid the mines, then returned to Rosyth for another load, passing south of the big North Sea mine area.[15]

HMS *Abdiel* was not hit during the battle, and did not participate in any action with German warships, but did get "a very good view of the whole show between 6 and 8 p.m." Naval combat unwitnessed by *Abdiel* persisted throughout the night and following morning, as both fleets continued in smaller actions to suffer damage and ship losses. In concluding his modest account, Commander Curtis wrote, "We had 80 ordinary mines and 10 Leon mines on board, all primed, so perhaps it is just as well that we weren't hit. The ship did exactly what she was intended to do, justified her existence, and that's all there is to it."[16]

SMS *OSTFRIESLAND* DAMAGED BY BRITISH MINE

At 0620 on 1 June, as the German battle fleet retired, pursued by the British, the battleship SMS *Ostfriesland* struck a mine believed to be one previously laid by *Abdiel* on 4 May 1916. The explosion tore a 40 foot by 16 foot hole in her starboard side, allowing 500 tons of water into the ship. Further flooding occurred after her torpedo bulkhead gave way. The damaged battleship made port, but required drydocking in Wilhelmshaven for repairs, which lasted until 26 July 1916.[17]

SIGNIFICANCE OF THE BATTLE OF JUTLAND

Based on the greater losses inflicted against the larger British fleet, the German Navy claimed victory. However, the battle was a strategic success for Britain. After the battle, the Grand Fleet remained a powerful fighting force whereas the German High Seas fleet by choice was not. Having been bloodied, the German Naval Command did not want to endure the risk of further losses so the fleet remained in port, preserving British naval supremacy for the remainder of the war.[18]

Photo 14-3

German battle cruiser SMS *Seydlitz* badly damaged but under way while en route to port after the battle of Jutland, circa 1-2 June 1916. Her bows are nearly submerged due to torpedo and shell hits forward.
Naval History and Heritage Command photograph #NH 59637

Comdr. Berwick Curtis was promoted to the rank of Captain on 30 June 1916, and also became a Companion of the Distinguished Service Order. At least one of his crew, Leading Stoker Harold Wright, was also awarded the DSO. Among his officers and crew, there were likely other recipients of awards for valour, but the *London Gazette* in providing notice of such events to its readers, usually did not associate particular individuals with the command to which they were assigned when they earned the award.   Curtis would eventually retire as Vice-Admiral Berwick Curtis, CB, CMG, DSO, Royal Navy.

Photo 14-4

Dockyard hands standing by the side of the light cruiser HMS *Chester*, where a shell impacted during the Battle of Jutland, 31 May 1916. Note the missing rivets. Naval History and Heritage Command photograph #NH 50164

GERMANY ISSUES COMMEMORATION RIBBONS TO RAISE MONEY FOR CHARITIES

Like other countries, German did various things to raise money on the home front during World War I. Each drive for the German Red Cross or other charities was called a Stiftung. One of the more interesting ways to solicit donations was the Nagelpfosten, or nail post. A ribbon (like the one for the *U-Deutschland* on the far right in the set of five, below) was pasted on a post and people bought nails to drive into them. The nail drivers had to follow the picture, so that when the picture was fully nailed, the rim, ocean, and submarine were covered, leaving the sky and the lettering visible. The center commemoration ribbon was issued following the Battle of Jutland.

Photo 14-5

World War I Commemoration Ribbons issued to raise money for the German Red Cross and other relief societies. These examples memorialise L-R: the loss of the raider SMS *Möwe*, February 1916; the Naval Airship Service; the Battle of Jutland (Skagerrak) 1916; the submarine *U-21*; and the merchant submarine *U-Deutschland*.
Naval History and Heritage Command photograph #NH 2733 (first four ribbons from left to right); photograph on the far right, courtesy of Dwight Messimer

15

British Mining Policy, First Use of Submarines, 1916

Submarine E.24 is to leave Harwich at 5 p.m. on March 4 and proceed past Amrum Bank to the east of Heligoland to lay mines ENE from lat. 54.1½ N, long. 8.14 E, in 8 fathoms.

The mines should be laid within one hour of slack water.

It is most important that the limits of the minefield as laid should be known, and that no mines should be laid unless the accurate depth of water is known.

After the mines are laid you are to return to Harwich.

—Operation orders for HMS *E-24*'s first minelaying mission.[1]

BRITISH BEGIN USE OF SUBMARINE-MINELAYERS

At the beginning of 1916, British mining policy was: (1) to reinforce the offensive minefields in the Heligoland Bight on the routes leading north and west from German ports, and of the defensive minefields across the southern parts of the North Sea; (2) to lay deep mines, reinforced by mine nets, around the occupied part of the Belgian coast; (3) to lay deep and shallow independent minefields as required off the English and Scottish coasts, and (4) to mine the entrance to the Dardanelles.[2]

Much of this agenda could be carried out by surface ships, but such operations in the Heligoland Bight were becoming increasingly hazardous. Needing a stealthier means to mine the Bight, the British developed a special S-type mine (employing German type Hertz horns) to be laid by specially configured *E*-class submarines. Recognisable by their bulbous sides, flat deck, and general whale-like appearance, the "E boats" were the backbone of the Royal Navy's submarine fleet. Six under construction in 1916 were modified to carry twenty "S" mines, by fitting vertical chambers into the submarines' ballast tanks. Ultimately, this adaption proved ineffective. The mine carrying capacity of the submarines was limited, and the mines had to be of special design to fit into the chutes.[3]

The mine in each chamber was carried upside down, resting on a pad at the bottom, and held in position by a pin penetrating into its side near the top of the chamber. In dropping, the pad was swung clear, and the pin withdrawn, releasing the mine. The mines fell from their chambers with a loud clatter. Submariners dislike unnecessary noise, particularly in enemy waters. Although pertaining to British E-class submarines, a 1918 U.S. Office of Naval Intelligence publication highlighted this flaw to its readers. "Incidentally, this noise is quite distinctive and can be heard for some distance by surface craft, but more especially by submarines and hydrophone flotillas. Mining operations are often given away by this means when no occular evidence of the submarine exists. Hydrophones are being rapidly developed, and with some types, flotillas can now detect at a distance of 6 miles a submarine proceeding submerged at 2 knots."[4]

Photo 15-1

British E-type submarine (probably HMS *E-1*), circa 1913-1914.
Naval History and Heritage Command photograph #NH 43131

When completed, the six submarines were allocated to the 9th Flotilla, based at Parkeston Quay (now Harwich International Port) at Harwich. *E-24* was ready for service in February 1916. Conditions aboard all E-class submarines were pretty rudimentary and extremely cramped for the 30-man crew, there was just one bunk which the three officers shared; the ratings slept where they could. The heads (toilets) were more often than not a bucket.[5]

The table below provides summary information about the British and German submarine-minelayers. The latter's large ocean minelaying submarines (UE I/UE II) are included for reference purposes, but are not discussed in the book.

British Minelaying Submarines

Type Class	Length feet oa	Displ. tons sm	Speed knots sm/sf	No. Mines	No. Deck gun/ Torpedoes	Crew Size O/E
E-class	181	807	15/10	20	1 12-pounder 10 torpedoes	3-O/27-E

German Minelaying Submarines

Type Class	Length feet oa	Displ. tons sm	Speed knots sm/sf	No. Mines	No. Deck gun/ Torpedoes	Crew Size O/E
UC I	111	183	6.2/5.2	12	0/0	1-O/13-E
UC II	162	493	11.6/7.0	18	1-88mm/7	26 men
UC III	184	560	11.5/6.6	14	1-88mm/7	32 men
UE I	186	832	10.6/7.9	38	1-105mm/4	32 men
UE II	267	1,512	14.7/7.0	42	1-150mm/14	40 men[6]

Key: sm (submerged), sf (surfaced), oa (overall), O (officer), E (enlisted)

E-24's career was short-lived. She left Harwich the morning of 21 March, on her second mission to lay mines in the Heligoland Bight. Lt. Comdr. George Naper's orders were to arrive at the Bight via the Amrum Bank, and to enter on the surface in darkness. He was to lay his mines in a zigzag pattern, and return via the same route. *E-24* failed to arrive back at Harwich, and was logged as missing on 24 March 1916. The cause of her loss was unknown, but believed likely due to mines and perhaps her own. No additional mines were laid by British submarines until June 1916.[7]

Decades later, divers hunting for a World War II-era U-boat found a submarine wreck broken into three pieces. During recovery in July 1974, only the midship section, that included the conning tower, was raised. The wreckage was towed to Cuxhaven on Germany's North Sea coast, where it was identified as a British *E*-class rather than a German submarine. Inspection of the hull indicated that *E-24* had indeed hit a mine. The remains of twenty-five of the crew were recovered and buried in Hamburg Ohlsdorf Cemetery. Artifacts from *E-24* and her crew, such as tobacco pipes belonging to Lieutenant Commander Naper, the sextant, a pistol, and boots are on display at the Wrackmuseum (Wreck Museum) in Cuxhaven, as are also the conning tower and propellers.[8]

   Three more submarines—*E-41*, *E-45*, *E-46*—were commissioned as minelayers in 1916, and two—*E-34*, *E-51*—in 1917. Later in the war, *E-34* would also be lost to a mine. She sailed from Harwich the morning of 14 July 1918 (on her twenty-fourth trip to the Bight) to lay mines off the Dutch island of Vlieland. On the morning of the 20th, she was mined near the Eijerlandse Gronden (a sandbank located between Texel and Vlieland, in the Dutch West Frisian islands); there were no survivors.[9]

BRITISH SUBMARINE-MINING RESUMES

British use of submarines to mine German waters resumed in June 1916. On 10 June, *E-41* laid seventeen mines some eight miles southeast of Amrum Light. Returning from her mission, *E-41* set off again on 21 June, and deposited another nineteen mines just off Norderney. While she had been laying her mines on 10 June, German minesweepers fifty miles northwest of her had just found the mines laid by HMS *Abdiel* on 3 May. The flotilla leader had been commissioned a fast minelayer in March 1916 to provide a suitable surface ship for operations in the Bight. She and the submarines carried out the bulk of the remaining operations that year. However, HMS *Princess Margaret* also laid two fields, and *Biarritz* one that year. In total, seventeen fields comprising 1,782 mines put in the Bight in 1916.[10]

Photo 15-2

Load of mines aboard the destroyer-minelayer HMS *Abdiel*.
Naval History and Heritage Command photograph #NH 540

There were other changes as well that year outside of the forces employed in the Bight.   At the beginning of 1916, the minesweeper *Gazelle* (converted to lay mines off the Dardanelles) was replaced by *Perdita*, a 500-ton former merchant vessel fitted out to carry 500 mines. In April the 4,500-ton *Wahine*, formerly of the Union Shipping Company of New Zealand, took the place of *Orvieto*.[11]

E-41 OVERCOMES DIFFICULTIES IN LAYING MINES

In July, *E-41* (Lt. A. M. Winser) laid two fields, each of twenty mines, in the Bight. The first was put down on 5 July, some ten miles northeast of Heligoland, and the second, six miles north of Borkum, on the 22nd. She experienced difficulties in laying the second field. As the submarine reached the area she was to mine on 22 July, she had to dive. (There is no explanation of why this occurred in official British Naval history consulted.) "A bad bump caused one of the bow tube torpedoes to override its stop, and it started running. The inboard vent of the tube was open, and exhaust gases filled the boat, making the men sick." Lieutenant Winser, however, laid his mines and coming to the surface off the Ems River mouth, aired out the boat. While on the surface, *E-41* was sighted by a seaplane, which dropped ten bombs around her. Fortunately she suffered no damage and was able to return to port.[12]

UC-7 FAILS TO RETURN FROM MINING MISSION

To the south, in July, UC minelayers from Flanders were carrying their loads with ant-like assiduity across the North Sea to an area south of Flamborough Head. Some thirteen fields (of twelve mines each) were laid during the month: 5 off Yarmouth, 2 off Southwold, 1 off Aldborough, 4 in the Calais and Dover area, and 1 off the Thames. These were responsible for mining five ships making their way up the east coast in the War Channel. However, one of the enemy submarines responsible paid dearly.[13]

UC-7 (Oberleutnant zur See Georg Haag) left Zeebrugge with *UB-19* on 3 July, to lay mines off Elbow Buoy at the north entrance to the Downs. She never returned. On the night of the 6th, the motor boat *Salmon* (192) commanded by Lt. Temple West, RNVR, was patrolling off Southwold. She was one of the ex-civilian pleasure craft making up the Yacht Patrol Organisation. Their craft, crewed by RNVR personnel with yachting experience, carried out local and harbour patrol duties. At midnight, West was monitoring the vessel's hydrophone and heard an underwater noise like "a wind whistling through a pipe." The noise gradually grew louder until the dull hum of what seemed to come from an electric dynamo (used by submarines when running submerged) could be heard.[14]

West decided to make a depth-charge attack and increased speed before the drop to get the boat safely away. The charge exploded 100 yards astern; followed almost immediately by a terrific explosion, which threw up a column of water fifty feet high and gave the *Salmon* a violent shake. Myriad large bubbles rose to the surface, and nothing more was heard in the hydrophone. A ship transiting the area that forenoon (the period of daylight before noon) reported seeing a great circle of oil close to the spot.[15]

Whatever *Salmon* destroyed, or exploded, in darkness apparently was not the lost coastal minelaying submarine. The Germans doubted the claim that *UC-7* had been depth-charged off Southwold, because the position was so far west of her operational area. Their doubt was supported by the fact that the bodies of two members of her crew washed ashore on the Flanders coast on 19 July, suggesting that she had hit a mine off the Belgian coast. This has now been confirmed. The wreckage of *UC-7* was found by marine archaeologist Tomas Termote off the Belgian coast, near Rabs Bank at the mouth of the Scheldt River.[16]

Minefields regularly and persistently laid by UC boats off the east coast during the summer proved clearly that a net zareba constructed earlier in the year off Zeebrugge had not fulfilled its purpose.[17]

BELGIAN COAST "ZAREBA"

I often had visions of finishing the war in a German prison camp. On many occasions our little fleet would consist of three paddlers and the old Marshal Soult, *or some other monitor equally fast and furious (about five knots), and our own escort of destroyers often out of sight on some job or another. Twelve miles away on our starboard beam was Zeebrugge with all its ultra-modern [German] destroyers. Why the Germans never tried to cut us off was a mystery. It would have been simple.*

—Comdr. Alexander D. Thompson, RNR, who in 1917 commanded
the hired paddler *Duchess of Montrose* as a lieutenant,
recalling duty off the Belgian coast.[18]

The principal British minelaying task of 1916 was establishing a complex of mines, nets and buoys in the North Sea off Belgium intended to curtail German movements off the occupied coast where her submarines were based. The British referred to this barrier as a zareba—in reference to improvised stockades constructed of thorny bushes in parts of Africa. The first minefields were laid on 24 April, and the barrier of double lines of deep contact mines and fifteen miles of mined nets between Ostend and the River Scheldt was virtually complete by the end of May. It was patrolled all summer.[19]

The nets, which were intended to ensnare and destroy enemy submarines, were fitted with a new type of 65-lb electro-contact mines. The batteries for the mines were housed in empty mine cases secured to the jackstays supporting the nets. Maintenance was difficult in the German-occupied waters, and stretched the resourcefulness of the British torpedomen involved. Periodic servicing of batteries and testing of electrical connections and insulation, when carried out under enemy fire and in rough seas was extremely difficult.[20]

No new German minefields were found in the English Channel between 17 April and 17 May, suggesting to Admiral Bacon that the barrage was fulfilling its intended purpose. However, it was later learned that on 29 April: *UC-10* had mined Southwold, and *UC-1* north of *Galloper* light vessel. In May, various UC boats visited points from Margate on England's southeast coast, northward to the Corton Sands, demonstrating that the Flanders boats were finding a way around the barrage without prohibitive difficulty. *UC-5* discovered the zareba on 25 April 1916. After informing Zeebrugge, she proceeded along the barrier until she found a gap, then passed through and continued toward the English east coast. It was on this mission that she grounded and was captured by HMS *Firedrake*; see Chapter 13.[21]

PADDLE-SWEEPERS SENT TO BELGIAN COAST

For many months, from April 1916 until the end of the war, British paddle-sweepers (a half-dozen or more at a time) were stationed at Dunkirk. They were employed sweeping northeast from Nieuport, up the Belgian coast to the approaches to Antwerp in the Scheldt Estuary, along the barrier laid to stop Zeebrugge-based U-boats from entering the English Channel. The route—also regularly patrolled by British destroyers and monitors—lay an average distance of twelve miles off the coast, meaning on a clear day, it was possible to count the individual windows in the hotels and other large buildings on the waterfront in Ostend.[22]

The first six of the paddle-sweepers had arrived at Dover on 14 July 1915. They were acquired and fitted out by Lt. Comdr. Walter Rigg, who was also occupied in training newly-reported officers and men. These sweepers were the *Albyn* (ex-*Albion*), *Balmoral*, *Duchess of Montrose*,

Jupiter II, *Marmion II*, and *Ravenswood*. All were familiar to excursionists on England's south coast and Bristol Channel. They were augmented by six more paddlers with names equally familiar. Commanded by RNR officers, with crews comprised of officers of the RNVR, and manned by volunteers from every walk of life and every profession, the paddlers had earlier done yeoman service off Dover, and the Belgian coast during bombardments of Zeebrugge and Ostend. The paddlers could sweep at 10-11 knots, and thus cut the moorings of mines, instead of dragging them in their gear as was the case for the slower trawlers. Additionally, because they drew no more than 9½ feet of water, they were at much less risk of being blown up by mines than were trawlers which drew 14-15 feet.[23]

However, paddlers, like all minesweepers, were not immune from hazards of their tasking including being destroyed by the mines they were trying to remove. The first paddle-sweeper lost was the *Brighton Queen* on 6 October 1916. While sweeping at night off Nieuport, she hit a mine and sank almost immediately, with the loss of six crewmen. One additional man died the following day from his wounds. Their deaths reminded everyone of the great danger associated with mine clearance operations after dark, when cut mines could neither be seen, destroyed by rifle fire, nor evaded if lying in the path of a vessel.[24]

The paddle-minesweepers *Albyn*, *Brighton Queen*, *Cambridge*, *Devonia*, *Duchess of Montrose*, *Glen Avon*, *Jupiter II*, *Kempton*, *Lady Ismay*, *Marmion II*, *Ravenswood*, and *Westward Ho* all received Battle Honours BELGIAN COAST, 1914-18 during the war.[25]

BRITISH MINELAYERS RESUME MINING OF BIGHT

The British policy of laying extensive minefields in the Bight was not pursued in early 1916, because the surface minelayers were working mostly off the Belgian coast. In the latter part of the year however, effort was renewed in the Bight with surface ships working in concert with submarines. *E-45* (Lt. Comdr. Geoffrey R. Watkins) laid a small field about fourteen miles northeast of Heligoland on the night of 24-25 November.[26]

This effort was immediately followed up by *Abdiel*, which had last put down a field on 31 August on the Horn Reefs route. Sailing from Scapa on 24 November, Capt. Berwick Curtis laid a field of ninety service mines about twenty-five miles south of Horn Reefs. The weather was bad, with a considerable sea. Nonetheless, the mines went over the ship's stern, ten to the mile, set for 15 feet LWOS with 38-day sinking plugs. (Low Water Ordinary Springs is a tidal datum based on low water of ordinary spring tides. Water soluble sinking plugs were designed to deactivate mines laid in enemy waters after a predetermined period of time. They were used to allow minelayers to revisit areas already mined for the purpose of reinforcement.) No enemy forces were encountered and *Abdiel* got safely home. The light cruisers HMS *Galatea, Inconstant* and four destroyers from Rosyth were in position to support her 130 miles northwest of the reefs, but were unnecessary.[27]

Another large field was laid a few days later by *Princess Margaret*. She sailed from Immingham, a coastal town on the Humber Estuary, on 28 November. Escorted by the three Harwich destroyers—HMS *Sandfly, Ferret,* and *Moorsom*—Comdr. Lockhart Leith sowed 500 British Elia mines about twenty miles west of *Borkum* light vessel. The mines were laid at various depths from 7 to 15 feet below LWOS, with all but ninety-nine fitted with 38-day sinking plugs. A southwest gale was blowing, and there was again an absence of enemy forces.[28]

Map 15-1

Frisian Islands off the Netherlands and Germany

Only two minefields were laid in the North Sea in December. In early morning on 3 December, *E-45* deposited her twenty mines about six miles northwest of Nordeney. On her way home, she ran around at 1445 on Terschelling Bank in the northern Netherlands, owing to a defect with her magnetic compass. Eleven hours later, the tide lifted her off without damage, and she made it safely back to Harwich. *Abdiel* laid the final field of the year on the night of 29-30 December. It was a v-shaped pattern of eighty mines, each leg about four miles in length, with apex pointed toward the Jade Bight. She sighted nothing but a single British trawler on her way home.[29]

MINING SCHOOL ESTABLISHED AT PORTSMOUTH

By 1916, expansion of the British minelaying program imposed a significant burden on the nation's munitions manufacturing capacity, and HMS Vernon's ability to conduct development and trials. With insufficient space in Vernon afloat, it was decided to set up a mining establishment ashore. The new facility would still be a branch of Vernon, but located at the Old Gun Wharf at Portsmouth, instead of collocated with Vernon at Portchester Creek four miles to the northwest. Rear Adm. Robert S. Phipps Hornby, RN, orchestrated the move which took place in December 1916. Responsibility for the design, testing and development of mining materiel was henceforth the responsibility of the new Mining School which—with ample space and a large, new specialist staff—would now have the opportunity to greatly improve Britain's mines.[30]

Germany's Unrestricted Submarine Campaign Begins and Mine Warfare intensifies in 1917

The situation was bad enough before February 1, 1917; but on that date the enemy started his unrestricted submarine campaign in which any ships—British, Allied or Neutral—round about the British Isles, France and in the Mediterranean, were liable to be sunk on sight, entirely without regard to the lives of their non-combatant crews and passengers.

—Capt. Henry Taprell Dorling, RN, in *Swept Channels*.[1]

In February 1917, shortly before the United States declared war on 6 April, Germany began pursuing an unrestricted campaign against Allied ships. Within a couple of months, it appeared possible with the greatly increased losses of shipping, that submarines would win the war for Germany. Achieving devastating results, they were being built and pressed into service faster than they could be destroyed. In 1914-15, enemy submarines sent 568 Allied or neutral merchant vessels to the bottom. For 1917, this total doubled (or nearly doubled, cited numbers vary). In February 1917, the first month of unrestricted warfare, 260 merchant vessels were sunk. Shipping losses increased to 338 in March, and 430 in April. On 19 April, the worse day of the worse month of the war, eleven British merchantmen and eight fishing vessels were destroyed. One out of every four merchant ships that left the British Isles that month never returned.[2]

As German attack boats sent scores of Allied ships to the bottom with torpedoes and gunfire, the submarine-minelayers continued to deposit deadly cargoes with equal efficiency. In April, during the height of the unrestricted submarine campaign, an average of one mine was laid off the English coast every hour of the day, and each day the British lost one minesweeper. Throughout 1917, an average of one submarine's cargo of mines was deposited every 30 hours. On a broader perspective, there was hardly an important harbour, headland, or channel in the

British Isles which was not mined at least once. Denser traffic areas were mined more or less continuously.[3]

BRITISH IMPLEMENT SHIP CONVOY SYSTEM

The hemorrhaging of ships was partially abated by implementation of a convoy system, where merchant vessels were grouped together and escorted through particularly dangerous areas by Navy cruisers and patrol craft. When the U-boats took a heavy toll of the cross-channel coal colliers during the last quarter of 1916, the British instituted the coal trade convoys, using instead, the term "controlled sailing" to avoid giving the Germans legal grounds for torpedoing the colliers without warning.   In March the use of convoys was extended to the Scandinavian traffic route.   By the end of April, these and other measures had been incorporated into Britain's general convoy system.[4]

DEVELOPMENT OF H2 MINE SPURS MINELAYING

In 1917, in addition to the ship convoy system, the British took a number of other important steps to combat the German submarine campaign, including several related to minelaying. HMS Vernon (with the backing of the new Mining School at the Gun Wharf) finally produced a reliable mine. The British H2 was a spherical contact-type mine (copied from the successful German Hertz-horn mine) which utilised a 320-lb explosive charge. Production started in early 1917, but significant numbers of mines were not available until November. The first use of the H2 mines occurred on 24 September 1917, when this new type was deployed in the Heligoland Bight as part of a greatly intensified mine laying campaign in those waters.[5]

Because of Admiralty fears that their mines laid in 1915-16 might pose danger to British minelayers, new fields were put down farther off the German coast than the original ones.   In addition to the fields targeting German submarines, a barrier stretching from Terschelling to the Horn Reefs (with mines laid thickly and at shallow depths) was intended to damage or destroy enemy minesweepers and patrol craft.[6]

German vessel losses to British mines increased greatly in 1917, and enemy minesweepers, which had little rest, began to suffer serious losses as well. The sweepers became less and less inclined to venture far from their harbours and morale began to suffer. From the winter of 1917-18 onward, the German policy of clearing minefields was abandoned and diminishing efforts concentrated on keeping swept routes open.[7]

INCREASED MINELAYING DETERS GERMAN SHIPS, BUT NOT SUBMARINES

Other British mining initiatives were unsuccessful. A mine and net barrier constructed in the Dover Straits in December 1916-February 1917 proved untenable, because strong tidal currents displaced mines making maintenance of the barrier hazardous. Following the loss of the British tender *Albert* to a mine gone astray, the remaining ones were swept and the nets relaid in a new location to the south. In other actions, deep minefields were laid in the English Channel; construction began of a deep mine barrier between Folkestone and Cape Gris Nez; and deep and shallow fields were laid off the English east coast. Yet, despite all these efforts, the movements of German submarines were not greatly impeded.[8]

Photo 16-1

Former German submarine (either the *U-119* or *U-121*) at Cherbourg, France. This view of the bow shows a net cutter attached to the submarine's hull. Naval History and Heritage Command photograph #NH 43785

The longer the nets were in place the easier it became to pass through them because they deteriorated so quickly. Strong currents, storms, and heavy seas tore apart the nets. Many of the Flanders boats, particularly the UB boats, were equipped with net cutters, but they were largely unused. The device was roundly hated by U-boat skippers who complained that they were worthless and often came loose in rough seas, causing unwanted drag when running submerged.[9]

The British later embarked on a top secret project to replace the defective Dover barrage defences with a series of five armed submersible platforms joined by submarine nettings. Two of these structures were constructed in 1918 at Shoreham but the end of the war intervened and they were never put in place. One, only partially completed, was demolished but the other was eventually towed to the Solent near the Isle of Wight and sunk and used as a base for a lighthouse that is still in use at Nab Rocks.[10]

ADDITIONAL VESSELS ALLOCATED TO MINING, AND COMMANDER'S POSITION UPGRADED

Photo 16-2

Engraving of Beachy Head, England, *The Naval Chronicle*, Vol. 18, London, 1807. Naval History and Heritage Command photograph #NH 66786

In support of the expanded minelaying campaign, the Royal Navy allocated additional vessels to this function. The old, protected cruiser HMS *Ariadne* was converted to a minelayer, but her career was short-lived. She was torpedoed and sunk by *UC-65* off renowned Beachy Head (on the southeast coast of England) on 26 July 1917, with thirty-four killed. The prominence of Britain's highest chalk sea cliff had long made it a landmark for sailors in the English Channel, as noted in "Spanish Ladies," a traditional British naval song, describing a voyage from Spain to the Downs. Many readers will be familiar with the first verse, but perhaps not the one which mentions "Beachy."

> Farewell and adieu to you, Spanish ladies,
> Farewell and adieu to you, ladies of Spain;
> For we have received orders
> > For to sail to old England,
> But we hope in a short time to see you again.

> The first land we sighted was called the Dodman,
> Next Rame Head off Plymouth, off Portsmouth the Wight;
> We sailed by Beachy, by Fairlight and Dover,
> And then we bore up for the South Foreland light.[11]

HMS *Ariadne* was replaced by a sister ship, *Amphitrite*, in August. Eleven light cruisers and a dozen destroyers were equipped to serve as temporary minelayers, though not all were called upon to function in this role. Twelve motor launches were fitted out in England and two in the Mediterranean as coastal minelayers. For operations in shallow waters off the Belgian coast, nine coastal motor boats were configured to lay from one to four mines (according to the type of boat).[12]

In recognition of the increased importance of minelaying, the Royal Navy upgraded the Captain (M) position to Rear Admiral (M) in August 1917. Rear Adm. Lewis Clinton-Baker took up these duties on 24 January 1918, at Grangemouth on the Firth of Forth.[13]

Photo 16-3

UC-56 (a UC II-class minelaying submarine like *UC-65*) at Christabel, Spain, where she interned herself on 24 May 1918; due to casualties to both her port and starboard electrical motors, preventing the submarine from operating submerged.
Naval History and Heritage Command photograph #NH 111101

Photo 16-4

Minelayer HMS *Amphitrite* sporting a coat of dazzle camouflage paint.
Naval History and Heritage Command photograph #NH63009

MINESWEEPERS TO THE FORE

In 1917, British minelayers created more and more fields in German waters in an effort to restrict the movements of enemy submarines, and thereby reduce shipping losses. These efforts were only partially successful, due to Germany's greatly expanded submarine construction program, and because her attack boats and submarine-minelayers were able to broach barriers with near impunity. The enemy's dramatically increased submarine-minelaying efforts and extension of minefields to distant areas in the first half of 1917, overwhelmed the already heavily burdened British Minesweeping Service.[14]

Requiring still greater numbers of minesweepers (in addition to the hundreds already in service), every available civilian paddle steamer and motor fishing boat was commandeered, and those incapable of utilising the standard minesweep were fitted with lighter gear and employed for searching. Aircraft and motor launches were sent out at low water, to visually locate fields for subsequent destruction. Related efforts included better organisation of shipping traffic, and improved communication and coordination between adjacent areas.[15]

HUNT-CLASS MINESWEEPERS JOIN THE FLEET

With Britain desperate for additional minesweepers, the construction of a new class of vessels had been undertaken in 1916. The first of the resultant *Hunt*-class ships began reporting for duty in mid-1917. There had been recognition in early 1916 of the need for a twin-screw minesweeper, after experience had shown that the paddlers were unsuitable for operations in bad weather, and were susceptible to ensnaring mines in their paddle-wheels. The essential characteristics of the new ship was a shallow draught with a sweeping speed of 12 knots.[16]

Photo 16-5

British minesweeper HMS *Belvoir* under way; date and location unknown. Imperial War Museums photograph SP 109 (collection no. 1900-01)

Twenty *Hunt*-class minesweeping sloops were delivered to the Royal Navy in 1917. Built to a design drawn up by Ailsa Shipbuilding, they were termed the Belvoir group—another ninety-five sloops were subsequently built, based on a modified Admiralty design. A majority of these somewhat larger *Hunt*-class vessels (the Aberdare group) were not completed before war's end. In total, 115 *Hunt*-class sloops were constructed, some of which later served in World War II.[17]

Hunt-class (Belvoir Group) Minesweeping Sloops

Ship	Builder	Completed	Disposition
Belvoir	Ailsa Shipbuilding Co.	Jun 1917	Sold 1922
Bicester	Ailsa Shipbuilding Co.	Sep 1917	Sold early 1923
Blackmorevale	Adrossan Shipbuilding Co.	Aug 1917	Sunk 1 May 1918
Cotswold	Bow, McLachlan	Mar 1917	Sold early 1923
Cottesmore	Bow, McLachlan	May 1917	Sold early 1923
Cattistock	Clyde Shipbuilding Co.	May 1917	Sold early 1923

Croome	Clyde Shipbuilding Co.	Aug 1917	Sold 1922
Dartmore	Dunlop, Bremner	Jun 1917	Sold early 1923
Garth	Dunlop, Bremner	Aug 1917	Sold early 1923
Hambledon	Fleming & Ferguson	Jun 1917	Sold 1922
Heythrop	Fleming & Ferguson	Aug 1917	Sold 1922
Holderness	Henderson	Mar 1917	Sold Aug 1924
Meynell	Henderson	Apr 1917	Sold 1922
Muskerry	Lobnitz	Jan 1917	Sold early 1923
Oakley	Lobnitz	Mar 1917	Sold early 1923
Pytchley	Napier & Miller	Jul 1917	Sold 1922
Quorn	Napier & Miller	Sep 1917	Sold 1922
Southdown	Simons	May 1917	Sold Dec 1926
Tedworth	Simons	Jun 1917	Sold Nov 1946
Zetland	Murdoch & Murray	Sep 1917	Sold early 1923[18]

The first of the *Hunt*s were of 220 feet length, 28-foot beam, 7-foot draught, and 730-ton displacement. The ships had a top speed of 16-17 knots, and were fitted with standard minesweeping gear (with paravane sweeps in later vessels). They had depth charges for use against submarines, and two 12-pounder guns and two 2-pounder pom-poms (anti-aircraft guns) for employment against surface ships and aircraft. The Belvoir group ships were laid down in builders yards between June and October 1916, and were completed in March through September 1917.[19]

The ships of the Belvoir group were named after British fox hunts, while those of the Aberdare group were originally named after coastal towns, watering places and fishing ports, some of which happened to be hunts, by coincidence. All the Aberdare ships were soon renamed after inland locations. The sloops' boilers burned pulverised coal using forced draft air to increase the rate of combustion, thereby increasing steam production and associated turbine-horsepower. Turbine output is directly related to the speed of a ship. However, the boosted combustion (from the use of both forced air and pulverised coal) resulted in production of additional smoke, sufficient for the sloops to become known as "Smokey Joes." Ships dislike emitting excessive smoke from their funnels in wartime—which might give away their position to the enemy—as much as submarines abhor making excessive noise.[20]

The *Hunt*-class sloop HMS *Blackmorevale* was mined and sank in the North Sea (off Montrose on Scotland's east coast) on 1 May 1918. Of her ship's complement of seventy-two officers and men, twenty-six perished, including her captain, Lt. Comdr. Geoffrey A. Luscombe. The casualty list provides an inkling of her crew composition (heavy on deck and engineering ratings), as well as the sources of these personnel. Two temporary lieutenants were lost, one RNR and the other RNVR. The remaining crew casualties were also all reservists: RNR (Royal Naval Reserve), RNVR (Royal Naval Volunteer Reserve), and MMR (Mercantile Marine Reserve).

HMS *Blackmorevale* Casualties

Name	Position	Name	Position
William G. Blanch, RNR	Deck Hand	Robert E. Jones, MMR	Greaser
William Bodinar, RNR	Deck Hand	David M. Lewis, MMR	Greaser
Arthur C. Bridgewater, RNVR	Ordinary Telegraphist	Geoffrey A. Luscombe	Lt. Comdr.
Alexander S. Brown, RNR	Deck Hand	James Martin, MMR	Trimmer
James Butler, MMR	Leading Fireman	Robert C. Menelaws, MMR	Fireman
Reginald T. Canton, MMR	Fireman	Joseph G. Neville	Signalman
Wilfred G. Chalk, RNR	Deck Hand	James Pearson, MMR	Leading Fireman
John J. Donnelly, MMR	Fireman	Arthur Phillips, MMR	Greaser
Lewis M. Evans, MMR	Greaser	Edward Phillips, MMR	Leading Fireman
George Hall, RNR	Temporary Lt.	Edgar Redman, RNVR	Signalman
John Henderson, MMR	Trimmer	Edward Timmins, MMR	Fireman
Edward Hughes, MMR	Leading Fireman	John Williams, RNVR	Temporary Lt.
John Jones, MMR	Fireman	James Windram, RNR[21]	Deck Hand

BRITISH MERCANTILE MARINE RESERVE

The Mercantile Marine Reserve, the source of *Blackmorevale*'s engineers, had come into existence in 1916 through wartime expediency. During 1916-1920 the MMR was used to engage officers and seamen on board vessels employed on government service. The crews of vessels commissioned as auxiliaries by the Admiralty were signed on under an agreement, whereby they agreed to serve in any commissioned vessel, but retained aspects of their civilian pay and benefits.[22]

Mercantile Marine War Medal

In 1919, the British Board of Trade instituted a Mercantile Marine War Medal to recognise war service of the officers and men of the Mercantile Marine. Altogether 133,135 of these medals were awarded; 624 to Canadians. On the front of the medal was an effigy of King George V, with, in Latin, "George V, King of all the British Isles and Emperor of India." On the back was a laurel wreath around a merchant ship on a stormy sea with an enemy submarine and an old sailing ship to the right of the merchant ship. Below the image were the words, "For War Service/Mercantile Marine 1914-1918."[23]

British Raids on Zeebrugge and Ostend, 1918

Captain William V. Howard, DSO, [RN] of the Trawler Patrol, accompanied the expedition in the paddle minesweeper "Lingfield," and did valuable work in keeping touch with the force, giving assistance by towing, and otherwise helping small craft in trouble while on the passage to and from Zeebrugge, also in receiving the surplus crews from blockships, and escorting motor launches. This veteran officer has been on patrol work off the southeast coast of England during the whole of the war. His energy and example are great incentives to the officers and men of the Trawler Patrol which he commands.[1]

I may say here that I regarded the chances of escape from any of the blocking ships as very slender, and this was well known to those who so readily volunteered for this hazardous service and to the volunteer crews of the motor launches who ran equal risks in their work of rescue.

—Vice Adm. Roger Keyes, RN, commander Dover Patrol, citing in
a despatch, the service of Capt. William V. Howard, and bravery
of the skeleton crews aboard ex-minelayers *Intrepid, Iphigenia,*
and *Thetis* during a raid on Zeebrugge in April 1918.[1]

On 23 April 1918, British naval forces carried out coordinated raids on Zeebrugge and Ostend, in an effort to deny German naval units continued use of these Belgian ports. Submarines, torpedo boats, and ships based inland at Bruges had long accessed the English Channel via canals leading to the sea openings at Zeebrugge and Ostend. Over the course of the war, approximately one-third of all Allied merchant vessels would be sunk by German torpedo boats and submarines based at Bruges-Zeebrugge. By 1918, shipping loses were of such magnitude, it was feared that Britain would be starved into submission unless the enemy raiders could be stopped. In an effort to rectify this situation, Vice Admiral Keyes, commander of the Dover Patrol, devised a plan to block the ports at Zeebrugge and Ostend in a coordinated night-time operation, code named Operation Z-O.[2]

The main objectives were to block the Bruges ship-canal entrance inside the harbour at Zeebrugge, block the Ostend harbour from the sea, and inflict as much damage as possible upon the two ports. Old British cruisers filled with concrete ("blockships"), escorted by a naval force, were to proceed across the English Channel to the ports, and force their way inside. Upon arrival at key locations, the crews aboard the blockships would scuttle them. Three of the sacrificial ships were to blockade Zeebrugge, and two Ostend. At Zeebrugge, explosives-filled submarines were to blow up the viaduct, a steel railroad bridge that connected the mole to the shore, while HMS *Vindictive* landed three companies of the 4th Battalion, Royal Marines (750 men total), and two companies of naval infantrymen on the mole to destroy German gun positions at the entrance to the Bruges Canal and blow up as many installations as possible before withdrawal. A mole is a massive structure, usually constructed of stone or concrete, used as a pier, breakwater, or a causeway between places separated by water.[3]

Aiding *Vindictive* would be the river ferries *Daffodil* and *Iris II*. In addition to the landing force of three companies of Royal Marines and the two companies of naval infantrymen aboard the *Vindictive*, there was one company of naval infantrymen each in the smaller vessels. The sailors comprising the assault force of four rifle companies were each organised with two officers and fifty men. During the actual assault, only one of the submarines, *C-3*, participated in blowing up the railroad viaduct. Lt. Richard D. Sandford rammed her between two of its iron piers, and he and his crew abandoned after lighting the fuses. (For this heroic action, he later received the Victoria Cross.) Five minutes later, the explosives detonated, destroying communications between the mole and the shore. The other submarine intended for the operation, *C-1*, suffered a mishap while under tow to Zeebrugge, and did not arrive until just before retirement of the force.[4]

The inland docks at Bruges were connected to Zeebrugge via a straight, deep ship-canal and to Ostend by a considerably older, shallower and more crooked canal. The whole resembled a triangle. The eight-mile long canal from Zeebrugge to Bruges formed the eastern side, and the eleven mile Bruges-Ostend Canal the southern side. Facing northwest, twelve miles of heavily fortified coastline between Ostend and Zeebrugge shaped the base. Blocking the Zeebrugge entrance to the Bruges ship-canal was of the greatest importance, but it was also necessary to obstruct the entrance to the Ostend harbour; for unless this were done, smaller craft would still be able to pass freely through the narrower waterway.[5]

FIRST ATTEMPT CANCELLED, PLANS CAPTURED

A naval force had earlier sailed on 11 April for the attack. Comprising it were 1 cruiser, 28 destroyers, 8 monitors (bombardment vessels), 61 motor launches, 24 coastal motor boats and 1 minesweeper. Early the next morning, with the force just sixteen miles from Zeebrugge, the wind began blowing from the south. Because the shifting winds would dissipate the smokescreens to be generated by motor launches and coastal motor boats, to impede visual sighting of the force by enemy shore batteries, the attack was cancelled. The coastal motor boat *CMB-33* failed to return, having run aground near the harbour entrance. In addition to capturing the boat and crew, the Germans obtained copies of the operational orders; specifically prohibited to be aboard the vessel.[6]

ATTACKS ON ZEEBRUGGE AND OSTEND, 23 APRIL

Although suitable conditions of tide and moon would not occur for another month, Keyes convinced the Admiralty that the operation should be attempted some two weeks later, when the tides would be suitable, irrespective of the fact that the date chosen would coincide with a full moon. The blocking ships and storming forces (Royal Marines) had assembled toward the end of February. From 4 April onward they had been located in the West Swin Anchorage, in the outer passages of the Thames River. The remaining naval forces were staged at Dover and Dunkirk prior to depature.[7]

Photo 17-1

A British paddle minesweeper; date photograph taken and identify of ship unknown. Among their other attributes, these vessels only drew six feet of water.
Naval History and Heritage Command #NH 110566

Among the ships and craft at Dover—which included the flagship *Warwick* (D25) as well as several other destroyers, monitors, coastal motorboats, and motor launches—was the paddle minesweeper *Lingfield*. Her tasking was to take off surplus steaming parties aboard the blockships after arrival of the naval force off the Belgian coast. Extra watch sections of engineers were needed to steam the ships, and make any necessary repairs to their propulsion plants during the passage, but not for port entry and scuttling. It was also advantageous to have a minesweeper along, should any mines be encountered in the approaches to the harbours.[8]

Much of the passage of the force, once joined, had to be carried out in daylight, with the associated likelihood of discovery by enemy aircraft or submarines. This risk was largely countered by the escort of all the scouting aircraft under Vice Admiral Keyes' command. On arrival at a position one and one-half miles short of designated point G, the force stopped to enable the surplus steaming parties to be disembarked and coastal motor boats under tow slipped. On resuming passage, *Warwick* and *Whirlwind*, followed by the other destroyers, drew ahead on either bow of the formation to neutralize any German outpost vessels.[9]

BLOCKING OPERATIONS

Several books are devoted to the raids on Zeebrugge and Ostend, and to the associated heroic actions of personnel drawn from the British Grand Fleet, the three Home Depots, the Royal Marine Artillery and Light Infantry. The force also included men from the Royal Australian Navy and the Admiralty Experimental Stations at Stratford and Dover. The ships and torpedo boats were provided by the Dover Patrol, reinforced by vessels from the Harwich Force and the French Navy. This overview of the operations is largely devoted to describing only the execution and results of the blockading actions.[10]

The bombardment of Zeebrugge by monitors began at 2320, simultaneously with that of the Ostend defences by monitors, and by shore batteries in Flanders. The attack upon the Zeebrugge Mole, as well as the bombardment of the port, was designed to distract German defence forces from the main operations. Without this diversion, shore batteries would likely have thwarted the attempt of the blocking ships to pass round the end of the mole, to enter the harbour, and to reach the ship-canal entrance in the inner area. One of the grim realities of this operation is that over half of the Royal Marines and the Naval Landing Force who were aboard the *Vindictive* were killed or wounded before they could get onto the mole, and those who reached the upper parapet were almost entirely wiped out. The Germans were impressed by the British, as evidenced by the 24 April 1918 edition of the *Hamburger Nachrichten*, which noted, "The attack was carried out by the British with great skill and extraordinary valour." Echoing these sentiments, Kapitän Eduard von Pustau in a letter to *Die Tageszeitung*, wrote, "Their gallant action merits all recognition." Von Pustau was a holder of the Order of the Red Eagle, 1st Class, with swords, one of Prussia's highest valour awards.[11]

Photo 17-2

Photograph taken on 6 June 1918 of the blockships sunk six weeks earlier on 23 April, at the entrance to the Bruges ship-canal inside Zeebrugge Harbour, Belgium.
Naval History and Heritage Command photograph #NH 121373

Thetis, the first of the blocking ships, got by the end of the mole twenty-five minutes after midnight; already in a sinking condition from enemy gunfire. Making her way toward the entrance to the canal, she sank just shy of it. *Intrepid*, following a few minutes later, was scuttled by her crew in the ship-canal; and at forty-five minutes past midnight, *Iphigenia* settled to the bottom across the narrowest part of the canal. The three ships were formerly part of the seven ex-2nd-class protected cruisers that had constituted the Royal Navy's entire minelaying force when Britain entered the war four years earlier.[12]

FAILURE AT OSTEND

It was expected that by heading southwest along the coast, the blockships *Brilliant* and *Sirius*—old second-class protected cruisers of the *Apollo*-class—would have found the entrance to Ostend harbour by midnight. However, as the naval force of which they were a part, neared Ostend, winds from the north-northeast (which had been favourable for purposes of the smoke screen) had begun blowing from the south-southwest, exposing the British ships to enemy fire. To make matters worse, the Stroom Bank buoy marking the channel entrance to Ostend harbour, had been repositioned 2,400 yards farther east; apparently as a ruse by the enemy.[13]

As the two blockships steered to pass northward of the buoy, they came under fire from shore batteries, and set a course for the believed position of Ostend. When the Ostend Piers should have been visible aboard *Brilliant*, breakers were observed on her starboard bow, and she grounded. *Sirius* (following astern and badly damaged by gunfire and sinking) put her helm hard over and her engines full astern, but the rudder failed to respond to the order from the ship's wheel, and she collided with the port quarter of *Brilliant*.[14]

The two ships were blown up at 0300 where they stranded (about 2,400 yards east of the entrance to the harbour) to avoid capture by the Germans. Their crews—excepting a relative few casualties—were taken off by motor launches which had been standing by under heavy fire of every calibre. One of the launches, under the command of Canadian Lt. Rowland Richard Lewis Bourke, RNVR, retrieved thirty-eight sailors from the *Brilliant* and towed the crippled *ML-532* out of the harbour, while under heavy enemy fire.[15]

BATTLE HONOURS

Intrepid, Iphigenia and *Thetis* received Battle Honours ZEEBRUGGE, 23 Apr 1918, as did also the paddle minesweeper *Lingfield*. Their captains, Lt. Stuart Bonham-Carter, Lt. Edward Billyard-Leake and Comdr. Ralph Wykes-Sneyd, respectively, fought their way into a heavily defended port to sacrifice their former minelayers. Capt. William V. Howard of the Trawler Patrol aboard *Lingfield* gave assistance to the naval force by towing, and otherwise assisting small craft while on the passage to and from Zeebrugge, also in receiving the surplus crews from blockships, and escorting motor launches.[16]

Photo 17-3

Photograph of old British cruisers sunk as blockships at Zeebrugge; taken sometime after the raid on 22-23 April 1918, when the ships had been partially dismantled. Naval History and Heritage Command photograph #NH 60070

Intrepid had not disembarked her spare stokers, owing to a delay in the motor launch, that was to take them off, arriving alongside; and apparently, also because the men were disinclined to miss the action. The cruiser had therefore proceeded with eighty-seven officers and men aboard instead of fifty-four. Approaching the mole she came under heavy fire, before rounding the lighthouse and, directed by *Thetis*, steering for the canal. On reaching the correct position, *Intrepid*'s commanding officer, Lt. Stuart Bonham-Carter, gave the order to abandon, and then went full ahead with the starboard engine, and full astern with the port one, with the helm "hard a starboard," while waiting for the crew to get into the boats. But, finding the ship was making sternway he had to blow the demolition charges before the steaming party could get out of the engine-room.[17]

Nevertheless, Engineer Sub-Lieutenant Edgar V. Meikle and his engine room crew made it into a cutter, and proceeded out past the *Thetis* until picked up by a motor launch. Another cutter was picked up by the destroyer *Whirlwind* and a skiff by the motor launch *ML 282*. With two officers and four petty officers, Bonham-Carter launched a Carley life-raft and proceeded out the canal until retrieved by *ML 282* as well; which coming in under heavy fire, had passed under the stern of *Iphigenia*.[18]

Vice Admiral Keyes recommended the commander of the motor launch, Lt. Percy Dean, RNVR, for promotion and receipt of the most prestigious award for heroism in the face of the enemy, noting, "I consider his gallant conduct is well worthy of the Victoria Cross." (With the exception of Stoker Petty Officer Harold L. Palliser, killed in the launch by machine gun fire, *Intrepid*'s whole crew got away.)[19] Dean's citation for the Victoria Cross follows:

> Lieutenant Dean handled his boat in a most magnificent and heroic manner when embarking the officers and men from the blockships at Zeebrugge. He followed the blockships in and closed '*Intrepid*' and '*Iphigenia*' under a constant and deadly fire from machine and heavy guns at point blank range, embarking over 100 officers and men. This completed, he was proceeding out of the canal, when he heard that an officer was in the water. He returned, rescued him, and then proceeded, handling his boat throughout as calmly as if engaged in a practice manoeuvre. Three men were shot down at his side whilst he conned his ship. On clearing the entrance to the canal the steering gear broke down. He manoeuvred his boat by the engines, and avoided complete destruction by steering so close in under the mole that the guns in the batteries could not depress sufficiently to fire on the boat. The whole of this operation was carried out under a constant machine-gun fire at a few yards range. It was solely due to this officer's courage and daring that *M.L.282* succeeded in saving so many valuable lives.[20]

SECOND ATTEMPT TO BLOCK OSTEND

After learning on 23 April that the enterprise to block Ostend had failed, Keyes advised the Admiralty of his desire to repeat the operation at once, and received concurrence to do so. With the cruiser *Vindictive* being the only available candidate for use as a blockship, every effort was made to repair and fit her out before seasonal changes in the tides and periods of darkness precluded undertaking the mission. *Vindictive* had been badly damaged by gunfire at Zeebrugge, as attested to by Artilleristmaat August Policke, a gun captain on one of the mole battery's two 88mm guns positioned nearest the lighthouse at the end of the mole:

> Suddenly a ship emerged from the fog scarcely 1,000 yards away and proceeded at full speed toward the harbour entrance. She was identified as a light cruiser (HMS *Vindictive*).... Our rounds exploded in the cruiser's upper works and into the deck that was crowded with men. Automatic cannons from the antiaircraft battery Baden added their weight and the carnage on the cruiser's deck was horrible to behold. The cruiser changed course to the west until she passed out of our field of fire.[21]

In addition to the other work *Vindictive* required, hundreds of tons of concrete were placed in her after magazines and upper coal bunker, which was all her increased draught would permit in the shallow approaches to Ostend. She was ready by the desired date, but as a result of unfavourable weather, the operation had to be postponed. However, this delay made it possible to prepare a second ship, the old cruiser *Sappho*, for blockship duties. She was taken from Southampton to Chatham and fitted out in the Chatham Dockyard.[22]

Aerial reconnaissance on 9 May revealed that many torpedo boats and submarines were shut up in Bruges, which seemed to indicate that the blocking of the Zeebrugge branch of the canal had been effective. The craft at Bruges had also been unable to use the small waterways to Ostend, but the latter port was being used by other enemy torpedo craft and submarines. On the evening of 9 May, *Vindictive* and *Sappho* sailed in company to join Commodore Hubert Lynes, RN, at Dunkirk. Under his command were the monitors, destroyers, motor launches and coastal motor boats assigned as supporting forces, Keyes had placed Lynes in overall command of the raid.[23]

Vindictive and *Sappho* arrived in Dunkirk Roads, disembarked their surplus crews, and proceeded with their escorts for Ostend at the appointed time. *Sappho* had scarcely left the anchorage when a man-hole joint in the side of her boiler ruptured, reducing her speed to about six knots and precluding her from participating in the operation. Her absence halved the chances of success, leaving blocking duties solely to *Vindictive*. Undeterred by this setback, the naval force pressed onward. Vice Admiral Keyes aboard *Warwick* and a division of destroyers, consisting of HMS *Whirlwind*, *Velox*, and *Trident*, cruised midway between Ostend and Zeebrugge to prevent interference from a German destroyer force newly arrived at the latter port.[24]

SECOND RAID ON OSTEND

The British force arrived off Ostend in the early hours of 10 May, while the coastal motor boat and motor launch divisions were sent in to create smoke screens. The signal to open fire was given at 0143, followed by immediate action from the monitors, Royal Marine Artillery siege guns, and Royal Air Force squadrons. During the ensuing action, the enemy almost certainly realised the nature of the attack. Since the smoke and fog prevented shore guns from aiming at definite targets, a continuous barrage of fire poured from the array of batteries in the Ostend area directed at the harbour entrance.[25]

For the critical twenty minute period in which *Vindictive*'s mission would succeed or fail, the destroyer force offshore fired "star shells"

over the entrance of the harbour, and shelled the German batteries—
the former to illuminate the pier-heads for the cruiser, and the latter to
divert the gun crews' attention farther seaward. Despite poor visibility
due to darkness, fog, and smoke, enemy batteries found the blockship
with two hundred yards to go, and concentrated all efforts on her. The
blast from a shell burst apparently killed her commanding officer,
Comdr. Alfred E. Godsal, RN, and propelled him over the side. He was
not seen again, and a thorough search after the ship was sunk proved
fruitless. Lt. Victor Crutchley manoeuvred to place *Vindictive* across the
channel, and the demolition charges were fired by Engineer Lt. Comdr.
William A. Bury and preparations made to abandon.[26]

Motor launches *254* and *276* took all survivors off the *Vindictive*
while under heavy fire. The general retirement was executed without
further casualties or incident; the supporting forces remaining at sea
until daylight to pick up any disabled small craft. There were none,
however; those unable to return by their own power had already been
towed home. Commodore Lynes attributed the relative light casualties
suffered—2 officers and 6 men killed, 5 officers and 25 men wounded,
and 2 officers and 9 men missing, believed killed—to the efficient
smoke screen, and probably also to the fog.[27]

Lieutenant Bourke received the Victoria Cross for gallantry in the
face of the enemy during the second raid on Ostend. He had previously
earned the Distinguished Service Order for his actions on 23 April
during the raid on Zeebrugge. His medal citation follows.

> Volunteered for rescue work in command of *M.L. 276* and followed
> '*Vindictive*' into Ostend, engaging the enemy's machine-guns on
> both piers with Lewis guns. After *M.L. 254* had backed out, Lt.
> Bourke laid his vessel alongside '*Vindictive*' to make further search.
> Finding no one, he withdrew, but hearing cries in the water, he again
> entered the harbour, and after a prolonged search, eventually found
> Lt. Sir John Alleyne, and two ratings, all badly wounded, and in the
> water, clinging to an upended skiff, and he rescued them. During
> all this time, the motor launch was under very heavy fire at close
> range, being hit in fifty-five places, once by a 5 inch shell. Two of
> her small crew being killed and others wounded. The vessel was
> seriously damaged and speed greatly reduced. Lt. Bourke, however,
> managed to bring her out and carry on until he fell in with a
> Monitor, which took him in tow. This episode displayed daring and
> skill of a very high order, and Lt. Bourke's bravery and perseverance
> undoubtedly saved the lives of Lt. Alleyne and two of the
> '*Vindictive*'s' crew.

The officer Bourke saved, Lieutenant Alleyne, had volunteered from a monitor of the Dover Patrol for service in the *Vindictive*. He had navigated the blockship to the entrance to Ostend harbour, before being severely wounded, and rendered unconscious for a time, by the shell burst which killed his commanding officer.[28]

At the commencement of war, Bourke had tried to join the Canadian military. Rejected by all three arms due to poor eyesight, he, undeterred, had traveled to England at his own expense, where he joined the Royal Naval Volunteer Reserve serving on motor launches. King George V presented Bourke his Victoria Cross at Buckingham Palace on 11 September 1918.[29]

Photo 17-4

Canadian skippers of Royal Navy motor launches posing with the main armament of one of these type vessels. Fred MacFarlane is on the extreme right.
Courtesy of John MacFarlane

AFTERMATH

It had been Commander Godsal's intention to ram the western pier with the object of swinging the ship across the channel under port helm, a manoeuvre that would have been greatly assisted by the tide, which was setting strongly through the piers to the eastward. It would appear that when the "Vindictive" eventually found the entrance she was too close to the eastern pier to use port helm without risk of grounding broadside on. This would account for Commander Godsal's order "hard a starboard" a few seconds before he was killed. The "Vindictive" was thus committed to starboard helm when the command devolved on Lieutenant Crutchley, who very promptly put the port telegraph to full speed astern. Unfortunately the port propeller, which was very severely damaged against Zeebrugge Mole, was of little value. Due to this, and also to the fact that the tide was setting strongly against her starboard side, the ship's stern did not swing across the channel as desired, with the result that she grounded at an angle of about 25 degrees to the eastern pier, leaving a considerable channel between her stern and the western pier.

—Vice Adm. Roger Keyes, RN, commander Dover Patrol, assessment of why the sunken cruiser *Vindictive* failed to block the harbour entrance at Ostend, Belgium.[30]

Although the raids were carried out with great courage, they were not successful from an operational perspective. German naval forces were still able to utilise Zeebrugge, Ostend, and Bruges much as they had previously done. A third planned operation at Ostend was not carried out after British intelligence learned that a new channel carved out at Zeebrugge was sufficient to allow access for U-boats. Remedying this situation would have called for an even larger second assault, and would have stretched the resources of the Allies too far. British losses in the three futile attempts to close Bruges cost over 600 casualties and the loss of several ships; and the threat from the inland base was not eliminated until the last days of the war, when the area was liberated by Allied land forces.[31]

A painting by Charles de Lacy of HMS *Vindictive*, engaged in fierce action at Zeebrugge where she was badly damaged by gunfire alongside the mole, hangs in the Britannia Royal Naval College. The bow of *Vindictive* remains at Ostend as a memorial to the British Naval and Marine Forces who took part in the raids on Zeebrugge and Ostend. One of her 7.5-inch howitzers was acquired and preserved by the Imperial War Museum. Although the raids were not successful, they were represented as such to the British people, which gave Britain a much needed morale boost at that point in the war.[32]

The British casualties at Zeebrugge were 176 killed, 412 wounded, and 49 missing in action. The Royal Marine 4th Battalion company commanders were; A Company (Chatham) Maj. Charles E. C. Eagles; B Company (Portsmouth) Capt. Edward Bamford; C Company (Plymouth) Maj. Barnard G. Weller.[33]

18

North Sea Mine Barrage

Unsatisfactory.

—U.S. Navy's Bureau of Ordnance assessment of the situation in 1917 regarding the availability of mines. A few thousand mines were in stock in America, and approximately 140 per month were being manufactured, but were of a type that proved wanting during use by the British in the first three years of World War I.[1]

When World War I erupted in 1914, American President Woodrow Wilson pledged neutrality for the United States, a position that the vast majority of Americans favored. However, with continued German submarine attacks on shipping, public opinion in the United States began to turn irrevocably against Germany. When the British ocean liner RMS *Lusitania* was torpedoed without warning by *U-20* off the coast of Ireland on 7 May 1915, of the 1,198 passengers killed, 128 were Americans. On 8 November, *U-38* torpedoed the Italian passenger liner SS *Ancona* killing 208 people, including 25 Americans. Coming as it did six months after the sinking of the *Lusitania*, this act added to a growing outrage in the United States, and Secretary of State Robert Lansing protested yet another sinking of a passenger vessel with Americans on board.[2]

In February 1916, Germany announced that defensively armed merchant vessels would be liable to be torpedoed without warning, effective on 1 March. A written explanation of this policy concluded with the statement:

> In view of the aforesaid circumstances, enemy merchantmen carrying guns are not entitled to be regarded as peaceful merchantmen. The German naval forces, therefore, after a short interval in the interest of neutrals, will receive an order to treat such vessels as belligerents.[3]

Strained relations came to a head in early 1917 when Germany announced its intention to pursue a policy of unrestricted submarine warfare. The U.S. broke diplomatic relations with Germany on 3 February. Later that same day, *U-53* torpedoed the American liner SS *Housatonic*. In response to the latest provocation, Congress passed a $250 million arms appropriations bill intended to make the United States ready for war. However, this action failed to deter other attacks against American shipping. Between 12 and 18 March, German submarines sank the SS *Algonquin*, SS *Vigilancia*, SS *City of Memphis*, and SS *Illinois*. On 2 April, President Wilson appeared before Congress and called for a declaration of war against Germany, and his request was granted four days later on 6 April 1917.[4]

At that point in the war, there was every reason for a pessimistic view of the situation. The French and British land forces appeared to have a slight advantage over the enemy, having made small gains here and there; but they clearly had little or no prospect of obtaining an early military decision. The Italians were holding their own, but with no prospect of decisive victory. The military situation on the western front was practically a stalemate, and on the eastern front the Russians were holding, for the time being. But, there were indications that the newly established revolutionary government would be unable to overcome internal dissensions and that Russian power might crumble at any time. In the Balkans, the Allies had insufficient force to prosecute an offensive campaign. In the Mediterranean, the growing submarine menace threatened the lines of communication by which this force was sustained. In Turkey, the British were making some progress in Mesopotamia, but it was doubtful whether victory there would have any significant effect on conditions in Europe.[5]

There was no prospect of victory over the Central Powers unless, and until, heavy American forces were sent to Europe to turn the tide. The United States was not ready to do such, and could not create and equip an adequate army within a year, or probably two. It did, however, commit to sending a large force of troops to reinforce the French and British on the western front. The first 14,000 U.S. infantry troops landed in France at the port of Saint Nazaire on 26 June 1917, to begin training for combat. The entry of these and subsequent troops into the conflict marked a major turning point in the war and helped the Allies to victory. When war finally ended on 11 November 1918, more than two million American soldiers had served on the battlefields of Western Europe, and some 50,000 had lost their lives.[6]

U.S. NAVY WARSHIPS ARRIVE IN EUROPE

On May 1917, six destroyers of the Eighth Division, Destroyer Force, Atlantic Fleet, arrived at Queenstown on the southern coast of Ireland. They were the first units of a planned destroyer force of thirty-six that would arrive by the end of August.   The American destroyers worked under the command of British Vice Adm. Lewis Bayly, RN, commander-in-chief Coast of Ireland, supported by the destroyer tenders USS *Dixie* and *Melville*. Engaged first on patrol duties and later as convoy escorts, the success of the destroyers in hunting U-boats in British waters spurred the German Naval Command to despatch other submarines to North America. This action was taken in the hope that decimation of shipping off the Eastern Seaboard would result in sufficient public outrage to induce the U.S. government to bring the destroyers home to patrol and protect America's east coast.[7] (This submarine offensive is described in the following chapter.)

NORTH SEA MINE BARRAGE

> *Besides influencing an early armistice, this great minelaying operation marks an epoch in the use of submarine mines in warfare. It was an event in military history, as well as a prominent operation, and the credit for it belongs not alone to the officers and men who were actually present but also to those of the old mine force, to whose service in developing, in our navy, the art of handling and laying mines in large numbers, the success of the great operation was so largely due.*

—Rear Adm. Lewis Clinton-Baker, RN, the British Rear Admiral
of Mines and head of the British minelaying force which, in
company with the U.S. Minelaying Force,
laid the North Sea Mine Barrage.

> *It was the determination of every officer and man in the 14th Flotilla, who had the honour of being entrusted with the screening of the U.S. Minelaying Force, that no preventable attack by enemy submarine or surface vessel should inflict damage on any ship of the Force.*

—Capt. Harry R. Godfrey, Royal Navy,
commanding HMS *Vampire* and
the 14th Destroyer Flotilla.

The convoy and escort system implemented in 1917 eventually reduced ship losses to a manageable level, but the Allies wanted to bottle up U-boats in German ports. Unfortunately, the German High Seas Fleet controlled the adjacent waters. The next best option was to barricade the North Sea to keep U-boats out of the Atlantic, by laying a minefield stretching from Scotland to Norway across hundreds of miles of open sea. This idea was first suggested by the British First Sea Lord, Adm. Henry Jackson, but the Royal Navy was opposed to the idea. The number of mines that would be required to create such a barrier would be enormous, and with no guarantee of success, the Admiralty decided against it.[8]

Reportedly, Adm. John Jellicoe (who in November 1916 had replaced Jackson as the First Sea Lord) ultimately only agreed to the mine barrage to pacify his American counterparts. U.S. Navy "top brass," which believed the barrier would either act as a deterrent and keep U-boats from venturing out of German waters or destroy any that tried, wanted to use both shallow and deep mines in all three of the barrage's sections. The British viewed the barrage as a "bluff" that hopefully might draw the High Seas Fleet out into the North Sea and force a general fleet engagement.[9]

FLEDGLING PEACETIME U.S. NAVY MINE FORCE

In 1915, as the Allied and Central Powers waged war on land, at sea, and in the skies over Europe, and while America was still at peace, an initiative was begun within the U.S. Navy to develop doctrine and to acquire the ships, men, and infrastructure necessary to carry out minelaying at sea. Minelaying from a ship had previously received little attention, but Allied ship losses to U-boats clearly demonstrated the important role mines were likely to play in the future. Capt. George Ralph Marvell, a senior naval officer in the Navy Department, was assigned the principal duty of mining affairs: the acquisition and conversion of two additional ships to minelayers (the *Baltimore* and *Dubuque*, to join the hitherto solitary mine ship *San Francisco*) was pushed through, and mine training began in earnest in the fleet.[10]

The Mine Force did not have any wartime minelaying experience, but was able to gain practice in early December 1916, sowing a field of unarmed mines off the New Jersey coast, below Sandy Hook. The field (200 mines, in three parallel lines laid simultaneously) was taken up the next day, without notification to the press about the operation. Subsequent planning of mining installations, organisation, and training associated with the North Sea Mine Barrage was guided by the experience gained. Moreover, while the original Mine Force was too small for the task that lay ahead, its value as a nucleus and catalyst for the soon-to-be-formed enlarged mine squadron was invaluable.[11]

Photo 18-1

Capt. George R. Marvell, USN, 1 August 1917.
National Archives #24-P-42

OPERATIONAL COMMAND OF THE MINE FORCE

From autumn 1916 onward, the principal Mine Force officers were its commander, Capt. Reginald Belknap, Comdr. Henry Butler, the commanding officer of the flagship *San Francisco* and senior aid to Belknap, and Commanders Albert Marshall and Thomas Johnson of the *Baltimore* and *Dubuque*, respectively. These four men were to take part in the North Sea operation—and were involved with its preparation. Butler trained new crews, Marshall began experimenting with a new mine under development, and Johnson helped to select additional ships for use as minelayers. In October 1917, with approval to commence final arrangements to lay a mine barrier across the North Sea, the development of plans and coordination of preparations became the principal duty of Belknap, whose previous command of the *San Francisco* (12 December 1914-16 December 1915) and two years at the head of mining affairs in the Atlantic Fleet had provided him experience that was directly pertinent.[12]

Photo 18-2

USS *San Francisco* in 1915; her name was later changed on 1 January 1931 to *Yosemite*. Naval History and Heritage Command photograph #NH 67785

ADDITIONAL MINELAYERS REQUIRED QUICKLY

Following receipt of orders to lay the barrage as soon as possible, the Mine Force had much to do in preparation. Calculating that five days turnaround (involving provisioning, coaling, loading mines, transit out from port, laying mines, and return) would be the minimum amount of time necessary between minelaying operations; and that expected manufacturing output of mines would be 1,000 a day; a minelaying squadron capable of laying 5,000 mines at one time was required. The *San Francisco* and *Baltimore* together carried only 350 mines. The acquisition of eight additional ships would add another 5,350 capacity, providing a good margin for the loss of a ship or an acceleration in speed in the mining, if directed.[13]

Time was of the essence. Within ten days, the navy purchased the Eastern Steamship Corporation's fast passenger liners *Bunker Hill* and *Massachusetts* which (previously running daily between New York and Boston) became respectively the *Aroostook* and the *Shawmut*. The Southern Pacific freight steamers *El Cid*, *El Dia*, *El Rio*, and *El Siglo* were taken over within a month, becoming the *Canonicus*, *Housatonic*, *Roanoke*, and *Canandaigua*, respectively. With the capacity to carry 860 mines each, these ships soon became known as the Big Four. Lastly, the Old Dominion steamers *Jefferson* and *Hamilton* (familiar to passengers between New York and Norfolk) followed by 6 December 1917. Once converted, these sister ships became in turn *Quinnebaug* and *Saranac*.[14]

Mine Squadron 1: Capt. Reginald R. Belknap, USN

Minelayer/ former Ship	Length/ Displ.	Commis- sioned	Commanding Officer
Aroostook (ID 1256) SS *Bunker Hill*	395/3,800	launched 1907 7 Dec 1917	Capt. James Harvey Tomb, USN
Baltimore (CM 1) protected cruiser C 3	335/4,413	7 Jan 1890 8 Mar 1915	Capt. Albert W. Marshall, USN
Canandaigua (ID 1694) SS *El Siglo*	379/7,620	built in 1901 2 Mar 1918	Comdr. William H. Reynolds, USN
Canonicus (ID 1696) SS *El Cid*	405/7,620	built in 1899 2 Mar 1918	Capt. Thomas L. Johnson, USN
Housatonic (ID 1697) SS *El Dia*	405/7,620	built in 1899 25 Jan 1918	Comdr. John Wills Greenslade, USN
Quinnebaug (ID 1687) SS *Jefferson*	375/5,150	built in 1899 28 Mar 1918	Comdr. David Pratt Mannix, USN
Roanoke (ID 1695) SS *El Rio*	379/7,620	built in 1901 25 Jan 1918	Capt. Clark Daniel Stearns, USN
San Francisco (CM 2) protected cruiser C 5	324/4,083	15 Nov 1890 21 Aug 1911	Capt. Henry Varnum Butler Jr., USN
Shawmut (ID 1255) SS *Massachusetts*	386/3,746	built in 1907 7 Dec 1917	Capt. Wat Tyler Cluverius Jr., USN
Saranac (ID 1702) SS *Hamilton*	375/5,150	built in 1899 9 Apr 1918	Comdr. Sinclair Gannon, USN[15]

Length and displacement units are feet/tons; commissioning dates reflect the ships' original commissioning/completion dates, followed by the dates the converted vessels were recommissioned as minelayers.

SHIPYARD CONVERSION

The momentous task of making the freight ships—*El Cid*, *El Dia*, *El Rio*, and *El Siglo*—habitable for 400-man crews, while providing them capability to carry twice as many mines as other vessels their size, was both challenging and lengthy. With regard to the larger passenger ships (*Bunker Hill*, *Hamilton*, *Jefferson*, and *Massachusetts*), they were gutted like fish, with saloons and cabins ripped out before their conversion could begin. The winter of 1917-18 was memorable for its many shortfalls—scarcity of materiel, congested transportation of materiel, unsettled labour disputes, fuel shortages, severe weather, and high prices—

compounded by a general lack of interest among many workmen. Belknap explained:

> There was insufficient supervision, the contractors were converting vessels to a type for which no model existed, and plans were not forthcoming as fast as wanted, often not in logical order. Besides delays and losses of material in transportation, one trade in which labour was shortest—shipfitter—was the one on whose work much of the other had to wait.[16]

Photo 18-3

Freight ship SS *El Dia* in service, before World War I and her subsequent acquisition by the Navy and conversion to the minelayer USS *Roanoke*.
Naval History and Heritage Command photograph #NH 100250

Nevertheless, by constant urging and anticipation of probable delays, the work progressed, even if at times slowly. As soon as possible, the commanding officers of the ships, and their principal officers, came aboard, followed by members of their crews. By 25 January 1918, two of the largest ships (*Roanoke* and *Housatonic*) were commissioned. Living conditions were rough amid the dirt and disorder, made worse by slush and mud in unpaved shipyards, but the presence of sailors aboard helped push things along and provided them opportunity to become acquainted with their ships.[17]

In the conversion of sister ships *Aroostook* and *Shawmut* at the Boston Navy Yard, sailors worked in industrial gangs alongside civilian employees. This effort markedly advanced the date of completion. At the same time, other members of the ships' crews underwent training at

Newport, Rhode Island, under the tutelage of Mine Force officers, with practical instruction given aboard the *San Francisco* and *Baltimore*, supplemented by other training elsewhere. Three gun crews for each minelayer were trained aboard battleships, and engineering personnel were kept under training at Philadelphia, until needed. The officers undertook similar training to acquaint themselves with the methods and experiences of the Mine Force, so far as could be done with ships in yards, fitting out/under conversion.[18]

Photo 18-4

USS *Shawmut* at the Boston Navy Yard, Massachusetts, 4 June 1918, following conversion to a minelayer. Her sister ship, *Aroostook*, is in the background. Naval History and Heritage Command photograph #NH 41959

FLAG OFFICER ORDERED TO HEAD MINE FORCE

Unlike the old Mine Force which consisted solely of ships afloat, the new one was to be comprised of supporting organisations ashore as well as the ships afloat. For this upgrade an officer of flag rank was warranted, and Rear Adm. Joseph Strauss, USN, was selected to command the Mine Force. He was detached from duties as commanding officer of the battleship USS *Nevada* in February 1918, for the assignment as commander, Mine Force, Atlantic Fleet. During temporary duty in the Office of Naval Operations, Strauss familiarised himself with information related to the establishment of the North Sea Mine Barrage and the preparation's in-hand for its laying. After a tour of the ships, and acquainting himself with the mine supply situation, he sailed for England. Arriving at Liverpool on 23 March, he travelled to London to report for duty to Vice Adm. William S. Sims, USN, commander U.S. Naval Forces, European Waters.[19]

Photo 18-5

Rear Adm. Joseph Strauss, USN, commander Mine Force Atlantic Fleet, 1918. Naval History and Heritage Command photograph #NH 50491

Rear Admiral Strauss assumed command of the Mine Force on 29 March 1918, with headquarters at U.S. Naval Base 18, Inverness, Scotland. Thereafter, the original Mine Force, consisting only of ships afloat, became Mine Squadron 1. It became the duty of Captain Belknap (formerly the Mine Force commander and now commodore of the Mine Squadron) to complete its preparations in the United States and command the forces afloat.[20]

Photo 18-6

Capt. Reginald Rowan Belknap, USN, circa 1918.
Naval History and Heritage Command photograph #NH 56134

BALTIMORE LAYS FIELD IN ENGLISH WATERS

While U.S. Mine Force preparations were in progress in America, across the Atlantic in the early spring of 1918, German submarines were very active in the Irish Channel. To counter shipping losses, the Admiralty decided to lay a deep minefield off the north coast of Ireland in the North Channel. As all British minelayers were employed elsewhere, the Admiralty approached Vice Admiral Sims about the possibility of the U.S. Navy lending them a minelayer for this purpose. *Aroostook* and *Shawmut* were then still undergoing work at the Boston Navy Yard, but *Baltimore* was available. She was promptly ordered to these duties and sent to the Firth of Clyde (an inlet of the Atlantic on the southwest coast of Scotland). Upon her arrival, she became the first American minelayer to enter British waters.[21]

Baltimore remained on the Clyde for about three weeks while being fitted out with paravanes and taut wire measuring gear (used to enable the positions, in which minefields were to be laid, to be located with greater accuracy). Her stay there provided opportunity to send parties of officers and men to Grangemouth for instruction at the mining depot, and aboard the minelayer HMS *Princess Margaret*, on the British H2 mine and its Mk XII sinker. Located near Rosyth, on the Firth of Forth, Grangemouth was home to the British Minelaying Squadron. During this period, Capt. Albert Marshall met with Rear Adm. Lewis Clinton-Baker, RN, who was responsible for overall details of laying the minefield. Marshall and Capt. Lockhart Leith, RN, then visited Larne and Buncrana in Northern Ireland, Ardrossan on Scotland's southwest coast, and Lamlash on the Isle of Arran, to discuss the procedure for carrying out the minelaying operation with the senior naval officers at these ports bordering the new north Ireland field.[22]

Lamlash, a village off the west coast of Scotland, was selected as the base from which *Baltimore* should operate. Mines were supplied by train from the mine depot at Immingham, England, situated on the southwest bank of the Humber Estuary. The mines were British H2 star (with Mk XII fixed moorings) fitted with deep switches and calibrated so as to be inoperative when nearer the surface than fifty feet. Sinking plugs were not used.[23]

Map 18-1

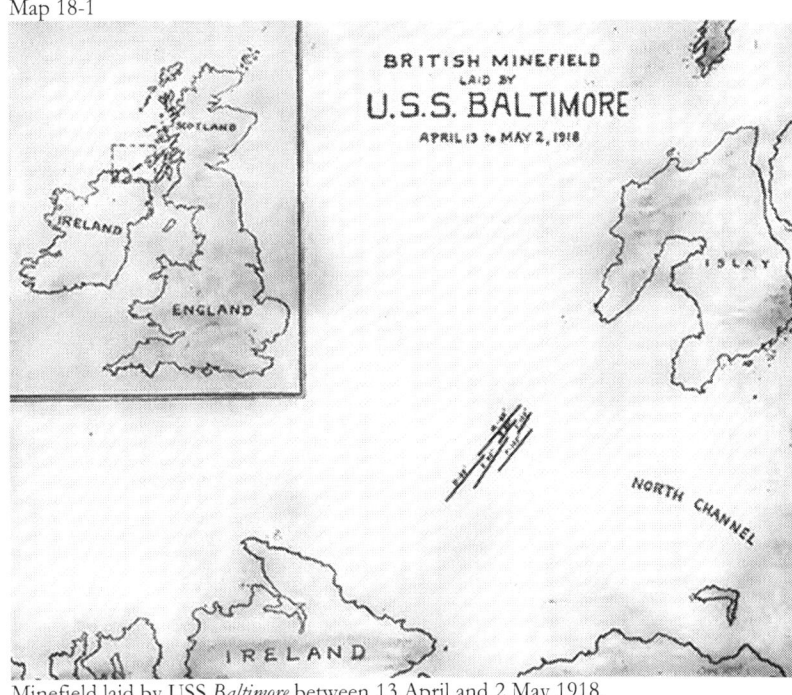

Minefield laid by USS *Baltimore* between 13 April and 2 May 1918.

Baltimore laid the minefield between 13 April and 2 May 1918, with all operations conducted at night and with two British destroyers screening her from possible attack. On orders from the Admiralty, minelaying was discontinued after 2 May, because a skimming sweep of the field had disclosed several shallow mines at its northern end, due in all probability to the very uneven nature of the bottom. Because the mines in the field were set for fixed moorings of approximately 45 fathoms, tests were conducted at Grangemouth to ascertain the reliability of the locking device in the Mk XII sinkers. The results revealed the possibility of the locking nut stripping the threads and allowing the full length of the cable on the reel to run out, thereby positioning the mine body too close to the water's surface.[24]

Sweeping for shallow mines continued until 29 May, when the entire North Channel deep minefield had been swept at a depth of approximately 36 feet. A few shallow mines were found in lines D and E, but not nearly so many as were found in the other lines. Depth soundings obtained by the vessels engaged in the skim sweep showed considerable irregularity in the bottom and much variation from the survey soundings which were used for setting the fixed moorings.[25]

Prior to discontinuation of the laying operations for the North Irish field, it appeared that *Baltimore* would not be able to complete the minefield in time to join Mine Squadron 1 for the first operation in laying the North Sea Barrage. Accordingly, *Roanoke* was despatched from the United States on 3 May—based on an inspection following her departure from the shipyard which found her to be in excellent condition—to assist the *Baltimore*. Before her arrival, the operations in the Irish Channel had been discontinued. *Roanoke* remained for several days at Lamlash, and then sailed for Invergordon, Scotland. She arrived there a week ahead of Mine Squadron 1, which at that time was making the Atlantic crossing from America.[26]

Baltimore remained on Ireland's west coast for several weeks performing experiments for the British in connection with minelaying and minesweeping, then proceeded to Inverness, Scotland.[26]

MINE SQUADRON 1

Mine Squadron 1 had been established at Hampton Roads, Virginia, on 10 April 1918 aboard the flagship *San Francisco*. The first minelayer, *Roanoke*, joined the squadron on 12 April, followed closely by the *Housatonic* and the *Canandaigua* the following day. Arrangements were made for them to load mines, and it began at once. Within a week, *Quinnebaug* and *Canonicus* also arrived, thus completing the squadron— with the exception of *Shawmut* and *Aroostook* which were still undergoing work at the Boston Navy Yard. *Baltimore* and *Roanoke* were already in Europe.[27]

When ready to proceed, the squadron sailed from the United States, and arrived in Scotland in the early morning on 26 May. The flagship and minelayer *San Francisco*, minelayers *Canandaigua* and *Canonicus*, and the fleet tug *Sonoma* entered Inverness (Overseas Base 18), and the minelayers *Housatonic* and *Quinnebaug*, along with collier *Jason* entered nearby Invergordon (Base 17) to join *Roanoke*.[28]

OVERSEAS BASES 17 AND 18

The American squadron was to use Invergordon and Inverness in the Scottish Highlands as mine assembling and operating bases. The two ports were situated about eight miles apart on the Cromarty Firth and Inverness Firth, which emptied into Moray Firth. The bases, which utilised the facilities of the Dalmore Distillery at Dalmore, Alness, at Invergordon, and those of the Glen Albyn Distillery at Inverness, had not sprung up overnight. Months earlier, two parties of men, led by lieutenant commanders Edwin Wolleson and L. M. Stewart, had arrived at Invergordon and Inverness, respectively, on 8 January, to begin development of Bases 17 and 18.[29]

Map 18-2

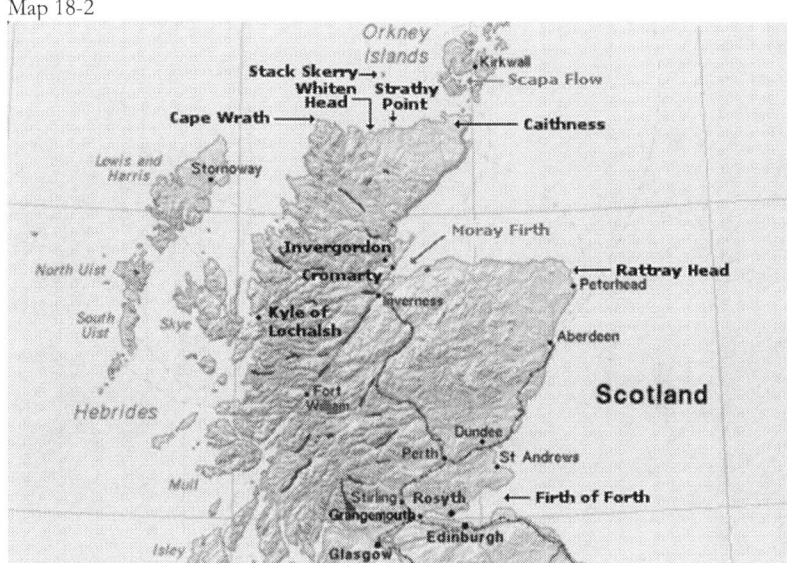

American Overseas Bases 17 and 18 were at Invergordon and Inverness, Scotland. To the southwest, on the west coast of Scotland, was the village of Kyle of Lochalsh, where supplies were landed for transport inland to the bases.

The first stores sent from the United States arrived on 20 January 1918 by way of Liverpool. The American flag was raised over Base 18 on 9 February; and three days later "Old Glory" was flying at Base 17. The mine carrier *Ozama* arrived at Kyle of Lochalsh (a village on the northwest coast of Scotland, sixty-three miles southwest of Inverness) on 18 February, with stores and equipment for the bases. By 1 March, the two bases were ready to receive mine components and begin assembly when needed. Mine components began to be delivered soon after. The mines to be employed were the U.S.-manufactured Mk VI type. (A description of these mines may be found in the Preface.) Most construction work was completed by 1 April, shortly after the arrival of the squadron.[30]

Following his arrival with the squadron, Belknap had reported to higher command that his ships would be ready to commence minelaying as soon as they had been watered and refueled. The lack of a critical mine part, however, prevented the immediate start of operations. For safety reasons, mines were shipped from the U.S. unassembled, in loads of individual parts. All of the parts were on hand except the requisite number of antenna floats for mines, and it was necessary to wait until a mine carrier had arrived before sufficient floats would be available to assemble the large quantity of mines needed for the first excursion.[31]

Photo 18-7

Harbour scene in 1918 at Invergordon, Scotland, from a U.S. Navy minelayer. A 3"/50 AA gun is visible at the right; and a British battleship in drydock at the left. Naval History and Heritage Command photograph #NH 89509

Photo 18-8

Assembling mines at Base 18, Inverness, Scotland.
History and Heritage Command photograph #NH 123961

SHIPPING MINE COMPONENTS TO SCOTLAND

The Mk VI mines were all assembled at Bases 17 and 18, using components from many points of manufacture in the United States. The materiel was transported to Norfolk, Virginia, and loaded aboard mine carriers for transatlantic shipment. Since an inventory of all components had to be available constantly at these bases, regular deliveries by a fleet of cargo vessels was essential. This was accomplished by vessels of the "Lake" class acquired by the Navy Department for exclusive use as mine carriers.[32]

The 251-foot cargo ship *Ozama*, built by Detroit Shipbuilding Co., Wyandotte, Michigan, in 1916, was one such American mine carrier. She had been acquired by the Navy on 24 December 1917 and commissioned that same day with Lt. Comdr. P. E. Crosby, USNRF, in command. Following her initial voyage from Hampton Roads to Scotland with a cargo of minelaying equipment, she had returned to Norfolk. After loading and transiting the Atlantic again, she arrived at Corpach, Scotland, on 21 May with the first Mk VI mine spheres for Base 18. Thereafter, she continued to ply the Atlantic keeping the bases in Scotland supplied with mine materiel. On 13 February 1919 following the war, she was decommissioned and returned to her owner, the Atlantic, Gulf, and West Indies Steamship Line.[33]

These supply ships—armed for defence against submarines, and manned by Naval Reserve crews—were small, averaging about 3,000 tons, but by reason of their shallow draughts were well suited for their intended purpose. Larger and deeper draught vessels could not have been so readily loaded or discharged at all designated terminals. In fact, one of the harbours designated by British authorities could not accommodate ships drawing more than twenty feet. Further, smaller vessels carrying fewer mines each, would also minimise the effect on the whole project in the event of a ship loss.[34]

Fortunately, of the twenty-four carriers, only *Lake Moor* was lost in the war. She was torpedoed by the German submarine *UB-73* on 11 April 1918 and sank three miles off Corsewall Point Light, Scotland, killing five officers and 41 men and taking her cargo of Mk VI mine components, mostly anchors, to the bottom. The following month, *UB-57* torpedoed the armed merchant cruiser RMS *Moldavia* off Beachy Head on 23 May. Aboard her were men of the U.S. Army 4th Infantry Division, fifty-six of whom perished. These incidents reinforced the importance of measures to combat U-boats, one of which was the laying of the mine barrage.[35]

SQUADRON 1 BEGINS MINELAYING OPERATIONS

The first sowing of mines in the North Sea Barrage was to be a joint operation between the British minelaying squadron, which had been designated by the Admiralty as the 1st mine laying squadron, and the American minelayers the 2nd minelaying squadron. Both squadrons were assigned separate mining areas for the concurrent laying of both shallow and deep mines. Mines to be laid were to be supplied by each squadron's country. (To minimise confusion, U.S. Squadron 1 will henceforth be referred to in the book as the American squadron.) On 7 June 1918, the minelayers of the American squadron left their bases, rendezvoused outside Cromarty Firth with the British destroyers sent to escort them, and proceeded across the North Sea until Udshire Light was sighted on the coast of Norway. The light was used as a reference, being the nearest point of land to the position in which the minelaying was to commence.[36]

Map 18-3

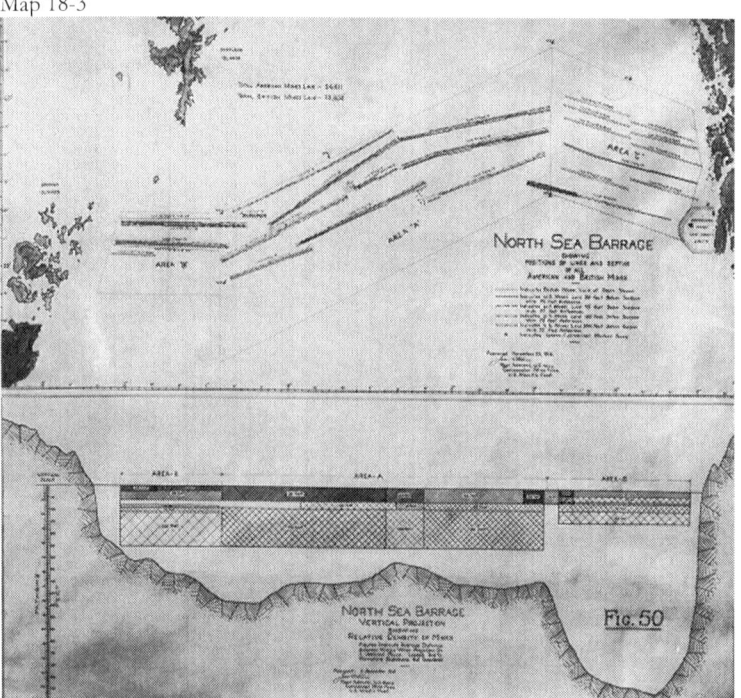

Chart of North Sea Barrage, showing positions of lines and depths of American and British mines, with a vertical projection displaying the relative density of mines. Area A lies in the center, Area B is toward the Orkney Islands, and Area C toward Norway. Source: *The Northern Barrage and Other Mining Activities*

During the initial U.S. operation, no difficulties were encountered by any of the ships with their mining installations because of the lack of experience of their crews. The mines were laid with accuracy and precision and the minelayers, in spite of the various types of vessels which constituted the American squadron, manoeuvred well together. However, shortly after operations began, some of the Mk VI mines began to explode prematurely—perhaps 3-4 percent of the 3,385 mines that were laid. Some of the mines exploded almost immediately after they went overboard, severely shaking the ships from which they were laid. Others did not blow up until days later. These explosions were baffling, and efforts immediately began to determine the cause.[37]

NORWAY PROHIBITS PASSAGE OF BELLIGERENT SUBMARINES THROUGH ITS TERITORIAL WATERS

The British minelaying squadron proceeded separately to Area C, where their mines were laid on the same date that the American ones were put down. Shortly after the minelaying began, the Norwegian government issued a declaration to the effect that belligerent submarines equipped for use in warfare must not traverse or stay in Norwegian territorial waters except by reason of extreme weather or to save life. Breach of this prohibition would subject them to armed attack without warning. This decree, rigidly enforced, would have the same result as if mines had been laid right up to the Norwegian coast instead of stopping at their territorial waters, three miles offshore.   It later became apparent, however, that this policy was not enforced against German submarines.[38]

After the completion of their first operation, further minelaying by the American mine force was delayed by a shortage of mining materiel. The first excursion had used up all but three of the antennae floats for the lower-level mines. There were plenty of floats on hand for the upper-level mines, but tests performed in Loch Ness revealed that they would not, however, hold up when submerged to the necessary depth. Meanwhile, the British minelaying squadron completed its second and third operations on 18 and 30 June.[39]

Four American minelayers got under way on 30 June for Area C, and laid their cargoes on 1 July. Once again, about four percent of the mines exploded prematurely. These deficiencies had been thought to be caused by inaccuracies in assembly and testing, inaccuracy of the depth-taking mechanism, or inability of the mine cases to withstand the water pressure when planted at 240 feet. The possible causes of premature explosions were many, and it was impossible to attribute them to any one mine component. It was hoped that utmost care in the assembly, adjustment, and planting of the mines would reduce the percentage of premature explosions.[40]

Photo 18-9

American Mk VI mines in storage for the North Sea Mine Barrage.
Naval History and Heritage Command photograph #NHF-136

Photo 18-10

Mines being loaded onto lighters (at the Base 18 loading basin on the Caledonian Canal at Inverness, Scotland) for transfer to minelayers.
Naval History and Heritage Command #NH 123965

Following the first two American excursions, a homeward bound German submarine, *U-86*, was damaged on 9 July while transiting Area C. She reached port successfully, exhibiting tangible proof that the North Sea Barrage was a reality.[41]

CONTINUED SEARCH FOR CAUSE OF PREMATURE EXPLOSIONS

The fourth British operation was carried out on 12 July in Area C. The American squadron got under way for its third excursion on 14 July. The following day 5,395 mines were laid in 4 hours and 22 minutes (the largest number planted to that date in a single operation). The ships all laid their entire quotas of mines in one continuous string at a speed of 12½-13 knots. Approximately 5 percent of the mines exploded prematurely. The slight increase over previous performances was because some of the explosions were caused by countermining. This term refers to the explosion of one mine inducing the detonation of several others. Curiously, mines as far distant as a half-mile were countermined, while others only 300 feet away remained intact.[42]

Photo 18-11

USS *Shawmut* laying mines in the North Sea, with a British V-W type destroyer laying a protective smoke screen at right.
Naval History and Heritage Command photograph #NH 99410

The fifth British operation in Area C was carried out on 21 July. Several days' delay was encountered before the fourth American one, owing to the necessity to wait for mining materiel. The squadron was ready to sail on 25 July, but had to wait four additional days for the availability of escorting and supporting forces from the Grand Fleet. The British and American operations had, to that point, been overlapping, with one squadron at sea while the other was loading in port. As this necessitated keeping a large part of the Grand Fleet supporting force at sea almost constantly, it was decided that the

Americans should wait until the British had again loaded, so that it would only be necessary to send one force to support both squadrons.[43]

The American squadron sailed on 29 July, and laid 5,399 mines the following day. However, the premature explosions were much more numerous than on previous excursions, with approximately 14 percent of the mines going off. This was very troubling. Instead of the explosions decreasing as experience was gained in the assembly and laying of the mines, the percentage had dramatically increased. The Force commander ordered the suspension of further minelaying operations until the cause was found and corrected. Two possible causes seemed to be the most likely. One prospect was the circuit breakers in the antennae circuits. They were being used for the very first time and it was thought that they possibly might adversely affect the firing device. But, it was not obvious how. The other possible cause was believed to be the improper installation of horn bushings in the mine case. Unless carefully installed there was danger of electrically grounding the firing device, which could cause the mine to fire as soon as the soluble washer had dissolved.[44]

Photo 18-12

U.S. Navy minelayers steaming in two parallel columns of four, during the laying of the North Sea Mine Barrage in the summer and fall of 1918. In the left column (from front to rear) are *Saranac*, *Roanoke*, *Housatonic*, and either *Shawmut* or *Aroostook*. The right column contains (front to rear) *Canandaigua*, *Canonicus*, *Quinnebaug* and (perhaps) *Baltimore*.
Naval History and Heritage Command photograph #NH 41736

Believing that further actual experience might help identify the problem, arrangements were made for the next laying mission to begin on 8 August. To eliminate one potential cause of the premature explosions, the mines were assembled with the electric circuits to the horns disconnected, but everything else remained as before. This excursion was again a joint one, with the British laying surface mines in Area C. The American portion of the operation was discontinued with only 1,596 mines laid, after about 19 percent of them exploded prematurely.[45]

Evidently the horn circuit was not at fault, and in the following days, numerous experiments were carried out in search of another possible cause. It was found that the vulcanised rubber insulation between the copper plates on the firing device caused the formation of sulphates and sulphides on the copper which, when immersed in salt water, set up a slight current in the firing circuit. Although small, if the current created was eliminated, the mines might have sufficient stability to not explode after they had been planted.[46]

On 10 August, U-113 was damaged proceeding outbound through the barrier, and was forced to turn back. Meanwhile, minemen cleaned the copper plates on their charges, and the American squadron sailed on its sixth excursion on 18 August. The British squadron proceeded at the same time to complete laying their surface mines in Area C. Twelve percent of the American mines exploded prematurely. Subsequently, it was learned that the first lots of firing devices shipped from the United States to the bases were set to fire at between 25 and 40 millivolts. The Bureau of Ordnance had subsequently reduced the voltage to between 10 and 15 millivolts. Apparently, it was the use of these latter firing devices that had dramatically increased premature detonations.[47]

Additionally, tests conducted to ascertain the effect of the copper sulphate deposits on the plates of the firing device showed that as much as 10 millivolts could be generated. This was sufficient voltage to rotate the armature of the firing device through a considerable portion of its arc so that a slight additional shock, which might readily be caused by the explosion of a nearby mine, would be sufficient to shake the firing ball from its cup and detonate (countermine) the mine. By adjusting the tension of the hair spring on the armature, the voltage necessary to fire a mine could be increased to the desired amount, so that this stray voltage would not inadvertently do so.[48]

These adjustments were made before the American squadron's seventh excursion (on 26 and 30 August). Using the higher voltage settings, only about three percent of the mines exploded prematurely, the same as with the original lots of firing devices.   This was undoubtedly of great relief to sailors aboard the ships. Those sailors pushing mines overboard did not welcome the possibility that these explosives could blow up after hitting the water, before their ship was well clear of them. Duty aboard any minelayer was dangerous, but assignment to one carrying large quantities of high explosives was particular so. Enemy gunfire or a torpedo could detonate the deadly cargo, instantaneously obliterating the ship and her crew.   The assignment of units of the British Grand Fleet to screen minelayers from German combatants largely eliminated the possibility of an attack by surface ships—although not one by submarines.[49]

MINES SINK *U-92*, DAMAGE SECOND SUBMARINE

The eighth excursion, one in Area B, was meant to surprise German submarines. They had been passing through this area on their way to the Atlantic. After secretly routing Allied shipping around it, and mining it, it was the hope that the subs would continue their practice of using it. The British and American mining squadrons rendezvoused off the Orkneys on 7 September and carried out the operation. The USN ships laid six lines of surface mines across Area B, and those of the RN one parallel to these. Admiral Strauss was in charge of both squadrons, while the minelaying was in progress.[50]

The following day, *U-92* was sunk in Area B. She had been outward bound. After this, it appeared that the enemy began to attempt passage directly across Area A, which was relatively poorly mined. The tenth, eleventh, and twelfth excursions in the latter part of September and early October greatly increased the effectiveness of this portion of the barrier. The losses of *U-156* and *U-123* respectively, on 25 September and 18 October, were attributed to mining in this area.[51]

RESULTS OBTAINED BY THE BARRAGE

It is well to remember that a mine barrage of this nature can never be an absolute barrier possessing 100 percent efficiency. On account of the necessity of laying the mines at a distance of approximately 300 feet apart in order to reduce the possibility of countermining, it would always be possible for a submarine with a beam of approximately 30 feet to successfully cross such a barrier no matter how many parallel lines may be laid.

The danger in crossing, of course, increases with the number of rows of mines but not in direct proportion. The object, then, in constructing a barrage must be to make the danger incurred by the passage of a vessel sufficiently great to prevent submarines from taking the risk involved.

—Rear Adm. Joseph Strauss, USN, commander U.S. Mine Force, in his summary of the final status of the North Sea Mine Barrage and the results obtained from it.[52]

When hostilities ceased following the signing of an armistice on 11 November 1918, with 56,760 American Mk VI and 16,300 British H2 mines laid, the North Sea Mine Barrage remained incomplete. Although there were no gates, there was free passage through a 10-mile wide gap at the western extremely; left open to allow movement by the British Fleet. Additionally, because Norway had apparently neither mined, nor vigourously patrolled its territorial waters (until perhaps very late in the war), it was believed German submarines had been passing through them to bypass the barrier.[53]

British intelligence and German records following the war indicated that six submarines were likely casualties of the North Sea Mine Barrage:

U-boats Believed Lost to North Sea Mine Barrage

Date	Area	U-boat	Commanding Officer
9 Sep 1918	B	*U-92*	Kptlt. Günther Ehrlich
19 Sep 1918	B	*UB-104*	OLt. z. S. Ernst Berlin
25 Sep 1918	A	*U-156*	Kptlt. Konrad Gansser
September	B	*UB-127*	OLt. z. S. Walter Scheffler
30 Sep 1918	A	*U-102*	Kptlt. Ernst Killmann
19 Oct 1918	A	*UB-123*	OLt. z. S. Robert Ramm[54]

For all the mining, the British H2 and H4 mines sank more German U-boats between November 1917 and November 1918 than the unreliable Service and Elia mines had since October 1914, by a wide margin. There were four confirmed losses of German submarines to mines up to November 1917 and sixteen during the last twelve months of the war. In recent years, these numbers have gradually increased as submarine wreckage is found by divers and inspection reveals that the losses of some submarines to previously unknown causes were the result of mines. For readers desiring more information about U-boat losses in World War I, attributable to all causes, Dwight R. Messimer's book, *World War I U-boat Losses* (Naval Institute, 2002) is a seminal reference.[55]

Presumably, the existence of the North Sea Mine Barrage and the desire of some submarines to avoid it resulted in their losses in other minefields, in particular the enormous Folkstone to Cape Gris Nez deep mine barrage, which replaced the failed barrier/net system. This barrage, which became operational in December 1917, was intended to close the Dover Strait to U-boats. Two factors made it extremely effective. One was the availability of H2 mines in large quantities. The other was the British practice of illuminating the barrage at night and patrolling it continuously day and night. The result was U-boats had to dive as they approached the barrier, forcing them down into a minefield. The mines were laid in a ladder-pattern to a depth of 200 feet, and any submarine attempting to pass through the barrier would almost certainly hit a mine.[56]

Submarine Offensive off North America's Eastern Seaboard

The Germans have completed a number of cruising submarines of large radius and large capacity, and these may be used on our coast with a view to divert some of our military activity away from European waters. The constant increase of antisubmarine forces abroad may compel an enemy effort to cause such a diversion, and the comparative openness of American waters offers a good field for submarine activities.

Their aim will be to destroy shipping, interrupt the transport of troops and supplies to Europe, interfere with our coastwise shipping, by these means causing the recall from abroad of some of our naval force for defense of home waters. Bombardment of coast towns may also be done, with a view to heighten popular demand for local protection, and thereby embarrass the naval administration.

The general policy of the United States is to send the maximum possible force abroad for offensive operations in the active theater of war. This policy the Board has kept constantly in mind to the end that there might be no weakening of it.

—Excerpts from a report (Defense against submarine attack in home waters, Navy Department, Office of Naval Operations, Washington, 6 February 1918) by a special board convened by the Chief of Naval Operations to formulate a plan of defense in U.S. home waters.[1]

When the U.S. entered the war in April 1917 the naval assets of most value to the Allies was a fleet of destroyers equipped with the latest sonar devices and armed with depth charges. By August, thirty-six were deployed to a base in Queenstown, Ireland; to guard Allied convoys and attack German submarines in the western approaches to Europe where they were wreaking havoc on Allied supply shipping. The deployment was successful and losses of shipping diminished significantly. To counter the threats to their U-boats in the most fruitful hunting grounds, the Germans began sending submarines to attack shipping in North American waters hoping to prompt U.S. withdrawal of the destroyers to their home waters.

In spring and summer 1918, the German Naval Command sent seven U-boats to the North American East Coast. The first, *U-151*, left Kiel (a German port on the Baltic Sea) on 18 April, on an eastern route around the Shetland Islands. After passing through the Sund (a strait between Sweden and Denmark) and around the Skagen Peninsula, on the northern tip of Denmark, she entered the North Sea and set a course to pass round the Shetland Islands before turning southwest, bound for America's east coast. (The Shetland Islands, which lie some 50 miles northeast of the Orkney Islands and 170 miles southeast of the Faroes, form part of Scotland. The Faroe Islands, situated about halfway between Norway and Iceland, are an autonomous country within the Kingdom of Denmark.)[2]

Map 19-1

U-boats leaving Kiel or Warnemünde, Germany, for North America transited the Sund and passed around the Skagen Peninsula, before entering the North Sea

Of the remaining six boats, five departed from Kiel. The other submarine, *U-140*, sailed from Warnemünde, a port town on the Baltic about eighty miles (as the crow flies) to the east of Kiel. The submarines took routes that passed between the Shetlands and the Faroe Islands; or north of the Faroes, passing between Iceland and the Faroes. A summary of the U-boats' individual departure dates, arrival dates off the Atlantic Coast (or at Longitude 40° West), departure dates for return transit to Germany, and arrival dates in Germany is provided in the table.[3]

Map 19-2

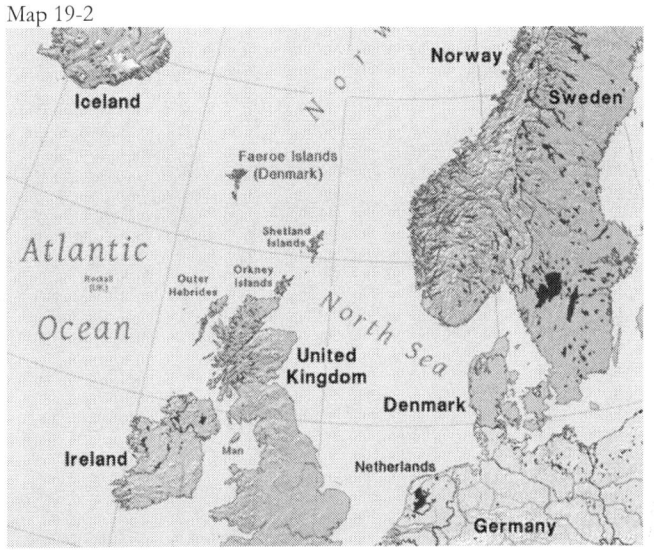

Eastern North Atlantic and North Sea

Summary of German Submarine Movements

U-boat	Left Germany	Arrived off Atlantic Coast or Long. 40°W	Left Atlantic Coast	Arrived Germany
Deutschland (first visit)	14 Jun 1916	9 Jul 1916	1 Aug 1916	23 Aug 1916
U-53	20 Sep 1916	7 Oct 1916	7 Oct 1916	1 Nov 1916
Deutschland (second visit)	10 Oct 1916	1 Nov 1916	21 Nov 1916	10 Dec 1916
U-151	18 Apr 1918	22 May 1918	1 Jul 1918	20 Jul 1918
U-156	16 Jun 1918	5 Jul 1918	1 Sep 1918	Sunk on 25 Sep 1918 in North Sea Mine Barrage

U-140	2 Jul 1918	14 Jul 1918	1 Sep 1918	20 Sep 1918
U-117	11 Jul 1918	8 Aug 1918	1 Sep 1918	22 Sep 1918
U-155 (former Deutschland)	11 Aug 1918	7 Sep 1918	20 Oct 1918	14 Nov 1918
U-152	5 Sep 1918	29 Sep 1918	20 Oct 1918	14 Nov 1918
U-139	11 Sep 1918	Did not get west of 43°40'N, 30°50'W	Not on Atlantic Coast[4]	14 Nov 1918

Of the seven submarines that sailed for North America only five would make it to their assigned area. The exploits of those that did are discussed later in this chapter. *U-152* arrived on station, but was redirected back to the Azore Islands after inflicting considerable damage on shipping including the sinking of the transport USS *Ticonderoga* as discussed in a subsequent section. *U-139* was heavily damaged en route, necessitating her to proceed and remain in the Azores because she was unable to dive. The damage occurred after torpedoing the British cargo ship SS *Bylands* on 1 October. Her commander Kptlt. Lothar von Arnauld had dived deep to avoid an expected depth charge attack; remarking as he did so, "A bit close, hopefully, she won't sink on top of us." This premonition was realised when the bow of the *Bylands* struck *U-139*'s conning tower.[5]

Photo 19-1

Kptlt. Lothar von Arnauld de la Perière
Naval History and Heritage Command photograph #NH 65859

The damaged submarine surfaced to find the convoy, of which the *Bylands* had been a part, moving quickly away. Despite the ruin of *U-139*'s three periscopes, a large dent in her pressure hull at the control room, and water seeping in through hundreds of unseated rivets, von Arnauld reported to Nauen that he could continue his mission and operate on the surface in the Azores. (Nauen is a radio transmitter twenty-six miles west of Berlin. It is the oldest radio transmitter in the world. Telefunken built the station in 1907, but during WWI, the German Navy took it over. It was through Nauen that the U-boats received radio messages from German naval headquarters, and it was to Nauen that the U-boats sent their messages.)[6]

U-139 remained on station and sank the Portuguese sailing vessel *Rio Cavado* on 2 October, and twelve days later the Portuguese minesweeper *Augusto de Castilho*. Von Arnauld received a recall order on 21 October, and brought the submarine into Kiel on 14 November 1918. He was the leading German submarine "Ace" of World War I (with a total of 200 vessels, of about a half-million tons, sunk).[7]

Photo 19-2

Unarmed German cargo submarine *U-Deutschland* proceeding up the Weser River to Bremen, Germany, on 25 August 1916, on her return from Baltimore. She became the *U-155* on 10 February 1917.
Naval History and Heritage Command photograph #NH 43611

The submarines sent to America were all relatively new. The oldest, *U-155*, had been launched on 28 March 1916 as the unarmed submarine freighter *U-Deutschland*. Skippered by Merchant Navy Capt. Paul König, she departed Kiel on 11 July and arrived that night in Heligoland. Before departing Heligoland on 14 June, she took on additional fuel, and König was given a thorough briefing on British anti-submarine patrols and minefields. He was also briefed on German intelligence estimates about British and Canadian patrol strength and activity along the North American east coast. *U-Deutschland* reached Baltimore, Maryland, in July. She returned to Germany in August with a cargo of vital war materiels estimated to be worth ten times her building cost. In autumn 1916, she made a voyage to New London, Connecticut.[8]

U-Deutschland was taken over by the German Imperial Navy on 10 February 1917 and was fitted with six bow torpedo tubes (18 torpedoes), and two 155mm SK L/40 naval guns from the pre-dreadnought battleship SMS *Zähringen*. Her sister, *Bremen*, scheduled for a similar conversion, was lost in early 1917 under uncertain circumstances (possibly mined) before acquisition by the German Navy. Having been requisitioned before entering their intended merchant service, the other five submarine freighters were converted into *U-151* class boats, equipped with two 150mm deck guns, and 18 torpedoes to be fired from 2 bow tubes.[9]

Of the seven boats discussed: one was a UE 2 type submarine, two were *U-139* class submarines, and the remaining three (like *Deutschland*) were of the *U-151* class. The submarines' length and displacement in the table, refers to their overall length and submerged displacement.

U-boat/ Type	Length Displ.	Date Comm.	Commanding Officer
U-117 (UE 2)	267 feet 1,512 tons	28 Mar 18	Kptlt. Otto Dröscher
U-139 (*U-139*)	301 ft. 2,483 tons	18 May 18	Kptlt. Lothar von Arnauld de la Perière
U-140 (*U-139*)	301 ft. 2,483 tons	28 Mar 18	KKpt. Waldemar Kophamel
U-151 (*U-151*)	213 feet 1,875 tons	21 Jul 17	KKpt. Heinrich von Nostitz und Jänckendorff
U-152 (*U-151*)	213 feet 1,875 tons	17 Oct 17	Kptlt. Adolf Franz
U-155 (*U-151*)	213 feet 1,875 tons	19 Feb 17	Kptlt. Karl Meusel, KKpt. Erich Eckelmann, KKpt. Ferdinand Studt
U-156 (*U-151*)	213 feet 1,875 tons	22 Aug 17	Kptlt. Richard Feldt[10]

WAR PATROL OF *U-151*

Once clear of the European war zone, heavy traffic was encountered all along the route to, in, and from the patrol area. All the ships steamed alone and unprotected. The traffic off New York is particularly heavy. For the time being, there are only weak patrols and no aircraft.

—KKpt. Heinrich von Nostitz und Jänckendorff,
commanding officer of *U-151*.[11]

Cruising in U-151 with a heavy sea is no picnic, for the U-boat with its broad upper deck tends to drive her bows under.

—First officer Martin Niemöller commenting on the difficulties *U-151* faced in any type of sea. When the submarine's bows dove under waves, it was necessary to reverse her engines to regain her trim. It was found that in a storm, it was more economical to run submerged than on the surface.[12]

U-151 left Kiel on 18 April 1918. During her ninety-four day cruise, she would account for 51,929 tons of shipping sunk by torpedoes, gunnery, and scuttling charges, and an additional 4,000 damaged by mines she laid. She and the other four U-boats collectively destroyed ninety-six vessels in the western Atlantic: eighty-one by gunfire, depth charges, or a combination of both; and fifteen larger ships by torpedo. Six vessels were damaged by mines the submarines laid. These losses do not include vessels sunk by submarines while they were en route to America's east coast, or returning to Germany.[13]

Appendix C provides a listing of these victims. Of those attacked on the surface, three-quarters were relatively small: sailing vessels, tugs, barges, and motor-propelled boats. Many of the sailing vessels were schooners from 100 tons up. The motor boats varied from 18 to 117 tons. All the vessels torpedoed were steamships of moderate to large size. The U-boats typically only used their scarce torpedoes if a ship appeared large enough to be armed, whereas small helpless craft were openly attacked and ruthlessly destroyed. The listing of vessels sunk or damaged was compiled from information found in the U.S. Navy's 1920 publication *German Submarine Activities on the Atlantic Coast of the United States and Canada* and U-boat war logs.[14]

Intelligence from Room 40 at the Admiralty provided U.S. Naval headquarters in Washington, D.C., foreknowledge of *U-151*'s voyage. On 16 May, a warning was transmitted to all bases, alerting them that an enemy submarine could be encountered anywhere west of longitude 40°W, and that ships should tow paravanes at their bows as defence against mines and show no lights except as immediately necessary to avoid collision. Most of *U-151*'s victims lacked radio communications equipment and thus would not have received this information.[15]

Map 19-3

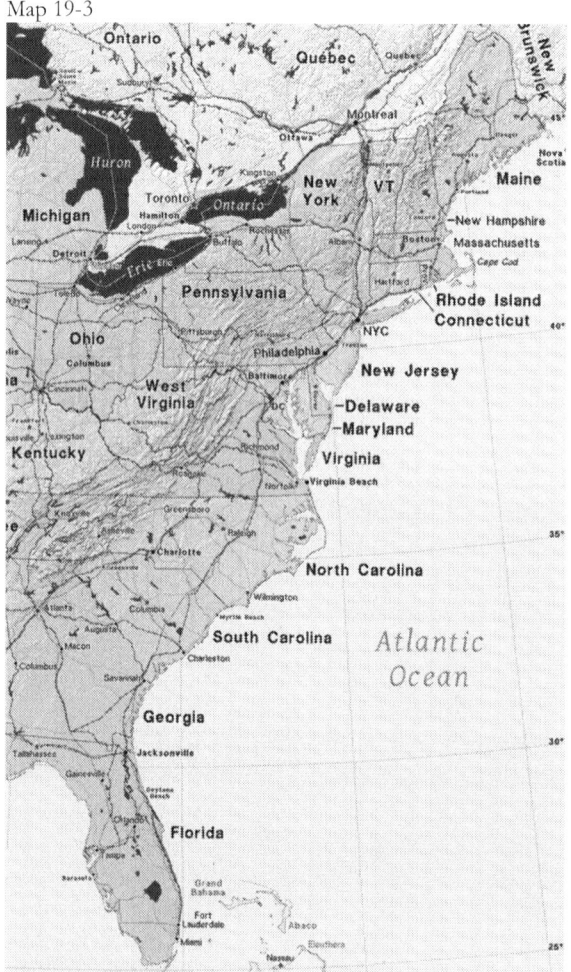

East Coast of the United States. The entrance to the
Chesapeake Bay lies just northward of Virginia Beach.

MINING CAPABILITIES OF *U-151* SUBMARINES

U-151 and her sister ships normally carried fourteen mines (six in deck
lockers for surface operations, and eight tube-launched mines in the
torpedo stowage room)—additional mines could be brought aboard if
some torpedoes were left behind.   Although each mine carried a
powerful 200 lb-TNT charge, there was little chance that an Allied ship
would stumble into an indiscriminate area sown with so few of them.
Accordingly, the mines were laid in areas of high vessel density.   The

first target specified by the German Naval Command was an area south of the *Five Fathom Bank* lightship in Chesapeake Bay.[16]

Upon arriving in this area and finding heavy shipping traffic and a cruiser engaged in gunnery practice, *U-151* lay on the bottom of Chesapeake Bay in about nine fathoms of water awaiting a chance to lay mines. (This bay is a large estuary, inland from the Atlantic.) She surfaced at 2130 on 24 May in a calm sea with bright moonlight. Because of the illumination, time was of the essence if she wished to remain undetected. Finding that use of her deck minelaunchers proved to be painfully slow, crewmen resorted to simply pushing the mines over the deck edge at 900-1,000 metre intervals. The water in this location was 11-14 metres in depth. This operation took just eight minutes, with the submarine making 18 knots. Whether due to haste or inefficiency, the resultant field did no damage. All of the mines were discovered either afloat or washed ashore, between 22 June and 9 September.[17]

Toward midnight on 26 May, KKpt. Heinrich von Nostitz und Jänckendorff approached the *Overfall* lightship in Delaware Bay to lay his remaining mines. Navigating by periscope sightings of the lights and beacons was easy but strong currents made it difficult to maintain proper depth, and frequently lifted *U-151*'s bow to break the surface. When within about 600 metres of the lightship, eddies repeatedly plunged her downward, then rebounded her upward and back down again. In daylight, this could have been catastrophic, if she had been observed broaching the surface.[18]

In any case, just before 0100 on 27 May, as fog began to obscure the lightship, *U-151* laid four mines at intervals of 150-250 metres in water depths of 20-22 metres. She lay on the bottom to counteract the currents while loading her last four mines in torpedo tubes, then launched them at locations determined by dead reckoning. The depth settings, intended to place the mine bodies 5 metres below the surface, were also aimed at deep-draught vessels. Von Nostitz's skill in laying the mines was all the more impressive in light of his submarine's limited manoeuverability. The American steamship SS *Herbert L. Pratt* struck one of the mines on 3 June, but was beached safely; after repairs were made, she was refloated and towed to Philadelphia. Of the seven remaining mines, one washed ashore and the others were destroyed by U.S. Navy minesweepers.[19]

CABLE-CUTTING MISSION

On the morning of 28 May, *U-151* hove to off New York, while crewmen rigged heavy cable-cutting gear on deck, consisting of a derrick, winches, greased flexible wire rope, and pressure cutters. Her second mission after the mining one was to interrupt trans-Atlantic communications by cutting telegraph cables. The cables in this location with their thick protective skin and armoured strands lay on the seafloor 25 fathoms below the surface. Shortly after 1100, sailors cut what they believed to be the southern cable of Western Union Cable 1889; nine hours later the southern German cable was similarly cut; and by 0100 (early the following morning), the northern German cable was severed.[20]

American authorities recorded only two interrupted cables: the Central and South American Cable Company's New York-Colon link, and the Commercial Cable Company's No. 4 Canso-New York link. Both were repaired by 5 July. Apparently the intended targets had been missed.[21]

U-151 SINKS TWENTY ALLIED VESSELS IN JUNE

As understandable as such a procedure is from the human standpoint, it is detrimental to the intended effect of u-boat warfare.

—Admiral Henning von Holtzendorff, head of the Imperial Admiralty Staff, censuring the commanding officer of *U-151* for his actions in broadcasting an SOS in English with precise positions of drifting lifeboats from the Norwegian sailing vessels *Samoa* and *Kringsjaa*, which he sank on 14 and 15 June 1918.[22]

Photo 19-3

U-151, taken from the Spanish passenger steamer *Isabel de Bourbon*.
Naval History and Heritage Command photograph #NH 114

In the month of June, Von Nostitz sank twenty Allied vessels ranging from the 124-ton Canadian schooner *Dictator* to the 5,093-ton American passenger ship *Carolina* and the 8,173-ton British troop ship *Dwinsk*. In doing so, he observed prize rules meticulously, making provisions for the safety of abandoned crews and passengers in their lifeboats, offering medical attention where needed, and freeing prisoners. On 1 July, he let "a large hospital ship fully illuminated according to regulations" pass.[23]

Von Nostitz's most important coup occurred on 9 June. After stopping the 3,197-ton Norwegian *Vindeggan*, he transferred 70-tons of pure copper bars from his victim, before scuttling her with depth charges. To compensate for the weight of this incredibly valuable cargo, *U-151*'s crew jettisoned water, iron ballast and trim weights. The submarine returned to Kiel on 20 July 1918, having expended six torpedoes and two hundred eighty-eight 150mm gun rounds.[24]

U-156 NEXT SUBMARINE TO SAIL FROM GERMANY

The second submarine sent to North America, *U-156*, had departed Kiel on 16 June 1918. Her captain's orders were to mine the approaches to New York Harbour prior to engaging in warfare against shipping in four areas: the Gulf of Maine, and approaches to Boston, Halifax, and Saint John. Kptlt. Richard Feldt was also to attempt to cut the overseas cables at Canso, Nova Scotia, and if able, capture a prize vessel and transform her into an auxiliary warship in support of extended operations. During her voyage, *U-156* would destroy twenty sailing vessels, nine merchant vessels, and the armoured cruiser USS *San Diego*. Unfortunately for her she did not enjoy any immediate acclaim for her efforts as on return passage to Germany, she went missing—believed sunk in the North Sea Mine Barrage.[25]

Near the latter part of July, *U-156* laid eight mines near the *Fire Island* lightship in the approaches to New York. One sank the *San Diego*, which had been based at Halifax the previous winter for convoy escort duties. The loss of the armoured cruiser greatly concerned Vice Adm. William L. Grant, RN (commander-in-chief, North America and West Indies) as did intelligence that *U-140* was approaching coastal waters. With a majority of U.S. Navy anti-submarine vessels overseas in Europe, there were no more than eighteen destroyers available on the whole of the Eastern Seaboard.[26]

Grant had communicated to the British Admiralty earlier that spring that the "present inadequate anti-submarine forces on this side [North American waters] can no longer be justified"—and had been sharply rebuked. He now argued that some of the new destroyers being built in the United States should be retained in the western Atlantic. The response was even more barbed, "As you are not in a position to form a true appreciation of the submarine situation generally, it is essential that you should not express any opinion to the US Authorities on the subject of retention or otherwise of US destroyers in American waters." (The Admiralty believed that all U.S. destroyers should be in Europe).[27]

Photo 19-4

The armoured cruiser USS *San Diego* sinking off Fire Island, New York, on 19 July 1918; after striking a mine laid by the *U-156* (painting by Francis Muller, 1920). Naval History and Heritage Command photograph #NH 55012-KN

CANADIAN FISHING VESSEL *TRIUMPH* TAKEN

While Grant was trying in vain to get additional anti-submarine assets, *U-156* was destroying Allied ships and craft with gunfire and scuttling charges, and the 4,139-ton British cargo ship SS *Penistone* with a torpedo. On 20 August, Kptlt. Richard Feldt apparently found a suitable vessel to transform into an auxiliary warship, per his orders. During the early hours of 21 August, crewmembers of the 236-ton Canadian trawler SS *Triumph* arrived in their dories at Canso, Nova Scotia, with a startling story. A prize crew from a huge submarine had captured her the previous day and left them in their boats to find their way home across sixty miles of open ocean.[28]

Triumph had been fishing with her side trawls down (and thus was unable to manoeuvre) some thirty miles southeast of Cape Canso, when *U-156* surfaced near her and fired a shot across her bow. The fishermen could do nothing but destroy their confidential books and submit. Within twenty-five minutes of boarding, the Germans had equipped her with a wireless radio, two light guns and three or four boxes of 3-pound shells, and twenty-five depth charges.[29]

Map 19-4

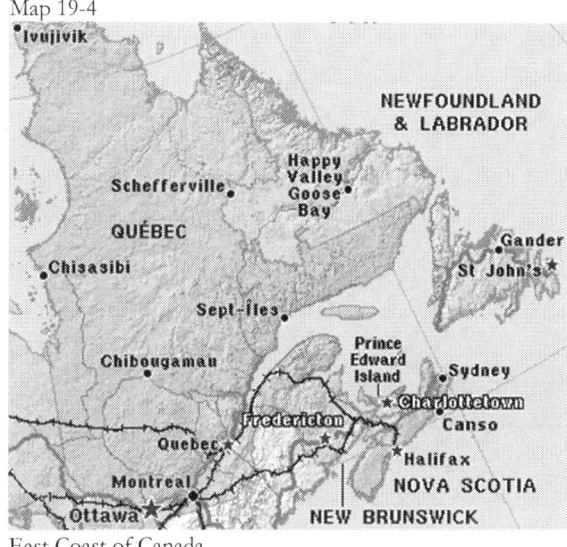

East Coast of Canada

CANADIANS DESPATCH PATROL VESSELS

Capt. Walter Hose, RCN (the founder of the RNCVR, and currently Captain of Patrols) immediately ordered three auxiliary patrol ships—*Cartier*, *Hochelaga*, and *Stadacona*—and the trawlers *TR-22* and *TR-33* to sea. At the time, all five vessels had recently completed local escort missions and were available. Three Halifax-based U.S. Navy submarine chasers under Hose's operational control joined the forces tasked with patrolling the east coast fishing banks later that day. The sub-chasers were small, 110-foot wooden vessels designed for rapid wartime construction, which owed their existence in large measure to Assistant Secretary of the Navy Franklin D. Roosevelt, an avid yachtsman. Their principal value lay in their availability in large numbers. When built, their armament consisted of two 3"/23-calibre guns and two machine guns. Later on, a depth charge projector was substituted for the after 3-inch gun.[30]

The Canadian vessels were an unimpressive force to send against a U-boat. The unnamed minesweeping trawlers HMCS *TR-22* and *TR-33* were copies of the Royal Navy's *Castle* class, constructed in Canadian yards (Canadian Vickers Ltd., Montreal, and Government Shipyard, Sorel, Quebec). Although newly built, they were both slow and minimally armed. The auxiliary patrol ships HMCS *Cartier*, *Hochelaga*, and *Stadacona* were slightly faster by two knots but, with one exception, also armed with a single gun. The most formidable of the vessels, the ex-survey ship *Cartier*, boasted three 12-pounder guns. In the following table, the units for ship's length, displacement, and speed are feet, tons, and knots, respectively.

Vessel	Formerly	Launched Completed	Length/ Displ./Speed	Armament
Cartier	survey ship CGS *Cartier*	1910 L	164/556/12	3 x 12-pounder guns
Hochelaga	yacht *Waturus*	1900 L	193/628/12	1 x 12-pounder gun
Stadacona	yacht *Columbia*	1899 L	196/693/12	1 x 4-inch gun 1 x 12-pounder gun
TR-22	newly built	31 May 18 C	133/279/10	1 x 3-inch gun
TR-33	newly built	4 Jun 18 C	133/279/10	1 x 3-inch gun[31]

As soon as the Sydney, Nova Scotia-based forces returned from their local missions and escort of an HC (Halifax later Quebec) and an HS (Sydney) convoy, they too were sent to sea. The patrols against *U-156* and *Triumph* were more extensive than any previously mounted in Canadian waters. The enemy could be in search of prey anywhere in the vast North Atlantic fishing banks which stretched southward to the Gulf of Maine, northward to the vicinity of St. Pierre et Miquelon, and eastward to the Grand Banks of Newfoundland.[32]

TRIUMPH LURES/DESTROYS THE UNSUSPECTING

Over a three-day period while *U-156* remained hull awash three or more miles away, *Triumph* preyed on unsuspecting vessels. Known by sight to almost the entire fishing fleet, she stopped and destroyed the American schooners *A. Piatt Andrew*, *Francis J. O'Hara Jr.*, *Sylvania*, and the Canadian schooners *Lucille M. Schnare*, and *Pasadena*. *Uda A. Saunders*, another Canadian schooner, was sunk by the submarine.[33]

Capt. Wallace Bruce, of the *A. Piatt Andrew*, later described the ease by which his vessel was taken and destroyed:

> The schooner was about 55 miles south half east [SSE] off Canso, Nova Scotia, when the beam trawler *Triumph* approached to within about one half mile of my schooner and suddenly commenced firing shots or shells, which fell in the water ahead of the schooner. I thereupon caused the schooner to lie to and shortly thereafter was ordered by an officer on board the trawler to come alongside in a dory with my ship's papers. I carried out these instructions and upon arriving alongside the *Triumph*, I found that she had been

seized by the crew of a German submarine and converted into a raider—with a rapid-fire gun fore and aft.

Three members of the German crew, armed with revolvers and carrying bombs, then got into my dory. We were ordered to abandon ship and take to our dories. We were given only a few minutes and had not sufficient time to save but very little of our personal effects.

About 15 minutes after we abandoned ship the bombs which had been placed amidships exploded and the schooner sank; we saw the submarine, painted a dark color, about 4 or 5 miles south by southwest.

The German officers and crew appeared to be healthy and well fed, the crew wearing soiled white uniforms and the officers dark colored uniforms; there were about 15 German officers and men on board the *Triumph*.[34]

Once the *Triumph* had exhausted her coal supplies, her German crew scuttled her and rejoined *U-156*. On 25 August, the submarine was in the process of destroying a group of four fishing trawlers—the Canadian *E. B. Walters*, *C. M. Walters*, and *Verna D. Adams*, and the American *J. J. Flaherty*—when a four-ship *Canadian* patrol appeared on the scene. Auxiliary patrol ships HMCS *Cartier* and *Hochelaga*, and the trawlers *TR-22* and *TR-32* were steaming in a line abreast at four-mile intervals. HMCS *Hochelaga* sighted two schooners six miles away and left the formation to head due east toward them. Within about four miles, it was possible to see a U-boat, just as one of the schooners disappeared from view. Facing the formidable submarine alone, the skipper of the lightly armed patrol ship, apparently not liking his chances of survival, turned back and hoisted signal flags.[35]

On seeing *Hochelaga* alter course, the senior officer, Lieutenant McGuirk (*Cartier's* commanding officer) brought the formation around to intercept her and read her flags. *Hochelaga* reported the "submarine bearing East" whereupon McGuirk ordered the patrol to proceed directly toward her at high speed. *Hochelaga* held back and signaled to *Cartier* the greater wisdom of awaiting reinforcements. By the time, the other patrol ships reached the scene, *U-156* was gone.[36]

A court martial held in Halifax on 5 October 1918, found that the commanding officer of HMCS *Hochelaga*, "did not, from negligence or other default, on sight of the enemy which it was his duty to engage, use his utmost exertion to bring his ship into action." He was dismissed from the Naval Service. Vice Adm. Horatio Nelson (the Royal Navy's greatest naval hero, who was fatally wounded at the Battle of Trafalgar in 1805) once observed, about similar circumstances in which the disgraced officer had found himself, "No captain can do very wrong if he places his ship alongside that of an enemy."[37]

U-156 SAILS FOR HOME, BUT NEVER MAKES PORT

On 7 September, Nauen received a transmission from *U-156* reporting that she was homeward bound, and had sunk 41,000 tons of shipping including the USS *San Diego*. The submarine subsequently reported her position on 25 September, as northwest of the Shetlands and that she would be at the *Skagen* lightship on 27 September. It is believed that she struck a mine while attempting to run the North Sea Mine Barrage, and sank due to damage received.[38]

WAR PATROL OF *U-140* COMMENCES ON 2 JULY

Two weeks after *U-156* had sailed from Kiel for the American Atlantic coast, *U-140* (KKpt. Waldemar Kophamel) departed Warnemünde. Mounting two 150mm deck guns and carrying 24 torpedoes, she sank 30,594 tons of shipping during her eighty-one day cruise.[39]

Kophamel despatched *Porto*, *Stanley M. Seaman*, and *Merak* with scuttling charges; and *O. B. Jennings*, *Diamond Shoals* light vessel *71*, *Diomed*, and *Tokuyama Maru* by gunfire. He had torpedoed the latter ship, and then resorted to gunfire, as she stubbornly remained afloat[40]

Date	Type Ship	Name	Displ.	Nationality
27 Jul 18	sailing vessel	*Porto* (S)	1,079	Portuguese
2 Aug 18	steamer	*Tokuyama Maru* (TG)	7,029	Japanese
4 Aug 18	tanker	*O. B. Jennings* (G)	10,289	American
5 Aug 18	sailing vessel	*Stanley M. Seaman* (S)	1,060	American
6 Aug 18	light vessel	*Diamond Shoals LV71* (G)	590	American
6 Aug 18	steamer	*Merak* (S)	3,024	American
21 Aug 18	steamer	*Diomed* (G)	7,523	British

Key: G (sunk by gunfire), S (scuttled with depth charge), T (torpedoed)

U-140's patrol was cut short on 10 August by damage she suffered at the hands of a U.S. destroyer. While attempting to stop the Brazilian cargo ship SS *Uberaba*, she had been forced to dive by the attacking destroyer, which then conducted a depth charge attack on her. Sixteen explosions created leaks in her pressure hull, and opened seams in a fuel tank. Her crew was able to deal with the water, but the continued loss of fuel forced *U-140* to end operations twelve days later and begin her return trip. She arrived back at Kiel on 20 September.[41]

U-117 DEPARTS FOR AMERICA, 11 JULY

The fourth submarine to sail for America, *U-117* (Kptlt. Otto Dröscher) departed Kiel on 11 July; taking the eastern route around the Shetlands, as was the convention. During her cruise, she would sink twenty vessels (27,459 tons) and damage four others (30,845)—one of the latter being the 18,000-ton battleship USS *Minnesota*.[42]

Photo 19-5

German submarine *U-117*, location and date unknown.
History and Heritage Command photograph #NH 92862

U-117 was a 267-foot ocean minelayer, armed with one 150mm deck gun, 14 torpedoes, and 42 mines. Arriving off New York on 10 August, she moved north and sank nine fishing vessels with gunfire and scuttling charges in the vicinity of Georges Bank (between Cape Cod, Massachusetts, and Cape Sable Island, Nova Scotia). She next came across two ships, which she torpedoed—the Norwegian SS *Sommerstadt* on the 12th, and the American tanker *Frederic R. Kellog* the following day on 13 August.[43]

On the same day that she sank the tanker, the submarine laid nine mines at the *Barnegat* lightship off New Jersey. Two of these mines later sank the cargo ships SS *San Saba* and SS *Chaparra*, respectively, on 4 and 27 October. Of the remaining mines: one was cut loose by the paravanes of the battleship USS *South Carolina*; one was destroyed 14.5 miles northeast of Brigantine Shoals Buoy; four were destroyed by USS *Teal* (a *Lapwing*-class minesweeper commanded by Lt. (jg) Frederick Meyer); and one went unlocated. *Teal* was assigned to the 4th Naval District, patrolling off the shores of New Jersey, Delaware, and Pennsylvania. She would later be part of the force of U.S. minesweepers sent to Europe to clear the North Sea Barrage.[44]

On 15 August, *U-117* laid mines south of the *Fenwick Island Shoal* lightship, as well as south of the *Winter Quarter Shoal* lightship (located off Virginia as a reference point for coastal traffic and shipping approaching Chesapeake Bay from the north). One of the first mines laid in the Fenwick field damaged the battleship USS *Minnesota* on 29 September, and the cargo ship USS *Saetia* was sunk in the same field on 9 November. The remaining five mines in the field were cleared by *Teal*, and the seven in the Winter Quarter field by the *Lapwing*-class minesweeper USS *Rail* (Ens. R. E. Allen, USNRF). She too was sent to Europe.[45]

The following day, 16 August, the industrious submarine sowed mines in Wimble Shoal off Cape Hatteras. While doing so, she sighted and torpedoed the British tanker SS *Mirlo*, then returned to her mining. The U.S. Navy 1920 publication *German Submarine Activities on the Atlantic Coast of the United States and Canada* identifies seven minefields. Of the sixty-two mines attributed to the activities of U-boats, three were found off Nova Scotia. *U-155* was apparently responsible for the mines found outside the reported fields.

U-boat Laid Minefields off North America

U-boat	Locations of Minefields	No. Mines Laid
U-155	Mines found outside reported fields	6
U-151	Vicinity of *Overfalls* lightship	7
U-117	Vicinity of Wimble Shoal	10
U-151	Vicinity of Chesapeake Bay	7
U-117	Vicinity of *Winter Quarter Shoal* lightship	9
U-117	Vicinity of *Fenwick Island Shoal* lightship	7
U-117	Vicinity of Barnegat	8
U-156	Vicinity of *Fire Island* lightship	8
	Total[46]	62

The last two victims of *U-117* on this side of the Atlantic were the Canadian fishing schooners *Elsie Porter* and *Potentate*, sunk on 30 August by explosives. The sinking of the two schooners evidently took place after the submarine had begun her homeward trek. On 9 September, *U-117* went to the aid of the *U-140* which was forced to call for assistance because of her fuel leak, also on return voyage. The two spent the day in company at latitude 54°10'N, longitude 22°30'W, and then proceeded into the North Sea. *U-117* arrived at Kiel on 22 September, completing a seventy-four day patrol.[47]

WAR PATROL OF *U-155* (FORMER *DEUTSCHLAND*)

U-155 left Kiel on 11 August, bound for North America via passage around the Faroes. The last boat that would hunt in American waters, the formerly unarmed *U-Deutschland* now sported two 150mm deck guns, mines, and eighteen torpedoes for firing from two bow tubes. KKpt. Ferdinand Studt's orders were to lay mines, cut cables, and conduct U-cruiser (submarine) warfare.[48]

Studt would sink eight vessels, and damage one during his cruise. The first one in the western Atlantic was the 3,245-ton SS *Leixoes* on 12 September. After despatching her, the sub commander turned to mining Canadian waters and severing communication cables.

Victims of *U-155*

Date	Type Ship	Name	Displ.	Nationality
31 Aug 18	sailing vessel	*Gamo* (S)	343	Portuguese
2 Sep 18	steamer	*Stortind* (G)	2,510	Norwegian
7 Sep 18	sailing vessel	*Sophia* (S)	162	Portuguese
12 Sep 18	steamer	*Leixoes* (T)	3,245	Portuguese
20 Sep 18	trawler	*Kingfisher* (S)	353	American
3 Oct 18	steamer	*Alberto Treves* (T)	3,838	Italian
4 Oct 18	sailing vessel	*Industrial* (S)	330	British
12 Oct 18	steamer	*Amphion* (G) (damaged)	7,409	American
17 Oct 18	steamer	*Lucia* (T)	6,744	American[49]

Key: G (sunk by gunfire), S (scuttled with depth charge), T (torpedoed)

Photo 19-6

U-155 at London, England, 4 December 1918.
Naval History and Heritage Command photograph #NH 111056

On 17 September, *U-155* sowed six mines off Betty Island near Halifax. The following day, she laid a string of four mines between the *Sambro* lightship and Sambro Ledges, outside Halifax Harbour, and two series of four mines each in the approaches to Halifax. The mines did no damage. Most broke free of their moorings, set adrift by wind and sea. Fishermen recovered several and received twenty-five dollars for their efforts (likely the six the U.S. Navy cited as found outside identified minefields). Others may have sunk; washed ashore and remained unfound; or have been recovered, but not reported.[50]

U-155 torpedoed the 6,744-ton American freighter *Lucia* on 17 October—the last ship to be sunk by a German submarine in North American waters. By this point, submarine warfare could not help prevent the inevitable defeat of Germany. An Allied drive opening on 25 September in the Argonne Forest, in northeastern France, against German ground forces had pushed on into the battle of Cambrai-St. Quentin from 27 September-10 October. These advances would continue to press hard on retreating German forces until the armistice on 11 November 1918.[51]

TRANSPORT *TICONDEROGA* SUNK WITH MANY CASUALTIES IN FIGHT WITH *U-152*

I, Mr. Muller, was a gunnery officer at the Battle of Jutland. But during the years since, I have been in submarines. And the submarines have been doing all the Navy's work in the war. The battleships and cruisers of the High Seas Fleet have been doing next to nothing.

—Kptlt. Adolf Franz, commanding officer of *U-152*, addressing Lt. Frank L. Muller, USNRF, executive officer of the transport USS *Ticonderoga* before she was sunk by the submarine, and he and another officer were taken prisoner. The feeling of chagrin and anger expressed by Franz, was prevalent aboard *U-152* and ships visited by the two men following arrival at Kiel, Germany.[52]

On 30 September, *U-152* (Kptlt. Adolf Franz) was en route to North America, having left Kiel on 5 September. She had encountered the Danish sailing vessel *Constance* and the American tanker *George G. Henry*, and had damaged but not sunk both of them. Her luck changed at 0520 that morning when the submarine found the 5,212-ton USS *Ticonderoga* of the Naval Overseas Transportation Service. *Ticonderoga* was alone in the vast Atlantic, having fallen behind the convoy of which she was a part (bound for Europe), due to engine troubles.[53]

Photo 19-7

The former German merchant ship SS *Camilla Rickmers* at Boston, Massachusetts, 27 November 1917. She was placed in commission as USS *Ticonderoga* on 5 January 1918, and sunk by the *U-152* on 30 September 1918.
Naval History and Heritage Command photograph #NH 42415

The transport was the former SS *Camilla Rickmers*, built in 1914 by Rickmers Aktien Gesellschaft, at Bremerhaven, Germany. Seized by U.S. Customs officials in 1917, she had been turned over to the Navy, renamed *Ticonderoga*, and commissioned at Boston on 5 January 1918. Lt. Comdr. James J. Madison, USNRF, was in command. The 401-foot ship was manned by a Navy crew. She had been fitted with a 3-inch naval gun forward and a six-inch gun aft during her conversion.[54]

That morning, *Ticonderoga* was proceeding in fairly rough seas (at position 43°05'N, 38°43'W) when at 0520 an enemy submarine suddenly appeared close aboard, just off the transport's port bow. Upon receiving this report, Lieutenant Commander Madison ordered the general alarm sounded and the helm put hard to starboard, in an attempt to ram the submarine. (This rudder order implies the sub had right bearing drift, and that the ponderous ship did not react quickly to large course changes.) Ens. Gustav Ringelman, the officer of the deck of the *Ticonderoga*, described the ensuing rapid death dealt by the U-boat's 150mm (6-inch) guns:

> The submarine was sighted at first about 200 yards off our port bow awash, the whole length showing. I reported to the commanding officer immediately and ordered the forward gun crew to open fire.

The forward gun had its gun cover on because during the night it had rained, and there was a heavy spray, and we needed the gun cover on to protect the gun. Immediately the captain put his helm hard to starboard and came within 25 feet of ramming the submarine. Before we could get a shot off the submarine fired an incendiary shell which struck our bridge, killing the helmsman [as well as severely wounding the commanding officer] and practically putting the navigation of the ship out of commission, crippling the steering gear and setting the amidships section ablaze.

This all took place in just as short a time as I am telling you this. I was going back—I had charge of the 6-inch gun aft. [Ringelman was en route to his battle station.] The submarine fired with the aft gun at our 3-inch forward gun, killing the gun crew. They fired six shots putting the gun out of commission. She then steamed around our starboard side and opened up her distance a little bit, opening fire again. We replied with our 6-inch gun.[55]

The distance between the *Ticonderoga* and her attacker was then about 4,000 yards—before *U-152* gradually opened to about four miles. As she continued to shell *Ticonderoga*, the transport answered with gunfire from her after mount. Ringelman continued his narrative:

During this time most everybody on board our ship was either killed or wounded to such an extent that they were practically helpless from shrapnel. The lifeboats hanging on the davits were shelled and full of holes, others carried away. However, we kept the submarine off until our fire was put out and our boats swung out on the davits, ready to abandon the ship with the few men left on board. Possibly 50 were left by that time—the rest were dead. Well, at 7 o'clock up comes the submarine again, off the starboard quarter.

Meanwhile we had also several boats which were swamped immediately, due to the falls carrying away—the submarine had shot them away before—and holes in the boats, and there was not another boat got away that I could see. Every boat that attempted to get away was either swamped, or something happened to it. The submarine fired at us again for the second time at a range of 10,000 to 12,000 yards, and there were only three left on our 6-inch gun as a gun crew—a chief boatswain mate, a gunner's mate, and myself. We manned that gun until a shell struck us underneath the gun and put the gun out of commission, as well as ourselves, disabling us. The submarine still continued to shell us, and then came alongside off our starboard beam and fired a torpedo which struck amidships in the engine room. The ship thereafter slowly settled.[56]

Approximately fifteen minutes elapsed from the time the torpedo hit *Ticonderoga* and she sank at about 0745. The battle with *U-152* had raged for over two hours—since the sighting of the submarine at 0514. Third engineer, Ens. Clifford T. Sanghove, USRNF, and others got some of the wounded together along with some water and blankets, lashed the wounded to the life raft, and shoved the raft (stored above the deckhouse) off the ship from twenty feet above the water. Only one of the boats had got clear, lowered away at about 0715 with the wounded captain and fourteen soldiers in it.[57]

Sanghove describes being aboard the raft (after climbing onto it from the water), and of the submarine coming alongside both the raft and the lifeboat and taking men off for interrogation:

> A few minutes after getting on the raft the vessel went down, stern first, sinking completely in about 10 seconds. We then drifted off on the raft. I saw the submarine fire two shots at the only open boat left.
>
> The submarine then went alongside the lifeboat and inquired for the captain, chief engineer, and gunner. On being told that the captain was not aboard [Lt. Comdr. James J. Madison was lying on the bottom of the boat], they took aboard the submarine two seamen, tying the boat to the stern of the submarine. The last I saw, the two seamen were on the submarine. The submarine then went over to the driftwood, and picked up considerable potato crates, etc., from the water, also picking up the executive officer and taking him prisoner. In about 15 minutes the submarine came over to the raft on which we were, tied up alongside, and took on board Chief Machinist Mate, Rudolph Alicke. They questioned him for some time, he being of German extraction, and then put him back on the raft.
>
> They asked for the captain, chief engineer, and gunner, all the time keeping us covered with revolvers. We told them the chief engineer had been killed, but that the first assistant engineer was on the raft, so they took him aboard the submarine, putting the two seamen back on board our raft. That left the first assistant engineer and executive officer on board the submarine.[58]

At 1400 that afternoon, the raft drifted toward the captain's lifeboat, and someone aboard the latter "shouted that there was no one in the boat who was able to man same, all of them having been wounded." Five men then left the raft and got into the lifeboat (Turner, Chief Quartermaster George S. Tapley, the carpenter Edward J.

Willoughby, and Ensigns Ringleman and Sanghove). Those still on the raft would later all perish. Tapley describes the inability of the men in the boat to help their shipmates aboard the raft; and of the rescue of the boat's occupants on their fourth day on the sea:

> The only boat that got away was about 1 mile to windward of us, but all the time drifting nearer. When it came alongside five of us from the raft got in the boat, intending to tie a line to the raft, but the wind was so strong that we couldn't do so. We tried for four hours to get back to the raft to give her a line, but the wind prevented us from doing so. We then hoisted a small sail on the bow of the boat, in order to keep her stern to the wind, and this way we spent the night…. There were 22 men in all, including the captain, who was very badly wounded.
>
> We at first decided to try and make Newfoundland, but the captain said northwest winds started blowing about this time of the year, so we abandoned the idea and commenced to steer east-southeast for Spain. Bad weather had set in and we thought we saw two ships on the horizon, but were not sure…. We continued pulling on our course all that day. That night the sea started to run very high, and we had great difficulty in keeping the boat from swamping. On the third day the sea became more moderate, and we made perhaps 60 miles to the eastward. The captain was feverish and delirious at times, and it was necessary to give him water at frequent intervals to keep his fever down. The men in the boat were behaving as well as could be expected, except that they were constantly complaining about not having water.
>
> On the fourth day the weather calmed down, and the sea was moderate. At about 7 a. m. we sighted a ship away off on the horizon heading west, but apparently, she did not see us. At about 1 o'clock smoke was sighted dead ahead, and in the course of an hour's time the [British cargo ship] S.S. *Moorish Prince* came alongside and picked us up. Everybody was very weak, and the captain was in an extremely bad condition. They kept us on board for three days and then transferred us to the [Norwegian liner S.S.] *Grampian*.[59]

U-152 (with the two American naval officers aboard as prisoners) steered a southwest course between 30 September and 11 October, speed 4 knots, on the lookout for Allied shipping. Because she was continually in the Gulf Stream, her position did not vary much. The submarine's engines were in bad shape, and she could not make more than 10 knots on the surface. On 11 October, the Admiralstab (German Admiralty) ordered the *U-152* to proceed to the Azores to attack shipping there. On 13 October, she stopped and by gunfire sank the Norwegian sailing vessel *Stifinder*. Two days later, the submarine attacked the British SS *Messina* with gunfire but was forced to break-off the attack and dive upon the arrival of a British auxiliary cruiser. On 17 October she made a submerged torpedo attack on the British SS *Briarleaf*, then surfaced and finished the job with gunfire.[60]

Kptlt. Adolf Franz later commented about his boat:

The helplessness of the old commercial U-boats under the present circumstances was clearly evident. Extremely limited surface and submerged speed; difficult to get the boat under in any sort of sea, and very difficult to handle when submerged. Her poor submerged handling resulted in failures to successfully make torpedo attacks on several occasions.

On a glass-calm surface, the *U-152* needs 40 to 60 seconds to get under. By normal weather—wind strength 3 to 4—it can take 3 to 4 minutes to get under. The slow diving time makes the *U-152* very vulnerable to ramming.[61]

Photo 19-8

U-152 on 16 October 1918. Seated are Lt. Frank L. Muller, USNRF, *Ticonderoga*'s executive officer, and first assistant engineer Lt. (jg) Junius H. Fulcher, USNRF. Naval History and Heritage Command photograph #NH 2472

U-152 received the message on 20 October, "All submarines return to Kiel," whereupon Franz set a course northeast until rounding the Faroe Islands. *U-152* entered the North Sea Mine Barrage at 1600 on 11 November, proceeding at full speed on the surface, through its center. The American prisoners on the *U-152* woke the following day to learn that the German crew had heard of the signing of the armistice. All hands seemed pleased that "the war was over." Lieutenant Schwartz, the radio officer, admitted that Germany had been waging a losing fight for months, because the United States had intervened.[62]

The submarine reached Kiel in late afternoon on 15 November. The two U.S. naval officers were quartered on the submarine mother ship *Kronprinz Heinrich*, but they continued to mess on *U-152*, which was the outboard submarine of the seven U-boats alongside. The executive officer of the *Heinrich* released them as prisoners. Blaming the collapse of Germany upon the United States entry into the War, he stated, "You have ruined our country. See what you have done." He told them that they were free to go ashore, but advised against it. The Americans left Kiel aboard the *U-152* on 20 November. She was part of a group of twenty-four submarines, preceded by a transport, bound for England to surrender. The group arrived at Harwich on the 24th.[63]

AFTERMATH

Although they succeeded in sinking numbers of vessels as enumerated in this chapter, the German U-boat campaign on the Atlantic coast of Canada and the United States, so far as concerned the major operations of the war, was a failure. Every transport and cargo vessel bound for Europe proceeded as if no offensive was in progress. All coastwise shipping kept to their schedules, a little more care in routing vessels being observed. There was no panic on the Atlantic coast; no excitement; and, above all, this enemy expedition did not succeed in retaining on the Atlantic coast any vessels designed for duty in European waters, or cause the return of any. This retention of U.S. antisubmarine forces, principally destroyers that diminished the sinking of supply ships as they approached Europe, may have been one of the United States greatest contributions to winning the war.[64]

CDR. JAMES JONAS MADISION, USNRF, 1888-1922

Lieutenant Commander Madison survived his injuries, was promoted to commander in mid-1919, and was awarded the Medal of Honor, the text of which follows:

> The President of the United States of America, in the name of Congress, takes pleasure in presenting the Medal of Honor to Lieutenant Commander James Jonas Madison, United States Navy (Reserve Force), for exceptionally heroic service in a position of great responsibility as Commanding Officer of the U.S.S. *TICONDEROGA*, when, on 4 October 1918, that vessel was

attacked by an enemy submarine and was sunk after a prolonged and gallant resistance. The submarine opened fire at a range of 500 yards, the first shots taking effect on the bridge and forecastle, one of the two forward guns of the *TICONDEROGA* being disabled by the second shot. The fire was returned and the fight continued for nearly two hours. Lieutenant Commander Madison was severely wounded early in the fight, but caused himself to be placed in a chair on the bridge and continued to direct the fire and to maneuver the ship. When the order was finally given to abandon the sinking ship, he became unconscious from loss of blood, but was lowered into a lifeboat and was saved, with thirty-one others, out of a total number of 236 on board.[65]

Photo 19-9

Commander James Jonas Madison, USNRF,
wearing the Medal of Honor (Tiffany Cross).
Naval History and Heritage Command photograph #NH 48048

Madison was retired in August 1920. The effects of his combat injuries kept him hospitalised for much of his remaining short life, and he underwent several operations, one involving the amputation of a leg. Commander James J. Madison died on 25 December 1922 at the U.S. Naval Hospital, Brooklyn, New York. The destroyer USS *Madison* (DD-425), of 1940-1969, was named in his honor.[66]

LEST WE FORGET

Mine Sweepers 1914-18 Sea Warfare by Rudyard Kipling

(Set to music by the English composer Edward Elgar in 1917, as the fourth of a set of four war-related songs, titled "The Fringes of the Fleet")

DAWN off the Foreland—the young flood making
  Jumbled and short and steep—
Black in the hollows and bright where it's breaking—
  Awkward water to sweep.
  "Mines reported in the fairway,
  Warn all traffic and detain.
Sent up *Unity, Claribel, Assyrian, Stormcock,* and *Golden Gain.*"

Noon off the Foreland—the first ebb making
  Lumpy and strong in the bight.
Boom after boom, and the golf-hut shaking
  And the jackdaws wild with fright.
  "Mines located in the fairway,
  Boats now working up the chain,
Sweepers—*Unity, Claribel, Assyrian, Stormcock,* and *Golden Gain.*"

Dusk off the Foreland—the last light going
  And the traffic crowding through,
And five damned trawlers with their syreens blowing
  Heading the whole review!
  "Sweep completed in the fairway.
  No more mines remain.
Sent back *Unity, Claribel, Assyrian, Stormcock,* and *Golden Gain.*"

The famous poem by Rudyard Kipling pays homage to the hundreds and hundreds of vessels, taken from every port and harbour in Britain for service as minesweepers. Although the origin of *Claribel* seems to be a mystery, it appears that the other four of the famous craft were drifters and trawlers. Kipling apparently shared the sentiments of Lord Jellicoe, who declared that the Royal Navy had saved the Empire, but it was fishermen in their boats who had saved the Royal Navy.

Minesweeper	Type Vessel	Admiralty No.	Built
Unity	hired drifter	784	1904
Claribel			
Assyrian (later *Spider*)	fishing trawler	54	1908
Storm Cock	fishing trawler hired	H.405 (hull-reg.)	1892
Golden Gain	hired drifter	1000	1911[67]

Postwar Mine Clearance

The British Mine Clearance Service had the advantage of war experience in minesweeping unrivalled among the world's navies. Its general direction at the Admiralty was also in the most capable hands of Captain Lionel G. Preston, C.B… who had been associated with minesweepers since before the war.

—Capt. Henry Taprell Dorling, RN, in *Swept Channels*.[1]

Following war's end, the Supreme War Council (a central command founded in 1917 to coordinate Allied military strategy) based in Versailles, France, allocated areas requiring mine clearance to specific countries. America became responsible for its portion of the North Sea Mine Barrage; France for an area between the Belgian and French coasts; and Germany the large area in the Heligoland Bight to the east of 4 Degrees East Longitude. Mine Forces clearing mines they knew best would presumably make the already dangerous work a little less hazardous.[2]

The British faced the most daunting challenge. At the end of the war there were only a few comparatively narrow lanes of water around the British Isles which could be guaranteed to be safe. The necessary clearance would be a laborious task, involving a search of over 40,000 square miles. A large portion of their area would have to be swept twice, and in some cases three times. To facilitate this work, a special "Mine Clearance Service" was established in February 1919.[3]

It required large numbers of people, involving all classes of officers and seamen, except active service ratings of the Royal Navy who could not be spared from the Fleet. The officers and men joining the Service received special rates of pay and conditions of leave. In testament to their dangerous duty, all those engaged in minesweeping were permitted to wear the Mine Clearance Badge approved by his Majesty, on their left sleeves.[4]

British Mine Clearance Service Badge

In June 1919, the Service numbered about 700 officers and 14,500 men under Mine Clearance Officers (MCOs) assigned in twenty-two different areas in British home waters and abroad. The MCOs that were associated with home waters are identified in the table. Of these thirteen individuals, nine were authorised to wear either the DSO or DSC, received during the war, on their uniform blouses. Fifty-five different flotillas/groups of vessels carried out the clearance work in home waters and overseas.[5]

British Postwar Mine Clearance, Home Waters

Mine Clearance Area	Commander
Area 1: Northern Area	MCO: Comdr. C. H. G. Benson, DSO, RN
Area 2: Eastern Scottish Area	MCO & Granton PMSO: Comdr. Leslie D. Fisher, DSO, RN
Area 3: North-Eastern Area	MCO: Comdr. Basil R. Brooke, DSO, RN
Area 4: Eastern Area	MCO: Capt. H. F. Cayley, DSO, RN (Retired)
Area 5: Dover Area	MCO: Lt. A. E. Buckland, DSC, RN
Area 6: Portsmouth Area	MCO: Comdr. F. E. Seymour, RN (Retired)
Area 7: Devonport Area	MCO: Comdr. Kennet Dixon, RN (Retired)
Area 8: Western England Area	MCO: Lt. Comdr. Thomas C. Macgill, RN
Area 9: South Ireland Area	MCO: Comdr. F. C. G. St. Clair, RN
Area 10: North Ireland, Clyde and West of Scotland Area	MCO: Comdr. Eric W. Harbord, DSO, RN
Scheveningen Area	MCO: Lt. Comdr. (acting) James Collis Bird, DSC, RN; relieved in April 1919 by Lt. Comdr. S. H. Simpson, DSO, RN
Scheldt Area	MCO: Lt. Comdr. H. T. Baillie-Grohman, DSO, RN[6]

Individual ships were paid off as they completed their work, and reductions in personnel took place. The clearance effort was finished by 30 November 1919, at which time British minesweepers had cleared over 23,000 Allied and 70 German mines since the Armistice.[7]

U.S. NORTH SEA MINESWEEPING DETACHMENT

The signing of the Armistice makes this the greatest day for our country since the signing of The Declaration of Independence. For the World there has been no day so momentous for liberty. I send greetings and congratulations to all in the Naval Establishment at home and abroad. The test of war found the Navy ready fit with every man on his toes. Every day all the men in the service have given fresh proof of devotion, loyalty, and efficiency. In America and in all other countries the people have applauded Naval initiative and Naval resourcefulness. As we rejoice in the victory for every principle that caused us to enter the war let us be thankful that when the American people needed a Navy we were rapidly creating all others that could be employed.

—Statement issued by Secretary of the Navy Josephus Daniels on 11 November 1918 to all civilian and uniformed members of the U.S. Navy.[8]

Photo 20-1

Surrender of German High Seas Fleet off the Firth of Forth, Scotland, 21 November 1918. Vice Adm. William S. Sims, USN, and Rear Adm. Hugh Rodman, USN, observe from aboard the battleship *New York* (BB-34).
Painting by Bernard F. Gribble, 1920; U.S. Naval History and Heritage Command Accession #NH 58842-KN

At the cessation of hostilities on 11 November 1918, the U.S. Navy's regular and reserve enrolled strength was 497,030 men and women, 32,474 officers, and 2,003 ships in commission. Ten days later, the U.S. Sixth Battle Squadron (Battleship Division Nine) witnessed the surrender of the Imperial German Navy's High Seas Fleet off the Firth

of Forth, Scotland. The Grand Fleet escorted the High Seas Fleet to
Scapa Flow the following day.[9]

On 22 November 1918, the Secretary of the Navy ordered
demobilisation to take effect "as fast as the exigencies of the service
permit and accomplishment is hereby directed." This included the
demobilisation of the North Sea Mine Barrage bases aside from
maintenance of minesweeping capabilities, and of all naval personnel
and equipment in France aside from minesweepers and destroyers, until
their services were no longer required.[10]

The Navy Department announced on 30 November that U.S. naval
losses for World War I included 44 ships lost and 10,521 Navy and
Marine Corps casualties. On 1 December, minelayers of the U.S. Mine
Force sailed from Scotland to return to the United States. Later that
month, on 22 December, the requisitioned British fishing smacks *Red
Fern* and *Red Rose* were towed by the tugs USS *Patapsco* and USS *Patuxent*
from Lowestoft, England, out to the North Sea Mine Barrage to assist
with its removal.[11]

AMERICAN MINES PRESENT GRAVE DANGER

The firing mechanism of the U.S. Mk VI mine consisted of an electrical
device inside the spherical mine case, and a connected thin wire antenna
of variable desired length, that was supported by a small buoy or float
which positioned the top of the antenna within eight or ten feet of the
surface. The mine itself had a destructive radius of about 100 feet, so it
was not necessary for a vessel to strike a mine for it to explode. If a
steel ship touched the antenna, the mine to which it was attached would
detonate.[12]

Because of the properties of these mines, they were dangerous to
any steel vessel, including the *Lapwing*-class minesweepers which would
perform the bulk of the clearance. Thus, much experimentation had to
be carried out, and protective measures identified before the actual
sweeping could commence. Successful measures found included
equipping the *Lapwing*s with an electrical device designed to prevent the
mine from firing within a certain distance.[13]

It was also necessary to determine the actual condition of the mines
in the barrage. Some had exploded after being laid, while others,
discovered on the Norway coast, had broken adrift. On 23 December,
while the *Patapsco* and *Patuxent* stood off, the wooden smacks began an
experimental sail-driven shared operation, one end of a sweep wire
made fast to each vessel. A few minutes past noon, as they crossed the
first invisible line of mines, a giant column of water sprang high into the
air astern of the *Red Rose*—the first mine in the North Sea Barrage to be

swept. As it were, the force of the explosion all but crushed her wooden hull; water spurted in between the timbers in countless places, and the pumps were barely sufficient to keep her dry.[14]

The actual mine clearance began on 29 April 1919, following the heaviest snowstorm of the year, when the sweepers and a division of sub-chasers set out for the barrage. The U.S. Mine Force was commanded by Rear Adm. Joseph Strauss who flew his flag in the *Black Hawk*. The North Sea Minesweeping Detachment, a subordinate force, was commanded by Capt. Roscoe Carlyle Bulmer, USN—the commanding officer of *Black Hawk*. Bulmer was critically wounded in an automobile accident on 3 August 1919, and died two days later at Kirkwall. Eighty-eight vessels comprised the Mine Force: 8 repair ships and auxiliaries; 34 minesweepers; 24 sub-chasers; 2 tugs; and 20 leased British trawlers manned by USN personnel. (The U.S. Coast Guard cutter *Seneca*, intended for salvage and general utility duty was only present 2-5 June 1919, before being recalled for other duties.)[15]

United States Mine Force

Repair Ships and Auxiliaries

USS *Black Hawk* (flagship, repair and supply ship for minesweepers)
USS *Chesapeake* (wrecking vessel, used as cargo carrier between Liverpool, Brest, and Kirkwood)
USS *Panther* (repair and supply ship for sub-chasers and trawlers)
SS *Aspenleaf* (British oiler, used as store ship for reserve supply gasoline)
SS *Crenella* (British oiler)
RFA *Hickorol* (British Royal Fleet Auxiliary petrol supply ship for sub-chasers and British motor launches)
RFA *Hopkiln* (British seagoing water vessel)
RFA *Petronel* (British seagoing water vessel)

Submarine Chasers: 110 feet, 70 tons, 16 knots

SC-37, SC-38, SC-40, SC-44, SC-45, SC-46, SC-47, SC-48, SC-95, SC-110, SC-164, SC-178, SC-181, SC-182, SC-206, SC-207, SC-208, SC-254, SC-256, SC-259, SC-272, SC-329, SC-354, SC-356

Minesweepers (*Lapwing*-class): 187 feet, 950 tons, 14 knots

USS *Auk, Avocet, Bobolink, Chewink, Cormorant, Curlew, Eider, Falcon, Finch, Flamingo, Grebe, Heron, Kingfisher, Lapwing, Lark, Mallard, Oriole, Osprey, Pelican, Penguin, Quail, Rail, Robin, Sanderling, Seagull, Swallow, Swan, Tanager, Teal, Thrush, Turkey, Whippoorwill, Widgeon, Woodcock*

Fleet Tugs: 157 feet, 917 tons, 12 knots; and 148 feet, 755 tons, 13 knots

USS *Patapsco*, USS *Patuxent*

Minesweeping Trawlers (leased from the British)

George Burton, George Clarke, George Cochrane, John Clay, John Collins, John Dunkin, John Fitzgerald, John Graham, Liam Duffey, Pat Caharty, Richard Bulkeley, Thomas Blackthorne, Thomas Buckley, Thomas Graham, Thomas Hendrix, Thomas Laundry, William Aston, William Caldwell, William Darnold, William Johnson[16]

Photo 20-2

USS *Black Hawk* moored at Inverness, Scotland, in September 1918, while serving as Mine Force repair ship and flagship.
Naval History and Heritage Command photograph #NH 56398

Patapsco and Patuxent left Inverness on 20 March for the North Sea Mine Barrage, to conduct experiments in Area "B" with minesweeping gear. Inverness was then the only remaining U.S. Overseas Base; Invergordon having been demobilised and turned over to the British government on 1 March 1919. During tests carried out by the fleet tugs from 22–24 March, twenty-one mines were exploded and seventeen more were cut adrift. On 20 April, the first twelve *Lapwings* steamed into Inverness Firth, from Boston, Massachusetts. The sub-chasers that would work astern of the sweepers (destroying cut mines with rifle fire and laying dan buoys to mark swept areas) had begun to arrive at Inverness in the latter part of February. By 1 March, nineteen chasers had reported, including three previously sent to Norway for exhibition and possible sale.[17]

In anticipation of the possible use of British trawlers crewed with American sailors, 400 trained petty officers and seamen had been taken from the minelayers before their departure on 1 December 1918 and transferred ashore.   These men carried out the minesweeping experimentation with the smacks and tugs, and would later form the nuclei of the trawler crews. When the minelayers sailed for America, *Black Hawk*, *Patapsco*, and *Patuxent* remained behind to support the minesweeping force. Since it had not been possible previously to grant leave to any of the officers and men due to the uncertainty of ship movements, the minelaying squadron was sent to Plymouth for a brief stay—providing all hands the opportunity to visit England before returning to the United States.[18]

Photo 20-3

Minesweeper USS *Tanager* circa mid-1919. The X identification mark on her bow and smokestack denoted that she was a unit of the North Sea Mine Clearance Force.
Naval History and Heritage Command photograph #NH 107315

The *Lapwing*s were 187 feet long, with a 35' 6" beam, and 9' 10" draught. They (like all minesweepers) were designed for pulling power and not speed, but could make 14 knots, propelled by two Babcock and Wilcox header boilers, one Harlan and Hollingsworth vertical triple expansion reciprocating steam engine producing 1,400 shaft-horsepower, and a single shaft and propeller. For armament, the ships were fitted with two 3"/50 mounts which were now unnecessary for self-defence. Crew complement was 78 officers and men.[19]

FIRST CLEARANCE OPERATION (29 APRIL-2 MAY)

In the first operation to remove the American portion of the North Sea Mine Barrage, twelve minesweepers and six submarine chasers sailed from Inverness on 29 April. That same day, *Black Hawk* and the remaining sub-chasers got under way for their new base at Kirkwall, Orkney. This base was selected as the primary base for operations because of its proximity to the barrage. A few hours after *Black Hawk* had anchored at Kirkwall, she was joined by *Auk*, *Heron*, *Oriole*, and *Sanderling*—newly arrived from the United States. The minesweeping operation was completed on 2 May. The Force proceeded to Kirkwall; having destroyed 221 Mk VI mines, twenty-five percent of those originally laid in the area swept.[20]

SECOND OPERATION (8-29 MAY)

The second minesweeping operation began from Kirkwall on 8 May. An explosion on the 12th damaged the minesweeping gear of the tug *Patuxent*. Her commanding officer ordered all hands forward to safety and joined the chief boatswain's mate on the fantail in clearing a mine fouled in the sweep gear behind the vessel. Without warning the mine exploded, shards severing the thumb of the commanding officer, but causing no other injuries. Up to this point, several ships had hauled in mines aboard which had fouled their sweep, as souvenirs. According to design, it had been believed that they were safe when they were within approximately thirty feet of the water's surface. Now, no one trusted the mines under any circumstance.[21]

In a similar incident on 14 May, the minesweeper *Bobolink* was damaged by a mine explosion, and her commander, Lt. Frank Bruce, USN, killed in the blast when he attempted to remove a mine caught in the sweeping gear. The boatswain and three other men were blown into the water. All four were rescued, although the former had been knocked unconscious by the shock. The ship suffered serious damage; her after hull plating driven in 2-3 feet in places; rudder and rudder post shorn away; propeller distorted and shaft bent; engine thrown out of alignment; and the towing engine, capstan, searchlights and many other fixtures broken or disabled.[22]

Teal took the *Bobolink* in tow and, accompanied by *Swallow* and *SC-45*, headed for port. After temporary repairs were made to *Bobolink* at Scapa, she was towed to Devonport, England, for more extensive work; which took over six months to complete. During the operation, a mine detonation under *Turkey*, on 16 May, caused her to leak so badly she also had to be docked.[23]

The operation concluded on 29 May with 1,672 mines swept and overall 1,750 destroyed. (Presumably, the additional 78 mines were ones found adrift. The 1920 U.S. Navy publication *The Northern Barrier (Taking up the Mines)* included the unattributed quote, "It is interesting to note that although far fewer British mines were laid in the barrage than American ones, a great many more of the former type were sighted afloat than our own." Four days later on 2 June, the last of the leased

British minesweeping trawlers with American crews arrived at Kirkwall, for duty assisting in clearing the North Sea Mine Barrage.[24]

The long hours of sunlight which existed in the summer months at that high latitude greatly assisted the operations, by enabling the vessels to operate up to the physical endurance of their crews. The added illumination was further beneficial (especially during the early work) because it enabled vessels to more easily spot and keep clear of the many floating mines which had broken adrift in the vicinity of the barrage. Weather permitting, the normal nighttime procedure was to anchor several miles from the minefield by means of a heavy weight or a kedge anchor made fast to the end of the sweep wire. (Ship's ground tackle was not used, for fear anchor and chain would be tangled in sweep gear.) When there was no wind, this makeshift method worked, but even a moderate breeze caused vessels to drag considerably.[25]

THIRD OPERATION (5 JUNE-1 JULY)

Photo 20-4

Band concert in 1919 for the crew of the repair ship *Black Hawk* (flagship of Rear Adm. Joseph Strauss), during the sweeping of the North Sea Mine Barrage. The *Heron*, one of three minesweepers in the background, is at left, with the identification letter U painted on her bow.
Naval History and Heritage Command photograph NH 101173

On 5 June, minesweepers and sub-chasers sailed once again from Kirkwall for another operation. (That same day, *Chewink*, *Flamingo*, *Penguin*, and *Thrush* arrived at Kirkwall; and *Black Hawk* sailors began the installation of electrical protective devices aboard them.) An interesting incident occurred on the second day of sweeping. The western part of the barrage contained more shoal water (shallow depths) than elsewhere. While operating there, *Heron* and *Sanderling* were suddenly brought almost to a standstill by something on the bottom having snagged their sweep. A few minutes later, a large patch of oil rose to the surface astern of them—apparently freed from a sunken submarine by their wire jostling it. Months earlier, the minelaying squadron upon passing this spot, had sighted the body of a German sailor floating in the water. It was believed that *UB-127* lay below them.[26]

The weather in the North Sea in the month of June 1919 was far worse than ordinary and this, coupled with the heavy currents flowing through the Fair Island passage (between Orkney and Fair Island to the south), greatly delayed the completion of the operation. The sweeping work finally finished on 1 July after twenty-six-and-a-half days at sea. Eleven days were lost on the account of storms, nevertheless 2,329 mines were destroyed. None of the vessels were seriously damaged except for the submarine chasers *SC-164* and *SC-208*. Mine explosions caused significant damage about the upper decks of the former, and opened hull seams of the latter. *SC-208* required escort to port by the *Teal* and another chaser, and docking before she could resume work.[27]

On 21 July at Scapa Flow, under the mistaken belief that peace talks had failed, Rear Adm. Ludwig von Reuter gave the order to scuttle the entire High Seas Fleet. The crews of all the ships in the Flow (by then totaling fewer than 2,000 men) raised the German flag, and opened seacocks, portholes, watertight doors, hatches, and torpedo tubes. As German sailors took to their lifeboats, ships began to sink with tremendous hissings of steam, spouts of water, and finally sucking and gurgling sounds as they slipped below the surface. Also during the third operation, representatives of the Allied and Associated powers signed a treaty of peace with Germany at Versailles, France, on 28 June.[28]

FOURTH OPERATION (7-17 JULY)

The fourth minesweeping operation beginning on 7 July brought much tragedy. Over several days, the North Sea Minesweeping Detachment suffered one minesweeper sunk (*Richard Bulkeley*), one permanently damaged (*Pelican*), four damaged (*Flamingo, Lapwing, Penguin,* and *William Darnold*), and seven personnel killed. Greater detail about portions of the following account may be found in Chapter One.[29]

On 9-10 July, *Pelican* exploded six mines beneath her or close by, which severely damaged the ship, rupturing her forward bulkheads and causing her to rapidly fill with water. *Auk* and *Eider* made up to *Pelican* to pump out the stricken vessel while a fourth minesweeper, *Teal,* took her in tow. All through the night and into the next day the men on board the vessels fought to keep her afloat until reaching Tresness Bay, Scotland. At Tresness, the holes in *Pelican*'s hull were plugged and patched, allowing her to be towed to Scapa Flow for repairs.[30]

On 12 July, the British minesweeping trawler *Richard Bulkeley* sank seven minutes after a mine, fouled in her kite, exploded. Comdr. Frank R. King and six of his crew were killed. The operation concluded on 17 July with 2,455 mines destroyed. Two days earlier, four additional minesweepers had arrived at Kirkwall, bringing to thirty-two the total force of sweepers.[31]

FIFTH OPERATION (22 JULY-7 AUGUST)

The fifth operation from 22 July-7 August was marred by the death of a sailor blown overboard and lost from the *Curlew*. Five thousand, five hundred, and eighteen Mk VI mines were destroyed, bringing to that date the removal of 55 percent of the mines planted in the barrage. Meanwhile, the Mine Force was increased by the addition of three sub-chasers—*SC-95*, *SC-256*, and *SC-354*—which had been on duty in Russia for several months.[32]

SIXTH OPERATION (13 AUGUST-10 SEPTEMBER)

We are getting along with the work much better now than at first. The weather is better and we have more ships to operate with. If the weather is extraordinarily good we may finish this year. It is quite possible, however, that the increased darkness and heavy gales that are almost continuous from the latter part of September on in the North Sea may compel us to send a small finishing expedition next spring. I am hoping that this will not be the case, and we are all bending our utmost energy to get through with it. As may be imagined, the work of gathering these thousands of mines scattered throughout an area in the North Sea of some 6,000 square miles is a big job and a hazardous one. The laying of the mines was accomplished in 50 or 60 working hours and the hazard was slight or nonexistent. We have had our losses, but are much more fortunate than the British, who lost two large minesweepers of the Flower *class last month, when 40 men were drowned.*

—Portion of a letter by Rear Admiral Strauss
to the Secretary of the Navy.[33]

The sixth operation began on 13 August. By 1 September, work in the eastern half of the North Sea Mine Barrage was practically complete. On 4 September, the submarine chaser *SC-38* was damaged by a mine explosion but was salvaged. Efforts concluded on the 10th with 10,397 mines destroyed. One week later, U.S. Navy Overseas Mine Base 18 at Inverness, Scotland, was demobilised and turned over to the British in anticipation of the impending completion of American mine clearance operations.[34]

SEVENTH/FINAL OPERATION (17-30 SEPTEMBER)

The seventh and final minesweeping operation from Kirkwall, which finished on 30 September, destroyed 1,761 mines. Of the 52,219 Mk VI mines that had survived premature explosions while being laid, the North Sea Minesweeping Detachment in all their seven operations accounted for 21,295 (42.7 percent) of their removal. Most of the others had gone adrift; ripped loose by heavy seas and strong currents. Some may have failed to deploy from their anchors, or had sunk after deploying, or were perhaps not swept during operations.[35]

U.S NAVY MINESWEEPING FORCE RETURNS HOME

Photo 20-5

Review of the U.S. Minesweeping Squadron on 24 November 1919, by Secretary of the Navy Josephus Daniels, following its return to the United States. Naval History and Heritage Command photograph #NH 44904

The minesweeping detachment from Kirkwall, Scotland, arrived off Tompkinsville, New York, on 19-20 November 1919, after having completed their work in the North Sea Mine Barrage. On the 24th, Secretary of the Navy Josephus Daniels reviewed the North Sea Mine Force from on board the destroyer USS *Meredith*—as the ships lay at anchor in the Hudson River off New York City. That evening, at midnight, the flag of Rear Adm. Joseph Strauss was hauled down and the following day, at noon, the force was disbanded.[36]

AMERICAN AWARDS FOR VALOR

The Medal of Honor is a valor medal; to win it, a man must have performed an act of Heroism under fire, above and beyond the call of ordinary duty and at the risk of his life. The Distinguished Service Medal is what its name implies and it was awarded to those who served with marked distinction in a position of great responsibility. The Navy Cross was awarded for both gallantry in action and conspicuous service. Where it was awarded for gallantry, it takes precedence over the Distinguished Service Medal, taking its place next to the Medal of Honor but where it was given for exceptional service, the Medal ranks first.

—*Navy Book of Distinguished Service*, 1921

The final few pages provide readers information about the command structure of the U.S. Navy's minelaying and minesweeping squadrons. The commanding officers of the minelayers and minesweepers are identified if known, as are awards received for valor. The list does not include the sub-chasers, tugs, and smacks which also participated in mine clearance.[37]

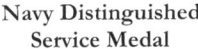

Navy Distinguished Service Medal

Navy Cross Medal

Laying of the North Sea Mine Barrage

Recipient	Positions/Duties
Comdr. William Lewis Beck, USN	Executive Officer, USS *Roanoke*, later Commander, 3rd Minesweeping Division, USS *Oriole* flagship

Capt. Reginald Rowan Belknap, USN	Commander, Mine Squadron 1
Capt. Roscoe Carlyle Bulmer, USN (posthumously)	Commanding Officer, USS *Black Hawk*; Commander Minesweeping Detachment
Capt. Henry Varnum Butler Jr., USN	Commanding Officer, USS *San Francisco*
Capt. Wat Tyler Cluverius Jr., USN	Commanding Officer, USS *Shawmut*
Lt. Noel Davis, USN	Aid to Commander, Mine Force; later the commander of a mine sweeping division
Comdr. Simon Peter Fullinwider, USN (Retired)	Meritorious service in the development of plans and material for the mine barrage
Capt. Sinclair Gannon, USN	Commanding Officer, USS *Saranac*
Capt. John Wills Greenslade, USN	Commanding Officer, USS *Housatonic*
Capt. Thomas Lee Johnson, USN	Commanding Officer, USS *Canonicus*
Capt. David Pratt Mannix, USN	Commanding Officer, USS *Quinnebaug*
Capt. Albert Ware Marshall, USN	Commanding Officer, USS *Baltimore*
Capt. William Herbert Reynolds, USN	Commanding Officer, USS *Canandaigua*
Capt. Clark Daniel Stearns, USN	Commanding Officer, USS *Roanoke*
Rear Adm. Joseph Strauss, USN	Commander Mine Force, U.S. Atlantic Fleet
Capt. James Harvey Tomb, USN	Commanding Officer, USS *Aroostook*

Clearance of the North Sea Mine Barrage

Minesweeping Divisions

1st Division: Comdr. John Rodgers, USN (DSM)

USS *Turkey* (flagship)	Lt. John B. Hupp, USN (Navy Cross)
USS *Robin*	Lt. Lewis Henry Cutting, USN (Navy Cross)
USS *Quail*	Lt. Robert Rohange, USN (Navy Cross)
USS *Kingfisher*	Lt. C. L. Green, USN; Lt. Earl Swisher, USN
USS *Finch*	Lt. Karl Rundquist, USN (Navy Cross); Lt. (jg) Gustav Adolf Curt Leutritz, USN (Navy Cross)
USS *Falcon*	Lt. John Conrad Lindberg, USN (Navy Cross)

2nd Division: Comdr. Walter Frederick Jacobs, USN (DSM)

USS *Eider* (flagship)	Lt. Arthur Edward Freed, USN (Navy Cross)
USS *Pelican*	Lt. George E. McHugh, USN (Navy Cross)
USS *Bobolink*	Lt. Frank Bruce, USN (DSM, posthumously)
USS *Woodcock*	Lt. Harry A. Wentworth, USN (Navy Cross)
USS *Rail*	Lt. Edwin Ray Wroughton, USN (Navy Cross)
USS *Teal*	Lt. Frederick Meyer, USN (Navy Cross)
USS *Seagull*	Lt. (jg) Frank Jurgenson, USN (Navy Cross)
USS *Swallow*	Lt. Bennie Clark Phillips, USN (Navy Cross)

3rd Division: Comdr. William Lewis Beck, USN (DSM)

USS *Oriole* (flagship)	Lt. Roy Melvin Cottrell, USN (Navy Cross)
USS *Auk*	Lt. Gregory Cullen, USN (Navy Cross)
USS *Heron*	Lt. Karl Rundquist, USN (Navy Cross)
USS *Sanderling*	Lt. Stanley Danielak, USN (Navy Cross)
USS *Chewink*	Lt. (jg) James Williams, USN (Navy Cross)
USS *Tanager*	Lt. (jg) Michael Higgins, USN (Navy Cross)
	Lt. Michael Joseph Wilkinson, USN (Navy Cross)

4th Division: Comdr. Edwin Armin Wolleson, USN (DSM)

USS *Thrush* (flagship)	Lt. (jg) Frederick Thomas Mayes, USN (Navy Cross)
USS *Avocet*	Lt. Christian Crone, USN (Navy Cross)
USS *Grebe*	Lt. Niels Dustrup, USN (awarded the Medal of Honor in 1924 for heroic action in 1914, and Navy Cross in 1919)
USS *Curlew*	Lt. John McCloy, USN (previously awarded two Medals of Honor, 1901 and 1914, and the Navy Cross in 1919)
USS *Cormorant*	Lt. John R. McKean, USN (Navy Cross)
USS *Mallard*	Lt. Robert Chester O'Brien, USNRF (Navy Cross)

5th Division: Comdr. Edward V. Keen, USNRF (DSM)

USS *Lark* (flagship)	Lt. Henry Aloysius Stanley, USN (Navy Cross)
USS *Swan*	Lt. (jg) Fredman Jerome Walcott, USNRF (Navy Cross)
USS *Widgeon*	Lt. Michael John Bresnahan, USN (Navy Cross)
USS *Whippoorwill*	Lt. Birney O. Halliwill, USN (Navy Cross)
USS *Flamingo*	Lt. Frederick J. Mayer, USN (Navy Cross)

Buoying Division

USS *Osprey*	Lt. Murray Wolffe, USN (Navy Cross)
USS *Patapsco*	Lt. William Edwin Benson, USN (Navy Cross)
USS *Patuxent*	Lt. Jesse Llewellen Harmer, USN (Navy Cross)
USS *Lapwing*	Lt. (jg) William Fremgen, USN (Navy Cross)
USS *Penguin*	Lt. (jg) Edgar Taylor Hammond, USN (Navy Cross)
	Lt. William Reginald Spear, USN (Navy Cross)

British Trawlers (operated by U.S. Navy Crews)

Division One

Trawlers	Class	Built	Commanding Officer
UST *Thomas Blackhorne*	Castle	1917	Lt. Floyd Scofield, USNRF
UST *George Clarke*	Castle	1917	Lt. (jg) Edwin Vernon Wilder, USN (awarded Navy Cross in 1920)
UST *John Collins*	Castle	1917	Lt. (jg) Fred O. Goldsmith (Navy Cross)
UST *Liam Duffey*	Castle	1918	Lt. (jg) Thomas Kennedy, USNRF (awarded Navy Cross in 1920)

UST *Thomas Laundry*	*Castle*	1918	Lt. (jg) Franz O. Willenbucher, USN; Lt. (jg) H. DeBarr, USNRF (awarded Navy Cross in 1920)

Division Two

UST *Thomas Buckley*	*Castle*	1917	Lt. Henry Y. McCowan, USN (awarded Navy Cross in 1920)
UST *George Cochrane*	*Castle*	1918	Lt. (jg) Richard Codwell Thompson, USNRF (awarded Navy Cross in 1920)
UST *John Graham*	*Castle*	1918	Lt. Leon H. Ackerman, USNRF (Awarded Navy Cross in 1920)
UST *William Caldwell*	*Castle*	1918	Ens. Charles A. Ryan, USNRF (awarded Navy Cross in 1920); Lt. (jg) Edmund DeLavy, USNRF (awarded Navy Cross in 1920)
UST *William Darnold*	*Castle*	1918	Lt. Edmund DeLavy, USN

Division Three: Comdr. Frank Ragan King, USN (DSM)

UST *Richard Bulkeley*	*Mersey*	1917	Lt. Frederick G. Keyes, USN (awarded Navy Cross in 1919)
UST *George Burton*	*Strath*	1917	
UST *Pat Caharty*	*Strath*	1918	
UST *Thomas Graham*	*Strath*	1918	
UST *William Ashton*	*Strath*	1917	

Division Four: Comdr. Ellis Lando, USN (DSM)

UST *William Johnson*	*Mersey*	1918	Lt. Valerious V. Black, USNRF (awarded Navy Cross in 1920); Lt. Albert Charles Fraenzel, USN (awarded Navy Cross in 1920)
UST *John Dunkin*	*Strath*	1918	Lt. (jg) J. G. Doerscburg, USN
UST *Thomas Henrix*	*Strath*	1918	
UST *John Fitzgerald*	*Strath*	1917	
UST *John Clay*	*Special*	1917	

Postscript

It is difficult to gain a full impression of all the toil and danger, the skill and devotion which went to make up what minesweeping flotillas were giving to the command cause. Their part was but the sober background against which the more conspicuous exploits of the navy are thrown into relief, yet, if we grasp what the sea service gave, we must never forget how that background was being worked in patiently, incessantly, stroke by stroke, in fair weather and in foul, with the old tasks never complete and new ones constantly being set.... We have been taught to be proud of how in days gone by the sea spirit of the nation answered the call at the hour of danger, but never in all our long story had there been such an answer as this.

—Julian Corbett, *History of the Great War Naval Operations Vol. II.*

This book, which is being launched on the 100th anniversary of the First World War, rightly pays tribute to the heroic efforts of Britain's Mine Forces between 1914-18, and during post-war mine clearance. It is therefore fitting to close out the book with a quick tour of the rich history of the Royal Navy's mine clearance forces, which were born out of necessity in WWI, to the present time. This section is most suited for readers with current or past mine warfare experience, and in particular Royal Navy Mine Warfare specialists and Clearance Divers. As a reminder to non-Royal Navy readers, the letters HMS followed by a name in italics refers to a ship. If the name following HMS is not italicised, it is a shore establishment, which RN personnel term a "stone frigate."

A similar account could easily have been written about the Allied personnel involved in mining and MCM (Mine Counter Measures) during the Second World War, especially the seafaring men of the trawlers, drifters and other auxiliary vessels engaged in the hazardous task of sweeping mines. As in the previous war, Britain was brought close to starvation by German mines while Allied-laid mines helped blockade Germany and prevent the free movement of U-boats. This time, the brunt of the minesweeping effort was borne by men of the RNPS (Royal Naval Patrol Service nicknamed "Harry Tate's Navy" or "Churchill's Pirates") whose usual day job was fishing.

ROYAL NAVAL RESERVE (TRAWLER SECTION)

It was Admiral Lord Charles Beresford, Commander-in-Chief of the Royal Navy's Home Fleet, who first recommended the use of trawlers for minesweeping duties after a visit to ports on the east coast of England in 1907. He wrote:

> Our fishing fleets, in war, will be rendered inactive and will, in consequence be available for war service. Fishermen, by virtue of their calling, are adept in the handling and towing of wires and trawls, more so than are naval ratings. Small naval vessels, if used in minesweeping, will be used at the expense of other urgent war requirements.

Admiral Beresford's prescience eventually led to the formation of the Royal Naval Reserve (Trawler Section)—the RNR(T). The Trawler Reserve was instituted with approval for 100 trawlers to be mobilised during any period of strained relations and for the immediate enrolment of 1,000 officers and ratings to man these vessels. This brought the new rank of 'Skipper' RNR into the Navy List and the first officer, a fishing boat skipper called Peter Yorston, enrolled at Aberdeen on 3 February 1911. By the end of 1911, fifty-three skippers had joined.

In 1912 a further twenty-five enrolled and the Trawler Section of the Royal Naval Reserve comprised 142 trawlers manned by 1,279 personnel. Thirty-one more skippers joined before the war started in August 1914 making a total of one hundred and nine. By the end of 1915 the Minesweeping Service employed 7,888 officers and men.

When the Armistice was signed in November 1918, the Trawler Reserve comprised 39,000 officers and men of whom 10,000 were employed in minesweepers and the rest in the auxiliary patrol. Total RN minesweeping forces included 762 ships stationed at 26 home ports and 35 foreign bases. A total of 214 RN minesweepers had been lost during the four years and three months of the war.

COMRADESHIP BETWEEN ALLIED NAVIES

There has always been a close association between the Royal Navy and the navies of the USA and Commonwealth nations including Canada, Australia and New Zealand; what thrives even now as the 'Five Eyes' intelligence alliance. These relationships proved particularly valuable in mine warfare, both mining and mine countermeasures (including bomb & mine disposal), during both world wars. Indeed, they persist to this day and RN, USN, RAN and RCN officers and ratings have often trained together and served in exchange posts ashore and at sea.

Although the U.S. Navy produced and sailed its own minelayers and minesweepers to Britain during World War I, much of the proficiency it gained in mine warfare was due to hard-won knowledge and expertise shared by the Royal Navy. This same knowledge and expertise formed the bedrock of mine warfare experience that RCN personnel serving aboard RN ships took back to Canada after the war.

The U.S. and Canadian navies have pursued robust mine warfare programmes in the intervening decades but they have only truly flourished in times of great need, like the Second World War, before lapsing into stagnation again.   In the UK, there is little glamour associated with mine warfare but there is a much greater appreciation for it, based on the vital role it played in two world wars in preventing Germany from starving Britain into submission.

As examples of the prowess of the Royal Navy in mine warfare, in 1991 during the first Gulf War, Commodore (Capt.) Chris Craig, CB, DSC, the RN's SNOME (Senior Naval Officer Middle East) described the RN mine countermeasures vessels as "the highest value units afloat in the Gulf" and was never contradicted. In 2011, Admiral Sir Trevor Soar, the RN's Commander-in-Chief Fleet, similarly described the role played by UK minehunters off Misrata as "the jewel in the crown of operations in Libya."

IMPORTANT ROLE OF HMS VERNON

The development of RN mine warfare began on 26 April 1876 with the commissioning of HMS Vernon as a torpedo and mining school at Fountain Lake within Portsmouth Harbour. The floating school was centred on the hulk of the 50-gun fourth-rate 'Symondite' frigate *Vernon*.

Like her predecessors, the fourth HMS *Vernon* was named after Admiral Edward Vernon (1684-1757). On 22 November 1739, he achieved fame by commanding a squadron of six ships which captured the Central American coastal fortress of Portobello from the Spanish. Although he suffered a later defeat at Cartagena, he was elected to Parliament on the basis of his previous success. He was known as 'Old Grog,' reputedly because of his penchant for wearing a cloak made of grogram (from the French 'gros grain'), a coarse fabric of silk or mohair and wool. In 1740, he had the sailors' neat rum ration diluted with water to prevent hoarding, a mixture known ever afterwards as 'grog.' Successive ships and the establishment ('stone frigate') called HMS Vernon adopted the same motto as the town of Vernon-sur-Seine in France where the Vernon family originated: "Vernon Semper Viret" or "Vernon Will Always Flourish."

Photo Postscript-1

The 50-gun fourth-rate frigate HMS *Vernon* designed by Sir William Symonds and launched at Woolwich on May Day in 1832.
Courtesy of Rob Hoole

Photo Postscript-2

Admiral Edward Vernon otherwise known as Old Grog (12 Nov 1684 – 30 Oct 1757)
Courtesy of Rob Hoole

The subsequent expansion of the floating school with other hulks was introduced in Chapter 3, with other references later in the text to the important role that Vernon played in World War I. Primary emphasis at the school was on torpedo trials and training and the research and development of anti-submarine devices and training in their use as well as mines, minesweeping and ships' electrics. In 1916, the second-class cruiser *Forte* was moored alongside *Warrior* (VERNON III) for use as offices and extra living accommodation. Between 1916 and 1923, various submarines and a barrage vessel were attached to the School to assist in providing electrical power.

Photo Postscript-3

12 Oct 1923 - HMS *Actaeon* (VERNON IV), the original HMS *Vernon*, under tow on her last journey to Castle's Shipbreaking Yard at Woolwich (where she had been built and launched in 1832) on 12 October 1923.
Courtesy of Rob Hoole

Post-war, HMS Vernon (or 'The Vernon' as it came to be known) was established ashore on 1 October 1923, at Portsmouth on the site of the old Gunwharf; and Mining, Whitehead [Torpedo] and Electrical departments were formed. The original 50-gun frigate HMS *Vernon*, since called *Actaeon* (VERNON IV), was sold and towed to Castle's Shipbreaking Yard at Woolwich to be scrapped. Similarly, *Marlborough* (VERNON II) was sold for scrap in October 1924 but capsized off Osea Island in the Blackwater Estuary on 28 November 1924 while being towed to the shipbreakers. *Donegal* (VERNON I) was sold on 18 May 1925 to Pounds Shipbreakers in Portsmouth.

IMPORTANCE OF HMS VERNON IN WORLD WAR II

Photo Postscript-4

19 Dec 1939 – Lt. Cdr. Ouvry at HMS Vernon showing King George VI the German magnetic ground mine he rendered safe on the mudflats at Shoeburyness on 23 November 1939. The projections were intended to prevent the cylindrical mine rolling across the seabed. The mine is displayed on board the museum ship HMS *Belfast*, a cruiser moored on the Thames in London which was severely damaged by an identical mine on 21 November 1939 and spent the next three years under repair. Courtesy of Rob Hoole

During the Second World War, HMS Vernon became responsible for mine disposal and mine countermeasures. Her officers and scientific staff achieved several coups involving the capture of mines and the development of countermeasures. One of the earliest of these was the rendering safe and recovery of the first German magnetic mine (Type GA) at Shoeburyness on 23 November 1939. For this deed, Cdr. John Ouvry, RN, was decorated with the DSO by King George VI at a ceremony on HMS Vernon's parade ground on 19 December 1939. Others decorated at the same time for this, and other tasks where mines were rendered safe for recovery and examination, were Lt. Cdr. Roger Lewis (DSO), Lt. J. E. M. Glenny (DSC), CPO C. E. Baldwin (DSM) and AB A. L. Vearncombe (DSM). Of particular note, these were the first Royal Naval decorations of the Second World War.

The recovery, investigation and exploitation of this first aircraft-laid German magnetic mine (British designation 'GA') enabled HMS Vernon to develop self-protective measures for Allied ships including degaussing coils that helped neutralise their magnetism. It also enabled the development of effective magnetic mine sweeps including the initial crude mine destructor ships containing huge electrical magnets in their holds, quickly superseded by minesweepers deploying the highly successful Double L (LL) electrode sweep, used throughout the war. Thus, the German stranglehold, on Allied shipping providing Britain's lifeblood at the outset of the Second World War, was relaxed considerably.

Photo Postscript-5

Electrically controlled mines on board HMS Vernon's minelaying tender
HM Trawler *Vernon* (ex-*Strathcoe*) between 1924 and 1938.
Courtesy of Rob Hoole

In June 1940, the first attempt to render safe a ground mine (which sits on the seabed, vice being suspended in the water column tethered to an anchor by a mooring cable) by divers was made in Poole Harbour, Dorset. A diving unit from HMS Excellent, supported by divers trained in RMS (Rendering Mines Safe) techniques from HMS Vernon, successfully removed the fuze from a Type GC magnetic mine underwater although the mine exploded as it was towed inshore. For his central role in this task, Able Seaman Diver R. G. Tawn was subsequently awarded the DSM. Tawn was later awarded the BEM "for gallant conduct and devotion to duty" but was killed, along with two other naval personnel, by an exploding mine in Falmouth Harbour on 6 March 1941 while manning a boat towed by 'The Mouse,' a small motor launch belonging to HMS Vernon which was specially fitted with Hotchkiss propulsion (no propeller). He was aged 24 and is buried in the Commonwealth War Graves part of Falmouth Cemetery.

On discovering the skill of HMS Vernon's mine technicians, the Germans placed booby traps in some mines. One was fitted with a small explosive charge that detonated when the mine was stripped in the mining shed at HMS Vernon on 6 August 1940. The explosion caused the deaths of Commissioned Gunner (T) Reginald A. Cook, PO Cecil H. Fletcher, AB William B. Croake, AB William J. Stearns and AB Alfred E. Stevens, and serious injuries to other personnel. Following this incident, mines were stripped and examined at a disused limestone quarry at nearby Buriton, which was nick-named HMS Mirtle (short for Mine Investigation Range).

Various sections of HMS Vernon were dispersed to sites throughout the country following heavy air raids on Portsmouth, one of which demolished Dido Building and killed 100 people in a single night. On 3 May 1941, the main part of HMS Vernon was evacuated to Roedean Girls' School at Brighton—HMS Vernon(R)—where bell pushes on the dormitory bulkhead were purportedly labelled 'Ring for Mistress." Other sites included Havant, Purbrook, West Leigh, Stokes Bay, Hove, Dartmouth/Brixham, Helensburgh, Edinburgh and Port Edgar.

Although many naval divers were trained at HMS Vernon in Rendering Mines Safe (RMS) procedures as members of the Mine Recovery Section during the Second World War, it was not until 1 October 1944 that responsibility for naval diving passed from the Gunnery Branch, still based at HMS Excellent, to the Torpedo Branch based at HMS Vernon. This brought mine warfare (both mining and mine countermeasures) and diving under the same organisation for the first time.

On 10 October 1946, the Torpedo Branch divested its Electrical responsibilities to the recently formed Electrical Branch and merged with the Anti-Submarine Branch (formerly based at HMS Osprey at Portland) to form the Torpedo and Anti-Submarine (TAS) Branch. Hence, the TAS Branch assumed responsibility for naval diving. HMS Vernon remained the home of the TAS Branch at Portsmouth until the summer of 1974 when it was devolved to HMS Dryad at nearby Southwick prior to the formation of the Operations Branch (now called the Warfare Branch) in early 1975.

Photo Postscript-6

HMS Vernon's coastal minelayer HMS *Plover*. Launched at William Denny & Brothers on the Clyde on 8 June 1937, sold on 26 February 1969 and subsequently broken up at Inverkeithing.
Courtesy of Rob Hoole

As the Royal Navy's *alma mater* of mine warfare and diving, HMS Vernon saw the development of clearance diving which originated with the 'P' Parties (Port Clearance Parties) that cleared European ports and their approaches of German ordnance and booby traps after D-Day in World War II. Until circa 2000, there were two types of diver in the RN. A Ship's Diver (formerly the Shallow Water Diver) could be of any rank or specialisation and was trained to use self-contained open-circuit compressed air diving apparatus to search the ship's bottom for explosive devices or perform simple underwater engineering tasks. The more advanced Clearance Diver (CD) was a specialist trained in the use of all types of service diving equipment including surface demand and closed-circuit mixture breathing apparatus to perform deeper diving, EOR (Explosive Ordnance Reconnaissance), EOD (Explosive Ordnance Disposal otherwise known as bomb & mine disposal), IEDD (Improvised Explosive Device Disposal), salvage operations and complex underwater engineering tasks. Today, only the Clearance Diver remains.

Warfare Branch ratings and warrant officers of the Royal Navy's CD Sub-Branch (formed in 1952) complement those of the Mine Warfare (MW) Sub-Branch (formed in 1975) while their officers, also members of the RN Warfare Branch, are usually trained in both disciplines as MCDOs (Mine Warfare & Clearance Diving Officers), able to turn their hand to minefield planning, minelaying, mine countermeasures (mine hunting using sonar & mine sweeping), diving, demolitions and EOD/IEDD.

Photo Postscript-7

HMS Vernon's waterfront in 1974, with RN, RNR and other NATO mine countermeasures vessels berthed alongside.
Courtesy of Rob Hoole

After the Second World War, HMS Vernon saw its progeny undertake the clearance of the Suez Canal in 1956, 1974 and again in 1975. In 1977, RN CDs co-operated with their U.S. counterparts to clear ex-U.S. and Japanese WWII ordnance from the waters of Tarawa and Tuvalu in the Gilbert and Ellis Islands. On a more peaceful note, thirty-five RN CDs worked with eighteen Egyptian divers in 1977/78 to shift 16,000 tons of mud and 320 blocks of stone during the movement of important Egyptian monuments submerged by the construction of the Aswan Dam to a site replicating Philae on Agilkia Island.

Royal Navy CDs, often accompanied by their MW comrades, have also undertaken the disposal of unexploded bombs in ships and the clearance of a minefield in the Falklands in 1982, the clearance of a minefield of Soviet mines laid by Gadhafi in the northern Red Sea in 1984, the clearance of Iranian or Iraqi mines in the Persian Gulf in 1987, 1991 and again in 2003 and the ongoing task of clearing legacy ordnance from on land and around the coast of the UK, in the Baltic and in the Mediterranean. MCDOs and CDOs have even deployed to Iraq and Afghanistan in a land-based counter-IED role and continue to undertake such tasks in the UK and worldwide today.

Photo Postscript-8

Two RN *Sandown*-class minehunters berthed alongside in Bahrain in 2017. Courtesy of Rob Hoole

Since 2006, the RN has stationed four minehunters and a support ship at Bahrain in the Arabian Gulf, an area of UK MCM operations harking back as far as 1963, with crews rotating every six or seven months. Based at the re-commissioned HMS Jufair (a base at the Mina

Salman Port) they are part of a multinational force whose command is shared between the Royal Navy and U.S. Navy.

DISESTABLISHMENT OF HMS VERNON

Training in Diving, Demolitions and Mine Warfare, along with Naval Control of Shipping and, for a time, Seamanship, continued on the site of HMS Vernon at Portsmouth even after it ceased to be an independent command on 31 March 1986 and was renamed HMS Nelson (Vernon Site). In 1987, the establishment was renamed HMS Nelson (Gunwharf) and briefly became Headquarters for the Commandant General Royal Marines before his move to more permanent accommodation at HMS Excellent on Whale Island.

In November 1995, Mine Warfare training was shifted to the School of Maritime Operations (SMOPS), HMS Dryad at nearby Southwick and subsequently to the Mine Warfare Operational Training Centre at the Maritime Warfare School in HMS Collingwood across the harbour from Portsmouth. Diving training, together with the Superintendent of Diving, the Fleet Diving Headquarters, the Fleet Clearance Diving Team and the Portsmouth Area Clearance Diving Team moved into new accommodation on Horsea Island in Portsmouth Harbour and the old Vernon establishment closed its gates for the last time on 1 April 1996.

The Ministry of Defence sold the site of HMS Vernon to a commercial property company to be redeveloped and rebranded as Gunwharf Quays, which then reopened in 2001 (see details at www.gunwharf-quays.com). Scattered in between the new luxury residential and retail property developments are some original, Royal Navy-era relics that remind one of the nautical history associated with this once famous establishment: some late-Victorian buildings; a few torpedo exhibits; a couple of famous figureheads from long-gone wooden-hulled warships; even the venerable red GPO telephone box has survived somehow. There are two mines: a refurbished British "M" Mk 1 moored magnetic mine found under rubble during some building works and a British Mk 17 moored contact mine.

EFFORTS TO ERECT A MONUMENT TO VERNON

There is no monument testifying to the tens of thousands of service personnel who passed through the gates of HMS Vernon, including the mine warfare and diving specialists, mine designers, minefield planners, bomb & mine disposal personnel and the crews of the minelayers, minesweepers and minehunters who were trained or based there. It was therefore decided to undertake a campaign called Project Vernon to erect a monument celebrating the heritage of HMS Vernon and as a suitable tribute to the people who have undertaken Mine Warfare and Diving in the past and will continue to do so for years to come.

Photo Postscript-9

Artist's impression of the planned Vernon Monument in situ at Gunwharf Quays in Portsmouth.
Courtesy of Rob Hoole

The planned 14-ton near-twice life-sized statue was designed by renowned Australian sculptor Les Johnson FRBS and was chosen by an all-ranks committee of serving and ex-serving Mine Warfare and Diving specialists after an open and transparent competitive tendering process. It comprises a diver wearing first generation Clearance Diver Breathing Apparatus, securing a plastic explosive demolition pack to a British Mk 17 moored contact mine that has been swept and is fouled on the timbers of a wreck. It incorporates a severed mechanical sweep wire fitted with an explosive cutter to indicate the mine has been swept.

To date (October 2017), Project Vernon's committee of volunteers has raised £260k of the £325k required to start work. The help of readers is requested in helping to reach the target and donations may be made via the Project's website (www.vernon-monument.org). Please assist in marking HMS Vernon's remarkable heritage and its legacy to today's proponents of mine warfare and diving.

ROYAL NAVY HUMOUR

For readers that made it through these last several pages of, for some, too much technical reference to mine warfare, the authors would like to leave you with some British humour of how the lower ranks sometimes view awards received by their seniors:

- MBE (Member) – My Bloody Efforts
- OBE (Officer) – Other Buggers' Efforts
- CBE (Commander) – Covers Bloody Everything
- Order of St Michael & St George which has three classes:
  CMG (Companion) – Call Me God
  KCMG (Knight Commander) or DCMG (Dame Commander) – Kindly Call Me God
  GCMG (Knight Grand Cross or Dame Grand Cross) – God Calls Me God

Appendix A: RN Mine Warfare Ships Awarded Battle Honours

BELGIAN COAST 1914-18

Albyn	paddle minesweeper
Brighton Queen	paddle minesweeper
Cambridge	paddle minesweeper
Devonia	paddle minesweeper
Duchess of Montrose	paddle minesweeper
Glen Avon	paddle minesweeper
Jupiter II	paddle minesweeper
Kempton	paddle minesweeper
Lady Ismay	paddle minesweeper
Marmion II	paddle minesweeper
Ravenswood	paddle minesweeper
Westward Ho	paddle minesweeper

BELGIAN COAST 1915

Brighton Queen	paddle minesweeper (sunk 6 Oct 1915)
Cambridge	paddle minesweeper
Devonia	paddle minesweeper
Duchess of Montrose	paddle minesweeper (sunk by a mine 18 March 1917)
Glen Avon	paddle minesweeper
Lady Ismay	paddle minesweeper
Marmion II	paddle minesweeper
Peary	paddle minesweeper
Ravenswood	paddle minesweeper
Westward Ho	paddle minesweeper

BELGIAN COAST 1915/16

Albyn	paddle minesweeper
Jupiter II	paddle minesweeper

BELGIAN COAST 1917

Kempton	paddle minesweeper

DARDANELLES 1915/16

Anemone	fleet sweeping sloop
Aster	fleet sweeping sloop
Gazelle	screw minesweeper
Heliotrope	fleet sweeping sloop
Honeysuckle	fleet sweeping sloop
Hussar	Minesweeper
Jonquil	fleet sweeping sloop
Peony	fleet sweeping sloop

JUTLAND, 31 May 1916

Abdiel	destroyer minelayer

ZEEBRUGGE, 23 April 1918

Intrepid	minelayer/blockship
Iphigenia	minelayer/blockship
Thetis	minelayer/blockship
Lingfield	paddle minesweeper

ZEEBRUGGE (OSTEND), 23 Apr 1918

Brilliant	minelayer/blockship
Sirius	minelayer/blockship

OSTEND, 10 May 1918

Vindictive	minelayer/blockship

Appendix B: Battle of Jutland Order of Battle

Royal Navy	Number of Ships	German Navy	Number of Ships
Dreadnoughts: *Agincourt, Ajax, Barham, Bellerophon, Benbow, Canada, Centurion, Collingwood, Colossus, Conqueror, Erin, Hercules, Iron Duke, King George V, Malaya, Marlborough, Monarch, Neptune, Orion, Revenge, Royal Oak, St Vincent, Superb, Temeraire, Thunder, Valiant, Vanguard, Warspite*	28	**Dreadnoughts and Pre-Dreadnought Battleships:** *Deutschland, Friedrich der Grosse, Grosser Kurfürst, Hannover, Helgoland, Hessen, Kaiser, Kaiserin, König, Kronprinz, Markgraf, Nassau, Oldenburg, Ostfriesland, Pommern, Posen, Prinzregent Luitpold, Rheinland, Schlesien, Schleswig-Holstein, Thüringen, Westfalen*	22
Battle Cruisers: *Indefatigable, Indomitable, Inflexible, Invincible, Lion, New Zealand, Princess Royal, Queen Mary, Tiger*	9	**Battle Cruisers:** *Derfflinger, Lützow, Moltke, Seydlitz, Von der Tann*	5
Armoured Cruisers: *Black Prince, Cochrane, Defence, Duke of Edinburgh, Hampshire, Minotaur, Shannon, Warrior*	8		
Light Cruisers: *Active, Bellona, Birkenhead, Birmingham, Blanche, Boadicea, Canterbury, Calliope, Caroline, Castor, Champion, Chester, Comus, Constance, Cordelia, Dublin, Falmouth, Fearless, Galatea, Gloucester, Inconstant, Nottingham, Phaeton, Royalist, Southampton, Yarmouth*	26	**Light Cruisers:** *Elbing, Frankfurt, Frauenlob, Hamburg, München, Pillau, Regensburg, Rostock, Stettin, Stuttgart, Wiesbaden*	11
Destroyers: *Acasta, Achates, Ambuscade, Acheron, Ardent, Ariel, Attack, Badger, Broke, Christopher, Contest, Defender, Faulknor, Fortune, Garland, Goshawk, Hardy, Hydra, Kempenfelt, Landrail, Lapwing, Laurel, Liberty, Lizard, Lydiard, Maenad, Marksman, Magic, Mandate, Manners, Marne, Martial, Marvel, Mary Rose, Menace, Michael, Midge, Milbrook, Mindful, Minion, Mischief, Mons, Moon, Moorsom, Moresby,*	77	**Torpedo Boats:** *B97, B98, B109, B110, B111, B112, G7, G8, G9, G10, G11, G37, G38, G39, G40, G41, G42, G86, G87, G88, G101, G102, G103, G104, S15, S16, S17, S18, S19, S20, S23, S32, S33, S34, S35, S36, S50, S51, S52, S53, S54, V1, V2, V3, V4, V5, V6, V26, V27, V28, V29, V30, V44, V45, V46, V48, V69, V71, V73, V186, V189*	61

Morning Star, Morris, Mounsey,
Munster, Mystic, Narborough,
Narwhal, Nerissa, Nessus, Nestor,
Nicator, Noble, Nomad, Nonsuch,
Obdurate, Obedient, Onslaught,
Onslow, Opal, Ophelia, Ossory, Owl,
Pelican, Petard, Porpoise, Shark,
Sparrowhawk, Spitfire, Termagant,
Tipperary, Turbulent, Unity

Destroyer-minelayer: *Abdiel*	1	
Destroyer tender: *Oak*	1	
Seaplane tender: *Engadine*	1	
Total Ships	151	99

Appendix C: Vessels sunk or damaged by U-boats in the western Atlantic in 1918

Nationality:
A (American), B (Belgian), Bn (Brazilian), Br (British), C (Canadian),
Cu (Cuba), D (Danish), F (French), I (Italian), J (Japanese), N (Norwegian),
P (Portuguese), S (Swedish)

Means of destruction:
G (gun), S (scuttled with depth charges), T (torpedoed)

Salved (salvaged after being sunk)

Vessels Destroyed by Gunfire or Depth Charges (81)

Name/Nationality	Gunfire or Bomb/Date	Name/Nationality	Gunfire or Bomb/Date
Hattie Dunn (A)	S/25 May 18	Sydland (S)	G/8 Aug 18
Hauppauge (A) salved	S/25 May 18	Katie L. Palmer (A)	S/10 Aug 18
Edna (A)	S/25 May 18	Reliance (A)	S
Isabel B. Wiley (A)	S/2 Jun 18	William H. Starbuck (A)	S/10 Aug 18
Jacob M. Haskell (A)	S/2 Jun 18	Progress (A)	S/10 Aug 18
Edward H. Cole (A)	S/2 Jun 18	Aleda May (A)	S
Texel (A)	S/2 Jun 18	Mary E. Sennett (A)	S/10 Aug 18
Winneconne (A)	SG/2 Jun 18	Earl and Nettie (A)	S
Carolina (A)	G/2 Jun 18	Cruiser (A)	S/10 Aug 18
Samuel C. Mengel (A)	S/3 Jun 18	Old Time (A)	S/10 Aug 18
Eidsvold (N)	G/4 Jun 18	Dorothy B. Barrett (A)	G/14 Aug 18
Edward R. Baird Jr. (A)	S/4 Jun 18	Madrugada (Bn)	Burned/15 Aug 18
Vinland (N)	S/5 Jun 18	San Jose (N)	S/17 Aug 18
Pinar Del Rio (A)	G/8 Jun 18	Nordhav (N)	S/17 Aug 18
Vindeggen (N)	S/10 Jun 18	Triumph (C) Captured	C/20 Aug 18
Henrik Lund (N)	S/10 Jun 18	Lucille M. Schnare (C)	S/20 Aug 18
Samoa (N)	G/14 Jun 18	Francis J. O'Hara Jr. (A)	S
Kringsjaa (N)	G/14 Jun 18	A. Piatt Andrew (A)	S
Chilier (B)	G/22 Jun 18	Uda A. Saunders (C)	S/20 Aug 18
Augvald (N)	G/23 Jun 18	Pasadena (C)	S/21 Aug 18
Marosa (N)	S/7 Jul 18	Sylvania (A)	S/21 Aug 18
Manx King (N)	S/8 Jul 18	Diomed (Br)	G
Perth Amboy (A)	G/21 Jul 18	Notre Dame de Lagarde (F)	S/22 Aug 18
Lansford (A)	S/21 Jul 18	Bianca (C) salved	S/24 Aug 18
Barge No. 403 (A)	G/22 Jul 18	E. B. Walters (C)	S/25 Aug 18

Barge No. *740* (A)	G/22 Jul 18	*C. M. Walters* (C)	S/25 Aug 18
Barge No. *760* (A)	G/22 Jul 18	*Clayton W. Walters* (C)	S/25 Aug 18
Robert and Richard (A)	G/22 Jul 18	*Marion Adams* (C)	S/25 Aug 18
Porto (P)	S/27 Jul 18	*Verna D. Adams* (C)	S/25 Aug 18
Dornfontein (C)	Burned/ 2 Aug 18	*J. J. Flaherty* (A)	S
Muriel (A)	S/3 Aug 18	*Eric* (Br)	S/25 Aug 18
Rob Roy (A)	S/3 Aug 18	*Gloaming* (C)	S/26 Aug 18
Sydney B. Atwood (A)	S/3 Aug 18	*Rush* (A)	S/26 Aug 18
Annie Perry (A)	S/3 Aug 18	*Potentate* (C)	S/30 Aug 18
Nelson A. (A)	G/4 Aug 18	*Elsie Porter* (C)	S/30 Aug 18
O. B. Jennings (A)	G/4 Aug 18	*Gamo* (P)	S/31 Aug 18
Agnes G. Holland (C)	S/5 Aug 18	*Constanza* (D)	S/11 Sep 18
Gladys M. Hollett (C)	S/5 Aug 18	*Kingfisher* (A)	S/20 Sep 18
Stanley M. Seaman (A)	S/5 Aug 18	*Industrial* (Br)	S/4 Oct 18
Merak (A)	S/6 Aug 18	*Stifinder* (N)	S/13 Oct 18
Diamond Shoal LS (A)	S/6 Aug 18		

Vessels Destroyed by Torpodoes (15)

Harparthian (Br)	5 Jun 18	*Mirlo* (Br)	16 Aug 18
Dwinsk (Br)	18 Jun 18	*Bergsdalen* (N)	27 Aug 18
Tortuguero (Br)	26 Jun 18	*Shortind* (N)	2 Sep 18
Tokuyama Maru (J)	1 Aug 18	*Leixoes* (P)	12 Sep 18
Luz Blanca (Br)	5 Aug 18	USS *Ticonderoga*	30 Sep 18
Penistone (Br)	11 Aug 18	*Alberto Treves* (I)	3 Oct 18
Sommerstadt (N)	12 Aug 18	*Lucia* (A)	17 Oct 18
Frederick R. Kellogg (A) Salved	13 Aug 18		

Vessels Damaged or Destroyed by Mines (6)

Herbert L. Pratt (A) salved	3 Jun 18	*San Saba* (A)	4 Oct 18
USS *San Diego* salved	19 Jul 19	*Chaparra* (Cu)	27 Oct 18
USS *Minnesota* salved	29 Sep 18	USS *Saetia*	9 Nov 18

Bibliography

PUBLISHED WORKS

Andrew, Christopher, Simona Tobia. *Interrogation in War and Conflict.* New York: Routledge, 2014.

Belknap, Reginald R. *The Yankee Mining Squadron or Laying the North Sea Mine Barrage.* Annapolis, Md: Naval Institute, 1920.

British Admiralty. *Handbook of Minesweeping 1917.* Admiralty, Gunnery Branch, G. 6999/17, May 1917

British Admiralty. *Naval Staff Monographs (Fleet Issue)* No. 1-13. Published between November 1920 and February 1921.

Campbell, John. *Jutland: An Analysis of the Fighting.* London: Conway Maritime Press, 1998.

Carpenter, A. F. B. *The Blockading of Zeebrugge.* London: Herbert Jenkins, 1921.

Chatterton, E. Keble. *Fighting the U-boats.* London: Hurst & Blackett Ltd, 1943.

Churchill, Winston S. *The World Crisis, 1915.* London: Thornton Butterworth, 1923.

Corbett, Julian S. *History of the Great War, Naval Operations Vol. I, To the Battle of the Falklands December 1914.* London: Longmans Green & Co, 1920.

—*History of the Great War Naval Operations Vol. II.* London: Longmans, Green, 1921.

Cowie, J. S. *Mines, Minelayers and Minelaying.* London: Oxford University Press, 1949.

Dorling, Taprell. *Swept Channels Being an Account of the Work of the Minesweepers in the Great War.* London: Hodder & Stoughton, 1935.

Duncan, Robert C. *America's Use of Sea Mines.* Washington, DC: U.S. Government Printing Office, 1962.

Friedman, Norman. *British Destroyers: From Earliest Days to the First World War.* Barnsley, UK: Seaforth Publishing, 2009.

Gardiner, Robert, Randal Gray, eds. *Conway's All the World's Fighting Ships 1906–1921.* London: Conway Maritime Press, 1985.

Gibson, R. H., Maurice Prendergast. *The German Submarine War 1914–1918.* Cornwall, UK: Periscope Publishing Ltd, 2002.

Gimblett, Richard H. *The Naval Service of Canada, 1910-2010: The Centennial Story.* Tonawanda, New York: Dundurn Press, 2009.

Goerlitz, Walter. *History of the German General Staff.* New York & Washington: Frederick A. Praeger, 1965.

Grant, Robert M. *U-Boats Destroyed The Effect of Anti-Submarine Warfare 1914-1918*. Cornwall, UK: Periscope Publishing, 2002.

Gröner, Erich. *Die deutschen Kriegsschiffe, 1815-1945, Vol. 1*. München: J. F. Lehmanns Verlag, 1966.

Gröner, Erich, Dieter Jung, Martin Maass. *German Warships 1815-1945 Vol. II: U-Boats and Mine Warfare Vessels*. London: Conway Maritime Press, 1991.

Hadley, Michael L., Roger Sarty. *Tin-pots and Pirate Ships: Canadian Naval Forces and German Sea Raiders 1880-1918*. London: McGill-Queen's University Press, 1991.

Hendrick, Burton J. and William Sowden Sims. *Victory at Sea*. London: John Murray, 1920.

Henry, Chris. *Depth Charge: Royal Naval Mines, Depth Charges & Underwater Weapons 1914-1945*. Barnsley, UK: Pen & Sword, 2005.

Herzog, Bodo. *Deutsche U-Boote, 1906-1966*. Herrsching: Pawlak, 1990.

Hurd, Archibald. *The Merchant Navy, Vol. I*. London: John Murray, 1921.

Langsdorff, Werner von. *U-boote am Frind: 45 deutsche U-Boat-Fahrer enzählen*. Barsinghausen: Unikum Verlag, 2013.

Lott, Arnold S. *Most Dangerous Sea: A History of Mine Warfare and an Account of U.S. Navy Mine Warfare Operations in World War II and Korea*. Annapolis, Md: Naval Institute, 1959.

Low, A. M. *Mine and Countermine*. London: Hutchison & Co. Ltd., 1944.

Massie, Robert K. *Castles of Steel, Britain, Germany, and the Winning of the Great War at Sea*. New York; Random House, 2003.

Messimer, Dwight. *Find and Destroy: Antisubmarine Warfare in World War I*. Annapolis, Md: Naval Institute, 2001.

—*Verschollen World War I U-Boat Losses*. Annapolis, Md: Naval Institute, 2002.

Muhlhauser, G. H. P. *Small Craft*. London: John Lane, 1920.

Poland, Nicho. *The Torpedoman – HMS Vernon's Story 1872-1986*. Great Britain: E. N. Poland, 1993.

Pollen, Arthur Hungerford. *The Navy in Battle (1918)*. Garden City, New York: Doubleday, 1918.

Potter, Elmer Belmont. *Sea Power: A Naval History*. Annapolis, Md: Naval Institute, 1981.

Smith, Peter C. *Into the Minefields: British Destroyer Minelaying 1916–1960*. Barnsley, UK: Pen & Sword Maritime, 2005.

Spindler, Arno. *Der Handelskrieg mit U-Booten, 1914-1918*. Berlin: E.S. Mittler & Sohn, 1934.

—*Der Handelskrieg mit U-Booten, 1914-1918, vol. 5.* Frankfurt am Mein: Verlag E. S. Lehmann, 1966.

Spragg, Iain. *London's Strangest Tales: The Thames: Extraordinary but True Stories.* London: Pavilion 2014.

Stringer, Harry R. *The Navy Book of Distinguished Service.* Washington, DC: Fassett Publishing Co., 1921.

Tucker, Gilbert Norman. *The Naval Service of Canada, Vol. I, Origins and Early Years.* Ottawa, Canada: King's Printer, 1962.

Tucker, Spencer C. *World War I Encyclopedia.* Santa Barbara, Ca: ABC-CLIO Inc., 2005.

U.S. Government Printing Office. *Antisubmarine Information O. N. I. Compilation No. 14 – 1918.* Washington, DC: Government Printing Office, 1918.

U.S. Government Printing Office. *German Submarine Activities on the Atlantic Coast of the United States and Canada.* Washington, DC: Government Printing Office, 1920.

U.S. Government Printing Office. *Mine Sweeping Manual United States Navy 1917.* Washington, DC: Government Printing Office, 1917.

U.S. Government Printing Office. *Northern Barrage and Other Mining Activities.* Washington, DC: Government Printing Office, 1920.

U.S. Government Printing Office. *The Northern Barrage (Taking Up the Mines).* Washington, DC: Government Printing Office, 1920.

PREFACE NOTES

[1] "The War Afloat, Kingston Upon Hull War Memorial 1914-1918" (http://www.ww1hull.org.uk/index.php/hull-in-ww1/the-war-afloat: accessed 2 July 2017).

[2] "Why did war break out in 1914?" (http://www.nationalarchives.gov.uk/education/greatwar/g2/backgroundcs1.htm: accessed 1 July 2017).

[3] Marek Pruszewicz, "The day the entire German fleet surrendered; Eric W. Osborne, Naval Warfare" (http://encyclopedia.1914-1918-online.net/article/naval_warfare: accessed 30 October 2016).

[4] ut supra.

[5] ut supra.

[6] Hendrick and Sims, *Victory at Sea*, 244-265. Heather Ramsey, "A Young British Officer's Account of the Awful Events at Scapa Flow" (http://knowledgenuts.com/2015/09/11/a-young-british-officers-account-of-the-awful-events-at-scapa-flow/: accessed 30 October 2016).

[7] Gibson and Prendergast, *The German Submarine War 1914–1918*, 2.

[8] "SS *Glitra* [+1914]" (http://www.wrecksite.eu/wreck.aspx?17922: accessed 2 July 2017).

[9] Tucker, *World War I Encyclopedia*, 836–837.

[10] Potter, *Sea Power: A Naval History*, 223.

[11] Jesse Greenspan, "Remembering the Sinking of RMS *Lusitania*" (http://www.history.com/news/the-sinking-of-rms-lusitania-100-years-ago; "WWI U-boats *U-20*" (http://uboat.net/wwi/boats/index.html?boat=20: both accessed 3 July 2017)

[12] "WWI U-boat Types" (http://uboat.net/wwi/types/: accessed 30 June 2017).

[13] Herzog, *Deutsche U-Boote, 1906-1966*, 62-65, 74-76; Gröner, *Die deutschen Kriegsschiffe, 1815-1945*, 369-76.

[14] Hendrick and Sims, *Victory at Sea*, 244-265.

[15] Ibid.

[16] "British Islands: Approximate Positions of Minefields. 19th August 1918." Hydrographic Department of the Admiralty, under superintendence of Rear-Admiral J. F. Parry, C.B. Hydrographer, August 6th, 1917. William Rea Furlong map collection, Geography and Map Division, Library of Congress.

[17] Nigel Wilson, "The First + Last Commonwealth Casualties" (http://www.gwpda.org/naval/flccaslt.htm: accessed 3 July 2017).

[18] "Germany Mines" (http://www.navweaps.com/Weapons/WAMGER_Mines.php); "Truth behind the sinking of HMS *Hampshire* revealed" (http://www.scotsman.com/news/truth-behind-the-sinking-of-hms-hampshire-revealed-1-4146171); "Curt Beitzen" (http://uboat.net/wwi/men/commanders/20.html: all accessed 3 July 2017).

[19] "SMS *Mowe* – German Raider" (http://navymuseum.co.nz/worldwar1/ships/hilfskreuzer-mowe/); "Marauders of the Sea, German Armed Merchant Raiders During World War I Moewe" (http://ahoy.tk-jk.net/MaraudersWW1/Moewe.html: both accessed 3 July 2017).

[20] ut supra.

[21] ut supra.

[22] Tucker, *World War I Encyclopedia*, 801-802.

[23] Dorling, *Swept Channels*, Appendix 3.

[24] Hendrick and Sims, *Victory at Sea*, 244-265.

[25] Grant, *U-Boats Destroyed The Effect of Anti-Submarine Warfare 1914-1918*, 43-44.

[26] Grant, *U-Boats Destroyed The Effect of Anti-Submarine Warfare*, 43-44; Hendrick and Sims, *Victory at Sea*, 244-265.

[27] Messimer, *Find and Destroy: Antisubmarine Warfare in World War I*, 187.

[28] Ibid, 186-188.

[29] U.S. Government Printing Office, *The Northern Barrage (Taking up the Mines)*, 7-8.

[30] Ibid, 62-63.

[31] "A Guide to British Awards for Gallantry or Meritorious Service in WW1" (http://www.greatwar.co.uk/medals/ww1-gallantry-awards.htm: accessed 1 August 2017).

CHAPTER 1 NOTES

[1] Stringer, *The Navy Book of Distinguished Service*, 20.

[2] U.S. GPO, *The Northern Barrage (Taking up the Mines)*, 42.

[3] Ibid, 11.

[4] Ibid, 40-43.

[5] Ibid, 40-41.

[6] Ibid, 7.

[7] U.S. GPO, *The Northern Barrage*, 7-8; "The Dover Barrage" (http://www.firstworldwar.com/atoz/doverbarrage.htm: accessed 28 June 2017.

[8] U.S. GPO, *The Northern Barrage*, 7-8.

[9] Ibid, 9.

[10] Ibid, 10-11, 18.

[11] Ibid, 23, 43.

[12] Ibid, 26.

[13] Ibid, 32, 35.

[14] *Richard Bulkeley, Directory of American Naval Fighting Ships* (DANFS).

[15] Ibid.

[16] U.S. GPO, *The Northern Barrage*, 15.

[17] U.S. GPO, *Mine Sweeping Manual United States Navy 1917*.

[18] U.S. GPO, *The Northern Barrage*, 42.

[19] *George Clarke, DANFS*.

[20] Stringer, *The Navy Book of Distinguished Service*, 28; "Casualties: US Navy and Marine Corps Personnel Killed and Injured in Selected Accidents and Other Incidents Not Directly the Result of Enemy Action" (https://www.history.navy.mil/research/library/online-reading-room/title-list-alphabetically/c/casualties-usnavy-marinecorps-personnel-killed-injured-selected-accidents-other-incidents-notdirectly-result-enemy-action.html: accessed 25 June 2017).

[21] U.S. GPO, *The Northern Barrage*, 42.

[22] Stringer, *The Navy Book of Distinguished Service*, 20, 30.

[23] *George Clarke, Pat Caharty, DANFS*.

[24] U.S. GPO, *The Northern Barrage*, 43; *George Clarke, DANFS*.

[25] U.S. GPO, *The Northern Barrage*, 42-43.

CHAPTER 2 NOTES

[1] Dorling, *Swept Channels*, 135, 285.

[2] Ibid, 8, 310, 336.

[3] Ibid, 17-18.

[4] Ibid, 18, 335.

[5] Ibid, 16.

[6] Ibid, 8.

[7] Dorling, *Swept Channels*, 29-30; Cowie, *Mines, Minelayers and Minelaying*, 37.

[8] U.S. GPO, *Antisubmarine Information O. N. I. Compilation No. 14 – 1918*; Cowie, *Mines, Minelayers and Minelaying*, 37-38.

[9] Cowie, *Mines, Minelayers and Minelaying*, 26-27.

[10] Dorling, *Swept Channels*, 30-31.
[11] Cowie, *Mines, Minelayers and Minelaying*, 203-204.
[12] Dorling, *Swept Channels*, 31, 47, 119.
[13] Ibid, 31-33.
[14] Ibid, 32.
[15] Ibid.
[16] Ibid, 110.
[17] Rob Hoole, "To Sweep No More"
(http://www.mcdoa.org.uk/To_Sweep_No_More.htm: accessed 3 September 2017).
[18] Dorling, *Swept Channels*, 80; *Handbook of Minesweeping 1917*, British Admiralty, Gunnery Branch, G. 6999/17, May 1917, 4.
[19] Dorling, *Swept Channels*, 79.
[20] Ibid, 316-317
[21] Ibid, 275-276.
[22] Ibid, 80.
[23] Ibid, 270-271.
[24] Ibid, 117-119.
[25] Ibid, 118-119.
[26] Dorling, *Swept Channels*, 117-119; British Admiralty, *Handbook of Minesweeping 1917*, 14.
[27] Dorling, *Swept Channels*, 117-118.
[28] Ibid, 118.

CHAPTER 3 NOTES

[1] Corbett, *History of the Great War, Naval Operations Vol. I, To the Battle of the Falklands December 1914*, 3, 5.
[2] Corbett, *History of the Great War, Naval Operations Vol. I*, 1.
[3] Corbett, *History of the Great War, Naval Operations Vol. I*, 3-4; Email from Rob Hoole to David Bruhn, 3 August 2017.
[4] Corbett, *History of the Great War, Naval Operations Vol. I*, 6.
[5] Ibid, 15-16.
[6] Ibid, 16.
[7] Ibid.
[8] Ibid, 16.
[9] Ibid, 22.
[10] Ibid, 11, 13, 22.
[11] Ibid, 22.
[12] Ibid, 25-26.
[13] Ibid, 26.
[14] Churchill, *The World Crisis, 1915*, 22-23.
[15] "Minesweeping and Minelaying"
(http://www.theodora.com/encyclopedia/m2/minesweeping_and_minelaying.html: accessed 5 July 2017).
[16] "Pink List – 5th August 1914" (http://www.naval-history.net/WW1NavyBritishShips-Locations2PL1408.htm; "Ships of the

Royal Navy – location/Activity Data, 1914-1918" (http://www.naval-history.net/WW1NavyBritishShips-Locations6Dist.htm: both accessed 22 July 2017).

[17] "Minesweepers, Torpedo Gunboat Conversions" (http://www.naval-history.net/WW1NavyBritishShips-Dittmar3WarshipsB.htm#151: accessed 21 July 2017).

[18] Corbett, *History of the Great War, Naval Operations Vol. I*, 17; British Admiralty, *Naval Staff Monograph, Vol. 3*, 83.

[19] "Thomas Parry Bonham" (http://dreadnoughtproject.org/tfs/index.php/Thomas_Parry_Bonham: accessed 2 August 2017); British Admiralty, *Naval Staff Monograph, Vol. 3*, 83.

[20] British Admiralty, *Naval Staff Monograph, Vol. 3*, 83-84.

[21] Corbett, *History of the Great War, Naval Operations Vol. I*, 17; Dorling, *Swept Channels*, 79.

[22] "Minesweeping and Minelaying" (www.theodora.com).

[23] Hoole, History of HMS Vernon (Email from Rob Hoole to David Bruhn, 3 August 2017).

[24] Hoole, History of HMS Vernon.

[25] "Minesweeping and Minelaying" (www.theodora.com).

[26] Corbett, *History of the Great War, Naval Operations Vol. I*, 38.

[27] Ibid, 38.

[28] Ibid.

[29] Ibid, 38-39.

[30] Corbett, *History of the Great War, Naval Operations Vol. I*, 39; Hurd, *The Merchant Navy, Volume I*, 1914 to Spring 1915, Chapter VIII.

[31] "Otto Weddigen, Sinking of the *Aboukir, Cressy* and *Hogue* by the *U-9*, 22 September 1914" (http://www.firstworldwar.com/source/u9attacks.htm: accessed 6 July 2017).

[32] "Minesweeping and Minelaying" (www.theodora.com).

CHAPTER 4 NOTES

[1] Corbett, *History of the Great War, Naval Operations Vol. I*, 176.

[2] Chatham House The Royal Institute of International Affairs, "International Law Applicable to Naval Mines" (https://www.chathamhouse.org/sites/files/chathamhouse/field/field_document/20140226NavalMines.pdf: accessed 24 July 2017).

[3] Chatham House The Royal Institute of International Affairs, "International Law Applicable to Naval Mines;" Low, *Mine and Countermine*, 85-86.

[4] Corbett, *History of the Great War, Naval Operations Vol. I*, 159-160.

[5] "World War 1 at Sea Royal Navy Vessels Lost and Damaged, June to December 1914" (http://www.naval-history.net/WW1NavyBritishBVLSaRN1408.htm: accessed 24 July 2017).

[6] Ibid.

[7] "World War 1 at Sea Royal Navy Vessels Lost and Damaged, June to December 1914" (www.naval-history.net); Len Barnett, "'Trial & Error' - The

Royal Navy and Mine Countermeasures 1904-1914"
(http://www.barnettmaritime.co.uk/Trial.pdf: accessed 26 July 2017).
[8] "*Cricket* coastal destroyers (1906-1909)"
(http://www.navypedia.org/ships/uk/brit_dd_cricket.htm: accessed 26 July 2017).
[9] "World War 1 at Sea Royal Navy Vessels Lost and Damaged, June to December 1914" (www.naval-history.net).
[10] Ibid.
[11] "World War 1 at Sea Royal Navy Vessels Lost and Damaged, June to December 1914" (www.naval-history.net); Barnett, "'Trial & Error' - The Royal Navy and Mine Countermeasures 1904-1914" (www.barnettmaritime.co.uk).
[12] Barnett, "'Trial & Error' - The Royal Navy and Mine Countermeasures 1904-1914" (www.barnettmaritime.co.uk).
[13] Ibid.
[14] British Admiralty, *Naval Staff Monograph, Vol. 3*, 110; "Battle of Heligoland Bight" (http://www.history.com/this-day-in-history/battle-of-heligoland-bight: accessed 24 July 2017).
[15] British Admiralty, *Naval Staff Monograph, Vol. 3*, 134; "Battle of Heligoland Bight" (www.history.com).
[16] "Battle of Heligoland Bight" (www.history.com).
[17] British Admiralty, *Naval Staff Monograph, Vol. 3*, 83.
[18] "World War 1 at Sea Royal Navy Vessels Lost and Damaged, June to December 1914" (www.naval-history.net); Barnett, "'Trial & Error' - The Royal Navy and Mine Countermeasures 1904-1914" (www.barnettmaritime.co.uk).
[19] Hurd, *The Merchant Navy, Volume I*, 1914 to Spring 1915, Chapter VIII.
[20] "World War 1 at Sea Royal Navy Vessels Lost and Damaged, June to December 1914" (www.naval-history.net).
[21] Ibid.
[22] Ibid.
[23] Barnett, "'Trial & Error' - The Royal Navy and Mine Countermeasures 1904-1914" (www.barnettmaritime.co.uk).
[24] Ibid.
[25] *History of the Great War, Naval Operations Vol. I*, 161.
[26] Ibid.
[27] *History of the Great War, Naval Operations Vol. I*, 161; Hurd, *The Merchant Navy, Volume I*, 1914 to Spring 1915, Chapter VIII.
[28] ut supra.
[29] *History of the Great War, Naval Operations Vol. I*, 161.
[30] Ibid, 177-178.
[31] "The German Invasion of Belgium in the First World War August 1914" (https://www.mtholyoke.edu/~jedzi20h/classweb/Index.html: accessed 28 July 2017); Goerlitz, *History of the German General Staff*, 146.
[32] "The German Invasion of Belgium in the First World War August 1914" (www.mtholyoke.edu); Goerlitz, *History of the German General Staff*, 146.

[33] Email from Dwight Messimer to David Bruhn, 28 July 2017.

[34] *History of the Great War, Naval Operations Vol. I*, 181, 190; Dwight Messimer, 28 July 2017.

[35] *History of the Great War, Naval Operations Vol. I*, 182; "World War 1 at Sea Royal Navy Vessels Lost and Damaged, June to December 1914" (www.naval-history.net).

[36] *History of the Great War, Naval Operations Vol. I*, 182; Cowie, *Mines, Minelayers and Minelaying*, 46.

[37] *History of the Great War, Naval Operations Vol. I*, 182-183.

[38] Ibid, 190.

[39] "World War 1 at Sea Royal Navy Vessels Lost and Damaged, June to December 1914" (www.naval-history.net).

[40] Dwight Messimer, 28 July 2017.

CHAPTER 5 NOTES

[1] Corbett, *History of the Great War Naval Operations Vol. II*.

[2] Massie, *Castles of Steel, Britain, Germany, and the Winning of the Great War at Sea*, 140.

[3] Massie, *Castles of Steel*, 140-141; Email from Dwight Messimer to David Bruhn, 7 August 2017.

[4] Massie, *Castles of Steel*, 317.

[5] Dwight Messimer, 7 August 2017.

[6] Massie, *Castles of Steel*, 141, 513-514; Hurd, *The Merchant Navy, Volume I, 1914 to Spring 1915*, Chapter VIII.

[7] Massie, *Castles of Steel*, 141, 513-514.

[8] Ibid, 513-514.

[9] Muhlhauser, *Small Craft*, 24-25.

[10] Massie, *Castles of Steel*, 146.

[11] Corbett, *History of the Great War Naval Operations Vol. II*, 7, 17.

[12] Ibid, 17.

[13] British Admiralty, *Naval Staff Monograph, Vol. 13*, 118.

[14] Corbett, *History of the Great War Naval Operations Vol. II*, 7, 17-18.

[15] Ibid, 18.

[16] Ibid, 18-19.

[17] Ibid, 22-23.

[18] Corbett, *History of the Great War Naval Operations Vol. II*, 23-24; "Yorkshire Coast Raid 15-16 December 1914" (http://www.historyofwar.org/articles/raid_yorkshire_coast_1914.html: accessed 4 August 2017); "World War I: Raid on Scarborough, Hartlepool, and Whitby" (https://www.thoughtco.com/raid-on-scarborough-hartlepool-and-whitby-2361385: accessed 6 August 2017).

[19] Corbett, *History of the Great War Naval Operations Vol. II*, 23-24.

[20] Ibid, 24.

[21] "Yorkshire Coast Raid 15-16 December 1914" (www.historyofwar.org).

[22] Ibid.

[23] Corbett, *History of the Great War Naval Operations Vol. II*, 45-46; "Yorkshire Coast Raid 15-16 December 1914" (www.historyofwar.org); World War I: Raid on Scarborough, Hartlepool, and Whitby (www.thoughtco.com).

[24] Corbett, *History of the Great War Naval Operations Vol. II*, 46.

[25] British Admiralty, *Naval Staff Monograph, Vol. 3*, 82-83.

[26] Ibid, 83.

[27] Hurd, *The Merchant Navy, Volume I*, 1914 to Spring 1915, Chapter VIII.

[28] Ibid.

[29] Corbett, *History of the Great War Naval Operations Vol. II*, 47.

[30] "Minesweeping and Minelaying," *The Encyclopedia Britannica, Vol. XXXI* (London: The Encyclopedia Britannica, Inc., 1922), 949-955.

[31] Corbett, *History of the Great War Naval Operations Vol. II*, 47; "World War 1 - Casualty Lists of the Royal Navy and Dominion Navies" (http://www.naval-history.net/xDKCas1914-12Dec.htm); East Coast Minesweeping Operations, Naval Despatch dated 19 February 1915, Admiralty, 19th February 1915 (http://www.naval-history.net/WW1NavyBritishLGDispatchesNavy1914-16.htm#29076: both accessed 6 August 2917).

[32] Corbett, *History of the Great War Naval Operations Vol. II*, 47; "East Coast Minesweeping Operations, Naval Despatch dated 19 February 1915, Admiralty, 19th February 1915" (www.naval-history.net).

[33] "World War 1 at Sea, Royal Navy Despatches, Part 1 of 3 *London Gazette* editions 28861-29654 (August 1914-July 1916)" (http://www.naval-history.net/WW1NavyBritishLGDispatchesNavy1914-16.htm#29076: accessed 6 August 2017).

[34] "World War 1 at Sea - Naval Battles, British East Coast Raid – 16 December 1914 and Minesweeping Operations" (http://www.naval-history.net/WW1Battle-German_Raid_English_East_Coast_1914.htm: accessed 6 August 2017); Lot 1005 (https://www.dnw.co.uk/auction-archive/lot-archive/lot.php?department=Medals&lot_id=135186: accessed 6 August 2017).

[35] "World War 1 at Sea - Naval Battles, British East Coast Raid – 16 December 1914 and Minesweeping Operations" (www.naval-history.net).

[36] Ibid.

[37] Hurd, *The Merchant Navy, Vol. I*, 1914 to Spring 1915, Chapter VIII.

[38] Corbett, *History of the Great War Naval Operations Vol. II*, 47; Hurd, *The Merchant Navy, Volume I*, 1914 to Spring 1915, Chapter VIII.

[39] "Casualty Lists of the Royal Navy and Dominion Navies" (www.naval-history.net).

[40] Corbett, *History of the Great War Naval Operations Vol. II*, 47-48.

[41] Hurd, *The Merchant Navy, Vol. I*, 1914 to Spring 1915, Chapter VIII.

[42] Corbett, *History of the Great War Naval Operations Vol. II*, 47-48; British Admiralty, *Naval Staff Monograph, Vol. 13*, 10; Hurd, *The Merchant Navy, Vol. I*, 1914 to Spring 1915, Chapter IX.

[43] "Minesweeping and Minelaying," *The Encyclopedia Britannica, Vol. XXXI*, 949-955.

[44] Corbett, *History of the Great War Naval Operations Vol. II*, 47-48; British Admiralty, *Naval Staff Monograph, Vol. 13*, 10.

[45] Hurd, *The Merchant Navy, Vol. I*, 1914 to Spring 1915, Chapter IX.

[46] "World War 1 at Sea - Naval Battles, British East Coast Raid – 16 December 1914 and Minesweeping Operations" (www.naval-history.net).

[47] Ibid.

[48] Ibid.

CHAPTER 6 NOTES

[1] Massie, *Castles of Steel*, 414.

[2] Ibid.

[3] Ibid, 293.

[4] Ibid, 310.

[5] Ibid.

[6] Massie, *Castles of Steel*, 309; Pollen, *The Navy in Battle (1918)*, 250.

[7] Massie, *Castles of Steel*, 309.

[8] British Admiralty, *Naval Staff Monograph, Vol. 3*, 92; Massie, *Castles of Steel*, 311.

[9] British Admiralty, *Naval Staff Monograph, Vol. 3*, 92; "Casualty Lists of the Royal Navy and Dominion Navies" (www.naval-history.net).

[10] British Admiralty, *Naval Staff Monograph, Vol. 3*, 92; Massie, *Castles of Steel*, 311. The website naval-history.net indicates that the minelayer was *Kolberg*, versus *Stralsund* as cited in other accounts.

[11] Massie, *Castles of Steel*, 312-313.

[12] Ibid, 313.

[13] "World War 1 at Sea, British Fishing Vessels Lost to Enemy Action Part 1 of 2 - Years 1914, 1915, 1916 in date order" (http://www.naval-history.net/WW1LossesBrFV1914-16.htm: accessed 9 August 2017).

[14] "Ships of the Royal Navy, British Naval Vessels Lost, Damaged and Attacked by Name, 1914-15, some 1916-19" (http://www.naval-history.net/WW1NavyBritishShips-Locations10Attacked.htm: accessed 18 August 2017).

[15] Massie, *Castles of Steel*, 312.

[16] Ibid.

[17] Ibid, 378.

[18] Corbett, *History of the Great War Naval Operations Vol. II*, 84; Massie, *Castles of Steel*, 375.

[19] Massie, *Castles of Steel*, 375-377.

[20] Corbett, *History of the Great War Naval Operations Vol. II*, 84.

[21] Corbett, *History of the Great War Naval Operations Vol. II*, 84-85; Massie, *Castles of Steel*, 378-379.

[22] Corbett, *History of the Great War Naval Operations Vol. II*, 85; Massie, *Castles of Steel*, 378-379.

[23] Corbett, *History of the Great War Naval Operations Vol. II*, 87; Massie, *Castles of Steel*, 382-383.

[24] Massie, *Castles of Steel*, 383-384.

[25] Ibid, 384.

[26] Corbett, *History of the Great War Naval Operations Vol. II*, 89; Massie, *Castles of Steel*, 384.

[27] Corbett, *History of the Great War Naval Operations Vol. II*, 87-88; Massie, *Castles of Steel*, 385-386.

[28] Corbett, *History of the Great War Naval Operations Vol. II*, 89; Massie, *Castles of Steel*, 386.

[29] Corbett, *History of the Great War Naval Operations Vol. II*, 89; Massie, *Castles of Steel*, 387-389.

[30] Massie, *Castles of Steel*, 392, 397.

[31] Corbett, *History of the Great War Naval Operations Vol. II*, 95; Massie, *Castles of Steel*, 398-399.

[32] Massie, *Castles of Steel*, 400-401.

[33] Ibid, 405-406.

[34] Massie, *Castles of Steel*, 406-407.

[35] Ibid, 355, 413-416.

[36] Ibid, 355, 414-415.

[37] John Blatherwick, "List of British Awards to the Royal Canadian Navy in World War One" (http://blatherwick.net/documents/Royal%20Canadian%20Navy%20Citations/a%20-%20Canadians%20in%20the%20RCN%20%26%20RN%20-%20WW1.pdf: accessed 10 August 2017).

[38] Ibid.

[39] Ibid.

[40] Ibid.

CHAPTER 7 NOTES

[1] Tucker, *The Naval Service of Canada, Vol. I, Origins and Early Years*, 114, 119.

[2] Email from George Duddy to David Bruhn, 12 August 2017.

[3] Tucker, *The Naval Service of Canada, Vol. I*, 119; Canadian Naval Operations in World War I (1914-18) (https://hmcssackville.ca/history/battles-and-conicts/world-war-i-1914-1918/: accessed 28 July 2017).

[4] Tucker, *The Naval Service of Canada, Vol. I*, 137.

[5] Ibid, 137-138.

[6] Ibid, 151.

[7] Tucker, *The Naval Service of Canada, Vol. I*, 152; Canadian Naval Operations in World War I (1914-18) (hmcssackville.ca).

[8] Tucker, *The Naval Service of Canada, Vol. I*, 153.

[9] Ibid, 177.

[10] Gimblett, *The Naval Service of Canada, 1910-2010: The Centennial Story*, 17; Tucker, *The Naval Service of Canada, Vol. I*, 217.

[11] Canadian Naval Operations in World War I (1914-18) (hmcssackville.ca).

[12] Canadian Naval Operations in World War I (1914-18) (hmcssackville.ca); "McBride, Sir Richard, Directory of Canadian Biography" (http://www.biographi.ca/en/bio/mcbride_richard_14E.html); "A post

from Dreadnought" (http://www.ornaverum.org/family/waddell-robert-two-tubs.html: both accessed 29 July 2017).

[13] "A post from Dreadnought" (www.ornaverum.org).

[14] Ibid.

[15] Ibid.

[16] "A post from Dreadnought" (www.ornaverum.org); Frank Rockland, "Canada's first submarines - CC1 & CC2" (http://www.sambiasebooks.ca/fire-on-the-hill/canada-ww1/submarines-cc1-cc2.html: accessed 29 July 2017).

[17] Rockland, "Canada's first submarines - CC1 & CC2" (www.sambiasebooks.ca).

[18] Ibid.

[19] "A post from Dreadnought" (www.ornaverum.org); Rockland, "Canada's first submarines - CC1 & CC2" (www.sambiasebooks.ca).

[20] Tucker, *The Naval Service of Canada, Vol. I*, 222.

[21] Ibid.

[22] John M. MacFarlane, Fred R. MacFarlane: A Canadian's Experiences in the RNVR in the First World War (http://www.nauticapedia.ca/Articles/MacFarlane_Fred_RNVR.php: accessed 4 August 2017).

[23] Ibid.

[24] Tucker, *The Naval Service of Canada, Vol. I*, 257.

[25] Ibid, 255.

[26] Ibid, 223-224.

[27] Ibid, 256-257.

[28] Ibid, 262,

[29] Ibid, 261.

[30] Ibid, 262.

CHAPTER 8 NOTES

[1] British Admiralty, *Naval Staff Monograph Vol. 13*, 35.

[2] Ibid, vii.

[3] Ibid.

[4] Ibid, 31-32.

[5] Ibid, 35.

[6] Ibid.

[7] Ibid, 35-36.

[8] Ibid, 36-37; "H.M.S. *Paris* (1913)" (http://www.dreadnoughtproject.org/tfs/index.php/H.M.S._Paris_(1913): accessed 13 August 2017).

[9] British Admiralty, *Naval Staff Monograph Vol. 13*, 36.

[10] Ibid, 37.

[11] British Admiralty, *Naval Staff Monograph Vol. 6*, 13.

[12] Tucker, *World War I Encyclopedia, Vol. 3*, 1102.

[13] British Admiralty, *Naval Staff Monograph Vol 13*, 190-191, 204.

[14] "Battle of the Yser/IJzer, 1914"
(http://www.greatwar.co.uk/battles/yser/yser-battle.htm: accessed 22
August 2017).
[15] "Battle of the Yser/IJzer 1914" (www.greatwar.co.uk); British Admiralty,
Naval Staff Monograph Vol. 6, 9, 14.
[16] "Battle of the Yser/IJzer, 1914" (www.greatwar.co.uk).
[17] British Admiralty, *Naval Staff Monograph Vol. 6*, 12.
[18] Ibid, 18.
[19] British Admiralty, *Naval Staff Monograph Vol. 13*, 63.
[20] Ibid, 63.
[21] "The Royal Naval Air Service, War Letters of Harold Roshier (London:
Chatto & Windus, 1916)"
(https://archive.org/stream/inroyalnavalairs00roshiala/inroyalnavalairs00ros
hiala_djvu.txt: accessed 19 August 2017).
[22] "Royal Naval Air Service" (http://www.historylearningsite.co.uk/world-
war-one/aerial-warfare-and-world-war-one/royal-naval-air-service/: accessed
19 August 2017).
[23] "Royal Navy Medals – Honours & Gallantry Awards, *London
Gazette* editions 29030-29423 (January-December 1915)"
(http://www.naval-
history.net/WW1NavyBritishLGDecorations1915.htm: accessed 19
August 2017).
[24] British Admiralty, *Naval Staff Monograph Vol. 13*, 63-64; "Claude
Grahame-White" (http://www.gracesguide.co.uk/Claude_Grahame-White:
accessed 20 August 2017).
[25] Muhlhauser, *Small Craft*, Preface.
[26] Hurd, *The Merchant Navy, Vol. I*, 1914 to Spring 1915, Chapter IX.
[27] Hurd, *The Merchant Navy, Vol. I*, 1914 to Spring 1915, Chapter IX;
"British Merchant and Fishing Vessels Lost and Damaged"
(http://www.naval-history.net/WW1NavyBritishBVLSMN1504.htm:
accessed 20 August 2017).
[28] British Admiralty, *Naval Staff Monograph Vol. 8*, 190, 192.
[29] Hurd, *The Merchant Navy, Vol. I*, 1914 to Spring 1915, Chapter IX.
[30] Muhlhauser, *Small Craft*, 22. 34; British Admiralty, *Naval Staff Monograph
Vol. 6*, 22.
[31] Muhlhauser, *Small Craft*, 1, 22.
[32] Dorling, *Swept Channels*, 86.
[33] Ibid, 86-87.
[34] Muhlhauser, *Small Craft*, 22, 23.
[35] Hurd, *The Merchant Navy, Vol. I*, 1914 to Spring 1915, Chapter IX;
Muhlhauser, *Small Craft*, 34.
[36] Hurd, *The Merchant Navy, Vol. I*, 1914 to Spring 1915, Chapter IX.
[37] Hurd, *The Merchant Navy, Vol. I*, 1914 to Spring 1915, Chapter IX;
"Memorials & Monuments on the Isle of Wight, Biography William Hubert
Stuart Garnett" (http://www.isle-of-wight-
memorials.org.uk/people_g/garnett_whs.html; "Garnett, K. G., Lieut., M.C.

Croix de Guerre with Palm (France). 1917"
(http://www.newmp.org.uk/article.php?categoryid=99&articleid=1635&disp
layorder=31: both accessed 30 August 2017).

[38] Hurd, *The Merchant Navy, Vol. I*, 1914 to Spring 1915, Chapter IX;
Muhlhauser, *Small Craft*, 35.

[39] Hurd, *The Merchant Navy, Vol. I*, 1914 to Spring 1915, Chapter IX; "Ships
of the Royal Navy, 1914-1919, Auxiliary Patrol Vessels, Part 1, Yachts to
Trawlers" (http://www.naval-history.net/WW1NavyBritishShips-
Dittmar4AP.htm#11; Nicho Poland, *The Torpedoman – HMS Vernon's Story
1872-1986* (Great Britain: E.N. Poland, 1993),77-78.

[40] "Casualty Lists of the Royal Navy and Dominion Navies; List of Battle
Honours and Single Ship Actions" (http://www.naval-
history.net/WW1NavyBritish-Royal_Navy_Battle_Honours.htm: accessed 23
October 2017).

[41] British Admiralty, *Naval Staff Monograph Vol. 8*, 202.

[42] Ibid.

[43] Ibid, 202-203.

[44] Ibid, 203.

[45] Ibid.

[46] British Admiralty, *Naval Staff Monograph Vol. 8*, 203; "*U 39*"
(http://uboat.net/wwi/boats/index.html?boat=39: accessed 23 August
2017).

[47] Hurd, *The Merchant Navy, Vol. I*, 1914 to Spring 1915, Chapter IX.

[48] British Admiralty, *Naval Staff Monographs Vol. 8*, 204-205.

[49] Ibid, 205-206.

[50] Ibid, 206.

[51] Messimer, *Find and Destroy: Antisubmarine Warfare in World War I*, 26-27.

[52] Hurd, *The Merchant Navy, Vol. I*, 1914 to Spring 1915, Chapter IX.

[53] Ibid.

[54] Ibid.

[55] "Ships of the Royal Navy, 1914-1919, Warships Part 2, Old Sloops to
Assault Ships" (http://www.naval-history.net/WW1NavyBritishShips-
Dittmar3WarshipsB.htm#12: accessed 24 August 2017).

[56] "Sloop Class (UK)"
(http://www.dreadnoughtproject.org/tfs/index.php/Category:Sloop_Class_(
UK); "HMS *Primula*"(http://uboat.net/wwi/ships_hit/4915.html); "HMS
Lavender" (http://uboat.net/wwi/ships_hit/3524.html); "Wartime
Construction Sloops and Escorts" (http://www.naval-
history.net/WW1NavyBritishShips-Dittmar3WarshipsB.htm#12: all accessed
24 August 2017).

[57] "Ships of the Royal Navy, 1914-1919 Warships, Part 2, Old Sloops to
Assault Ships" (www.naval-history.net).

CHAPTER 9 NOTES

[1] "Another Tragic Loss ~ The *Princess Irene*, Wessex Branch Western Front Association" (http://www.wessexwfa.org.uk/articles/princess-irene.htm: accessed 7 July 2017).

[2] Cowie, *Mines, Minelayers and Minelaying*, 50.

[3] Ibid, 37.

[4] Ibid, 50-51.

[5] "Category:Minelayer (UK)" (http://www.dreadnoughtproject.org/tfs/index.php/Category:Minelayer_(UK): accessed 8 July 2017); "HMS *Orvieto*" (http://www.naval-history.net/OWShips-WW1-08-HMS_Orvieto.htm: accessed 7 July 2017); Peter Manchester, "RMS *Orvieto*" (http://petermanchester.me.uk/index.php?page=rmsorvieto: accessed 7 July 2017); Cowie, *Mines, Minelayers and Minelaying*, 51.

[6] "H.M.S. *Princess Margaret* (1914)" (http://www.dreadnoughtproject.org/tfs/index.php/H.M.S._Princess_Margaret_(1914): accessed 7 July 2017); "Minesweeping and Minelaying" (www.theodora.com); Another Tragic Loss ~ The *Princess Irene* (www.wessexwfa.org.uk).

[7] "P&O Heritage Ship Fact Sheet *Angora* (1911)" (http://www.poheritage.com/Upload/Mimsy/Media/factsheet/92738ANGORA-1911pdf.pdf: accessed 7 July 2017).

[8] Ibid.

[9] "Clyde Built Ships" (http://www.clydeships.co.uk/view.php?year_built=&builder=&a1Page=2&ref=15465&vessel=PARIS: accessed 7 July 2017).

[10] "Clyde Built Ships" (http://www.clydeships.co.uk/view.php?year_built=&builder=&ref=15504&vessel=BIARRITZ: accessed 7 July 2017).

[11] "History of the *Orvieto*" (http://petermanchester.me.uk/index.php?page=rmsorvieto1: accessed 9 July 2017).

[12] Ibid.

[13] Ibid.

[14] Ibid.

[15] Cowie, *Mines, Minelayers and Minelaying*, 47; Henry, *Depth Charge: Royal Naval Mines, Depth Charges & Underwater Weapons 1914-1945*, 87.

[16] Cowie, *Mines, Minelayers and Minelaying*, 51.

[17] Another Tragic Loss ~ The *Princess Irene* (www.wessexwfa.org.uk).

[18] Ibid.

[19] Ibid.

[20] Lewis Dyson, "HMS Princess Irene exploded off Port Victoria on the Isle of Grain killing workers from Chatham and Sheerness dockyards" (http://www.kentonline.co.uk/sheerness/news/explosion-on-board-hms-37420/: accessed 9 July 2017).

[21] Another Tragic Loss ~ The *Princess Irene* (www.wessexwfa.org.uk).

[22] Ibid.

CHAPTER 10 NOTES

[1] British Admiralty, *Naval Staff Monograph No. 30, Vol. 14, Home Waters*, 112.

[2] Dorling, *Swept Channels*, 105-106.

[3] Ibid, 106-107.

[4] Dorling, *Swept Channels*, 85, 105; "Royal Naval Volunteer Reserve Personnel" (http://www.nationalarchives.gov.uk/help-with-your-research/research-guides/royal-naval-volunteer-reserve-personnel/: accessed 25 August 2017).

[5] Dorling, *Swept Channels*, 16, 85.

[6] Ibid, 7.

[7] Dorling, *Swept Channels*, 108-109; British Admiralty, *Naval Staff Monograph No. 30*, 55.

[8] Ibid.

[9] "Ships of the Royal Navy, 1914-1919, Warships, Part 2, Old Sloops to Assault Ships" (http://www.naval-history.net/WW1NavyBritishShips-Dittmar3WarshipsB.htm#16: accessed 26 August 2017).

[10] British Admiralty, *Naval Staff Monograph No. 30*, 55-56.

[11] Dorling, *Swept Channels*, 107-108.

[12] Dorling, *Swept Channels*, 108-109; "Casualty Lists of the Royal Navy and Dominion Navies; British Naval Vessels Lost, Damaged and Attacked, August 1914 to September 1915" (http://www.naval-history.net/WW1NavyBritishShips-Locations10AttackedDate.htm: all accessed 27 August 2017).

[13] "Type *UC I, UC* coastal minelayers class" (http://uboat.net/wwi/types/?type=UC+I: accessed 27 August 2017).

[14] Dorling, *Swept Channels*, 109, British Admiralty, *Naval Staff Monograph No. 30*, 93, 100.

[15] British Admiralty, *Naval Staff Monograph No. 30*, 59-60.

[16] Ibid, 60-61, 71.

[17] Ibid, 110.

[18] "Type UC I UC coastal minelayers class" (http://uboat.net/wwi/types/?type=UC+I: accessed 24 August 2017).

[19] "Royal House Order of Hohenzollern" (http://uboat.net/wwi/men/decorations/5.html: accessed 24 August 2017).

[20] British Admiralty, *Naval Staff Monograph No. 30*, 62

[21] Ibid, 62-63, 101.

[22] Ibid, 101-102.

[23] Muhlhauser, *Small Craft*, 44

[24] British Admiralty, *Naval Staff Monograph No. 30*, 109-110; Muhlhauser, *Small Craft*, 44.

[25] British Admiralty, *Naval Staff Monograph No. 30*, 110; Muhlhauser, *Small Craft*, 46-47.

[26] British Admiralty, *Naval Staff Monograph No. 30*, 110; Muhlhauser, *Small Craft*, 47.

[27] British Admiralty, *Naval Staff Monograph No. 30*, 73.

[28] Ibid, 63-64.

[29] Ibid, 64.

[30] Ibid, 92-93.

[31] Ibid, 95.

[32] Ibid, 95.

[33] British Admiralty, *Naval Staff Monograph No. 30*, 95, 99.

[34] "UB I Type Coastal UBoats UB 1 through UB 17, 1915" (http://www.dreadnoughtproject.org/models/ships/SMS_UB_2/: accessed 29August 2017).

[35] "Karl Grob" (http://uboat.net/wwi/men/commanders/99.html: accessed 29 August 2017).

[36] "UB I Type Coastal UBoats UB 1 through UB 17, 1915" (http://www.dreadnoughtproject.org/models/ships/SMS_UB_2/: accessed 29August 2017).

[37] Ibid.

[38] Ibid.

[39] Ibid.

[40] Ibid.

[41] "UB I Type Coastal UBoats UB 1 through UB 17, 1915" (www.dreadnoughtproject.org); UB 12 (http://uboat.net/wwi/boats/index.html?boat=UB+12: accessed 29 August 2017).

CHAPTER 11 NOTES

[1] British Admiralty, *Naval Staff Monograph No. 30*, 118.

[2] "Count Dohna and His SeaGull Ships – Meteor Vienna" (http://smsmoewe.com/ships/smsms85.htm: accessed 5 September 2017).

[3] British Admiralty, *Naval Staff Monograph No. 30*, 118.

[4] British Admiralty, *Naval Staff Monograph No. 30*, 119; *"Glitra"* (http://uboat.net/wwi/ships_hit/2544.html: accessed 6 September 2017).

[5] British Admiralty, *Naval Staff Monograph No. 30*, 119.

[6] Ibid, 119-120.

[7] British Admiralty, *Naval Staff Monograph No. 30, 120*; "British Naval Vessels Lost, Damaged and Attacked by Name, 1914-15, some 1916-19" (http://www.naval-history.net/WW1NavyBritishShips-Locations10Attacked.htm: accessed 7 September 2017).

[8] Dorling, *Swept Channels*, 110.

[9] "Ships of the Royal Navy, 1914-1919, Warships, Part 2, Old Sloops to Assault Ships" (http://www.naval-history.net/WW1NavyBritishShips-Dittmar3WarshipsB.htm#19: accessed 7 September 2017).

[10] British Naval Vessels Lost, Damaged and Attacked by Name, 1914-15, some 1916-19; British Admiralty, *Naval Staff Monograph No. 30*, 125-126.

[11] British Admiralty, *Naval Staff Monograph No. 30*, 126.

[12] Ibid, 122.

[13] Ibid, 123.

[14] Ibid.
[15] Ibid, 124.
[16] Ibid, 125.
[17] Ibid, 130.
[18] British Admiralty, *Naval Staff Monograph No. 30, 131-132*; "Casualty Lists of the Royal Navy and Dominion Navies" (www.naval-history.net); Dorling, *Swept Channels*, 110.
[19] British Admiralty, *Naval Staff Monograph No. 30*, 132; Dorling, *Swept Channels*, 110.
[20] British Admiralty, *Naval Staff Monograph No. 30*, 145.
[21] Ibid, 146.
[22] Ibid, 146-147.
[23] Ibid, 147-148.
[24] Ibid, 148.
[25] Ibid, 148-149.
[26] Ibid, 149.
[27] Ibid, 149-151.
[28] Ibid, 145, 150-151.
[29] Ibid, 152.
[30] Ibid.
[31] Ibid, 152-153.
[32] Ibid, 153-154.
[33] Ibid, 165-166.
[34] Ibid, 166.
[35] Ibid, 166-167.
[36] Ibid, 169.
[37] Ibid.
[38] Ibid.
[39] Ibid, 169-170.
[40] Ibid, 170.
[41] Ibid.
[42] Ibid, 170-171.
[43] Ibid, 171.

CHAPTER 12 NOTES

[1] British Admiralty, *Naval Staff Monograph No. 31*, 23.
[2] Ibid, 2.
[3] Ibid, 3.
[4] Ibid, 8.
[5] Ibid.
[6] Ibid, 13.
[7] Ibid, 13-14.
[8] "H.M.S. *Angora* (1910)" (http://www.dreadnoughtproject.org/tfs/index.php/H.M.S._Angora_(1910): accessed 23 September 2017).
[9] British Admiralty, *Naval Staff Monograph No. 31*, 14.

[10] Ibid, 13-15.
[11] Ibid, 15.
[12] Ibid, 17-18.
[13] British Admiralty, *Naval Staff Monograph No. 31*, 21; "*UC-6*" (http://uboat.net/wwi/boats/index.html?boat=UC+6); "*UC-7*" (http://www.uboat.net:8080/wwi/boats/index.html?boat=uc+7: both accessed 23 September 2017).
[14] British Admiralty, *Naval Staff Monograph No. 31*, 22; "*UC-9*" (http://uboat.net/wwi/boats/index.html?boat=UC+9: accessed 23 September 2017).
[15] British Admiralty, *Naval Staff Monograph No. 31*, 22; Dorling, *Swept Channels*, 275.
[16] British Admiralty, *Naval Staff Monograph No. 31*, 22.
[17] Ibid, 22-23.
[18] Ibid, 23-24.
[19] Ibid, 31, 23.
[20] British Admiralty, *Naval Staff Monograph No. 31*, 24; "*UC-8*" (http://uboat.net/wwi/boats/index.html?boat=UC+8: accessed 23 September 2017).
[21] British Admiralty, *Naval Staff Monograph No. 31*, 38.
[22] Ibid, 38-39.
[23] Dorling, *Swept Channels*, 273-275.
[24] British Admiralty, *Naval Staff Monograph No. 31*, 38-39.
[25] Ibid, 39.
[26] British Admiralty, *Naval Staff Monograph No. 31*, 39; "Casualty Lists of the Royal Navy and Dominion Navies" (www.naval-history.net).
[27] British Admiralty, *Naval Staff Monograph No. 31*, 39.
[28] Ibid, 39-40.
[29] Dorling, *Swept Channels*, 112.
[30] British Admiralty, *Naval Staff Monograph No. 31*, 47.
[31] Dorling, *Swept Channels*, 111-113.
[32] British Admiralty, *Naval Staff Monograph No. 31*, 48.
[33] Ibid, 48-49.
[34] British Admiralty, *Naval Staff Monograph No. 31*, 48-49; "A remarkable rescue off Sutherland's coast," *The Northern Times* (http://www.northern-times.co.uk/Features/Times-Past/A-remarkable-rescue-off-Sutherlands-coast-2851.htm: accessed 25 September 2014).
[35] British Admiralty, *Naval Staff Monograph No. 31*, 48-49; Dorling, *Swept Channels*, 113.
[36] British Admiralty, *Naval Staff Monograph No. 31*, 59.
[37] Ibid.
[38] Ibid, 59-60.
[39] Ibid, 60.
[40] Ibid, 60-61.
[41] "WWI U-boat Types" (http://uboat.net/wwi/types/: accessed 25 September 2017).

[42] Dorling, *Swept Channels*, 119.
[43] British Admiralty, *Naval Staff Monograph No. 31*, 66-67.
[44] Ibid, 67.
[45] Ibid, 67, 69.

CHAPTER 13 NOTES

[1] Andrew and Tobia, *Interrogation in War and Conflict*, 30.
[2] "*UC-5*" (http://uboat.net/wwi/boats/index.html?boat=UC+5); Tony Allen, "The story behind a Great War postcard - (20) The German submarine *UC-5*" (https://www.worldwar1postcards.com/german-submarine-uc5.php); "Johan Ryheul, The Flandern U-boat bases and U-Bootflottille Flandern" (http://uboat.net/articles/index.html?article=48: all accessed 12 July 2017); Email from Dwight Messimer to David Bruhn, 17 July 2017.
[3] "Type UC I UC coastal minelayers class" (http://uboat.net/wwi/types/?type=UC+I: accessed 12 July 2017).
[4] "Ships hit by *UC 5*" (http://uboat.net/wwi/boats/successes/uc5.html; Mike Scott, "Father and son killed in the war at sea. Son killed today. Both have no identified grave" (http://eyewitnesstours.com/father-son-killed-war-sea-son-killed-26-october-1916-no-identified-grave/: both accessed 12 July 2017).
[5] Chatterton, *Fighting the U-boats*, 185.
[6] Spindler, *Der Handelskrieg mit U-Booten, 1914-1918*, 57-59; The story behind a Great War postcard - (20) The German submarine *UC-5* (www.worldwar1postcards.com).
[7] Spindler, *Der Handelskrieg mit U-Booten, 1914-1918*, 57-59.
[8] Ibid.
[9] Ibid.
[10] Chatterton, *Fighting the U-boats*, 186.
[11] Allen, The story behind a Great War postcard - (20) The German submarine *UC-5* (www.worldwar1postcards.com); Spragg, *London's Strangest Tales The Thames Extraordinary But True Stories*.
[12] Email from Dwight Messimer to David Bruhn, 13 July 2017; Spragg, *London's Strangest Tales The Thames Extraordinary But True Stories*.
[13] Spindler, *Der Handelskrieg mit U-Booten, 1914-1918*, 57-59; Dwight Messimer, 13 July 2017.
[14] Allen, The story behind a Great War postcard - (20) The German submarine *UC-5* (www.worldwar1postcards.com); Spindler, *Der Handelskrieg mit U-Booten, 1914-1918*, 57-59.
[15] Allen, The story behind a Great War postcard - (20) The German submarine *UC-5* (www.worldwar1postcards.com).
[16] The Navy List. (November, 1917), 393u; Tillard Service Record. The National Archives, ADM 196/46, 95; "Aubrey Thomas Tillard" (http://dreadnoughtproject.org/tfs/index.php/Aubrey_Thomas_Tillard: accessed 13 July 2017).
[17] "Ulrich Mohrbutter" (http://uboat.net/wwi/men/commanders/211.html: accessed 13 July 2017).

CHAPTER 14 NOTES

[1] British Admiralty, *Naval Staff Monograph No. 32*, 5.

[2] C. N. Trueman, "The Battle of Jutland" (http://www.historylearningsite.co.uk/world-war-one/naval-warfare-and-world-war-one/the-battle-of-jutland/: accessed 16 September 2017).

[3] Ibid.

[4] Ibid.

[5] Ibid.

[6] Trueman, "The Battle of Jutland; Battle of Jutland - Order of Battle" (http://www.gwpda.org/naval/jutob.htm#RN: accessed 17 September 2017).

[7] Trueman, "The Battle of Jutland; Battle of Jutland" (http://www.history.com/topics/world-war-i/battle-of-jutland: accessed 27 September 2017).

[8] Trueman, "The Battle of Jutland" (www.historylearningsite.co.uk); "World War I: HMS *Queen Mary*" (https://www.thoughtco.com/world-war-i-hms-queen-mary-2361217: accessed 20 September 2017).

[9] Trueman, "The Battle of Jutland" (www.historylearningsite.co.uk); Innes McCartney, "Loss and Survival at Sea – The HMS *Invincible* at the Battle of Jutland, 1916" (https://news.bournemouth.ac.uk/2014/08/04/loss-and-survival-at-sea-the-hms-invincible-at-the-battle-of-jutland-1916/: accessed 22 September 2017).

[10] "Battle of Jutland" (http://www.history.com/topics/world-war-i/battle-of-jutland: accessed 27 September 2017).

[11] "HMS *Abdiel* – Her Role at Jutland" (http://www.jutland1916.com/ships-stories/hms-abdiel/: accessed 22 September 2017).

[12] "HMS *Abdiel* – Her Role at Jutland" (www.jutland1916.com).

[13] Friedman, *British Destroyers: From Earliest Days to the First World War*, 136-137, 296-297, 307; Gardiner and Gray, *Conway's All the World's Fighting Ships 1906–1921*, 77.

[14] Smith, *Into the Minefields: British Destroyer Minelaying 1916–1960*, 18, 86; Friedman, *British Destroyers: From Earliest Days to the First World War*, 153; Gardiner and Gray, *Conway's All the World's Fighting Ships 1906–1921*, 77.

[15] HMS *Abdiel* – Her Role at Jutland (www.jutland1916.com).

[16] Ibid.

[17] Smith, *Into the Minefields: British Destroyer Minelaying 1918–1980*, 21; Campbell, *Jutland: An Analysis of the Fighting*, 334-336.

[18] "Battle of Jutland War Game at the US Naval War College, Class of 1922" (https://www.history.navy.mil/research/library/online-reading-room/title-list-alphabetically/b/battle-jutland-war-game.html: accessed 15 September 2017).

CHAPTER 15 NOTES

[1] British Admiralty, *Naval Staff Monograph No. 31*, 152.

[2] Poland, *The Torpedoman – HMS Vernon's Story 1872-1986*, 76.

[3] Ibid.

[4] "ONI Compilation No. 14 – 1918" (Washington, DC: Office of Naval Intelligence, 1918), 15 (https://www.history.navy.mil/research/library/online-reading-room/title-list-alphabetically/a/antisubmarine-information-oni-no14-1918.html: accessed 2 October 2017).

[5] "Submarines World War I" (http://www.harwichanddovercourt.co.uk/submarines-ww1/: accessed 30 September 2017); Poland, *The Torpedoman – HMS Vernon's Story 1872-1986*, 76; British Admiralty, *Naval Staff Monograph No. 31*, 159.

[6] "Submarines World War I" (www.harwichanddovercourt.co.uk); WWI U-boat Types" (https://uboat.net/wwi/types/: accessed 30 September 2017).

[7] Poland, *The Torpedoman – HMS Vernon's Story 1872-1986*, 76; British Admiralty, *Naval Staff Monograph No. 31*, 159.

[8] "Submarines World War I" (www.harwichanddovercourt.co.uk); "Submarine Losses 1904 to Present Day" (http://www.submarine-museum.co.uk/what-we-have/memorial-chapel/submarine-losses?start=5; "Submarine E24, Great War Forum" (http://1914-1918.invisionzone.com/forums/topic/82106-submarine-e24/: all accessed 29 September 2017); Email from Dwight Messimer to David Bruhn, 2 October 2017.

[9] Poland, *The Torpedoman – HMS Vernon's Story 1872-1986*, 76; "Submarines World War I" (www.harwichanddovercourt.co.uk); "Submarine Losses 1904 to Present Day" (www.submarine-museum.co.uk).

[10] Poland, *The Torpedoman – HMS Vernon's Story 1872-1986*, 76-77; British Admiralty, *Naval Staff Monograph Vol. 17*, 50.

[11] Poland, *The Torpedoman – HMS Vernon's Story 1872-1986*, 76-77.

[12] British Admiralty, *Naval Staff Monograph, Vol. 17*, 67.

[13] Ibid, 72.

[14] British Admiralty, *Naval Staff Monograph, Vol. 17*, 72; Messimer, *Verschollen World War I U-Boat Losses*, 244.

[15] British Admiralty, *Naval Staff Monograph, Vol. 17*, 72.

[16] Messimer, *Verschollen World War I U-Boat Losses*, 244; and associated correspondence between Messimer and Michael Lowry of 14 December 2002, indicating that Tomas Termote had found the wreckage with small oiling can aboard marked UC 7.

[17] British Admiralty, *Naval Staff Monograph, Vol. 17*, 72.

[18] Dorling, *Swept Channels*, 283-284.

[19] Poland, *The Torpedoman – HMS Vernon's Story 1872-1986*, 76-77; Cowie, *Mines, Minelayers and Minelaying*, 54-55.

[20] ut supra.

[21] British Admiralty, *Naval Staff Monograph No. 31*, 143.

[22] Dorling, *Swept Channels*, 281.

[23] Ibid, 279-280.

[24] Ibid, 281.

[25] "Battle Honours and Single-Ship Actions of the Royal Navy 1914-18" (http://www.naval-history.net/WW1NavyBritish-Royal_Navy_Battle_Honours.htm#3: accessed 30 September 2017).
[26] British Admiralty, *Naval Staff Monograph, Vol. 17*, 219.
[27] British Admiralty, *Naval Staff Monograph, Vol. 17*, 219; Cowie, *Mines, Minelayers and Minelaying*, 55.
[28] Ibid, 219-220.
[29] British Admiralty, *Naval Staff Monograph No. 34*, 23.
[30] Poland, *The Torpedoman – HMS Vernon's Story 1872-1986*, 77.

CHAPTER 16 NOTES
[1] Dorling, *Swept Channels*, 17.
[2] Ibid.
[3] Dorling, *Swept Channels*, 18-19.
[4] British Admiralty, *Naval Staff Monograph No. 34, Vol. 17*, xiii; Dorling, *Swept Channels*, 18-19; Messimer, *Find and Destroy: Antisubmarine Warfare in WWI*, 150.
[5] Poland, *The Torpedoman – HMS Vernon's Story 1872-1986*, 77-78.
[6] Ibid, 77-78.
[7] Ibid, 78.
[8] Ibid, 78.
[9] Messimer, *Find and Destroy: Antisubmarine Warfare in WWI*, 44; Email from Dwight Messimer to David Bruhn, 14 October 2017.
[10] "The story of the Solent's Nab Tower lighthouse" (http://www.bbc.com/news/uk-england-hampshire-36533115: accessed 8 October 2017).
[11] Poland, *The Torpedoman – HMS Vernon's Story 1872-1986*, 78; "Casualty Lists of the Royal Navy and Dominion Navies" (www.naval-history.net); "Lewis Clinton-Baker" (http://www.dreadnoughtproject.org/tfs/index.php/Lewis_Clinton-Baker: accessed 2 October 2017).
[12] Poland, *The Torpedoman – HMS Vernon's Story 1872-1986*, 78; Cowie, *Mines, Minelayers and Minelaying*, 59.
[13] Poland, *The Torpedoman – HMS Vernon's Story 1872-1986*, 78.
[14] Dorling, *Swept Channels*, 122-123.
[15] Ibid, 123.
[16] "*Hunt* Class Minesweeper (1916)" (http://www.dreadnoughtproject.org/tfs/index.php/Hunt_Class_Minesweeper_(1916): accessed 3 October 2017).
[17] Dorling, *Swept Channels*, 371.
[18] Dorling, *Swept Channels*, 371-372; *Hunt* Class Minesweeper (1916).
[19] Dorling, *Swept Channels*, 371-372.
[20] *Hunt* Class Minesweeper (1916).
[21] "Casualty Lists of the Royal Navy and Dominion Navies" (www.naval-history.net).

[22] "Naval Reserve Forces"
(http://www.barnettmaritime.co.uk/reserves.htm#mmr: accessed 3 October
2017).
[23] "Mercantile Marine War Medal"
(http://www.greatwar.co.uk/medals/ww1-campaign-
medals.htm#mercantilemedal; "Campaign Stars and Medals (1866-1918)"
(http://www.veterans.gc.ca/eng/remembrance/medals-decorations/medal-
type/1: both accessed 3 October 2017).

CHAPTER 17 NOTES

[1] "Zeebrugge and Ostend Raids Naval Despatch dated 9 May 1918"
(http://www.naval-
history.net/WW1Battle1804ZeebruggeOstend.htm#31189: accessed 17 July
2017).
[2] "British Naval Raids on Zeebrugge and Ostend, 1918, The Great War
1914-1918" (http://www.greatwar.co.uk/battles/yser/zeebrugge-ostend-
raid.htm: accessed 15 July 2017).
[3] "Zeebrugge and Ostend Raids Naval Despatch dated 9 May 1918"
(www.naval-history.net); "Raid on Zeebrugge and Ostend, World War I New
Zealand's War at Sea" (http://navymuseum.co.nz/worldwar1/battles-
operations/battle-of-zeebrugge-and-ostend/: both accessed 17 July 2017);
Emails from Dwight Messimer to David Bruhn, 21 and 23 July 2017;
Carpenter, *The Blockading of Zeebrugge*, 120.
[4] "Zeebrugge and Ostend Raids Naval Despatch dated 9 May 1918"
(www.naval-history.net); Dwight Messimer, 21 July 2017.
[5] ut supra.
[6] Raid on Zeebrugge and Ostend, World War I New Zealand's War at Sea
(http://navymuseum.co.nz).
[7] Raid on Zeebrugge and Ostend, World War I New Zealand's War at Sea
http://navymuseum.co.nz); Zeebrugge and Ostend Raids Naval Despatch
dated 9 May 1918 (www.naval-history.net) .
[8] Zeebrugge and Ostend Raids Naval Despatch dated 9 May 1918
(www.naval-history.net).
[9] Ibid.
[10] Ibid.
[11] Zeebrugge and Ostend Raids Naval Despatch dated 9 May 1918
(www.naval-history.net); Email from Dwight Messimer to David Bruhn, 23
July 2017.
[12] Zeebrugge and Ostend Raids Naval Despatch dated 9 May 1918
(www.naval-history.net).
[13] Ibid.
[14] Ibid.
[15] Ibid.
[16] Zeebrugge and Ostend Raids Naval Despatch dated 9 May 1918
(www.naval-history.net); "World War 1 at Sea, Battle Honours and Single-

Ship Actions of the Royal Navy 1914-18" (http://www.naval-history.net/WW1NavyBritishBattleHonours.htm#3: accessed 30 June 2017).
[17] Zeebrugge and Ostend Raids Naval Despatch dated 9 May 1918 (www.naval-history.net).
[18] Ibid.
[19] Ibid.
[20] "Lieutenant Percy Thompson Dean VC, Lives of the First World War" (https://livesofthefirstworldwar.org/lifestory/7664317: accessed 18 July 2017).
[21] "Ostend Operations, May 10, 1918. Fleet House, Dover, June 15, 1918, No. 2305/003" (http://www.naval-history.net/WW1Battle1804ZeebruggeOstend.htm#ostend: accessed 18 July 2017); Artl. Mt. Policke, "Die Molenbatterie Zeebrugge beim englischen Angriff am 22./23. April 1918"; "Records of the German Navy, 1850-1945," RG242, Microfilm Publication T1022, Roll 1370, PG78417.
[22] Ostend Operations, May 10, 1918. Fleet House, Dover, June 15, 1918, No. 2305/003 (www.naval-history.net).
[23] Ibid.
[24] Ibid.
[25] "Enclosure to Vice-Admiral, Dover, letter No. 2305/003, dated 15th June, 1918, No. 053, Office of Commodore, Dunkirk, 10th May, 1918" (www.naval-history.net).
[26] Ibid.
[27] Ibid.
[28] "Lieutenant Commander Rowland Bourke VC DSO" (http://www.victoriacross.org.uk/bbbourke.htm: accessed 3 August 2017).
[29] "Zeebrugge and First Ostend Raid - 22nd/23rd April 1918, Second Ostend Raid - 10th May 1918" (http://www.naval-history.net/WW1Battle1804ZeebruggeOstend.htm: accessed 21 August 2017).
[30] Ostend Operations, May 10, 1918. Fleet House, Dover, June 15, 1918, No. 2305/003 (www.naval-history.net).
[31] "Raid on Zeebrugge and Ostend, World War I New Zealand's War at Sea; Oostende New Communal Cemetery West-Vlaanderen" (Belgiumhttp://www.ww1cemeteries.com/oostende-new-communal-cemetery.html: accessed 19 July 2017).
[32] Messimer, *Find and Destroy; Antisubmarine Warfare in World War I*, 57.
[33] Email from Dwight Messimer to David Bruhn, 21 August 2017.

CHAPTER 18 NOTES

[1] Duncan, *America's Use of Sea Mines*, 46.
[2] "U-Boat Sinks SS *Ancona* off Sardinia; 25 Americans Killed" (http://today-in-wwi.tumblr.com/post/132778954878/u-boat-sinks-ss-ancona-off-sardinia-25-americans: accessed 5 October 2017).
[3] British Admiralty, *Naval Staff Monograph No. 31*, 94-95.

[4] "1917 America enters World War I" (http://www.history.com/this-day-in-history/america-enters-world-war-i; "U.S. Merchant Ships, Sailing Vessels, and Fishing Craft Lost from all Causes during World War I" (http://www.usmm.org/ww1merchant.html: both accessed 5 October 2017).

[5] U.S. GPO, *Northern Barrage and Other Mining Activities*, 9.

[6] "1917 America enters World War I" (www.history.com).

[7] Paul G. Halpern, "Naval Warfare (USA)" (https://encyclopedia.1914-1918-online.net/article/naval_warfare_usa: accessed 5 October 2017).

[8] Lott, *Most Dangerous Sea*, 14; Duncan, *America's Use of Sea Mines*, 47.

[9] Chris Martin, "The Northern Barrage and Other Mining Activities Publication Number 2" (https://www.history.navy.mil/browse-by-topic/wars-conflicts-and-operations/world-war-i/tech/northern-barrage-other-mining-activities.html: accessed 20 June 2017).

[10] Belknap, *The Yankee Mining Squadron or Laying the North Sea Mine Barrage* (https://archive.org/details/yankeeminingsqua00belk: accessed 20 June 2017).

[11] Ibid.

[12] Ibid.

[13] Ibid.

[14] Ibid.

[15] "U.S. Naval Forces Operating in European Waters" (https://www.history.navy.mil/research/histories/ship-histories/us-ship-force-levels/wwiorgchart-1918.html: accessed 19 June 2017).

[16] Belknap, *The Yankee Mining Squadron or Laying the North Sea Mine Barrage* (https://archive.org/details/yankeeminingsqua00belk: accessed 20 June 2017).

[17] Ibid.

[18] Ibid.

[19] Belknap, *The Yankee Mining Squadron or Laying the North Sea Mine Barrage* (https://archive.org/details/yankeeminingsqua00belk: accessed 20 June 2017); Frank A. Blazich Jr., "United States Navy and World War I: 1914–1922" (https://www.history.navy.mil/research/library/online-reading-room/title-list-alphabetically/u/us-navy-world-war-i-redirect.html: accessed 23 June 2017).

[20] Belknap, *The Yankee Mining Squadron or Laying the North Sea Mine Barrage* (https://archive.org/details/yankeeminingsqua00belk: accessed 20 June 2017).

[21] U.S. GPO, *The Northern Barrage and Other Mining Activities*, 102.

[22] U.S. GPO, *The Northern Barrage and Other Mining Activities*, 102; Crowlie, *Mines, Minelayers and Minelaying*, 55.

[23] U.S. GPO, *The Northern Barrage and Other Mining Activities*, 102.

[24] Ibid, 103.

[25] Ibid, 103.

[26] Ibid, 104.

[27] U.S. GPO, *The Northern Barrage and Other Mining Activities*, 104; Belknap, *The Yankee Mining Squadron or Laying the North Sea Mine Barrage*

(https://archive.org/details/yankeeminingsqua00belk: accessed 20 June 2017).

[28] U.S. GPO, *The Northern Barrage and Other Mining Activities*, 104.

[29] Ibid.

[30] Belknap, *The Yankee Mining Squadron or Laying the North Sea Mine Barrage* (https://archive.org/details/yankeeminingsqua00belk: accessed 20 June 2017); Blazich, United States Navy and World War I: 1914–1922 (www.history.navy.mil).

[31] Belknap, *The Yankee Mining Squadron or Laying the North Sea Mine Barrage* (https://archive.org/details/yankeeminingsqua00belk: accessed 20 June 2017); Blazich, United States Navy and World War I: 1914–1922 (www.history.navy.mil).

[32] U.S. GPO, *The Northern Barrage and Other Mining Activities*, 58-60.

[33] *Ozama, DANFS*; Blazich, United States Navy and World War I: 1914–1922 (www.history.navy.mil); U.S. GPO, *The Northern Barrage and Other Mining Activities*, 104.

[34] Blazich, United States Navy and World War I: 1914-1922 (www.history.navy.mil); *Lake Moor, DANFS*; U.S. GPO, *The Northern Barrage and Other Mining Activities*, 60.

[35] U.S. GPO, *The Northern Barrage and Other Mining Activities*, 59-60.

[36] Ibid, 104-105.

[37] Ibid, 105.

[38] Ibid, 106-107.

[39] Ibid, 106-107.

[40] Ibid, 107-108.

[41] Ibid, 124.

[42] Ibid, 109-110.

[43] Ibid, 110.

[44] Ibid, 111-112.

[45] Ibid, 112.

[46] Ibid, 112-113.

[47] Ibid, 113, 124.

[48] Ibid, 113.

[49] Ibid, 114.

[50] Ibid, 115.

[51] Ibid, 124-125.

[52] Ibid, 125.

[53] Ibid, 121-123.

[54] "U-boat Losses 1914-1918" (https://uboat.net/wwi/fates/losses.html: accessed 8 October 2017); Erich Gröner, Dieter Jung, Martin Maass, *German Warships 1815-1945 Vol. II: U-Boats and Mine Warfare Vessels* (London: Conway Maritime Press, 1991), 25-30; U.S. GPO, *The Northern Barrage and Other Mining Activities*, 125.

[55] Messimer, *Verschollen World War I U-Boat Losses*, 4, 179.

[56] Messimer, *Verschollen World War I U-Boat Losses*, 4.

CHAPTER 19 NOTES

[1] U.S. GPO, *German Submarine Activities on the Atlantic Coast of the United States and Canada* (Washington, DC: Government Printing Office, 1920), 143.

[2] Spindler, *Der Handelskrieg mit U-Booten, 1914-1918, vol. 5*, 232-247, 252-269

[3] Ibid.

[4] Spindler, *Der Handelskrieg mit U-Booten, 1914-1918, vol. 5*, 232-247, 252-269; U.S. GPO, German Submarine Activities on the Atlantic Coast of the United States and Canada, 7.

[5] Spindler, *Der Handelskrieg mit U-Booten, 1914-1918, vol. 5*, 232-247, 252-269; *Werner von Langsdorff, U-boote am Feind: 45 deutsche U-Boat-Fahrer enzählen* (Barsinghausen: Unikum Verlag, 2013), 46-47.

[6] ut supra.

[7] Spindler, *Der Handelskrieg mit U-Booten, 1914-1918, vol. 5*, 232-247, 252-269.

[8] "His Imperial German Majesty's U-boats in WWI" (http://uboat.net/history/wwi/part5.htm: accessed 11 October 2017); Spindler, *Der Handelskrieg mit U-Booten, 1914-1918, vol. 5*, 232-247, 252-269; Email from Dwight Messimer to David Bruhn, 18 October 2017.

[9] "Type U 151" (http://uboat.net/wwi/types/?type=U+151: accessed 11 October 2017).

[10] "WWI U-boat Types" (http://uboat.net/wwi/types/); "WWI U-boat Commander Listing" (http://uboat.net/wwi/men/commanders/listing.html: both accessed 10 October 2017).

[11] Spindler, *Der Handelskrieg mit U-Booten, 1914-1918, vol. 5*, 232-247, 252-269.

[12] Michael L. Hadley and Roger Sarty, *Tin-pots and Pirate Ships: Canadian Naval Forces and German Sea Raiders 1880-1918* (London: McGill-Queen's University Press, 1991), 239.

[13] Spindler, *Der Handelskrieg mit U-Booten, 1914-1918, vol. 5*, 232-247, 252-269; U.S. GPO, *German Submarine Activities on the Atlantic Coast of the United States and Canada*, 7.

[14] U.S. GPO, *German Submarine Activities on the Atlantic Coast of the United States and Canada*, 139-141.

[15] Hadley and Sarty, *Tin-pots and Pirate Ships: Canadian Naval Forces and German Sea Raiders 1880-1918*, 239.

[16] Ibid, 240.

[17] Ibid.

[18] Ibid, 241-242.

[19] Ibid, 242.

[20] Ibid, 243.

[21] Ibid.

[22] Ibid, 244.

[23] Ibid.

[24] Ibid, 244-246.

[25] Ibid, 247-248.

[26] U.S. GPO, *German Submarine Activities on the Atlantic Coast of the United States and Canada*, 137; Hadley and Sarty, *Tin-pots and Pirate Ships*, 249.

[27] Hadley and Sarty, *Tin-pots and Pirate Ships*, 213, 250.

[28] Ibid, 263.

[29] Ibid.

[30] Ibid, 216, 264.

[31] "Canadian Naval Heritage Project" (https://web.archive.org/web/20111002013443/http://www.navy.gc.ca/project_pride/ships/ship_e.asp?shipNumber=78); "Converted Civilian Vessels" (http://www.hazegray.org/navhist/canada/ww1/convert/); "Miramar Ship Index" (http://www.miramarshipindex.nz/); "Ships and Shore Bases of the RCN" (http://www.forposterityssake.ca/RCN-SHIP-INDEX.htm#MINESWEEPERS: all accessed 13 October 2017).

[32] Hadley and Sarty, *Tin-pots and Pirate Ships*, 264-266.

[33] U.S. GPO, *German Submarine Activities on the Atlantic Coast of the United States and Canada*, 66.

[34] Ibid.

[35] Hadley and Sarty, *Tin-pots and Pirate Ships*, 268.

[36] Ibid.

[37] Ibid, 269.

[38] Spindler, *Der Handelskrieg mit U-Booten, 1914-1918*, 232-247, 252-269; Email from Dwight Messimer to David Bruhn, 14 October 2017.

[39] Spindler, *Der Handelskrieg mit U-Booten, 1914-1918*, 232-247, 252-269; "WWI U-boat Types" (http://uboat.net/wwi/types/: accessed 13 October 2017).

[40] Spindler, *Der Handelskrieg mit U-Booten, 1914-1918*, 232-247, 252-269; "U-140" (http://uboat.net/wwi/boats/index.html?boat=140: accessed October 13, 2017).

[41] Spindler, *Der Handelskrieg mit U-Booten, 1914-1918*, 232-247, 252-269.

[42] "U 117" (http://uboat.net/wwi/boats/index.html?boat=117: accessed 14 October 2017).

[43] "Type UE 2" (http://uboat.net/wwi/types/?type=UE+2: accessed 14 October 2917); U.S. GPO, *German Submarine Activities on the Atlantic Coast of the United States and Canada*, 82, 137.

[44] U.S. GPO, *German Submarine Activities on the Atlantic Coast of the United States and Canada*, 82, 137.

[45] Spindler, *Der Handelskrieg mit U-Booten, 1914-1918*, 232-247, 252-269; U.S. GPO, *German Submarine Activities on the Atlantic Coast of the United States and Canada*, 137.

[46] U.S. GPO, *German Submarine Activities on the Atlantic Coast of the United States and Canada*, 137-139.

[47] U.S. GPO, *German Submarine Activities on the Atlantic Coast of the United States and Canada*, 99-100; Spindler, *Der Handelskrieg mit U-Booten, 1914-1918*, 232-247, 252-269.

[48] Spindler, *Der Handelskrieg mit U-Booten, 1914-1918*, 232-247, 252-269; "Type U 151" (http://uboat.net/wwi/types/?type=U+151: accessed 14 October 2017).

[49] "Ships hit by *U 155*" (http://uboat.net/wwi/boats/successes/u155.html: accessed 14 October 2017); Hadley and Sarty, *Tin-pots and Pirate Ships*, 284-288.

[50] Hadley and Sarty, *Tin-pots and Pirate Ships*, 286-287.

[51] Ibid, 288.

[52] U.S. GPO, *German Submarine Activities on the Atlantic Coast of the United States and Canada*, 113-114.

[53] "Ships hit by *U 152*" (http://uboat.net/wwi/boats/successes/u152.html: accessed 14 October 2017); U.S. GPO, *German Submarine Activities on the Atlantic Coast of the United States and Canada*, 106.

[54] *Ticonderoga, DANFS*.

[55] U.S. GPO, *German Submarine Activities on the Atlantic Coast of the United States and Canada*, 106-109.

[56] Ibid, 107.

[57] Ibid, 107-110.

[58] Ibid, 110.

[59] Ibid, 109-111.

[60] U.S. GPO, *German Submarine Activities on the Atlantic Coast of the United States and Canada*, 112; Email from Dwight Messimer to David Bruhn, 15 October 2017.

[61] U.S. GPO, *German Submarine Activities on the Atlantic Coast of the United States and Canada*, 112-113; Spindler, *Der Handelskrieg mit U-Booten, 1914-1918, vol. 5*, 232-247, 252-269.

[62] U.S. GPO, *German Submarine Activities on the Atlantic Coast of the United States and Canada*, 112-113.

[63] Ibid, 114.

[64] U.S. GPO, *German Submarine Activities on the Atlantic Coast of the United States and Canada*, 141; Hadley and Sarty, *Tin-pots and Pirate Ships*, 239.

[65] Madison's medal citation appears to be incorrect in listing thirty-one as the number of survivors. Two officers were taken prisoner, and there were the commanding officer and fourteen soldiers originally in the lifeboat, joined later by five members of ship's company—for a total of twenty-two survivors.

[66] "Commander James J. Madison, USNRF, 1888-1922" (https://www.ibiblio.org/hyperwar/OnlineLibrary/photos/pers-us/uspers-m/jj-madsn.htm: accessed 14 October 2017).

[67] "Auxilary Patrol Vessels, Part 1, Yachts to Trawlers" (http://www.naval-history.net/WW1NavyBritishShips-Dittmar4AP.htm: accessed 14 October 2017).

CHAPTER 20 NOTES

[1] Dorling, *Swept Channels*, 311.

[2] Ibid, 310-311.

[3] Ibid, 310-311.

[4] Ibid, 311.

[5] Ibid, 311.

[6] Ibid, 353-355.

[7] Ibid, 311.

[8] Blazich, United States Navy and World War I: 1914–1922 (www.history.navy.mil).

[9] Ibid.

[10] Ibid.

[11] Ibid.

[12] Dorling, *Swept Channels*, 325.

[13] Ibid, 325.

[14] Ibid, 325-326.

[15] Dorling, *Swept Channels*, 324-326; *The Northern Barrage*, 62.

[16] Dorling, *Swept Channels*, 358-359; U.S. GPO, *The Northern Barrage*, 62, 78.

[17] Blazich, United States Navy and World War I: 1914–1922 (www.history.navy.mil); U.S. GPO, *The Northern Barrage*, 16.

[18] U.S. GPO, *The Northern Barrage*, 9-10.

[19] "Lapwing" (http://www.navsource.org/archives/11/02001.htm: accessed 18 October 2017).

[20] Blazich, United States Navy and World War I: 1914–1922 (www.history.navy.mil); U.S. GPO, *The Northern Barrage*, 19, 22.

[21] Ibid, 27.

[22] Ibid, 28.

[23] Ibid, 28-29.

[24] Blazich, United States Navy and World War I: 1914–1922 (www.history.navy.mil); U.S. GPO, *The Northern Barrage*, 30.

[25] U.S. GPO, *The Northern Barrage*, 29.

[26] Ibid, 33-34.

[27] Blazich, United States Navy and World War I: 1914–1922 (www.history.navy.mil); U.S. GPO, *The Northern Barrage*, 37.

[28] Richard Cavendish, "The German battle fleet scuttled at Scapa Flow," *History Today*, Volume 59 Issue 6 June 2009; Blazich, United States Navy and World War I: 1914–1922 (www.history.navy.mil); U.S. GPO, *The Northern Barrage*, 33.

[29] U.S. GPO, *The Northern Barrage*, 40-42.

[30] Blazich, United States Navy and World War I: 1914–1922 (www.history.navy.mil).

[31] Ibid.

[32] Blazich, United States Navy and World War I: 1914–1922 (www.history.navy.mil); U.S. GPO, *The Northern Barrage*, 50.

[33] U.S. GPO, *The Northern Barrage*, 51.

[34] Blazich, United States Navy and World War I: 1914–1922 (www.history.navy.mil).

[35] Ibid.

[36] Ibid.

[37] Stringer, *The Navy Book of Distinguished Service.*

Index

Note: Names containing von, such as von Arnauld, are alphabetized by the main last name, in this case, Arnauld.

About the Author

Rob Hoole joined the Royal Navy as a 'seaman officer' (later termed 'warfare officer') in 1971. He qualified as a Ships' Diving Officer in 1975 and as a Minewarfare & Clearance Diving Officer in 1976. In 1991, he co-founded the Royal Naval Minewarfare & Clearance Diving Officers' Association (MCDOA) of which he is Vice Chairman. Rob acquired an MBA from Oxford Brooks University in 2000 and left the Royal Navy in late 2002 after serving 32 years in all manner of operational and training roles at sea and ashore including Command of diving teams and mine countermeasures vessels. Rob lives in Waterlooville near Portsmouth with his wife Linda. They have three grown children and two young grandsons.

Aside from his family, his passions include country pubs & real ale, sailing, reading and maritime history, particularly the development of naval & military diving, minewarfare and explosive ordnance disposal (EOD) otherwise known as bomb & mine disposal. He has contributed to many books, journals and other publications covering different aspects of his favourite subjects and was the editor of the book *Last of the Wooden Walls – An Illustrated History of the TON Class Minesweepers & Minehunters*. Last but not least, he is a fierce supporter of Project Vernon, the campaign to erect a monument at Gunwharf Quays in Portsmouth, Hampshire, to commemorate the minewarfare and diving heritage of HMS Vernon which previously occupied the site.

About the Author

Commander David D. Bruhn, U.S. Navy (Retired) served twenty-two years on active duty and two in the Naval Reserve, as both an enlisted man and as an officer, between 1977 and 2001.

Following completion of basic training, he served as a sonar technician aboard USS *Miller* (FF 1091) and USS *Leftwich* (DD 984). He was commissioned in 1983 following graduation from California State University at Chico. His initial assignment was to USS *Excel* (MSO 439), serving as supply officer, damage control assistant, and chief engineer. He then served in USS *Thach* (FFG 43) as chief engineer and Destroyer Squadron Thirteen as material officer.

After graduation from the Naval Postgraduate School, Commander Bruhn was assigned to Secretary of the Navy and Chief of Naval Operation staffs as a budget analyst and resources planner before attending the Naval War College in 1996, following which he commanded the mine countermeasures ships USS *Gladiator* (MCM 11) and USS *Dextrous* (MCM 13) in the Persian Gulf.

Commander Bruhn's final assignment was executive assistant to a senior (SES 4) government service executive at the Ballistic Missile Defense Organization in Washington, D.C.

Following military service, he was a high school teacher and track coach for ten years, and is now a USA Track & Field official. He lives in northern California with his wife Nancy and has two sons, David and Michael.

Heritage Books by Cdr. David D. Bruhn, USN (Retired)

Battle Stars for the "Cactus Navy":
America's Fishing Vessels and Yachts in World War II

Eyes of the Fleet:
The U.S. Navy's Seaplane Tenders and Patrol Aircraft in World War II

Ingram's Fourth Fleet:
U.S. and Royal Navy Operations Against German Runners,
Raiders, and Submarines in the South Atlantic in World War II

MacArthur and Halsey's "Pacific Island Hoppers":
The Forgotten Fleet of World War II

Home Waters:
Royal Navy, Royal Canadian Navy, and U.S. Navy
Mine Forces Battling U-Boats in World War I
Cdr. David D. Bruhn, USN (Retired) and Lt. Cdr. Rob Hoole, RN (Retired)

We Are Sinking, Send Help!:
The U.S. Navy's Tugs and Salvage Ships in the African,
European, and Mediterranean Theaters in World War II

Wooden Ships and Iron Men:
The U.S. Navy's Ocean Minesweepers, 1953–1994

Wooden Ships and Iron Men:
The U.S. Navy's Coastal and Motor Minesweepers, 1941–1953

Wooden Ships and Iron Men:
The U.S. Navy's Coastal and Inshore Minesweepers,
and the Minecraft that Served in Vietnam, 1953–1976

90396340R00235

Made in the USA
Columbia, SC
07 March 2018